Tapping into
Unstructured Data

Tapping into Unstructured Data

Integrating Unstructured Data and Textual Analytics into Business Intelligence

William H. Inmon
Anthony Nesavich

PRENTICE
HALL

An Imprint of Pearson Education

Upper Saddle River, NJ • Boston • Indianapolis • San Francisco
New York • Toronto • Montreal • London • Munich • Paris • Madrid
Cape Town • Sydney • Tokyo • Singapore • Mexico City

The publisher offers excellent discounts on this book when ordered in quantity for bulk purchases or special sales, which may include electronic versions and/or custom covers and content particular to your business, training goals, marketing focus, and branding interests. For more information, please contact:

U.S. Corporate and Government Sales
(800) 382-3419
corpsales@pearsontechgroup.com

For sales outside the United States, please contact:

International Sales
international@pearsoned.com

Visit us on the Web: www.prenhallprofessional.com

Editor-in-Chief: Mark Taub
Acquisitions Editor: Bernard Goodwin
Development Editor: Michael Thurston
Managing Editor: Gina Kanouse
Project Editor: Betsy Harris
Copy Editor: Deadline Driven Publishing
Indexer: Cheryl Lenser
Proofreader: Anne Goebel
Technical Reviewers: Artur Dubrawski, Howard Rubin, Derek Strauss
Publishing Coordinator: Michelle Housley
Cover Designer: Alan Clements
Compositor: Bumpy Design

Library of Congress Cataloging-in-Publication Data
Inmon, William H.
  Tapping into unstructured data : integrating unstructured data and textual analytics into business intelligence / William H. Inmon and Anthony Nesavich.
     p. cm.
  Includes bibliographical references and index.
  ISBN 0-13-236029-2 (pbk. : alk. paper) 1. Business intelligence. 2. Data mining. 3. Management information systems. 4. Data warehousing. I. Nesavich, Anthony. II. Title.
  HD38.7.I536 2008
  658.4'72—dc22
                              2007040548

Pearson Education, Inc.
Rights and Contracts Department
75 Arlington Street, Suite 300
Boston, MA 02116
Fax: (617) 848-7047

ISBN-13: 978-0-13-236029-6
ISBN-10: 0-13-236029-2

Text printed in the United States on recycled paper at RR Donnelley in Crawfordsville, Indiana
First printing December 2007

 This Book Is Safari Enabled

The Safari® Enabled icon on the cover of your favorite technology book means the book is available through Safari Bookshelf. When you buy this book, you get free access to the online edition for 45 days. Safari Bookshelf is an electronic reference library that lets you easily search thousands of technical books, find code samples, download chapters, and access technical information whenever and wherever you need it.

To gain 45-day Safari Enabled access to this book:

- Go to http://www.prenhallprofessional.com/safarienabled
- Complete the brief registration form
- Enter the coupon code XXMN-SAEL-9FFA-FKLP-UTPL

If you have difficulty registering on Safari Bookshelf or accessing the online edition, please e-mail customer-service@safaribooksonline.com.

For Alice and David Glass, to whom it is a privilege to be related.
—William Inmon

For my wife Melissa whose love and support mean all the world, and for my parents,
John and Judy Nesavich, who are both as strong a role model a son could ever have.
—Anthony Nesavich

Contents at a Glance

Preface xvii

Acknowledgments xx

About the Authors xxi

Chapter 1 ■ Unstructured Textual Data in the Organization 1

Chapter 2 ■ The Environments of Structured Data and Unstructured Data 15

Chapter 3 ■ First Generation Textual Analytics 33

Chapter 4 ■ Integrating Unstructured Text into the Structured Environment 47

Chapter 5 ■ Semistructured Data 73

Chapter 6 ■ Architecture and Textual Analytics 83

Chapter 7 ■ The Unstructured Database 95

Chapter 8 ■ Analyzing a Combination of Unstructured Data and Structured Data 113

Chapter 9 ■ Analyzing Text Through Visualization 127

Chapter 10 ■ Spreadsheets and Email 135

Chapter 11 ■ Metadata in Unstructured Data 147

Chapter 12 ■ A Methodology for Textual Analytics 163

Chapter 13 ■ Merging Unstructured Databases into the Data Warehouse 175

Chapter 14 ■ Using SQL to Analyze Text 185

Chapter 15 ■ Case Study—Textual Analytics in Medical Research 195

Chapter 16 ■ Case Study—A Database for Harmful Chemicals 203

Chapter 17 ■ Case Study—Managing Contracts Through an Unstructured Database 209

Chapter 18 ■ Case Study—Creating a Corporate Taxonomy (Glossary) 215

Chapter 19 ■ Case Study—Insurance Claims 219

Glossary 227

Index 233

Contents

Preface   xvii

Acknowledgments   xx

About the Authors   xxi

Chapter 1 ▪ Unstructured Textual Data in the Organization   1

Unstructured Textual Data   2

Unstructured Textual Data and Organizational Functions   3

Unstructured Data and Its Characteristics   5

Updating Structured and Unstructured Data   9

The Challenges of Unstructured Textual Data and Analytical Processing   9

The Opportunities of Unstructured Textual Data   11

Summary   13

Chapter 2 ▪ The Environments of Structured Data and Unstructured Data   15

The Structured Environment   15

Databases   17

Speed of Storage, Retrieval   19

The Unstructured Environment   20

Emails   21

Spreadsheets   22

Transcripted Telephone Conversations   23

Medical Records   23

Legal Information   24

Corporate Contracts   25

Unstructured Data—Found Everywhere   26

The Analytical Environment   26

Doing Textual Analytics in the Unstructured Environment or the Structured Environment   28

Bringing Unstructured Data into the Structured Environment   30

Summary   31

Chapter 3 ▪ First Generation Textual Analytics   33

Simplicity   34

Search Engines That Look for Patterns   34

Search Engine—The Hit   35

Where Unstructured Data Resides   35

Searching an Index   36

A Crawler   37

Search Arguments and Schedulers   38

Tagging   38

Searching in Multiple Languages   39

Collecting Output in a Taxonomy   39

Hyperlink References   40

Federated Queries   41

Integration   41

Enhancing the Search Argument   42

Wild Cards   42

Boolean Expressions   43

Visualizing Text—First Generation   43

Understanding Context   44

Summary   45

Chapter 4 ▪ Integrating Unstructured Text into the Structured Environment   47

Possibilities of Unstructured Systems   47

Integrating Unstructured Textual Data   50

Reading the Unstructured Textual Data   50

Choosing a File Type   51

Reading Unstructured Data from Voice Recordings   52

The Importance of Integration   53
Simple Search   53
Indirect Search of Alternate Terms   53
Indirect Search of Related Terms   53
Permutations of Words   54

The Issues of Textual Integration   54

External Categorization   60

Simple Integration Applications   61
Examining the Contents of Existing Unstructured Data   61
Enterprise Metadata Repository   62
Customer Communications   62
The Resulting Architecture   64

Choosing the Best Types of Integration   65
Ways in Which Integration Occurs   66
Performance Limitations   66
Disadvantages to Integration   69

Summary   70

Chapter 5   ▪   Semistructured Data   73

The Many Forms of Semistructured Data   74
Common Patterns of Data   75
Prefacing Values   76
Default Values   77
Conflicting Values   77

The Degree of Accuracy   78

Preprocessing Semistructured Data   79
Variable Output   80
Semistructured Processing in an Unstructured Environment   81
Preparation Time   82

Summary   82

Chapter 6   ▪   Architecture and Textual Analytics   83

The Growth of Information Systems   83
The Maturing Need for Information   84
The Need for Data Integrity   86

The Need to Include Unstructured Data   87
A Fundamental Difference   88
First Generation of Analytical Processing   89
The Second Generation of Textual Analytics   89

DW 2.0—Data Warehouse Architecture   91

Summary   93

Chapter 7 ▪ The Unstructured Database   95

The General Flow of Data   96
Preventing a Blob of Unstructured Data   96

A Partial Relational Table   97
A Document/Word Table   98
The Key of the Relational Table   98

Different Indexes   99
Indexing Semistructured Data   100
Indexes for Both Semistructured and Unstructured Data   100

Managing Large Volumes of Data   101
Bring Everything into the Structured Environment   102
Selectively Storing Terms   103

Simple Pointer   104
Moving the Underlying Document   104
Alternatives to Moved Documents   105
Synonyms and Homographs   105
External Categories   106

Using the Unstructured Database for Analysis   108
Access Through a Standard SQL Interface   108
The High Level Design   109
Accessing Multiple Tables   109
"Hot" Data   111

Summary   111

**Chapter 8 ▪ Analyzing a Combination of Unstructured Data
and Structured Data   113**

Intersecting Structured and Unstructured Data   114
Linking Communications   114
Other Types of Linkages   116

A Probabilistic Link   116

Dynamic and Static Links   117

Accessing Linkages   118

Periodically Monitoring Linkage   119

Independently Processing the Static Link   120

A Join Based on the Link   120

Submitting Real-Time Online Queries   122

Enhancing Performance Through Priority Ranking   122

Filtering Data Based on Probability of Access   123

Looking at Links Partially   124

Unstructured Text and Future Capabilities   124

Summary   125

Chapter 9 ▪ Analyzing Text Through Visualization   127

Creating a Textual Visualization   128

Selecting Homogeneous Data   128

Integrating the Text   129

Creating a Database Format   130

Creating the Visualization   130

Other Types of SOMs   131

Iterative Development of the Visualization   131

Analytical Activities   132

Recasting a SOM Visualization   132

Creating a SOM for Semistructured Data   133

Summary   134

Chapter 10 ▪ Spreadsheets and Email   135

The Challenges of Spreadsheets   135

Strategies for Access   137

A Unique Spreadsheet Identifier   138

Unstructured Data in the Spreadsheet   138

Identifying Cells   140

Cross Equivalency   141

Global Spreadsheet Analysis   142

Emails   143

Screening Emails for Useful Data   144

Collecting Customer Communications   145

Summary   146

Chapter 11 ▪ Metadata in Unstructured Data   147

Metadata in the Unstructured Environment   147

Internal Metadata   148

External Metadata   149

Approaching Metadata Through the Data Model   150

The Basis for the Data Model   150

The Levels of the Data Model   152

How the Components Relate—The Larger Perspective   153

Two Types of Data Model—External and Internal   154

How Is the Internal Data Model Created?   155

Creating the External Data Model   156

Using Generic Data Models   156

The Corporate Glossary   158

Corporate Taxonomy   159

Corporate Ontology   159

The Role of the Data Model   160

Data Quality in the Unstructured Environment   161

Summary   162

Chapter 12 ▪ A Methodology for Textual Analytics   163

Preparing the Basic Components   163

Specifying the Processing   167

Organizing the Source Data   168

Analyzing the Results   170

Summary   173

Chapter 13 ▪ Merging Unstructured Databases into the Data Warehouse   175

The Data Warehouse   176

Linking Databases   176

Communications-Based Linkage Between Unstructured and Structured Data   177

Identifier-Based Linkage Between Unstructured and Structured Data   178

An Integrated Data Warehouse 179

Multi-Database Linkage 179

ETL for Unstructured Data 180

Housing Databases in DBMS Technology 180

Binding the Databases Together 181

Federated Analytical Technology 182

Simple Queries 182

Summary 184

Chapter 14 ▪ Using SQL to Analyze Text 185

A Simple Query 187

Indirect Query 189

Proximity Search 191

Basic Word String Snippet Report 192

Summary 194

Chapter 15 ▪ Case Study—Textual Analytics in Medical Research 195

Medical Records 195

The Cardiology Study 196

The Challenge of Terminology 196

Volumes of Data 197

Revealing a Strategy 197

The First Iteration 198

The Second Iteration 198

The Third Iteration 199

Fourth Iteration 200

Fifth Iteration 200

Textual Analytics 200

Standard Analytical Tools 201

Chapter 16 ▪ Case Study—A Database for Harmful Chemicals 203

The Institution's Data on Harmful Chemicals 203

An Abundance of Paper Reports 204

A Request for Analyses Leading to the Requirement for Storing Data Electronically   204

Putting Paper Data in an Electronic Format   205

Creating the Standard Set of Reference Tables   205

Text Editing and Integration   206

Textual Analytics   206

Periodic Additions   208

Chapter 17 ■ Case Study—Managing Contracts Through an Unstructured Database   209

A Hodgepodge of Contracts   209

A Plan for Textual Analytics   210

Iterative Development   211

Analytical Processing   212

Chapter 18 ■ Case Study—Creating a Corporate Taxonomy (Glossary)   215

A Technological Jumble   215

The IT Problem   216

The Issue of Terminology   217

Creating a Corporate Taxonomy (Glossary)   217

Creating Definitions and Equivocations   218

Using the Taxonomy   218

Chapter 19 ■ Case Study—Insurance Claims   219

A Collection of Inconsistent Claims   219

A Wealth of Information   220

Creating the Integrated Data Warehouse   221

First Iteration   221

Second Iteration   223

Third Iteration   223

Fourth Iteration   224

Glossary   227

Index   233

Preface

There have been two environments that have grown up side by side—the structured environment and the unstructured environment. The structured environment is typified by transactions, databases, records, keys, and attributes. The unstructured environment is typified by email, spreadsheets, medical records, documents, and reports.

It is amazing that at the same time that these worlds have grown up side by side, they have grown separately. It is as if these worlds exist in alternate universes.

The world of analytics and business intelligence has grown up around structured information. With business intelligence, we have displays of information, summaries, pivots, and an entire world of analytical processing. With business intelligence, we can make sense of the numbers, facts, and figures that hide out in the systems that run our corporations.

For analyses of text—unstructured information—there is nowhere near the amount of sophistication that exists in the structured environment. In the unstructured world, a few search engines can find documents and that is about it.

Does that mean that there is no important or useful information in the unstructured environment? The answer is—of course not. There is a wealth of important and useful information in the unstructured environment, but it is not as easily recoverable as information in the structured environment. The information in the unstructured environment is much more difficult to get a handle on.

There are many reasons why textual data is more difficult to handle than structured, transaction-oriented data. The primary reason is the lack of repeatability of textual data and the lack of predictability about the contents of the data. Textual data is hard to handle because it is hard to find, and it is hard to find because it does not entail repetition to any great degree.

This book is about doing textual analytics and the technologies that can be used to do textual analytics.

Two major architectural and technological approaches to doing textual analytics are used. One approach is to look at and gather the textual data in the unstructured environment. When there, the textual data is analyzed and manipulated in the unstructured environment. The unstructured environment seems like a natural place to do textual analytics because, after all, the text resides in the unstructured environment.

The other architectural approach is to look at and gather the textual data in the unstructured environment and then bring the textual data to the structured environment to do the textual analytics there.

It might seem strange or even unnatural to take the approach of accessing and gathering textual data in the unstructured environment and then bringing the textual data to the structured environment for analytical processing; however, there are good reasons for doing exactly that. Some of those reasons follow:

- The analytical environment has already been created in the structured environment. If we bring unstructured data to that environment, we can leverage existing investments. We already have trained end users, trained support staff, and licenses in place. So, why not bring the unstructured text to the structured environment where analytical tools are already in place?

- Proprietary software. When we bring in technology to do analytical processing in the unstructured environment, that technology is proprietary. Do we actually want more proprietary software in our world? Isn't it a much more rational approach to use open software that has thousands of users and uses around the world, rather than bring in proprietary software that might or might not meet the long-term goals of the organization?

- By bringing unstructured text to the structured environment, we can create links between the unstructured data and our structured data, making possible analysis that otherwise would not have been possible. In doing so, we can build an integrated data warehouse that takes into account both structured and unstructured data.

- If we don't bring unstructured data to the structured environment, we are going to have to re-create the analytical infrastructure in the unstructured environment. Is that advisable? We already have an analytical infrastructure. Why not use it?

For these reasons, this book is about what is required to go to the unstructured environment, find and integrate the textual data there, and then bring the unstructured textual data to the structured environment and organize it in a meaningful manner. After the textual data is in the structured analytical environment, a new world of analyses opens up.

One of the recurring themes of this book is the need for integration of text before it is useful. In most environments and in most circumstances, text is nonhomogeneous. People might talk in English, but for all practical purposes, they speak in dialects. Before analytical processing can be done effectively, there must be a common tongue established. Stated differently, if all you do is gather text and throw it into a database, you end up with the Tower of Babel. The Tower of Babel led nowhere, certainly not up to God.

One of the requirements of textual analytical processing is accessing and analyzing text in a colloquial vocabulary and a common vocabulary. The textual analyst needs *both* abilities.

The classical approach to text and text processing is to use semantics and natural language processing. This book describes a different approach. Without fail, the approach taken in this book is that text—made up of words—is just another form of data. The approach that looks at words as just another unit of data frees the analyst from the trap of context. It is true that words taken out of context can have twisted meanings in some occasions. It is also true that freeing words from context opens up the door to entirely new and novel kinds of processing that simply are not possible when having to stop and consider the context of text at every turn.

There is a tradeoff. Paying attention to context when dealing with text entails a certain set of opportunities and precision. However, freeing text from context opens up entirely new and exciting vistas.

This book assumes that words are treated as just another unit of data and does not take context into consideration in 99.99 percent of the cases.

This book is for a wide audience. It is for students of computer science, general managers, database designers, data modelers, database administrators, researchers, and end users—in short, it is for anyone facing the challenge of taking a body of text and trying to make sense of it. In addition, this book answers the questions, "How do we bridge the gap between structured and unstructured systems?" and "How do we create an integrated data warehouse that incorporates both structured and unstructured data?"

The discipline of textual analytics is in its infancy; it is entirely predictable that more discussion and more advances will be made in the future about this subject. This book represents merely the first step in what is likely to be a massive field of endeavor in years to come.

We hope that you find the book full of useful information. We hope the book at least sets you down the right path to enjoying the fruits of textual analytics.

Bill Inmon, January 11, 2007
Tony Nesavich, January 11, 2007

Acknowledgments

My most sincere thanks to Bill Inmon for affording me the opportunity to work with him at Inmon Data Systems.

—Anthony Nesavich

About the Authors

Bill Inmon—the "father of data warehousing"—has written 50 books and published in nine languages on subjects such as data warehousing, database design, and architecture.

For current events, seminars, conference speaking schedules, and a lot of other information related to data warehousing, unstructured data, and textual extract/transform/load (ETL), take a look at Bill Inmon's Web site at www.inmoncif.com.

Anthony AKA "Tony" Nesavich received his Master's degree in computer information technology from Regis University in Denver, Colorado. He worked with Bill Inmon at Inmon Data Systems (IDS) where he was instrumental in the development of the IDS Foundation software. Much of Tony's contributions to IDS are discussed in this book. Tony lives in Denver, Colorado, with his wife, Melissa, and his faithful dog, Lola.

I

Unstructured Textual Data in the Organization

Most organizations have two kinds of data: structured data and unstructured textual data. Because structured data preceded unstructured data in the workplace, unstructured data is often best understood in contrast to structured data. Structured data is data that is represented by numbers, tables, rows, columns, attributes, and so forth. Most IT professionals have spent the better part of their professional lives with structured data. As its name implies, structured data is usually disciplined, well behaved, predictable, and repeatable.

Structured data usually is generated as by-products of doing a transaction. A check is cashed, an ATM activity is done, an insurance claim is made, a production run is completed, a car is sold—these are typical transactions that generate a lot of structured data about the activity that has been done.

Structured data is made up of data types that are repeated continually. The same types of data are found in almost every transaction. The only things that differ from one transaction to the next are the values that the data types take. In addition to repeatability and predictability, the essence of the structured environment is numeric data. Although there is text in the structured environment, most text serves the purpose of identifying or describing some numeric data. The numeric data in the structured environment makes up the heart of the data that is found there and is heavily used for analytical purposes.

Unstructured Textual Data

The other major category of data found in the corporation is unstructured data. There are several forms—textual unstructured data and nontextual unstructured data, which includes images, colors, sounds, and shapes. This book is about textual unstructured data, which presents enough challenges on its own to fill a book (or even more than a book!).

Unstructured textual data is textual data found in emails, reports, documents, medical records, and spreadsheets. There is no format, structure, or repeatability to unstructured textual data. There is no one sitting on your shoulder telling you what to do when you write an email. You can write anything you want, however you want, and use any language you want. In addition, there are other forms of text that occur well outside the email environs, such as contracts, warranties, spreadsheets, telephone books, advertisements, marketing materials, annual reports, and many more forms of textual information that are the fabric of the organization. In short, unstructured textual data occurs almost everywhere and represents both a challenge and an opportunity to the organization that wants to use it for decision-making purposes.

It is true that many forms of unstructured data are not text-based. There are X-rays showing bones and breaks, real-estate listings with pictures, engineering change control documents mapping the structural changes made to complex edifices, MRIs that show detailed aspects of the human body, and scientific photos that help mankind unlock the secrets of the universe. But the most basic form of unstructured data is in the form of text. The focus in this book is on text, which presents its own set of challenges.

The purpose of this chapter is to provide an overview of unstructured textual data and the environment in which it sits. Unstructured textual data is so pervasive, is so ubiquitous, and has so many variations that it is hard to classify. In one place, unstructured textual data has one set of characteristics. In another place, unstructured textual data has a completely different set of characteristics. Because of this topsy-turvy, unpredictable nature, it is extremely difficult to generalize how to approach unstructured textual data.

Following are some examples of the nonuniform characteristics of unstructured textual data:

■ **Emails**—Emails are usually short relative to other documents. Emails usually contain a combination of business-related and nonbusiness-related information. There are usually a lot of emails, many of which are informal. Emails can be in any language (English, Spanish, German). In fact, emails can be in more than one language at the same time. Emails are normally identified by an email address and the time the email was sent.

- **Medical records**—Medical records can become quite voluminous and are full of medical jargon and terminology. Medical records are often quite large, some containing volumes of text. The reason why most medical records are text-based is that doctors prefer it that way. Most doctors prefer to write notes in text when dealing with a patient. In most environments, there are almost always fewer medical records than there are emails. (Although in the medical environment, there still are plenty of medical records.) Medical records are somewhat formalized, in the sense that doctors have a certain protocol that is used when writing a medical record. These records usually contain only information relevant to health and medicine.

- **Contracts**—Contracts are usually full of legal jargon and might contain business-related jargon as well. The text found in contracts usually has nothing but information relating to the contract. Contracts by and large vary greatly in size—some contracts are short, and some contracts are lengthy. Contracts are written in a legal style, according to the conventions of law and lawyers. There sometimes are a fair number of contracts in an organization, but never the number of contracts that there are emails. Contracts are almost always in a single language–for example, English, Spanish, or French.

And these are but a few of the types of unstructured textual data that exist in the organization. Each type of unstructured textual data has its own peculiarities and its own characteristics.

Unstructured Textual Data and Organizational Functions

To start to understand unstructured textual data, consider that there are different kinds of unstructured textual data associated with different functions within the organization. Table 1-1 shows some of the corporate functions and the unstructured textual data that is typical of those departments.

Table 1-1 Corporate Functions—Unstructured

Corporate Function	Unstructured Data Types
Accounting	Spreadsheets, notes, Word documents, audit trails, account descriptions
Call center	Conversations, notes, replies
Engineering	Bill of material, engineering changes, production archives, design specs
Finance	Spreadsheets, notes, annual reports
Human Resources	Emails, letters, hiring offers, termination documentation, evaluations, job specifications, employee manuals, holidays, policies
Legal	Agreements, amendments, proposals, contracts, meeting notes, telephone transcripts, patents, trademarks, nondisclosure

continues

Table 1-1 Corporate Functions—Unstructured   (continued)

Corporate Function	Unstructured Data Types
Marketing	Ads, spreadsheets, targets, accounts, forecasts, webinars, seminars, conferences, booth notes, feedback, customer contact notes
Operations	Manufacturing runs, defective products, reservations, claims processing, precious goods store, delivery notes, scheduling notes
Sales	Sales leads, sales calls, sales meetings, sales forecasts, spreadsheets, performance evaluations, customer meetings
Shipping	Delivery directions, fragile specifications, cooling temperature specifications, time of delivery specifications, speed of delivery specifications, tracking

The corporate function of accounting typically has spreadsheets, Word documents, audit reports, and audit trails associated with its activities. Call centers typically have recorded or transcribed conversations, replies, follow-up activities, and other notes associated with their activities. The engineering department typically has unstructured textual data associated with the bill of materials, engineering changes that have been made, production archives, and design specifications.

Each of these different forms of unstructured textual data has its own set of characteristics.

Unstructured textual data is not just endemic to different departments of the organization. Unstructured textual data appears in different forms and in different measures in different industries. Some industries have a lot of unstructured textual data while others have little. Table 1-2 shows unstructured textual data by industry and emphasizes the differences.

Table 1-2 Industries and Unstructured Data

Corporate Type	Type of Transaction Processing	Amount of Unstructured Data
Banking, finance	Heavy transaction (tx) processing	Light, scattered
Construction	Light tx processing	Light, scattered
Government	Tx processing	Heavy concentrations
Healthcare	Tx processing	In the fabric
Information processing	Heavy tx processing	Heavy concentrations
Insurance	Heavy tx processing	Heavy concentrations
Manufacturing	Tx processing	Heavy concentrations
Medicine	Light tx processing	In the fabric
Mining	Light tx processing	Heavy concentrations
Pharmaceuticals	Tx processing	Heavy concentrations
Real estate	Light tx processing	Light, scattered
Retailing	Heavy tx processing	Some pockets

Corporate Type	Type of Transaction Processing	Amount of Unstructured Data
Scientific	Light tx processing	Lots of heavy concentrations
Transportation	Heavy tx processing	Light, scattered
Utilities	Tx processing	Light, scattered

Table 1-2 shows that different industries have different mixes of transaction processing data and unstructured textual data. For example, banks are rich with transaction processing, checks, ATM activities, and other banking activities. Whereas banks certainly do have unstructured textual data, they do not have (relatively speaking) nearly as much unstructured textual data as they have structured data. On the other hand, medical environments are rich in unstructured textual data. The unstructured data is so ingrained in healthcare that it is part of the fabric of medicine and healthcare. Doctors write and take notes in a textual fashion, hospitals take notes textually, and so on. The world of medicine is rich in text, and certainly transactions occur in the medical environment. Patients get billed on a regular basis, for example. But—relatively speaking— the medical environment is heavily ingrained with textual data.

Unstructured Data and Its Characteristics

One of the perplexing aspects of unstructured textual data is that the characteristics associated with the different forms of unstructured textual data are mixed across the many different forms of the data. There is little uniformity among the different forms of unstructured textual data.

Table 1-3 on unstructured textual data and characteristics points out the extreme lack of uniformity of the characteristics. Table 1-3 is complex and deserves an explanation. The columns are as follows:

- Direct business relevance refers to the unstructured textual data. Unstructured textual data that is directly business relevant would include legal documents, customer credit reports, insurance claims, and airline reservations complaints. Indirect business relevance of unstructured textual data might include human resources, employee evaluations, and some email.

- Formal/informal refers to the way the unstructured textual data is written. Informal unstructured textual data would include email and letters. Formal unstructured textual data would include contracts and quarterly reports. (Note: Only Warren Buffet can get away with an informal annual report, and even then there is a section that is formalized.)

Table 1-3 Unstructured Data and Its Characteristics

Corporate Data Type	Direct Business Relevance	Formal/Informal	Jargon	Keys	Number of Documents	Repeated Data	Retention	Typical Storage	Updated	Volume
Advertising	High	Informal	Limited	Usually not	Few	Almost never	Long cycle	Electronic	No	Very limited
Company manuals	High	Formal/informal	Large	Limited	Few	Very small amount	Long cycle	Paper, electronic	Yes	Very limited
Contracts	Very high	Formal/informal	Large	Limited	Moderate	Almost never	Very long cycle	Paper	Occasionally	Very limited
Customer call feedback	High	Informal	Limited	Very infrequent	Moderate	Almost never	Limited	Electronic	Never	Can be voluminous
Customer complaints	High	Informal	Limited	Very infrequent	Moderate	Almost never	Limited	Electronic	No	Small to moderate
Descriptive text	High	Formal/informal	Large	Usually not	Large	Almost always	Long cycle	Electronic	Yes	Moderate to large
Email	Mixed	Informal	Some	Specialized	Very large	Almost never	Varies	Electronic	No	Can be very large
Employee files	Low	Mixed	Limited	Almost never	Small	Very limited	Long cycle	Paper, electronic	No	Relatively small
Engineering bill of matls	Very high	Formal/informal	High	Yes	Moderate	Yes	Varies	Electronic	Yes	Varies
Employee evaluations	Low	Mixed	Low	Almost never	Small	No	Long cycle	Paper, electronic	No	Small to moderate
Internet	Mixed	Informal	Mixed	Seldom	Small	No	Varies	Electronic	Infrequently	Moderate
Legal docs	High	Formal/informal	Large	Very few	Moderate	None	Very long cycle	Paper, electronic	Occasionally	Usually very small
Marketing materials	High	Informal	Some	Very few	Small	Almost never	Varies	Paper, electronic	Never	Usually very small
Memos	Usually high	Informal	Some	Very few	Small	Almost never	Varies	Paper, electronic	Never	Very small

Corporate Data Type	Direct Business Relevance	Formal/ Informal	Jargon	Keys	Number of Documents	Repeated Data	Retention	Typical Storage	Updated	Volume
Order information	High	Formal/ informal	Some	Lots	Moderate	Sometimes	Not long	Paper, electronic	Yes	Small to moderate
Presentations	High	Informal	Some	Infrequently	Small	Almost never	Short	Paper, electronic	Sometimes	Small
Quarterly report	High	Formal/ informal	Some	Infrequently	Small	Almost never	Very long cycle	Paper, electronic	Never	Very small
Reference tables	High	Formal/ informal	Large	Lots	Small	Lots	Varies	Electronic	Yes	Small
Reports	High	Informal	Large	Infrequently	Small	Sometimes	Varies	Paper, electronic	Sometimes	Small
Shipments	High	Formal/ informal	Some	Lots	Moderate	Sometimes	Short	Paper, electronic	Sometimes	Small to moderate
Spreadsheets	Usually high	Formal/ informal	Some	Frequently	Small	Yes	Short	Electronic	Yes	Small to moderate
Telephone transcripts	Varies	Informal	Limited	Occasionally	Moderate	No	Varies	Electronic	No	Small to moderate
Warranties	High	Informal	Some	Yes	Moderate	Seldom	Varies	Paper, electronic	Never	Small to moderate
Word docs	Varies	Informal	Varies	Varies	Moderate	Seldom	Varies	Electronic	Yes	Small to moderate

- Jargon refers to the type of language used. Some unstructured textual data tends to have a lot of jargon, and others tend to have very little. Contracts have a lot of legal jargon. Scientific research tends to have a lot of scientific jargon. Emails usually have a little jargon. Employee human resources files typically have little jargon.

- Keys refer to the ability of the analyst to tie the unstructured textual data to some singularly identifiable entity, such as a customer, product, or salesperson. Emails have keys such as the email address. The engineering bill of materials has lots of keys, referring to a product. Employee evaluations might refer to only an employee number. Telephone transcripts typically are identified only by a time and telephone number.

- Number of documents refers to the general number of documents on hand. There are usually a lot of email documents and only a relatively small number of contracts on hand (although there are exceptions to this).

- Repeated data refers to the repetition of data within the unstructured textual data. Phone books are full of repetitive data. Emails—as a rule—are not filled with repetitive data.

- Retention refers to how long unstructured textual data is kept. Internet text is not usually kept around for a long time, but quarterly reports are kept for a very long time.

- Typical storage media refers to the media on which the unstructured textual data is stored. Transcripted telephone conversations are stored almost exclusively electronically. Emails are usually stored electronically; although, they are occasionally printed out. Many forms of unstructured textual data are stored in both paper and electronic format.

- Update refers to whether the unstructured textual data can be changed when originally created. (Note: Update does not refer to adding unstructured textual data to an existing body of data. It refers to the changing of textual data when created.) Emails are almost never updated. In fact, in some cases it is illegal to update emails. On the other hand, ordinary Word documents are updated all the time.

- Volume of data refers to the total volume of data that is associated with a type of unstructured textual data. Typically, there is a large volume of data associated with email. But there would be a small volume of data for advertising, for example.

When you look down any of the columns, you see that there is little or no rhyme-or-reason to the characteristics. One form of unstructured textual data has one set of characteristics, and the next form of unstructured textual data has a completely different set of characteristics. It is this complete lack of characteristic pattern coupled with the complexity of language that causes the difficulty with the automated usage of data.

Updating Structured and Unstructured Data

One of the major differences between the structured and unstructured environments is that in the structured environment data is updated on a regular basis. Whenever your ATM is used, whenever a deposit is made, whenever a check is cashed, your bank account is updated. And it is at these times that structured data is commonly measured, or some record is created.

But unstructured data—for the most part—doesn't change after creation. After a contract is created and signed, it might be amended, but the original contract cannot have wording changed. After an email is written and sent, it is not changed. After a magazine article is written and published, it is not changed. In case after case, unstructured data is not changed when published. This difference between structured data and unstructured data creates many operating differences in the environments.

The Challenges of Unstructured Textual Data and Analytical Processing

Traditionally, analytic processing is used for business analysis of structured data. Structured data is particularly amenable to analytic processing because structured data is

- **Shaped by transactions**—Transactions are predictable in that the same types of data appear over and over again.

- **Shaped by numbers**—Transactions have a lot of numerical data, and in many cases, it is the numerical data that is of primary interest. Furthermore, numeric information can be easily manipulated—addition, subtraction, multiplication.

For these reasons, analytical processing is a natural partner with structured data. However, unstructured textual data has none of these characteristics. To do analytical processing against unstructured textual data, it is necessary to overcome or address several obstacles. Some of these challenges follow:

- **Physically accessing unstructured textual data**—Unstructured textual data is stored in a wide variety of formats. Some formats are easy to read and other formats are difficult to read. However, unstructured textual data must be accessible wherever it hides, whether or not it is easily accessible.

- **Terminology**—Terminology is a real issue. Three people call the same thing something different. If analytical processing is to be done against unstructured textual data, there must be a rationalization of terminology, or the analyst cannot recognize when the text illustrates the same thing.

- **Languages**—What if analysis must be done against unstructured textual data that is in English, French, and Japanese?

- **Volume of data**—The sheer volume of data that can be collected can defeat the efforts of the analyst who wants to see what is contained in a body of text. The sheer volume of unstructured textual data, coupled with the fact that analysis usually has to look at every word, makes the resources required for some kinds of unstructured analysis daunting.

- **Differing priorities of unstructured textual data**—Some unstructured textual data is "hot," meaning that the unstructured textual data needs to be treated with a great deal of sensitivity. Other unstructured textual data is merely normal, meaning that nothing is sensitive or urgent about it. The "hot" unstructured textual data usually has real and dire circumstances surrounding it, such that it must be handled in a completely different manner than other unstructured textual data.

- **Searchability of unstructured textual data**—It is one thing to do a simple search of unstructured textual data. In a simple search, some data—an argument—is passed onto the search engine, and a search is made on the basis of the argument. For example, a search is made on the term felony. In a simple search, the term felony is used, and everywhere there is a reference to felony, a hit to an unstructured document is made. But a simple search is crude. It does not find references to crime, arson, murder, embezzlement, vehicular homicide, and such, even though these crimes are types of felonies. A more sophisticated search—an indirect search— finds references to these types of felonies.

- **The economics of the infrastructure**—A cost of the infrastructure is required to support the unstructured textual environment. There is the cost of software, storage, and hardware. In addition, the cost of the personnel is required on an ongoing basis to make the unstructured environment operate on a daily basis.

- **Security**—Some unstructured textual data is not secure. Other unstructured textual data requires a careful consideration for how the unstructured textual data is to be handled and who has access to it. As the organization moves forward with the unstructured environment, it must not be assumed that all unstructured textual data is open and available to anyone who has access to the unstructured textual data.

This is just the short list of challenges that await the organization that attempts to come to grips with the unstructured textual data environment.

The Opportunities of Unstructured Textual Data

From the preceding discussion, it is obvious that there is a cost—in time, money, and manpower—to get a handle on the unstructured textual data environment. Why would an organization want to come to grips with the unstructured environment?

A world of promise and opportunity in information is buried in the unstructured textual data environment. Organizations have a tremendous opportunity at making better decisions—more timely, more accurate, more informed decisions—when they incorporate unstructured information into the decision-making process. That is the reason why organizations need to come to grips with the unstructured textual data environment. Stated differently, organizations that look only at their structured data—usually transaction-based data—miss an entire class of information that waits to be used for the decision-making process.

Organizations that base all their decisions on structured data use only a portion of the corporate information on which to base decisions. It is like a manager making decisions solely on revenues for this month. Although this month's revenues are an interesting figure and are certainly important, a lot of other types of information are factored in as well. There are monthly expenses, revenue figures for next year, the projections for next year, the size of the customer base, and new product announcements that need to be considered.

So exactly what kinds of useful information can be gained from looking at unstructured textual data? Some examples of useful information that might be buried in unstructured textual data include the following:

- **Customer feedback**—Do customers like or hate a new product? A new service?

- **Contractual commitments**—How many contracts have represented productive agreements? Unproductive agreements? How have corporations performed over many different contracts?

- **Warranties**—Is there a pattern to the warranties that are presented to a company?

- **Medical information**—What medical conditions correlate with other medical conditions? If a subpopulation of subjects is created, how does that change the correlations to medical conditions?

- **Compliance**—How has the corporation met reporting obligations?

- **Security**—Are employees saying and doing things that are not proper according to the guidelines for corporate conduct?

- **Marketing "buzz"**—What is said in the customer community about new products? New services? The company and its activities?

- **Competition**—What is known about new products? New promotions? New services?

- **Human resources**—Is the company actually living up to its obligations for hiring practices? To opportunity? To dismissals?

But perhaps the biggest promise of unstructured textual data lies in its ability to be combined with structured data. As a simple example of combining structured data and unstructured textual data, consider emails. How important are emails for the creation of the complete picture for a customer? The answer is that communications with the customer are important.

Consider the following simple example. An organization has a lot of demographic information about its customers. Suppose there is a Mrs. Jones who is a customer. The company knows that Mrs. Jones

- Is a mother of three
- Is a college graduate (Tufts, 1975)
- Is a systems analyst
- Works for Merrill Lynch
- Makes $105,000 per year plus commission
- Drives a Lexus
- Vacations in the Bahamas
- Pays her bills on time
- Is married to John Jones
- Invests in mutual funds

With this information, the company thinks that it is prepared to deal with Mrs. Jones, establishing a personal and long-term relationship with her.

So how important is demographic information in understanding Mrs. Jones? Very important. How important is Mrs. Jones' demographic information in the face of having no information about communications? Not important at all.

It seems that Mrs. Jones ordered some goods a month ago. The goods were late, sent to the wrong address, and broken when they arrived. And Mrs. Jones sent a scalding email last week to the corporation. How important is it to know about communications when trying to establish a relationship with Mrs. Jones? Vitally important.

And what are emails? They are nothing but a form of unstructured textual data. There are many cases where establishing a relationship between unstructured textual data and structured data leads to business opportunities that are today unimagined.

Summary

In this chapter, we examined the totality of the world of unstructured textual data. There are many difficulties with unstructured textual data. It has many characteristics, depending on the type of unstructured textual data that is discussed. Different industries have different needs for unstructured textual data. Different functional areas in the organization have various needs for unstructured textual data.

There are many different challenges when using unstructured textual data, such as challenges of terminology, volumes of data, and the cost of the infrastructure.

With the challenges, there is the promise of opening up an entirely different world of processing and opportunity. Unstructured textual data by itself contains much useful and interesting information. But unstructured textual data coupled with structured data opens up even more opportunities for unlocking the promise of unstructured textual data.

As powerful as the opportunity for unstructured data in the organization and business is, the technical environment that holds unstructured data must be understood, because many of the opportunities for exploiting unstructured data are shaped by, or certainly influenced by, the technical environment. Chapter 2, "The Environments of Structured Data and Unstructured Data," addresses the technology infrastructure appropriate to unstructured data.

2

The Environments of Structured Data and Unstructured Data

The essence of textual analytics for the world of unstructured data is the ability to analyze text in much the same way that numbers are analyzed by the classical Business Intelligence (BI) tools found in the structured data environment. To understand what the issues are for textual analytics—from an environmental perspective—there needs to be a firm understanding of the different environments—the unstructured data environment and the structured data environment.

The Structured Environment

The structured environment is one that has been the domain of the technician for years. From the first assembler programs and the COBOL programs of yesterday to the C++ and the vb.net programs of today, there is a world that is rooted in technology that operates on the basis of structure and discipline.

One of the fundamental building blocks of the structured environment is that of the computer and the different operating components of the computer. Figure 2-1 shows some of these basic components:

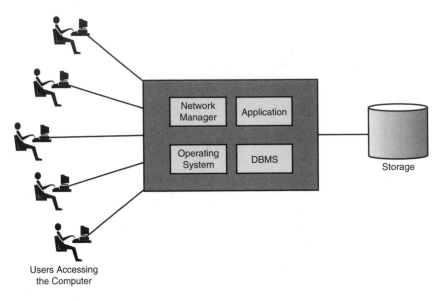

Users Accessing
the Computer

Figure 2-1   The basic components of a computer

- Network manager
- Operating system
- Application manager
- Database management system (DBMS)

Regardless of the size or even the age of the computer, you can find these basic components:

- **Network manager**—It is the job of the network manager to understand who is on the network and how messages can be sent and received to those nodes on the network. Some of the issues the network manager faces are the speed with which messages can be sent and received, the handling of large messages, the flexibility to add and delete nodes from the network, and the format of the messages sent and received.
- **Operating system**—The operating system is the software that manages the activities internal to the computer. It manages priorities of operation, sequencing of events, protocols and formats that are required for the communications internal to the computer, and starting and stopping of applications. Some of the benchmarks of an operating system are the speed of operation that can be achieved, bandwidth of the operating system, ability of the systems programmer to find and alleviate bottlenecks, events that occur upon encountering an error, and different technologies that can be integrated.

- **Application**—The application is the software that turns the general purpose computer into a specialized device dedicated to solving problems. The application takes business requirements and turns them into a solution. The application can perform a wide variety of tasks, such as gathering information from a diversity of sources, collecting information, restructuring that information, putting the information into storage in a meaningful manner, applying logic to show understanding of an issue, and speedily reading information. Some of the benchmarks of an application are the speed with which the application can be constructed, the speed with which the application can be run, the throughput that can be achieved by an application, and the grace (or lack thereof) with which an application can be modified.

- **DBMS**—The DBMS is the software that stores and retrieves data. It is responsible for taking data from the application and the operating system and placing the data on storage, usually disk storage. The DBMS is benchmarked by how much data it can handle, the rate at which the data can be handled, and the rate at which data can be placed on or retrieved from disk storage.

Databases

Both the structured and unstructured environments have operating systems, network managers, and applications. The primary difference between the structured and unstructured environments is the DBMS that organizes, manipulates, indexes, and sorts data.

Figure 2-2 shows that the tables that reside in the database are managed under a DBMS.

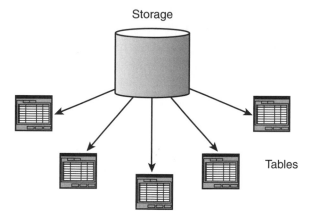

Figure 2-2   The DBMS manages tables.

The basic unit of information that the DBMS operates on is a table of data (or sometimes databases). A table is a collection of uniformly defined, repeatable data. Typically, tables relate to objects that, in turn, can be related to the world of business. Usually, there are customer tables, product tables, shipment tables, order tables, and manufacturing tables. However, you can find many other kinds of data in tables, such as reference data, control parameters, calendars, and summary data.

A database is composed of a table, and tables are composed of records, as shown in Figure 2-3.

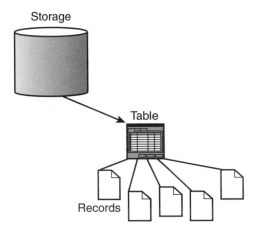

Figure 2-3 Tables contain records.

Tables, in turn, contain rows of data (or records). A row is a basic unit of information representing one finite event. There can be a row of data for the bank deposit made this morning, for a loan payment made this afternoon, and for an ATM activity made last night. Depending on the table, there will be a different kind of activity that triggers the creation of a row. If the table was for production control in a manufacturing environment, there might be a row created for the measurement of the work done by a shift, another row for the completion of a production run, and yet another row for the start of a manufacturing run.

Rows typically mark discrete events, such as the completion of a unit of business activity. Each row is identical in content to other rows in the sense that the same type of data is found in each row. The difference between rows is the values that are contained in each type of data.

Typically, rows have *keys*, which are identifiers for a record that might be unique. A row can have several keys or identifiers. The key can be a single identifier or a compound identifier. The row can be located by looking at a single key or multiple keys in tandem with each other.

Figure 2-4 shows the further breakdown of data in a database.

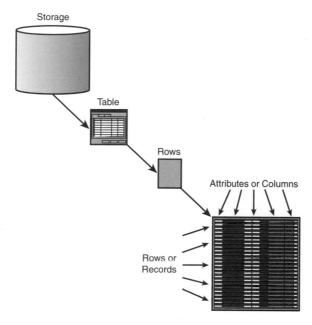

Figure 2-4   Tables are made up of rows or records.

A row (or record) consists of attributes or columns. The attribute has its own physical characteristics, such as NUMERIC, CHAR (character), or VARCHAR (a character set of varying length). Many specifications are possible for the definition of an attribute. An attribute is associated with a name—its metadata—and some counterpart in the business world. For example, an attribute might be called BALANCE (its metadata), and the attribute might hold the values that are in my account right now. If BALANCE is $5,000 for my account, the implication is that I have $5,000 in assets in my bank account.

Each row will normally have the same attributes as any other row. Because of this repetition, the environment is called the *structured environment*. The environment is structured because the end user can neither arbitrarily decide to create a new attribute for his private usage nor can the end user decide to put a social security number into the BALANCE field. (Unless, of course, the end user enters a large and specific amount of money into an account.) There is great discipline in the way data is structured and stored. That is why it is called the structured environment.

Speed of Storage, Retrieval

One of the advantages of the discipline required for the structured environment is the possibility of speed of storage and the speed of information retrieval. Because of the great discipline of the structured environment, data can be placed on disk storage with confidence and can be retrieved from there with confidence. Stated differently, when there is a desire to retrieve information in the structured environment, because of the discipline in storing data in a structured manner, the data that is sought can be retrieved because the system knows the meaning and significance of the data when it arrives at a physical address of storage.

In the unstructured environment, there is no discipline of storage as exists in the structured environment; therefore, data access is awkward and often sequential.

Figure 2-5 shows that in the structured environment there exists a correspondence of a business activity to the creation and storage of a row of data in a table. In Figure 2-5, a man has done some business with a clerk or bank teller, and in the row of data, there is a record of the particulars of the activity. The next customer and the next transaction cause one or more rows to be created as well and reflects that business activity.

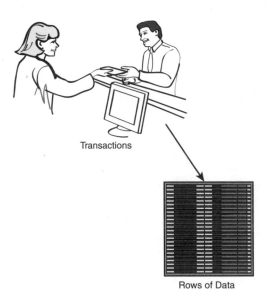

Transactions

Rows of Data

Figure 2-5 Each transaction results in the creation of a new row or record.

The Unstructured Environment

The other world of processing is the unstructured environment. In the unstructured environment, there is as much freedom and lack of discipline as there was discipline in the structured environment. Ironically, when measured from the volume of data found in the different environments, it is estimated that there is 2 to 10 times as much unstructured data as there is structured data. This, of course, varies tremendously, depending on the industry, number of users, and type of users.

The unstructured environment is typified by people "doing their own thing." There are few, if any, guidelines or rules as to how to create, store, or retrieve unstructured data. Unstructured data can be created at any pace, in any language, using proper or improper language, at any time of the day. Unstructured data is not created with any association or with any particular business event. Unstructured data is created when and however the end user wants and for whatever purpose the end user wants.

Unstructured data is often created for the purpose of communication. Some communication is direct; in other cases, communication is indirect. Or communication might be short, and in other cases, long. Or communication might be informal, and in other cases, formal. Another difference might be that in some cases communication is casual, and in other cases, legally binding.

Emails

One common form of unstructured communication is that of email, as shown in Figure 2-6.

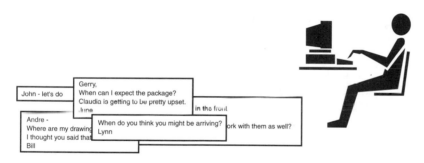

Figure 2-6   The unstructured world—email

Emails are the essence of informality. They occur often and are as casual as a chatty conversation. There are many emails that fly about the messaging systems of the corporation. Emails occur night and day, and on the weekends, too. Emails have both personal and private usage. One email might ask about the status of an account, and the next email might be an invitation to go on a date. Emails can be sent to many people at the same time. Emails have little or no identifying data in them other than an email address and the time of transmission.

There is valuable information that flows through the emails of the corporation. The trick is to find and recognize those emails that have useful corporate information.

There normally are so many emails flowing through a corporation that they have the tendency to "choke the system." It is like the canals and waterways in Florida being choked by plants that serve no useful purpose other than clogging up the normal flow of water. There are so many emails that there needs to be a process to weed out the unuseful emails so that information can flow efficiently.

As a rule, emails are short (although a few emails are very large). Emails contain attachments, and the attachments are an essential part of the email as well.

Spreadsheets

Spreadsheets are pervasive. Accountants, financial planners, managers, and many other people use spreadsheets. Spreadsheets are free form. When a person sets out to create a spreadsheet, the form and content are entirely up to the analyst (see Figure 2-7).

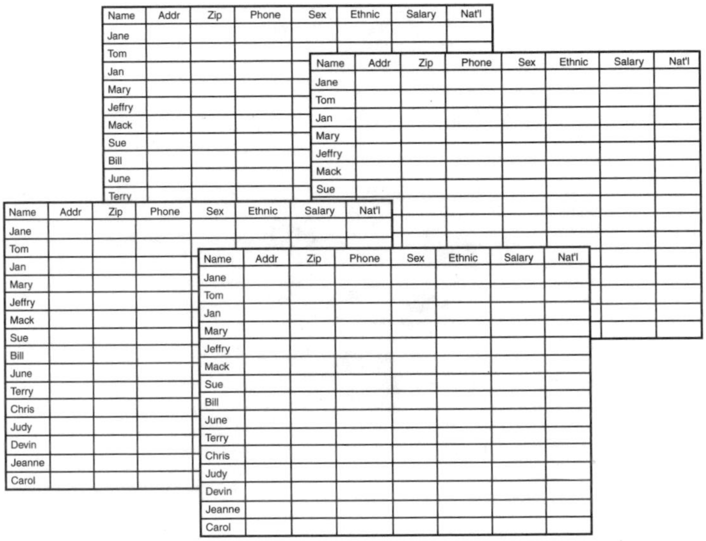

Figure 2-7   The unstructured world—spreadsheets

Spreadsheets can contain both numeric and character data and can be simple or complex. Spreadsheets can be large or small, and can exist on personal computers or on servers. There are usually keys or identifiers in spreadsheets. However, the keys that exist have been defined by the analyst creating the spreadsheet and might or might not be intelligible to the outsider.

In a word, spreadsheets are a regularly occurring form of unstructured data, or at least semistructured data.

The metadata in a spreadsheet is typically found in the column headings. There, however, might be metadata elsewhere in a spreadsheet depending on the needs of the creator.

Transcripted Telephone Conversations

Another form of unstructured data is that of transcripted telephone conversations in which the conversations are taped and then a transcript is made of the conversation. The transcripts of telephone conversations always have some degree of error. There are many reasons for the normal inaccuracy of transcripts—for example, inaudible words, garbled words, words spoken with a heavy accent, and words spoken in a different language. Even when humans listen to other humans, 100% of the words are not heard. The human brain listens to what is said and "fills in the blanks" when something is missed. Transcription technology cannot be expected to do better than the human brain. The object is not to have a perfect transcript, but to have a usable transcript (see Figure 2-8).

Figure 2-8   The unstructured world—transcripted telephone conversations

The conversation reflects what was said. There are no rules for speaking, so the content of transcripted conversations is completely unstructured. There might be a lot of data contained in transcriptions.

No keys exist in transcriptions. The only key information is the date of the phone call and the telephone numbers that have been connected.

No metadata regularly appears in transcripted telephone conversations.

Medical Records

Another regularly occurring form of unstructured data is the medical record. Medical records take on many different forms—from the structured data that result from the patient filling out a form at the emergency room to completely unstructured data that is created by the doctor taking notes in longhand during a patient visit (see Figure 2-9).

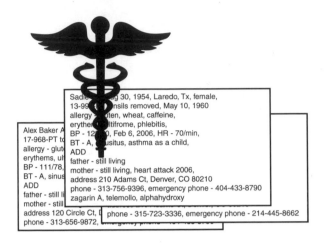

Figure 2-9 The unstructured world—medical records

In almost every case, there is at least some unstructured data in medical records. One of the issues of unstructured data in medical records is terminology. One doctor has one background and training whereas another doctor has another background. One part of the medical record is made by a nurse and another part is made by a hospital administrator. When there is a need to look across medical records, there is a need to "rationalize" the data—resolve the terminology into a standard set of terms.

The only consistent keys in medical records are the patient identifier and the doctor identifier. Any other keys are merely coincidental.

There is little or no metadata that has been placed in medical records on a disciplined basis.

There can be large volumes of medical records, depending on the number of patients dealt with and the length of time that those records cover.

Legal Information

Another normal and regularly occurring location of unstructured data is where corporate legal information resides (see Figure 2-10). The types of unstructured data in this category are varied. To protect the company and its best interests, the lawyer might want almost anything included as legally protected data—spreadsheets, emails, letters, transcripted telephone conversation, and many other forms of unstructured data. When declared vital to the legal interests of the company, unstructured data should not be altered or deleted. (Although in some cases, there might be a great temptation to do exactly that.)

Figure 2-10 The unstructured world—legal information

Because of the widely varying form of unstructured data that can come under the control of the lawyer, organizing and searching that unstructured data becomes a real challenge. The lawyer faces all the challenges of dealing with unstructured data that the textual analyst faces, except the lawyer faces *all* the challenges, whereas the analyst at least has the advantage of technology in overcoming some of the obstacles that come with a particular set of textual data.

Corporate Contracts

In the same vein as protected documents for litigation are corporate contracts. Corporate contracts are unstructured data that is definitely relevant to the business of the corporation. There usually are a number of contracts dating back to the early days of the corporation. The corporate contracts have a jargon of their own. The keys that are typically found in corporate contracts include the contract number and the parties that are part of the agreement, as shown in Figure 2-11.

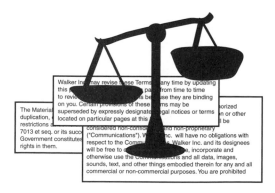

Figure 2-11 The unstructured world—corporate contracts

Metadata is often found in the contracts, but it is not identified as metadata. Instead, the metadata appears as section headings or even paragraph headings. There might be a considerable volume of data found in corporate contracts.

Unstructured Data—Found Everywhere

There are many places where corporate unstructured data is found. These simple examples are but a few of the common places where unstructured data resides. The common thread running through all occurrences of unstructured data is that the text is written at the will of the creator and follows no particular format or structure.

Unstructured data exists on, or at least passes through, a computer. However, unlike structured data, the data cannot be easily retrieved because there is no form or structure to the data. If unstructured data is to be retrieved, it is read and accessed sequentially and in its entirety. After the data has been read sequentially, tags or indexes can be created so that the data can be accessed easily thereafter. But there must be at least one complete pass of the unstructured data for the data to be accessible directly.

The Analytical Environment

Most corporations have created what can be termed the analytical environment. In some cases, the analytical environment is small and informal. In other cases, the analytical environment is large and very formal. In any case, the analytical environment is the place where information is generated for the purposes of corporate decision making. It is in the analytical environment that KPIs—key performance indicators—are calculated and made ready for decision makers. Some of these KPIs are created on a one-time-only basis. Other KPIs are generated on a regular basis—weekly, monthly, or quarterly.

Some typical KPIs include the following:

- Cash on hand
- Number of employees
- Monthly revenues
- Monthly expenses
- Expected sales
- Number of customers
- Number of repeat customers

The analytical environment uses technology typically known as Business Intelligence (BI) technology. BI technology is designed to capture information and then allow information to be analyzed and presented in many fashions. BI technology can produce reports. But the most elegant (and popular) output of BI technology is visualizations. The BI visualizations can take many different forms, as shown in Figure 2-12:

- Pareto charts
- Line graphs
- Scatter charts

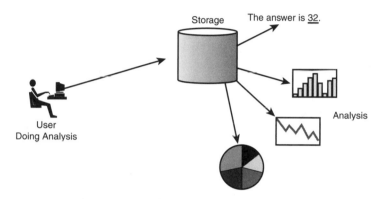

Figure 2-12 The DBMS manages tables.

The data that feeds the analytical environment is typically sourced from a data warehouse that contains granular information that has been integrated. The data warehouse also contains a wealth of historical information. The data inside the data warehouse is often called the "single version of the truth." Inside the data warehouse is where the bedrock data of the corporation resides.

Because data resides at a granular level, the same data can be shaped and reshaped as needed. One organization can look at data daily, whereas another organization can look at data monthly. One organization can look at data by sales territory, whereas another organization can look at data according to product line. In short, the granular data found in the data warehouse provides a foundation for many people looking at the same data in different ways.

The decision support analyst pulls data from the data warehouse and reshapes the data to suit the needs of the client. Then the decision support analyst puts the now-refined data into a *data mart*, which has data that is aggregated and summarized to suit the needs of a particular group of users. It is at this point—the data mart—that the end user has direct access to and direct analytical capabilities of corporate data.

Figure 2-13 shows that data marts are created from a foundation of a data warehouse.

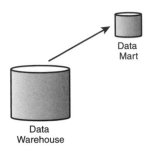

Figure 2-13 The BI foundation

Figure 2-14 shows that the direct access of the data is at the data mart level.

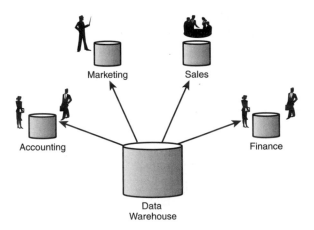

Figure 2-14 There are different data marts for different groups of users.

The analytical environment described is a depiction of the way that many organizations generate information for management decision making. But there is a great limitation to the environment that has been described: The analytical environment is fed by structured data only. It is transaction-oriented data exclusively that is used as a basis for decision making in the corporation. The implication of this limitation is that a great amount of useful information in the corporation is not found in the transaction processing environment.

Doing Textual Analytics in the Unstructured Environment or the Structured Environment

A major question arises in the building of the textual analytic environment. Where should you do textual analytics?

- In the unstructured environment?

- In the structured environment?

This issue is of major importance because it speaks directly to the reusability of an analytical environment that has already been created. Figure 2-15 shows that the placement of the textual analytical environment is of great strategic importance. There are multiple facets of consideration to both approaches.

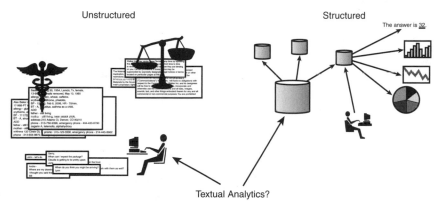

Figure 2-15   The issue is where to place textual analytics.

Textual analytics can be done in the unstructured environment. In many ways, this seems to be a natural place to do textual analytics because that's where the unstructured data resides. Therefore, it seems that doing textual analytics in the existing analytical environment is a sound proposition.

There is a major problem with this way of thinking, however. To do textual analytics in the unstructured environment, it is necessary to re-create much of the information analysis infrastructure that already exists in the structured environment. To do textual analytics properly, some of the components found in the structured infrastructure are needed:

- A DBMS that can handle large amounts of data

- Indexing capability that handles many different kinds of data

- Analytical tools that are capable of gathering, analyzing, and displaying information

These tools already exist as a standard part of the structured environment. The corporation has paid a large amount of money for installing and implementing the analytical environment in the structured environment. In addition, the end users are trained in the use of the technologies that are in the structured environment. There is already in place an environment for doing analytical processing, and that environment is the structured environment.

Therefore, it is much more appealing to bring the unstructured data to the structured environment than it is to re-create the analytical infrastructure in the unstructured environment.

Bringing Unstructured Data into the Structured Environment

Bringing unstructured data into the structured environment requires that the unstructured data be subjected to a rigorous process of integration and preconditioning. Merely bringing unstructured data into the structured environment without integrating and preconditioning the data produces little useful analysis. There is no question that unstructured data needs work to be useful in the analytical environment in the structured environment. But it is much easier to integrate and precondition unstructured data and to place it in the structured environment than it is to reconstruct the analytical environment elsewhere.

There is another reason why bringing unstructured data (after it has been integrated and preconditioned) into the structured environment makes sense. That reason is that there is the possibility that unstructured data can be integrated with structured data. And when structured and unstructured data can be analyzed together, all sorts of new possibilities for analysis arise. Figure 2-16 shows this possibility.

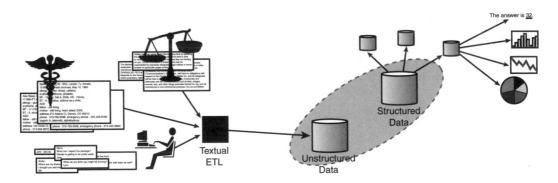

Figure 2-16   By creating a store of unstructured data, whole new possibilities for decision making are created.

When unstructured data is integrated and preconditioned to be placed in the structured environment for the purposes of analytical process, it is possible that unstructured data can be integrated with already existing structured data. There are many ways that this integration can occur:

- By email address
- By telephone number
- By employee number
- By social security number

If the data appears regularly in the unstructured environment, it can be used to match data in the structured environment. In doing so, a grand new possibility for information processing and analysis arises.

Summary

There are two environments that are very different from each other: the structured environment and the unstructured environment. The structured environment consists of disciplined and repeating data. The unstructured environment consists of free-form text.

To do textual analytics, the architectural decision must be made—should textual analytics be done in the structured environment or the unstructured environment? For a variety of good reasons, textual analytics is best done in the structured environment; however, it is necessary to read, integrate, and precondition the unstructured data before it can be used for the purposes of analytics in the structured environment.

The unstructured environment is rife with analytical potential. The next topic discussed is how to take the unstructured data and start to do something useful with it.

3

First Generation
Textual Analytics

Search technologies have existed for as long as there has been textual data. In time, these search technologies have become more powerful and more sophisticated. In many ways, it was with the Internet and the Internet search engines and the queries that they support that the world took its first good look at search technology.

The first generation of textual analytics is defined by technology whose primary purpose is to access and analyze unstructured textual information based on a search word. Figure 3-1 shows the basic form of first generation textual analytic technology.

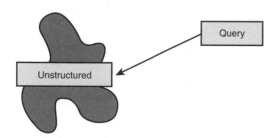

The Unstructured Environment

Figure 3-1 First generation unstructured processing

Simplicity

In concept, the first generation textual analytic software is simple. The purpose is to look at a body of unstructured information and to find the documents where certain unstructured information is located. The search is based on an *argument*. The argument is the search criteria that is defined by the analyst doing the search and has been passed to the search engine. The analyst defines the search argument, specifies the unstructured data to be analyzed, and then feeds that information into the search technology. The search technology then rummages through the unstructured documents and the text that is contained therein, and, upon finding a match with the search argument, creates a *hit*.

A hit simply means that the search argument is found in at least one place in the document.

In some cases, the search technology looks for only one occurrence of a hit within a document. In other cases, the search technology looks for all hits found in the document. Figure 3-2 shows the mechanics of the search technology and a hit that has been made.

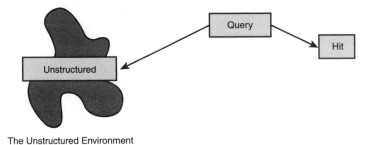

The Unstructured Environment

Figure 3-2   The query operates on unstructured data. Upon finding a match, a hit is created.

Search Engines That Look for Patterns

There is more than one type of search engine. The one that has been described is used for looking through documents in which there is little or no pattern of text. Occasionally, unstructured data occurs in a repeatable format. In some cases, the repeatable pattern is so prevalent that the data can be called semistructured data. In other cases, the patterns appear in only a small part of the unstructured data and are not considered to be semistructured data. An example of a pattern search in semistructured data is a collection of resumes. Each resume has a certain similarity. There might be a collection of chemical information sorted by chemical. Each chemical has essentially the same information about the properties of the chemical. There might be a collection of movie reviews sorted by movie.

In each of these collections of unstructured information, there is unstructured data. Each collection also has a certain sameness of text. In such a case, the search technology does not look for an argument. Instead, the search technology looks for patterns of data, such as a telephone number or a social security number. Or, the search technology looks for text that follows certain key text, such as the text that follows the following words: name, address, movie title, etc.

This type of search technology is called semistructured search technology. Of course, patterns might exist in unstructured text, too.

Search Engine–The Hit

The output of the search—the hit—can be formatted in many different ways. One way is to create the output in an XML format, as shown in Figure 3-3.

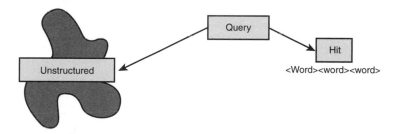

Figure 3-3 The format of the hit can be in XML.

When the hit is packaged in an XML format, it is wrapped up in a metadata infrastructure that identifies the meaning of the hits.

The hits can, however, be packaged in many other ways. A simple list displayed on a personal computer, an Excel spreadsheet, or an Access database are a few ways the hits can be gathered and delivered to the analyst.

Where Unstructured Data Resides

The unstructured data can reside in a wide variety of media. The classical media is in a textual format inside a server. In this case, the text might reside in a .doc format, .txt format, or some other format.

Text can reside in a wide variety of other formats. Another format text can reside in is a structured format where the text is collected and stored as a COMMENTS or MISCELLANEOUS field. In this case, each record in the file contains a field in which unstructured text can be stored.

Other places where you can find unstructured data might be in transcripted telephone conversations. In this case, the telephone conversations are taped, and the taped conversation is subjected to voice recognition software where the voiceover is converted into a textual form. Or, the conversation can be manually transcribed. One of the characteristics of voice transcription is the inevitable inaccuracy of the transcription. Because of accents, whispers, foreign language, and a variety of other reasons, there is no such thing as a 100 percent accurate transcription.

Another place where you can find unstructured text is in video and movie voiceovers.

All these places, and more, are where unstructured text can reside. They are also targets for a first generation search. Figure 3-4 shows that first generation textual analytic technology can be used against a wide variety of sources.

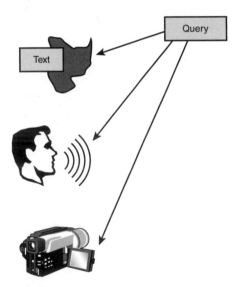

Figure 3-4   You can make a search on a variety of media.

Searching an Index

The diagram shown in Figure 3-4 is simplistic and, in a way, misleading. Although first generation search technology can do what has been described, it is much more normal for the search to go against an index that has been prepared in advance of the actual act of searching. The index is created by a one time pass through the base data where the index is created. Then subsequent passes through the search engine do not have to access the raw data but can access the index much more quickly.

Figure 3-5 shows an index that has been built for the purpose of supporting a search.

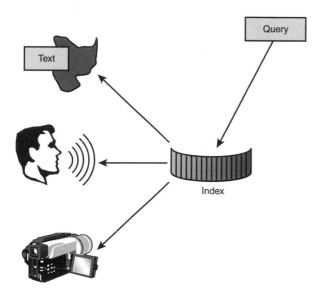

Figure 3-5   The search is often made against an index created by crawlers.

There is a good reason why search engines do not normally go against the actual unstructured text as it resides in the media in which it is found. The system performance of going against raw, native data would be poor. It might take an hour or more to find, read, and analyze the contents of a single source. No user wants to wait an hour or longer for his query to complete. People expect and demand fast response times.

A Crawler

To this end, the search technology creates a *crawler*. A crawler—in advance of any search—constantly goes after information at the raw level. The crawler loads the index that describes that information. The job of the crawler is to constantly look at new data and update existing data. When new or updated data is encountered, the crawler takes the resulting data and places it in the index.

Now, when the analyst wants to do a search using an argument, the search technology knows to go against the index, rather than the raw data. It is much faster to go against the index than it is to go against the raw data.

Furthermore, the index provides a basis for repeatability. If just one query has to be satisfied, the creation of an index might not be justified. However, when there are many queries that need to be satisfied, an index is the best way to satisfy the many permutations of arguments that are sent to the search technology.

Search Arguments and Schedulers

The search arguments can be submitted manually to the search technology. Another possibility is for the search arguments to be submitted according to a scheduler. With a scheduler, the query is submitted repeatedly according to the time set in the scheduler. The query might be submitted hourly, daily, weekly, or at whatever interval is needed. When the search technology finds a hit, the message that a hit has been found is sent to the analyst.

A scheduler submission of an argument is often called an *alert*. Figure 3-6 shows an alert.

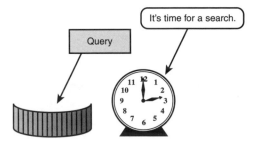

Figure 3-6   A search can be periodically triggered. This kind of search is typically called an alert.

Of course, with an alert, the message that is sent does not have to be sent to the analyst who initiated the job. Instead, the message can be sent to someone else—a manager, an auditor, a security specialist.

Tagging

In some cases, the source text can be *tagged*. When the source text is tagged, the search engine goes into the source text and adds markers to the source text that can be used in searching. At a later time, if a search is done, the source text can be directly and quickly referenced by use of the tags.

Of course, tagging depends on the ability of the source text to be modified. If the source text cannot be modified or if it is awkward to modify the source text, tagging is a less than desirable option.

Figure 3-7 shows tagged source text.

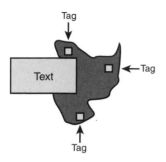

Figure 3-7 Textual data can be tagged.

Searching in Multiple Languages

Another feature of first generation search technology is the capability of the search technology to handle multiple languages. Some search engines can handle different languages and some cannot. Search engines that operate on the basis of natural language processing (or semantics) typically have a harder time handling multiple languages at the same time as do other search technologies.

Figure 3-8 shows a search technology that can handle multiple languages.

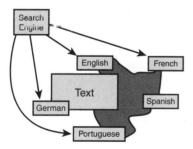

Figure 3-8 Search processing can be for many languages.

The output from a search is normally in the form of a hit. However, first generation search technologies are not limited to hits as the only form of output.

Collecting Output in a Taxonomy

Another form of output might be a categorization of words or a taxonomy of words that have been generated by the search technology. In this case, there are numerous hits that are made, and these hits are turned into a glossary or a taxonomy. Figure 3-9 shows such output.

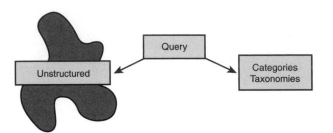

Figure 3-9   The output can also be formatted into a category or a taxonomy.

There are several ways that categories, or taxonomies, can be created. One simple way is by ranking words according to the number of occurrences. In this case, the document or documents that are used as the source contribute their words and are pooled together. The words are then counted and categorized by the number of occurrences.

Another way to create categorizations is by word proximity. In this case, the proximity of words to each other determines their categorization.

A simple form of a categorization is a taxonomy. Other forms of a categorization include a glossary or an ontology. A *taxonomy* is a collection of related words used by the corporation. Different corporations will have different taxonomies. The taxonomy can be generated by reading the unstructured documents and editing the words that need to go into the taxonomy.

Hyperlink References

Another task that can be assigned to the search technology is that of creating hyperlink references throughout the source documents and the output of the search, whatever its format. A hyperlink is merely a reference to a document or a location in a document than can be followed by the system. When the reader encounters a hyperlink, she has the choice of continuing to read the document or clicking on the hyperlink and having the system go to the document that is found in the hyperlink.

Figure 3-10 illustrates a hyperlink.

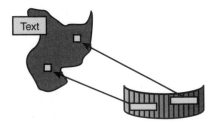

Figure 3-10   Hyperlinks can be created if desired.

Federated Queries

One of the features of first generation search technology is the support of federated queries. A *federated query* is a query that goes against multiple sources of data at the same time. The results are returned as if the query had operated against a single source. Figure 3-11 shows a federated query.

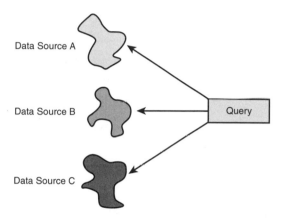

Figure 3-11   Federated queries can be created.

Federated queries have been around for a long time. They originated when queries went against multiple sources of data in the structured environment. However, federated queries that processed against legacy, structured applications always had a problem: With structured systems, there was no guarantee that there was any integration of data at the source level.

For example, in structured systems, suppose there are three sources of data: A, B, and C. Suppose A holds a record with a value of $400 US. B holds a record with a value of $1,000 Canadian. C holds a record with a value of $10,000 Australian. In a typical federated query against A, B, and C, the values are accessed and added together. The total dollar value is $11,400. The addition of money in different currencies, of course, makes no sense. If you want a meaningful result, you have to convert currencies to a common value.

Integration

The world of unstructured data does not have the integration problem, at least in the same way that the structured world does. The world of unstructured data operates against text. Assuming that text is in the same language—say, English—then the text is integrated. It doesn't matter that some of the text comes from a telephone conversation, email, a report, and spreadsheets. At the end of the day, it is still just text and is still subject to the rules of language. Therefore, the data in the unstructured environment is integrated because all of it is text, and a federated query against text is a far cry from a federated query against unstructured, legacy data.

Stated differently, because all text arrives at the same point of integration, and because all text obeys (to a smaller or a greater extent) the rules of grammar and punctuation, integration of text needs to be done only once. Contrast this with structured data that must be reintegrated each time a new source of data is added. Because of the uniformity of language, integration must be done only once, regardless of the physical source of unstructured data.

Enhancing the Search Argument

One of the features of first generation search technology is the enhancement of the search argument. In the simplest case, suppose the search argument is "Roy Rogers." A search can be made—literally—against the term "Roy Rogers." Wherever that exact phrasing is, a hit is generated. However, what if in the text there is the term "roy rogers?" Is a hit generated? The answer is no, unless case-sensitivity is removed as a consideration. If the search is case-sensitive, the system finds no match between "Roy Rogers" and "roy rogers."

Enhancing the search argument goes even further. Suppose the system recognizes "Roy Rogers" as a man's name. The system could suggest that a search be made on "R Rogers," "Mr. Roy Rogers," "Mr. R Rogers," and other permutations of "Roy Rogers." The system could query the analyst and ask if one or more of the permutations could be used as a search argument.

The first generation search technology system could go even further. It could suggest to the analyst that other permutations might also be used as a search argument. The system might suggest the use of wild cards.

Wild Cards

A wild card is a specification to the system that any letter found where the wild card is specified be accepted as satisfying the search criteria. For example, suppose the analyst specified "R*y R**ers." When the system encounters "Ray Rebers," the systems will qualify that entry as a hit.

In these ways, the first generation search technology can enhance the search argument to broaden the search to be much more analytical. Figure 3-12 shows the enhancement of the search argument.

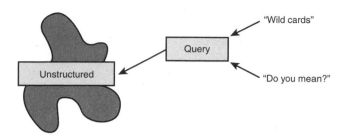

Figure 3-12 Some of the ways the argument can be extended and made more sweeping.

Boolean Expressions

Another standard feature of first generation search technology is that of the usage of Boolean expressions to qualify the search argument. Typical Boolean expressions are the AND function and the OR function.

The OR function says that if text from either A or B is found, then the source document will be included in the hit list. For example, if the search argument were "rocks OR stones," any document that contained either "rocks" or "stones" would be included in the hit list.

The AND function works differently. If the expression "rocks AND stones" were specified as a search argument, only if a document had both "rocks" and "stones" would it be included in the hit list.

Figure 3-13 shows the support of Boolean expressions.

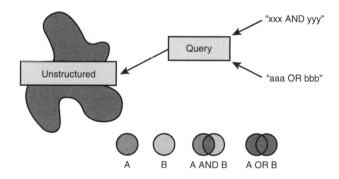

Figure 3-13 Boolean expressions can be used to qualify arguments.

Visualizing Text–First Generation

There have been attempts at visualizing text. One such attempt is a cluster diagram (see Figure 3-14).

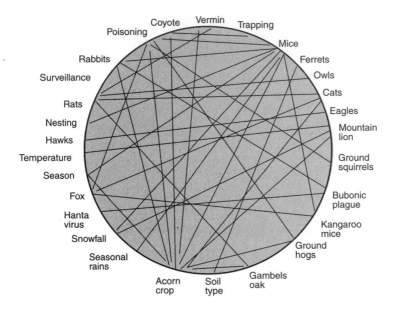

Figure 3-14 A cluster diagram

A cluster diagram takes a body of text and outlines the associations. The nouns that are in the body of text are positioned around a circle. When one word relates to another word, a line is drawn inside the circle. When one or two words start to have a majority of lines drawn in their direction, the implication is that there is a significant clustering of information around the words that are popular. When the clustering of the words is known, the first step has been taken to capturing and understanding the nexus of the text.

Understanding Context

Enterprise Content Management (ECM) is related to first generation search technology. ECM technology is essentially storage management technology that finds unstructured data and then stores it in a form that can be accessed at a later time. Typically, ECM technology provides a limited amount of first generation search functionality.

In some first generation search technology, one of the approaches to the management of text is called *natural language processing* (nlp). Another term sometimes used in conjunction with nlp is *semantic processing*. With nlp and semantic processing, the intent is understanding the context of language. The theory is that you can't understand language unless you understand the context of language.

As an example of the importance of the context of language, consider the short sentence— "She smacked him." What does this sentence mean? To understand the sentence, we have to understand the context of each word. Who is she? Is she someone who was mentioned before? Someone standing in the room whom we know is there? A ship on the ocean? When we understand who she is, we are on our way to making sense of the sentence. Then there is the word "smacked." What does it mean? Does it mean she killed him, as a gangster might say? Does it mean she kissed him? Does it mean she gave him dope as he was standing in line in an alley? Who is "him"?

It is obvious that to make sense of the sentence, it is necessary to understand the context of the words in the sentence. That is what natural language processing attempts to do.

In everyday life, we understand context. Our brains help us to resolve the different meanings of speech. Brains certainly use more than words. We use location, present company, the subject of discussion, past events, and many more factors to understand context. Our brains do it naturally.

For nlp to operate properly, the computer needs to be taught how to resolve context. One of the problems is that much of context resolution is not word- or text-related. In addition, trying to teach the computer how to do context resolution outside of text is difficult.

Unfortunately, there is a trap with nlp. The trap is that you have to consider context to understand words. When that assumption is made, the process of making sense of unstructured data—text—becomes a complex, involved process.

Summary

First generation search technology is technology that is used to operate directly on unstructured data. Here are many common features of first generation unstructured search technology:

- Support of many unstructured sources
- Enhancement of the search argument
- Creation of alerts
- Operation against indexes that have been prepared from the unstructured data sources
- Support of different languages
- Federated queries
- Boolean expressions

ECM technology is technology that captures and stores textual data. Nlp technology attempts to understand the context of data as part of the understanding of how to manage text.

There is another approach to the treatment of the unstructured environment. The key is the integration of textual data, as discussed in Chapter 4, "Integrating Unstructured Text into the Structured Environment."

4

Integrating Unstructured Text into the Structured Environment

The world of computing has grown from a small, unsophisticated world in the early 1960s to a world today of massive size and sophistication. Nearly every person worldwide—in one way or the other—is affected by or directly uses computation on a daily basis. Nothing less than national productivity from the 1960s to the present has been profoundly and positively affected by the widespread growth of the use of the computer.

The growth of computing can be measured in two ways: growth in structured systems and growth in unstructured systems.

Possibilities of Unstructured Systems

Structured systems are those for which the activity on the computer is predetermined and structured. Structured systems are designed by, built by, and operated by the IT department. ATM transactions, airline reservations, manufacturing inventory control systems, and point-of-sale systems are all forms of structured systems.

Structured systems are tied closely with the day-to-day operational activities of the corporation. Because of this affinity, structured systems grew quickly. Cost justification and return on investment for structured systems came easily because of the close tie-in with the day-to-day business of the corporation. The growth of the structured environment was fueled by the desire of the business world to be competitive and streamlined.

Unstructured systems are those that have no predetermined form or structure and are full of textual data. Typical unstructured systems include emails, reports, contracts, transcripted telephone conversations, and other communications. When a person does an activity in an unstructured environment, he is free to do or say whatever he wants. The person doing the communication can structure the message in whatever form is desired, using any language. In an unstructured environment, the communication can range from a proposal of marriage to a notification of a layoff to the announcement of the birth of a baby, and everything in between. There simply are no rules for the content of unstructured systems.

The growth of the unstructured environment has been fostered by the needs for communications, informal analysis (such as that found on a spreadsheet), and personal analysis (of finances, personal goals, personal plans). There was (and is) a different set of motivations for the growth of the two environments. Figure 4.1 shows the different environments.

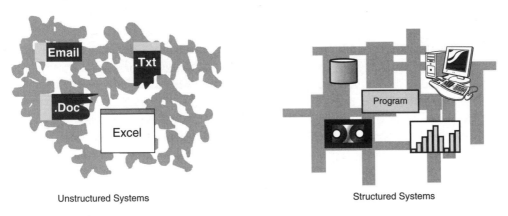

Unstructured Systems   Structured Systems

Figure 4-1   The two basic forms of data

From the beginning, the worlds of structured systems and unstructured systems have grown separately and apart and yet—at the same time—parallel with each other. It is no surprise that today each environment is separate from the other environment in many ways:

■ Technologically
■ Organizationally

- Structurally
- Historically
- Functionally

In truth, there is little overlap or connection between the two worlds.

Imagine what the world would look like if, indeed, there was overlap (or intersection) between the two environments. Imagine the possibilities if the two worlds could connect in an effective and meaningful way, the new types of systems that could be built, the new opportunities for the usage of computation, and the enhancements to existing systems in ways that are not possible using technology. When one accepts the limitations of today's technology and today's environment, there are only so many things that can be done. Imagine what would happen if those limitations suddenly disappeared.

If a bridge is to be built between the two environments, it makes sense to bring the unstructured text to the structured environment. In doing so, the decision support analyst can take advantage of the analytical processing capabilities that exist in the structured environment.

In most organizations an analytical infrastructure exists in the structured environment. This environment consists of things such as a database management system (DBMS), Business Intelligence (BI) software, hardware, and storage. Organizations have already invested millions in their analytical environment. The existing analytical infrastructure serves only structured systems, however. Data has to be put in a structure and a format that is particular and disciplined. Despite the particulars of the existing analytical infrastructure environment, it is less expensive to bring the unstructured data to the existing analytical infrastructure environment than it is to reconstruct the analytical infrastructure in the unstructured environment. By bringing unstructured data to the existing analytical infrastructure environment, the organization can leverage the training and the investment that has already been made in the existing analytical infrastructure environment.

When the gap between unstructured data and structured data is bridged, an entirely new world of possibilities and opportunity for information systems opens up. Figure 4.2 shows that a bridge between the structured and unstructured environments has many benefits.

The possibilities for new systems blossom when the gap between unstructured data and structured data is crossed. There are enormous and new opportunities that arise when the two types of data are merged.

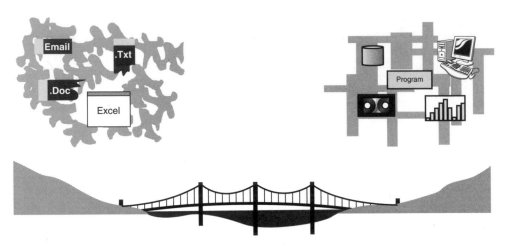

Figure 4-2 Forming the bridge between the structured and unstructured world

Integrating Unstructured Textual Data

In second generation textual analytics, the key to crossing the bridge between the two worlds is the integration of unstructured text before it is sent to the structured environment. Raw unstructured text cannot simply be placed into the structured world and still be meaningful and useful. Stated differently, unstructured text placed directly into a structured environment creates a mess. There is too much data—data that has different meanings and is recorded as a single name, alternate spellings, extraneous words, and documents that have no bearing on business. All these limitations of unstructured text become manifested when unstructured data is moved whole cloth into the structured environment.

To be effective, unstructured text must be integrated before it can be moved into the structured environment. By integrating unstructured text, the bridge between structured and unstructured data is created, and the stage is set for textual analytics.

Reading the Unstructured Textual Data

The first step in the integration of unstructured text is the physical reading of the text. To be integrated, raw text must first be read or "ingested."

In some cases, the text first appears in a paper format. In this case, the text on the paper must be read—scanned—and the text converted to an electronic format. This process is typically done in optical character recognition (OCR). There are quite a few challenges to this process of lifting text from a paper foundation:

- Sometimes the paper is old and brittle and is destroyed by the process of trying to read it. In this case, the analyst must not count on reading the paper more than once.
- Sometimes the print font on the paper is not easily recognizable by the scanner. In this case, there are a lot of manual corrections.
- Sometimes the scan process reads and interprets the words incorrectly.

As a rule, the process of converting from paper to electronics is one that involves a manual scan and correction after the electronic scan is done, if for no other purpose than to make sure the electronic scan is successful. In many cases, manual corrections must be made when the scanning and conversion process has made an error or the electronic scan process has made assumptions about what is read that are not true.

However it is done, the text needs to be lifted from the paper media and converted into an electronic format.

Then there is the case of voice recordings. Like data found on paper, voice data likewise needs to be lifted from the media in which it was stored and reset into an electronic format that is intelligible to a program that reads and analyzes text. Voice recordings can be converted to an electronic format by means of voice character recognition (VCR). Text can be lifted from VCR as well. The issues of quality and reliability for VCR are similar to OCR considerations.

Choosing a File Type

When the text is in an electronic format, the format and structure of the text needs to be taken into account. Some of the typical formats for the reading of electronic text follow:

- .pdf
- .txt
- .doc
- .ppt
- .xls
- .txt compatible
- Lotus
- Outlook

Often the vendor supplies software to read these file types. However, often the vendor does not guarantee a 100% successful reading. For this reason, third-party vendors supply software and software interfaces that are more efficient and more reliable than those supplied by the vendor. It is true that you have to pay for third-party solutions.

However, the third-party solutions are more reliable and more efficient than the vendor-supplied solutions. Also, the third-party vendor has the responsibility of keeping up with the different releases of the base software as new releases are made.

ALTERING THE ORIGINAL SOURCE

One of the issues faced by the systems programmer is whether to allow the original source text to be altered. In some cases, the software reading a source file wants to add data to or otherwise alter the source text. In other cases, the source text is never altered. It is read, but not altered.

By far, the safest policy is never to alter the source text, even at the expense of having redundant copies of data lying around.

Reading Unstructured Data from Voice Recordings

In some cases, where the text does not reside on paper, the text resides on tapes. Typical of this usage of tapes are telephone conversations that are taped and then transcribed. In this case, the tapes must be converted into an electronic format, much like scanning data, except the scan is not text. Typical software in this case includes VCR. VCR technology has many liabilities associated with it. VCR is subject to being fooled by accents, by people talking too softly, and other issues. As a rule, if a transcription can be done with 95% accuracy, that is considered to be good.

It is an interesting point that humans do not hear and understand 100% of the words that are spoken. Our brains "fill in the blanks" frequently. So it is not unreasonable that VCR does not do a 100% job of accurate transcription.

However it is accomplished, the original source text must be read and entered into the component that will begin the process of textual integration.

After the source text has been read, the next step is to actually integrate the text.

The purpose of textual integration is to prepare the data for textual analytics. It is true that raw text can be subjected to textual analytics. However, the reading, integration, and preconditioning of the raw source text sets the stage for effective textual analytics. Stated differently, textual analytics can be done on raw textual data, but not effectively. The data itself defeats much of the purpose of textual analytics. To be effective, textual analytics must operate on textual data that has been integrated and preconditioned.

The Importance of Integration

It is not always obvious why raw text needs to be integrated and preconditioned before it is useful and most effective for textual analytics. The following cases make the point of why integration of text is a necessary precursor to effective textual analytics.

Simple Search

A simple search is to be conducted on the name "Osama Bin Laden." Operating on unintegrated data, the search fails to find references when the name "Usama Bin Laden" appears or the name "Osama Ben Laden" appears. If textual integration had been done properly, the search for "Osama Bin Laden" would have turned up all occurrences of all spellings of his name.

Indirect Search of Alternate Terms

Suppose an analyst wants to find all places where there is a mention of a broken bone. If the analyst searches for "broken bone," the analyst finds all the places where there are permutations of the term. However, if data is integrated first, an indirect search for "broken bone" turns up the many terms that also mean "broken bone." Operating on integrated data, an indirect search on broken bone finds "fractured radius," "lacerated tibia," "oblique fractured ulna," and so forth.

Indirect Search of Related Terms

In addition to looking for alternate terms, related terms can also be accessed by the textual analyst. Consider the term "Sarbanes Oxley." If a direct simple search is made on the term "Sarbanes Oxley," the search will turn up the many places where that term is found. Consider what happens when raw textual data is integrated before the search is done. An indirect search can discover the many terms that are related to Sarbanes Oxley. For example, when the raw text is integrated and a search is done on related terms, an indirect search on "Sarbanes Oxley" finds items such as the following:

- Contingency sale
- Revenue recognition
- Promise to deliver

Permutations of Words

Another interesting aspect of integrating text is the recognition of the roots of words. When raw unintegrated text is searched for the phrase "moving the needle," if that phrase is used anywhere, the search finds it. When raw text is integrated, permutations of the base word are recognized as well. For example, when a search is made for "moving the needle" on integrated text where the stems of words have been recognized, the results find the following:

- Moves the needle
- Moved the needle
- Move the needle

From these simple examples of analysis of text against raw textual data and integrated textual data, it becomes obvious that if you are going to do effective textual analytics, the data that will be operated on must first be integrated.

The Issues of Textual Integration

The kinds of issues that must be addressed in the integration of unstructured text into the structured environment include the following:

- **Determining if the unstructured document has any relevance to the business**—If the unstructured document is not relevant to the business conducted, the unstructured document does not belong in the structured environment as a candidate for textual analytics. Figure 4-3 shows that raw unstructured data is fed to the integration component. The integration component then screens the data based on business relevance. For example, an email that said "I love you, darling" would not be deemed to have business relevance and would not be placed in the textual analytical database.

- **Removing stop words from the unstructured environment which are extraneous to the meaning of the text**—Typical stop words are "a," "and," "the," "is," "was," and "which." Stop words are used to lubricate language, but add little or nothing to the subjects that are discussed. Figure 4-4 shows that stop words need to be filtered out so that they don't get in the way of arriving at the heart of the matter when it comes to analyzing unstructured text.

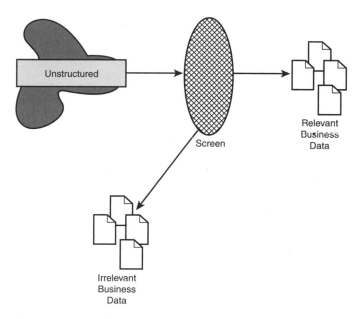

Figure 4-3   Relevant business data needs to be screened from irrelevant business data.

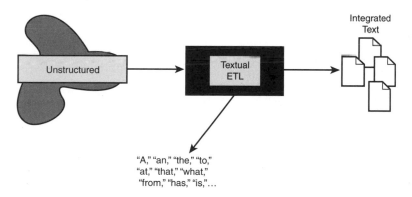

Figure 4-4   Stop words are removed.

- **Reducing words to their Greek or Latin stems**—By reducing the words found in unstructured text to a common stem, the commonality of words can be recognized when the words are literally not the same. Figure 4-5 shows that several ordinary words have a common Latin stem. The figure shows that the words "Moving," "Move," "Moved," and "Mover," all have a common stem—"Mov."

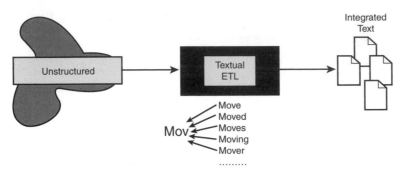

Figure 4-5   Words are reduced to a common stem.

■ **Resolving synonyms**—Where there are synonyms, the reduction of the synonym to a common foundation allows for the possibility of a common vocabulary. It is only through the establishment of a common vocabulary that meaningful searches can be done. There are two basic ways for synonyms to be resolved. One of those ways is through synonym replacement. With synonym replacement, when a synonym is recognized, it is replaced by the more common (or more general) form of the word, as shown in Figure 4-6. The problem with synonym replacement is that after the replacement is made, a search for the original synonym cannot be made. After a word is replaced, it cannot be found by a search.

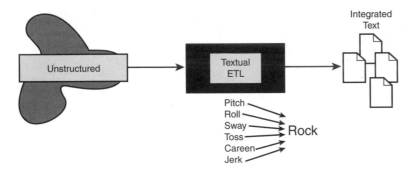

Figure 4-6   Synonym replacement is another activity that can be done to precondition unstructured data.

SYNONYM CONCATENATION

The other way for synonyms to be resolved is through synonym concatenation. In synonym concatenation, synonyms are not deleted. Instead, synonyms are concatenated with their original word, as shown in Figure 4-7. By using synonym concatenation, either the specific word or the synonym can be accessed and analyzed.

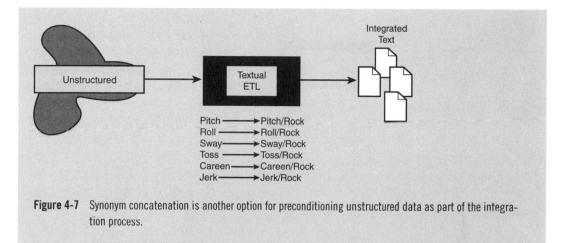

Figure 4-7 Synonym concatenation is another option for preconditioning unstructured data as part of the integration process.

The problem with synonym concatenation is that the texture of the original English sentence is destroyed. Usually, this doesn't matter. However, if there is a need to preserve the original texture of the English sentence, synonym concatenation is not useful.

As a rule, synonym concatenation is the best choice for managing synonyms.

■ **Resolving homographs**—In the case of words that have multiple meanings, the correct and unique term replaces the nonunique common term. This is the second ingredient needed for the establishment of a common vocabulary in raw text. In many regards, homographic resolution is the reverse of synonym resolution. In Figure 4-8, the term "ha" is replaced with different medical terms based on the person who originally wrote the term.

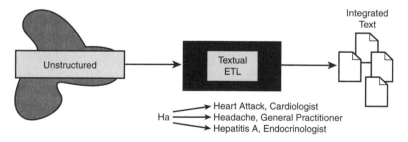

Figure 4-8 Homographs are expanded to a more precise meaning.

■ **The capability to handle both words and phrases**—It is not sufficient to support textual analytic processing by using just words. Phrases need to be supported as well, as shown in Figure 4-9.

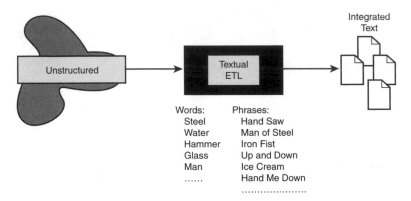

Figure 4-9 Both words and phrases need to be handled.

■ **Allowing for multiple spellings of the same name or word**—Some names and words can be spelled in many different ways. Common misspellings need to be included as well. In Figure 4-10, some of the many common misspellings of "Osama Bin Laden" are incorporated into the integrated text. In doing so, the textual analyst is sure to find the references even if they are not spelled correctly or spelled as the person initiating the search thinks they should be spelled.

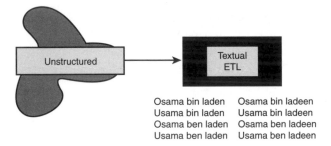

Figure 4-10 Alternate spellings should be handled as well.

■ **Negativity exclusion**—In the case of negativity exclusion, where there is a negative, the words that follow the negative expression are removed from any indexing or other reference. In Figure 4-11, cancer is not included in the indexing process because it is preceded by a "not."

■ **Punctuation and case-sensitivity**—Punctuation and case-sensitivity need to be removed as a consideration for searching. In Figure 4-12, the term "asher lev" can be found even though the term is written "Asher Lev" in the unstructured text. Punctuation and case are eliminated as a basis for finding a match between search argument and the text operated on.

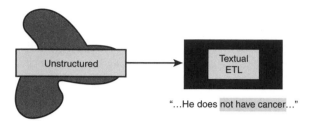

Figure 4-11 Negativity exclusion is another aspect of textual integration.

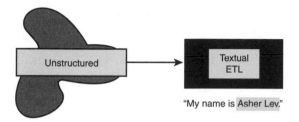

Figure 4-12 Punctuation and case-sensitivity should not be a factor in doing textual analytics.

- **Document consolidation**—On occasion, document consolidation is a useful aspect of textual integration. When textual consolidation is done, documents that hold like information are logically consolidated into a single document, as shown in Figure 4-13. The grouping of like documents can have the effect of enhancing the manageability of the process of textual integration.

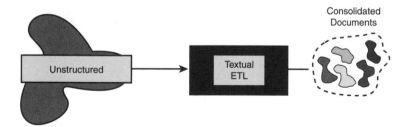

Figure 4-13 Document consolidation is sometimes a good thing to do as part of the textual integration process.

- **Themes of data**—Another important aspect of textual integration is that of determining basic themes of data. The themes can be discovered in a document or in the text that has been gleaned from multiple documents. In Figure 4-14, data is clustered around water and steel.

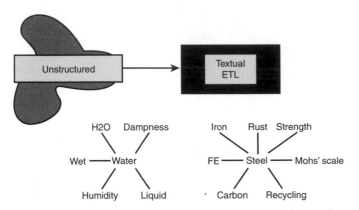

Figure 4-14 Creating themes for documents and groups of documents is another aspect of textual integration.

These basic activities of integrating unstructured text are the minimum subset of processes that need to occur to provide a sound foundation in the preparation of text for textual analytics. Many other related processes can be applied to unstructured text as it is prepared for movement to the structured environment.

External Categorization

An important process that needs to occur for the preparation for the movement of unstructured data into the structured environment is that of the creation of external categorizations (or indirect indexes).

The starting point for external categorization occurs when a topic is associated with multiple words. When the topic is associated with multiple words and phrases, the unstructured text is examined with the associated words and phrases. As a simple example, consider the topic "Sarbanes Oxley:"

> Topic—Sarbanes Oxley
>> Associated words and phrases:
>>> Promise to deliver
>>> Contingency sale
>>> Revenue recognition
>>> Contract terms

The unstructured data is examined, and wherever a word or phrase is found that is indirectly related to Sarbanes Oxley, a reference is made from that document to Sarbanes Oxley. This is an example of an indirect index. Now, when an indirect search of unstructured data is made on Sarbanes Oxley, all the references to terms that relate to Sarbanes Oxley are found.

Contrast an indirect search to a direct search. In a direct search, if the search were made on Sarbanes Oxley, only text where the term Sarbanes Oxley is found would be referenced. Such a direct reference has limited usefulness.

As data is placed in the structured environment from the unstructured environment, not only is the unstructured text integrated, but external categorization of the data is done as well. By integrating the unstructured text and creating indirect indexes, the gap between the two environments is bridged.

Simple Integration Applications

The first step in creating an integrated textual environment is accessing and gathering the unstructured documents to be processed. If an organization has many unstructured documents lying around in many different places, the ability to find, access, and gather those documents into a single location is an important feature.

After the raw documents have been gathered, the next step is to integrate them. The simplest kind of application that can be created from integrated unstructured text is one where data is simply integrated into the structured environment and then accessed and analyzed. When text has been integrated, there are many uses of the data. A standard BI tool can be used to create queries against the textual data.

As an example of a simple application, suppose there is a toxic chemical that has just been unearthed as a threat. The integrated text can be used as a basis for a search. It can take a matter of seconds to find out what information there is about this newly uncovered chemical.

A second simple use of integrated textual data in the structured environment is doing an indirect search. For example, suppose there is a need to do an indirect search on "toxic chemical." All the different kinds of toxic chemicals and all the information about the toxic chemicals can be accessed and organized quickly.

A third valuable use of unstructured data that has been integrated and placed in the structured environment is the ability to link that integrated text to other structured data. As a simple example, suppose there is text about "nitroglycerine." This text can be connected to and related to other occurrences of "nitroglycerine" in the structured environment, forming a robust query.

There is widespread applicability of simple unstructured integration. All companies that have unstructured data in any form need this capability.

Examining the Contents of Existing Unstructured Data

Another example of the use of integrating text and placing it in the structured environment is looking at large repositories of unstructured text. Many organizations collect unstructured data in the form of emails. Other corporations collect unstructured text in software such as Documentum. Over time, these collections of unstructured text grow large.

The problem is that as these collections of data grow large, the content becomes unintelligible. Stated differently, there is so much content and the content is so scattered and disparate that it becomes impossible to find anything in the files of unstructured data.

By integrating the large volumes of unstructured text and then bringing the text over to the structured environment, the unstructured text is meaningfully read and examined.

There is a widespread need for the ability to look into large volumes of unstructured data. All corporations that have large stores of unstructured data—emails, documents—need this capability.

Enterprise Metadata Repository

There is a great need for the ability to find and integrate and gather enterprisewide metadata. Metadata is a special class of unstructured text. Metadata refers to the classes of data, not to the data itself. Metadata—wherever it is found—is nothing but unstructured text. The same tools that can enter the unstructured environment and integrate content of text can also be used for enterprisewide metadata gathering. When gathered, the enterprisewide metadata can be used for the creation and population of a repository.

All organizations that have metadata need this capability.

Customer Communications

One of the most important sources of information is the communications found in the corporation. Communications can be between employees of the corporation or between the employees, customers, and prospects of the corporation. Typically, communications are stored in emails or transcripted telephone conversations. In truth, these communications can be found practically anywhere.

These communications can be integrated and brought into the structured environment and used to form the 360-degree view of the customer.

One of the most obvious ways that unstructured data can be used to enhance existing analytical systems is in terms of the creation of an unstructured customer contact file, which is a file of every contact or communication the customer has had with the corporation. This can include emails, letters, and other documents. The unstructured customer contact file is an index of the date of the contact, the nature of the contact, and to whom the contact was made.

There are many and powerful uses of the customer contact file. One of the most powerful uses is supplementing a customer relationship management (CRM) system. Figure 4.15 shows that a true 360-degree view of the customer is desirable for many businesses.

Figure 4-15 The 360-degree view of the customer

The essence of the CRM systems is to create a 360-degree view of the customer, thereby opening many avenues and opportunities. Some of the reasons why the 360-degree view of the customer is appealing follow:

- **Cross selling**—If you understand a lot about the customer in one arena, the opportunity to sell to the same customer in another arena will materialize.
- **Prospecting**—The more you understand about a customer, the better you can qualify a sales or sales prospect list.
- **Anticipation**—By understanding a lot about the customer, you can anticipate future needs.

One of the basic tenets of CRM is that it is much easier to sell into an established customer base than it is to bring in new customers. In this regard, creating a long-term and real relationship with the customer is certainly a worthwhile objective.

So exactly how is this relationship established? The basis of the relationship is the integrated knowledge about the customer. The integrated knowledge includes many different facets about the customer:

- Age
- Education
- Occupation
- Marital status
- Address
- Net worth
- Income
- Spending habits

- Children
- Car
- Cost of home

The idea behind creating the 360-degree view of the customer is to bring together data from many different places to integrate the data and achieve a truly cohesive and comprehensive view of the customer, as shown in Figure 4-16.

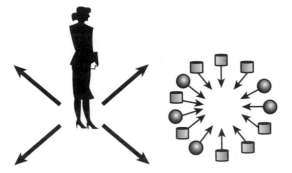

Figure 4-16   To achieve the 360-degree view of the customer, lots of different kinds of data are integrated together.

So exactly how does the unstructured contact file enhance the 360-degree view of the customer? The unstructured contact file adds the dimension of communication. Now, instead of just knowing odd facts about the customer, the corporation can know what the customer has been saying—what communications have transpired. If the customer has been irritated, the corporation can know that. If the customer has been especially pleased, the corporation can know that. If the customer has been trying to get through and talk to the corporation, the corporation can know that. In short, the unstructured contact file allows the corporation to know the recent state of mind of the customer. No 360-degree view of the customer comes anywhere close to knowing that kind of valuable information about the customer.

The Resulting Architecture

The resulting architecture that is created looks like Figure 4-17. By integrating unstructured text and organizing into the structure as shown, the following are possible:

- The unstructured data can be analyzed.
- The unstructured text can be accessed by direct or indirect searches.
- The unstructured text can be linked to structured databases and a composite query can be created.

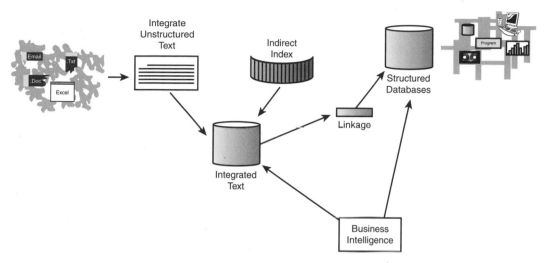

Figure 4-17   The architecture for textual analytics

Choosing the Best Types of Integration

There is no question that there is value to integration. Bringing together the many sources of unstructured data is no exception. When sources of unstructured data are integrated, it is possible to see a complete picture of whatever subject is captured. Different perspectives can be gathered together and compared and contrasted.

A lot of good things can happen when information is integrated. Figure 4-18 shows the integration of unstructured data.

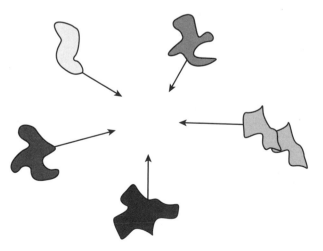

Figure 4-18   One of the values in the creation of the unstructured data warehouse is the integration of the data.

There are two basic forms of integration. One form of integration occurs when many different unstructured sources are integrated together. Another form occurs when unstructured data is integrated with structured data.

Figure 4-19 shows these two basic forms of integration.

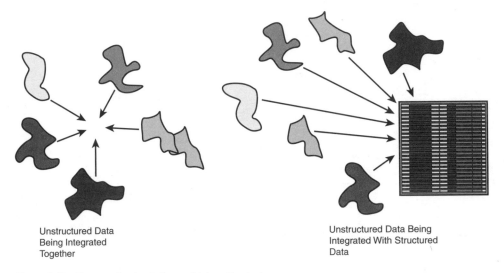

Unstructured Data
Being Integrated
Together

Unstructured Data Being
Integrated With Structured
Data

Figure 4-19   There are two basic forms of integrating text.

Both of these forms of integration are valuable; however, they essentially serve the same purpose.

Ways in Which Integration Occurs

There are at least two ways that integration can occur. One way is where data is accessed, gathered, and used to form a result. This can be called *access integration*. EII is a form of access integration. In access integration, the integration is done on-the-fly. The data is accessed, integrated, and then sent to the requesting party.

The other form of integration is *foundation integration*. With foundation integration, the sources of data are accessed in their entirety, the data is integrated in its entirety, and a foundation of integrated data is created. Then when it comes time to access integrated data, the foundation is accessed.

Figure 4-20 shows the two means by which data can be integrated. In general, when the data is integrated into a foundation, it is placed in a database.

Performance Limitations

There are two schools of thought as to which form of integration is better: the access-oriented integration or the building of a foundation.

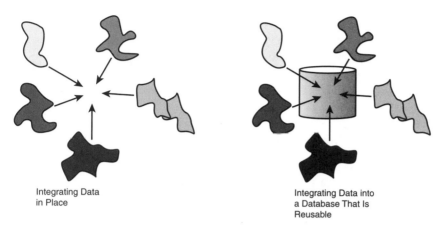

Integrating Data
in Place

Integrating Data into
a Database That Is
Reusable

Figure 4-20 Two basic approaches to integration

At first glance it appears that access integration is superior because a lot of data doesn't have to be integrated. When a foundation is built, a lot of data has to be integrated. Furthermore, the data that is integrated does not have an analyst querying the data, so building a foundation is a large undertaking. Doing access integration takes far fewer resources, at least on the surface.

However, consider this: Every time a query is made to data, the same data has to be reaccessed. Figure 4-21 shows the many accesses to the same data.

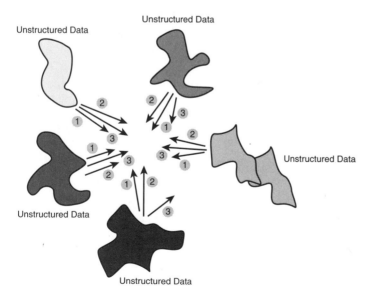

Unstructured Data

Unstructured Data

Unstructured Data

Unstructured Data

Unstructured Data

Figure 4-21 Every time there is a need for access, a whole new set of queries is made.

If only a few accesses/searches must be made, the work the system has to do, as shown in Figure 4-21, is not much. However, if there are many accesses/searches to be made, or if the accesses/searches actually go after the same data, the system must do an extraordinary amount of work to create access integration. The work the system has to do can result in poor performance and a need for large amounts of machine resources.

However, performance can be an issue for other reasons than a lot of queries being run. Another reason why performance can be a problem is that an integration access query runs at the speed of the slowest transaction. Consider the circumstances seen in Figure 4-22.

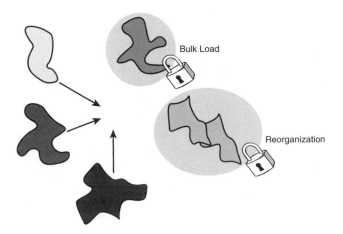

Figure 4-22 The speed of access is only as fast as the slowest source of data.

In Figure 4-22, a query has been submitted to access several sources of data. The query will not be complete until all other data is collected. The problem is that two of the sources of data are busy doing something else. One source of data is being reorganized while another source of data is busy with a bulk load. It might be hours before the data will be ready to be accessed. Performance is an issue that relates to more than just the total workload passing through the system.

However, there are other issues. In some cases, a heavy amount of processing must be done to integrate the data. The processing can take many different forms:

- Aggregation
- Summarization
- Conversion logic
- Reformatting
- Restructuring
- Addition of new fields

There are many activities that might have to occur when data is integrated.

Disadvantages to Integration

There are some problems. The first problem is that the same work must be done repeatedly. Every time the same data is accessed, the same integration activities have to occur. This is a waste of resources. Figure 4-23 shows this circumstance.

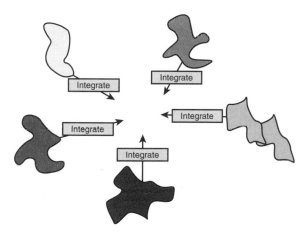

Figure 4-23   When integration must be done, it must be done repeatedly.

However, there is another related problem. If integration is done on-the-fly, what happens when the integration is done differently from one access of the data to the next? For example, at 10:41 AM the data is accessed and integrated. At 11:43 AM the same data is accessed, except this time the integration is done differently. If there is to be integrity of results, the same integration must be done each time. Otherwise, a query will yield one result one time and another result another time.

In the same vein is the circumstance where data is updated between different accesses of data. Figure 4-24 shows this instance.

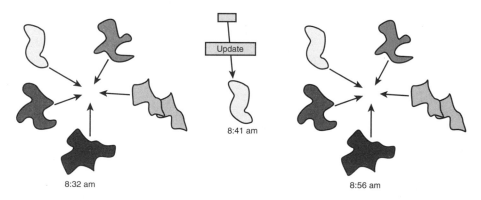

Figure 4-24   By accessing data from the source every time, if a change is made to the source data, the data has now become irreconcilable.

In Figure 4-24, you can see that data is accessed at 8:32 AM. An update is made to the source data at 8:41 AM. Then another access is made to the same data at 8:56 AM. The results at 8:56 AM will be different from the results of the access made at 8:32 AM.

If integrity of data is an issue, access data and then integrating it has a problem. However, when data is placed in a foundation database, as shown in Figure 4-20, the data does not have the problems that have been illustrated.

At first glance, it appears that building a foundation database of integrated data is an expensive, wasteful activity. However, when the limitations and disadvantages of access integration are considered, the foundation approach to integration starts to look really good.

Summary

Before textual analytics can be done properly, text must be integrated.

The first step in integration is the process of capturing the text in an electronic format. If the text is not in an electronic format, it must be lifted from the paper and produced electronically. OCR processing automates some of this process.

The next step is to physically read the data in whatever native format the data is in. Formats such as .doc, .txt, .ppt, .pdf are all common formats.

Next, the data is screened to separate the unneeded data from the relevant data. After the data is checked for relevancy, the next step is to read and analyze the text with the following criteria:

- Stemming
- Homographic resolution
- Synonym concatenation
- Synonym replacement
- Alternate spelling concatenation
- Negativity exclusion
- Punctuation, case, and font insensitivity
- Basic theming
- External categorization

After the text has been analyzed in accordance with these variables, the next step is to prepare the data for entry into a DBMS.

The different forms of search that can be done include the following:

- Simple direct searches
- Indirect searches
- Indirect searches based on external categorization
- Search on word permutations

As important as unstructured data, there are important considerations to semistructured data as well. Chapter 5, "Semistructured Data," addresses the "cousin" of unstructured data—semistructured data.

5

Semistructured Data

Accessing and integrating unstructured data is a powerful activity that sets the stage for all sorts of other analytical processing. With the ability to transform unstructured data into a form that is useful to analytical processing, whole new arenas of opportunity open up.

Figure 5-1 shows some unstructured data that might be accessed and integrated into a useful analytic form.

This agreement is a settlement between the two parties-
Jason Alexandria of Burton, Missouri, and Marie Toulon
of New Orleans. The two parties agree not to carry on
and fight and make a general public nuisance of themselves.
They agree not to drink on Saturday nights or to throw up in
public. Further and herewith, to wit the parties and all children,
including Judy Toulon, sometimes known as the "White
Phantom," and Samuel "Tomcat" Alexandria of Whitcomb,
Mississippi, on the river and south of the state line, just two
miles from Memphis, right down from the bridge and near
Interstate 40...

Figure 5-1 Unstructured data

Other forms of data other than unstructured data can greatly benefit from analytic processing. One of those forms of data is *semistructured data*, which has some of the characteristics of structured data and some of the characteristics of unstructured data. Semistructured data consists (either entirely or partially) of text, and in that sense, it is unstructured data. However, semistructured data also has a repeating format so that it appears to be structured data.

The Many Forms of Semistructured Data

Semistructured data is quite common. As a simple example of semistructured data, consider the data found in a resume, as shown in Figure 5-2.

The Resume of Greg Halstrom

Name—Greg E. Halstrom
Address—1713 North Wind Street
        Terrell, MN 09674
Phone—419-667-9822
        419-728-9916 cell
Email—ghalst@aol.com
Education—
      1975 Bemidji State
       BS—Accounting
      1981 U Minn
       MS—Computer Science
      2001-current
       Supervisor, Database Administration
       Fleury Systems, Inc.
       Halforence, MS

Gina Halbedl

Name—Gina L. Halbedl
Married—Three children
Address—19213 Lemon Drop Drive
        Orlando, FL 06876
Phone—639-688-2822
        639-550-5555 cell
Email—ghalbedl@msn.com
Education—
      1993 Georgia Tech
       BS—Engineering
      1981 Emory Univ
       MS—Medical Sciences
      2000-current
       Consulting Engineer
       Martin Aero Systems
       Badlington, FL

Figure 5-2 Resumes—semistructured data

Figure 5-2 shows two resumes. Each resume is written by the person whom the resume represents. The resume is made entirely of text, so in that sense, it is unstructured data. The precise format of the resume is made by the creator, and necessarily, there is no common format. It might happen that two or more people use the exact same format. However, if two or more people happen to use exactly the same format, that is pure coincidence.

Even though the exact same format is not used, there is a sameness to each of the resumes. The same types of data appear repeatedly:

- Name
- Date of birth
- Education
- Current position

- Salary

- Job description

Although each document is different in content and structure, each document is similar in terms of types of content. There is a certain repeatability of data in all the resumes that a corporation gathers.

However, there are, in fact, many other forms of semistructured data. Figure 5-3 shows a catalog of sorts where there are chemicals and descriptions of those chemicals. In the catalog is a designation of the melting point for the chemical. Some chemicals have no melting point designation, and others have two or more. The melting point designation does not occur at any set position in the description of the chemical. Instead, the melting point designation can appear almost anywhere in the text that describes the chemicals and their properties.

```
CAS 94.341................
...............MP 640........
......BP 790...................;
CAS 890.G65....................
....BP 980......................
...............................;
CAS 89.8876.................
.............Melting 120.......
.......Boiling 145.............
.......................;
CAS 10687A...................
.....MP 135.............BP 180..
.........................;
CAS 190.665.....MP 89.......
.........................;
```

Figure 5-3 A list of chemical properties found in the format of semistructured data

In the case of resumes, a separate document separated each resume. In the case of the chemical descriptions, all the descriptions were in the same document. There were other delimiters that delineated the boundary where one chemical description stopped and another description started.

There are then a wide variety of useful pieces of information that can be found in semistructured data. Reading the semistructured data and plucking all the discernible values becomes a useful thing to do. When the discernible values can be isolated and pulled from the semistructured data document, classical structured processing can occur.

Common Patterns of Data

One of the simplest ways that discernible data can be found and pulled from semistructured data is by looking for a common pattern in data. Figure 5-4 shows some common and simple patterns of data that can be pulled from semistructured data.

Telephone—999 999 9999
SSN—999 99 9999
Email—xxxx@yyyy.com

Figure 5-4 Some common recognizable patterns

One recognizable pattern is the telephone number (or at least the American version of the telephone number). The pattern is delineated by three numerics, followed by a sequence of three numerics, followed by a sequence of four numerics. Sometimes the sequences are separated by a blank. Other times the sequences are separated by a hyphen. The European phone number has a somewhat less defined structure as the total of numbers varies but is usually a sequence or sequences of numbers beginning with +.

The American social security number is similar to the telephone number except that there are only two numerics in the second sequence of digits. As in the case of telephone numbers, the digits of the social security number can be separated by a space or a hyphen.

The pattern created by an email address is an alphanumeric sequence uninterrupted by a space, followed by an @, followed by another alphanumeric sequence uninterrupted by a space, and ending with .com, .net, or some other Internet-approved symbol. There are, of course, no spaces in the address. In these cases, an element of data is recognizable merely by the pattern of its existence of data.

It is, of course, one thing to recognize a symbol or pattern; it is quite another thing to understand its context and meaning. In any case, the first step to organizing data is the recognition of the data pattern.

Prefacing Values

Another way that data elements are recognized in semistructured data is through a *prefaced value*, which is merely a recognizable text string that always precedes the value that is referenced. In Figure 5-5, you can see two prefaced values: melting point and boiling point. The melting point is 120 degrees, and the boiling point is 135 degrees. Note that degrees are inferred. The inference does not tell you that the measurement of the melting point or the boiling point is in Celsius or Fahrenheit degrees. The larger context of the document is used to determine those inferences.

Melting Point—120
Boiling Point—135

Figure 5-5 Some word-prefaced values

In the same document, there might be more than one way to provide a preface for a value. Figure 5-6 shows that in the same document there can be two specifications for the melting point—melting point and MP.

Melting Point—120
MP—120

Figure 5-6 The same value with different prefaces

When more than one value can be used for the same data element, there needs to be some logic to determine what value is to be assigned to the structured record that will be created. The logic can be simple or complex. Simple logic might be the first value encountered in the record; complex might be the value that follows the text "unch," except where there is a value of "not" preceding the data value.

Default Values

Part of the discovery and assignment of data values in the semistructured environment is the assignment of default values. When a record is created for the structured database from semistructured data, there will be occasions when no value is found. Because the final format of the data is structured, a data element value must be created whether there is one in the semistructured data document. For this reason, the analyst must define (or the system must define) some default value if the analyst wants to create a structured record.

Figure 5-7 shows that the value "unknown" has been defined as a default value if the semistructured data document does not contain a value for the data element in question.

Default—unknown

Figure 5-7 A default value

The default value that is assigned can be simple or complex. Figure 5-8 shows that a standard default value has been assigned. However, under certain conditions, the default value can be reassigned.

Default—unknown
If weight > 200 then default = Male

Figure 5-8 A default value that varies by values

Conflicting Values

Usually, when a data element has been assigned a value found in the semistructured data document, that is all there is to the creation of a structured record. However, on occasion, there might be a conflict in one or more values recognized by the system. Suppose the system is reading a semistructured data document, and suppose that two gender occurrences are found. The problem is that one gender is male and the other gender is female. If gender refers to a single person, this cannot be true because a person is normally either male or female (at least at the same time).

Logic must be inserted if one or more data elements are in conflict with another data element. Figure 5-9 shows a conflict between two occurrences of the same data element.

Gender = Male
Gender = Female

Figure 5-9 The same data element with conflicting values

On occasion, different documents will have a different preface for the same value. Figure 5-10 illustrates the case for having different specifications across documents for the same data element. In one type of document, melting point is designated as "melting point," and in another type of document, melting point is designated as "MP."

Document 1 ....melting point—120....
Document 2 ....MP—135

Figure 5-10 Different designations for the same set of values

When the system specifies the final structured record, the different prefaces must result in the same data type defined to the structured record.

The Degree of Accuracy

Creating a structured record from a semistructured data document or set of documents often is not perfect. There might be missed assignments due to:

- Incorrectly spelled preface
- Missing punctuation mark
- A preface that has not been defined

The analyst must decide at the beginning what degree of accuracy is acceptable. If an extremely high degree of accuracy is mandated, the analyst might want to assign two or more algorithms to create the structured record. Or, the analyst might want to have the computer create the first pass of transformations and manually verify the transformations using humans for a second pass.

As an example, it is possible to do an automated range-checking analysis after the structured records have been created. Such an automated procedure for auditing the results might look like the following:

- Gender must be male, female, or unknown.

- Weight must not be greater than 600 lbs or less than 80 lbs.

- Age must not be greater than 110.

- Hair must be one of the following: bald, black, brown, red, blonde.

The degree of accuracy is a function of what is needed and the amount of resources needed for the problem. The lower the degree of accuracy needed, the less expensive it is to capture, edit, and place the data into usage. The higher the degree of accuracy, the more expensive. Figure 5.11 shows that moving semistructured data to a textual analytical environment is less than a perfect activity. Inevitably, there will be errors.

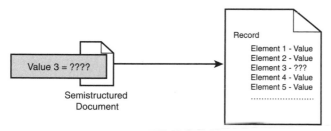

Figure 5-11   There is less than perfection in making the transformation from semistructured document to semistructured record.

Preprocessing Semistructured Data

On occasion, the easiest way to process semistructured data into a structured record format is to read and process semistructured data in a two-part process. The two-part process consists of a preprocessor followed by standard unstructured data processing. The advantage of a two-step process is that it is simple to do and can avoid great complexity. The disadvantage of the two-step process is that it requires two passes of the same data. The tradeoff is one that the analyst needs to make knowingly.

Typical of the processing done in a preprocessor step is the division of a single document into multiple documents. In many cases, the unstructured data processor requires that data be divided into documents. This works well for many document types. What happens when a document is created that needs to be treated as multiple documents? Suppose there is a document that contains a list of chemicals and their properties. First, one chemical is described and then another chemical is described in the document, but all the descriptions are in one document. To be processed, the original document must be broken into a series of smaller, separate documents.

What is needed is the ability to have only one chemical represented in a document. So what transpires is that the preprocessor reads the semistructured data document, and upon sensing that a description of a chemical is finished, creates a new document for the next chemical to be analyzed. The input is one document with descriptions of many chemicals. The output is many documents, each with only a description of one chemical.

To do such processing requires that the program have the capability to demark when the description of one chemical ends and the next chemical begins. The demarcation might be something obvious and formal or something as simple as the start of a new paragraph, as shown if Figure 5-12.

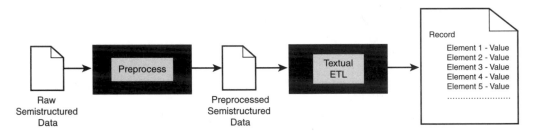

Figure 5-12   A two-step process is sometimes the best way to proceed.

Variable Output

One consequence of reading semistructured data documents and creating structured records is that the output can vary. One possibility for output is an entirely structured record where the data elements in the structured record have been gleaned from the semistructured data documents. Another possibility is a structured set of records where there are some data elements and the rest is classical unstructured data (as defined and described in Chapter 4, "Integrating Unstructured Text into the Structured Environment").

Figure 5-13 shows that there are two types of possible output. Of course, there is always the possibility of *both* types of output being produced at the same time.

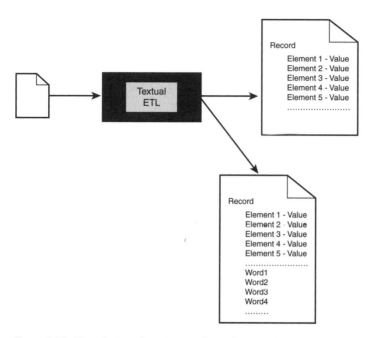

Figure 5-13 The output can be a structured record or a semistructured record.

Semistructured Processing in an Unstructured Environment

One other seldom-used possibility is that of semistructured data processing being done on a purely unstructured data record, as shown in Figure 5-14.

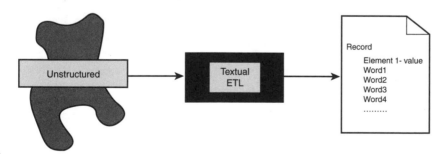

Figure 5-14 Semistructured processing can also be done on purely unstructured data.

The reason why the processing described in Figure 5-14 is not common is that there is no repeatability of data in the source. Unless special care is taken, there will be only one output record created. This, of course, is usually not helpful. However, this configuration of processing is a possibility that needs to be mentioned.

Preparation Time

There is one major difference between the input of unstructured data and the input of semistructured data. That difference is in terms of preparation time. To process unstructured data requires a minimum of initial preparation time. The first time that unstructured data is processed requires preparation of stop words, external categories, synonyms, and homographs. However, successive passes of processing against unstructured data require only minor touchups to the initial parameters.

Preparing for the processing of semistructured data is another story altogether. Preparing for semistructured data requires that the analyst have a working and intimate knowledge of the data as it exists in the unstructured environment. The analyst must know all the patterns that data can fall into, all the prefaces, and other information. It is not likely that after the first or even the second iteration of building the semistructured interface that the analyst will have all the different data elements in the semistructured environment identified completely and correctly.

Therefore, the preparation of the semistructured environment for processing can be a laborious thing. In addition, as changes are made to the unstructured data, those changes must be manually reflected in the parameters that have been set for the semistructured environment.

Summary

Not only can unstructured data be transformed into a structured file for the purposes of analytical processing, but semistructured data can also be defined in a like manner. Semistructured data is textual data that appears in a repeating format.

Data elements are lifted from a semistructured file to create a structured file. Data can be lifted and recognized because of the pattern of the data or because of the prefacing data preceding (or following) a recognizable data element.

The result of reading and analyzing a semistructured file is a structured database. Chapter 6, "Architecture and Textual Analytics," addresses the topic of unstructured data in a structured database.

6

Architecture and
Textual Analytics

Textual analytics fits comfortably within the framework of modern information systems architecture. To see how that fit is made, it is a good idea to look back to the beginning of information systems architecture and to view the progression of architecture leading up to the advent of textual analytics.

The Growth of Information Systems

In the earliest days of information technology, the first information systems consisted of some simple components. Figure 6-1 shows the components of punched cards, programs, magnetic tape files, and reports.

In these early and simple days, there was only a handful of data, a few programs, and some reports. People were grateful to get out of the computer whatever they could get. The reports were mostly tabulations and listings. About the best that could be said was that the early systems were automated and simple.

However, technology did not stand still. Soon there was disk storage with the ability to access data directly. This brought database management systems and online processing on to the scene. At this point, systems became both more complex and much more powerful. With the capability to do online processing, the computer entered the day-to-day business of the corporation. Soon corporations were sensitive to online response time and online availability. Bank teller systems, airline reservation systems, and insurance claims processing systems are a few of the applications that wedded the computer to business.

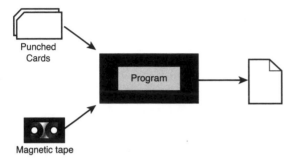

Figure 6-1 Early decision making

With the growing sophistication of information systems came the hue and cry for more information. Unfortunately, information systems were built such that each application served only a set of users—usually clerical workers. It was at this moment that the words were heard: "I know the information is somewhere in my corporation. If I could just get at it!"

The Maturing Need for Information

The end user had been promised much, but the IT department had delivered little. In response to this conundrum came more new technology. Figure 6-2 shows the advent of new technology that addressed the end users' plea for more information.

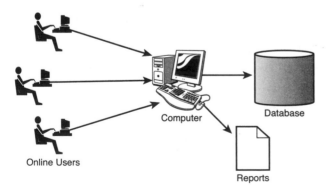

Figure 6-2 With online systems came much more sophisticated systems with more sophisticated decision-making capabilities.

The thirst for information became so great that corporations turned to a new technology—the personal computer, which allowed the individual to control her own destiny. With the personal computer, the individual had complete control of the environment (or so it appeared). The individual had data, a processor, and input and output devices. Figure 6-3 shows the personal computer.

Figure 6-3   Then came the personal computer.

One important ingredient was missing with the personal computer—the access to corporate data. Although the personal computer gave the end user control over his information processing environment, the control was not meaningful without access to corporate data. So the next step in the evolution of information architecture was to allow the end user to bring corporate data into the personal computer. Figure 6-4 shows corporate data being allowed to join the other analytical processing that was occurring in the corporation.

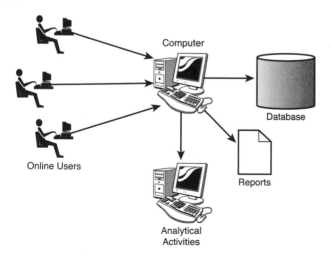

Figure 6-4   Soon the PC was integrated with the mainline systems of the corporation.

The Need for Data Integrity

When personal computers were allowed access to the corporate data, another limitation of the corporate computing environment was exposed: Even though the end user had access to corporate data, the corporate data had no integrity. There were ten different values for the same element of data at any one time in different places throughout the information processing environment, and no one knew the correct values. It was discovered that access to corporate data with no integrity was an exercise in frustration.

Other issues existed also. Corporate data was not accessible in an online environment. The demands and costs of high-performance processing meant that data in the high-performance environment was accessible only for short periods of time, if it was accessible at all. Another issue was the historical nature of the data. When data first entered an environment, it was treated one way. However, as the data aged, it needed to be treated differently. Another issue was the need for looking at data in different ways; but the biggest issue in the access of corporate information was the lack of integration—the lack of integrity of the corporate data.

For all these reasons and more, there was a basic need for a change in paradigms in end-user analytical processing. Figure 6-5 shows that change.

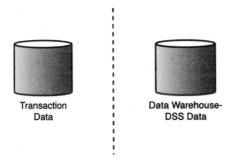

Transaction
Data

Data Warehouse-
DSS Data

Figure 6-5   It was recognized that there were two distinctly different kinds of data needed.

Figure 6-5 shows that there was a need to divide data into two categories: transaction-processing data and decision-support data. Transaction processing is done in high-performance response mode, where data can be updated and there is direct interaction with the end user or consumer. The decision support data is called a data warehouse. It is the decision-support data that provides a solid foundation for the informational processing of the corporation.

Figure 6-6 shows the evolution of data from applications to a data warehouse.

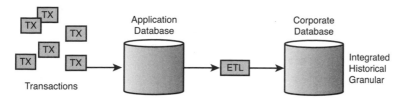

Figure 6-6 The evolution of the data warehouse

In Figure 6-6, you can see that the data warehouse consisted of data that was integrated, historical, and granular. The integrated foundation of data and its low level of granularity allowed different departments to look at the same data and to shape and reshape that data to fit the departments' needs for information. At the same time, there was a single version of the truth that could always be used for reconciliation should there be a difference of opinion in analyses among the different departments and different analysts.

At the same time, there was transaction processing that was physically separate from informational processing. A technology called ETL (extract/transform/load) was used to collect and integrate different application views of data and create a truly corporate view of data.

The Need to Include Unstructured Data

The simple architecture shown in Figure 6-6 served the needs of the corporation for many purposes. Now information could be available and distributed over the corporation. However, there was a great limitation of the architecture shown in Figure 6-6. The information in the architecture was limited to the data that was found in transaction processing systems. Now, the information found in transaction processing systems is useful and is the basis for many corporate decisions. However, at the end of the day, there was a completely different set of data that needed to be included, but wasn't. The data that was not included in the architecture shown in Figure 6-6 is unstructured data.

Figure 6-7 shows that there is a completely different type of data other than transactional data that needs to be included in the infrastructure.

Unstructured data has a textual nature, not a transactional nature. Unstructured data includes emails, medical records, legal documents, contracts, warranties, etc. A wealth of information in unstructured data is very different from transactional data.

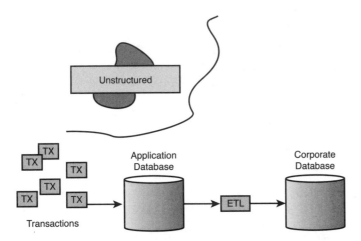

Figure 6-7   What about unstructured data being included in the collection of data going into a data warehouse, in the same fashion that transaction data is included?

A Fundamental Difference

There is an important technological distinction between transaction-based data and unstructured data. Transaction data tends to be repetitive; the same types of data appear over and over again. The only thing that is different from one transaction to the next is in the values of data, not the types of data. Contrast transactional data with unstructured data. With unstructured data, there is no repetition of data. There simply is no discernible or repeatable pattern of data that is associated with unstructured data.

The lack of repetition of data in the unstructured environment is foreign to the way that many technologies operate. Most analytical technologies in the existing environment depend on numeric data being repetitive, but, when there is unstructured data, there is frustration because unstructured data simply does not lend itself to processing by existing technology.

The difference between transaction data that is repetitive and unstructured data that is not is as fundamental a difference as appliances that run on AC or DC currents. It is a profound difference from the standpoint of technology.

If unstructured data did not contain valuable information, there would be no problem. It could be ignored. However, unstructured information does contain useful information; it simply belongs with the other useful information found in the corporation.

First Generation of Analytical Processing

Because of the profound differences of technology between the different environments, the first attempts at using unstructured information consisted of looking at it in isolation. This was the first generation of unstructured analytical processing, as shown in Figure 6-8.

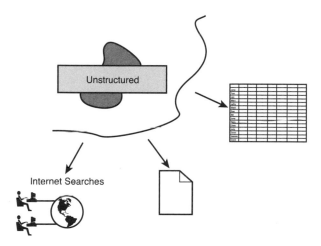

Figure 6-8 First generation textual analytics

The first generation of analytical processing consisted of search engines and "tagging" engines. Search engines include technology such as Google, Yahoo, and Altavista. Tagging technologies consist of technologies such as Clear Forest and others.

The first generation of unstructured analytical tools were primarily engines that could search for documents that had a word or a permutation of a word in the document. These were basic functions. They were certainly useful; however, they had one great limitation: The tools did not operate on integrated data and could not integrate seamlessly with structured data.

The Second Generation of Textual Analytics

Then appeared a second generation of unstructured analytical tools, which had two major distinguishing characteristics—the integration of unstructured data before it was searched and the ability to integrate unstructured data with structured data at the point of analysis.

Figure 6-9 illustrates the second generation of unstructured (textual) analytics.

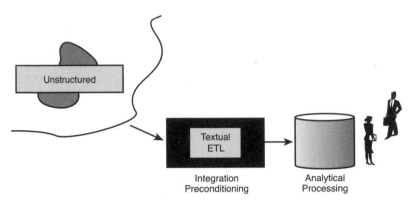

Figure 6-9 Second generation unstructured processing

The first characteristic of second generation textual analytics is that the textual data that is operated on is integrated. This is a fundamentally different consideration than that found in first generation systems. A second characteristic of second generation systems is that the integrated data is capable of being integrated with structured data. A third characteristic of second generation systems is that unstructured data is available for access and analysis in the structured environment.

The first two characteristics are explained in depth:

- **Integration of unstructured data**—This means—among other things—that the terminology that unstructured data is couched in is rationalized. There is a common language representing *all* the unstructured data. Terminology resolution includes resolution of synonyms through either replacement or concatenation, resolution of homonyms, and resolution of alternate spellings and common misspellings.

- **Integration with structured data**—Not all unstructured data can be integrated with structured data, but some can. Two common ways of integrating unstructured with structured data is through common email addresses or common telephone numbers. However, occasionally there are other ways to integrate the data through common social security numbers, common employee numbers, or common key identifier numbers.

Figure 6-10 shows that unstructured data can sometimes be integrated with structured data.

After unstructured data is integrated, it is placed in the structured environment, usually in a relational database. After the integrated unstructured data is placed there, it can be accessed and analyzed by commonly used BI tools such as Business Objects and Cognos.

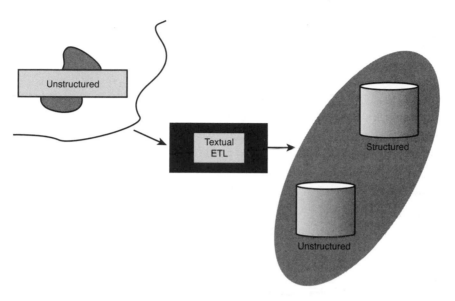

Figure 6-10   It is possible to integrate structured and unstructured data.

Figure 6-11 shows that unstructured data—after it has been integrated and placed in a structured technology—can be accessed and analyzed by BI tools.

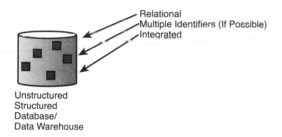

Figure 6-11   Unstructured data can be accessed and analyzed by BI tools when the unstructured data has been restructured into a standard format, such as a relational format.

DW 2.0–Data Warehouse Architecture

The architecture that includes unstructured data in a structured format is DW 2.0, the architecture that describes the next generation of data warehousing. DW 2.0 is described in much greater detail at www.inmoncif.com in the section for DW 2.0.

Although the inclusion of unstructured data in the data warehouse environment is one of the more important features of DW 2.0, other important components are the following:

- The recognition of the life cycle of data in the data warehouse
- The inclusion of metadata as an essential part of the data warehouse environment
- The foundation of data warehousing that is capable of changing gracefully as business conditions change

The table that unstructured data is placed in after it has been integrated is merely a relational table. There is nothing extraordinary about the table. Figure 6-12 shows some of the columns and rows of the relational table that has been created.

Document ID	Fullpath	Size	Date Created	Date Modified	Date Last Indexed			
{382CE20B-8E	\\DSTNES	22016	7/11/2006 11:08	7/5/2006 13:22	7/11/2006 12:58	1	0	1{39A9575E-EFC2-45C
{A301EE5-D!	\\DSTNES	135680	7/11/2006 11:08	7/5/2006 13:22	7/11/2006 12:58	1	0	1{39A9575E-EFC2-45C
{8DCE271C-D	\\DSTNES	33792	7/11/2006 11:08	7/5/2006 13:22	7/11/2006 12:58	1	0	1{39A9575E-EFC2-45C
{D551D2CB-2	\\DSTNES	27136	7/11/2006 11:08	7/5/2006 13:22	7/11/2006 12:58	1	0	1{39A9575E-EFC2-45C
{B5BAC059-2	\\DSTNES	23040	7/11/2006 11:08	7/5/2006 13:22	7/11/2006 12:58	1	0	1{39A9575E-EFC2-45C

Figure 6-12 Part of a relational table that contains the words that have been extracted and integrated from the unstructured environment

The kinds of queries that can be created to access and analyze the relational table that holds unstructured integrated data are written in SQL. Figure 6-13 shows that an SQL-based query might be run against the data because the data is in a relational format and has been integrated.

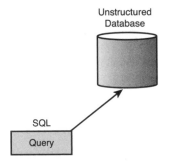

Unstructured
Database

SQL

Query

Figure 6-13 Querying unstructured data

Although access and analysis can be done to the relational table by itself, an even more powerful way to access and query data is to access both structured and unstructured data at the same time. Figure 6-14 shows that both kinds of data—structured and integrated unstructured data—can be accessed at the same time by the same query, doing a join on common data.

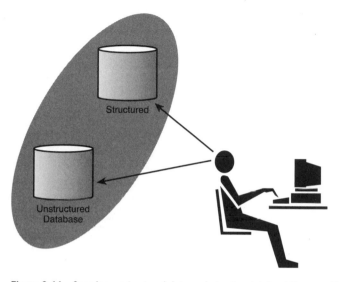

Figure 6-14 Querying unstructured data and structured data at the same time

Summary

Unstructured data fits with structured data in an architected manner. Unstructured data is integrated and then placed in a relational format, where it can be accessed and analyzed in a singular fashion, or the access and analyses can be done against structured and integrated unstructured data simultaneously.

The unstructured integrated data fits architecturally into the DW 2.0 environment as an essential component.

There are many reasons why unstructured data needs to be placed in an architecture. The primary reason is that the existing environment can be leveraged if unstructured data can be integrated and brought to the structured environment.

When the unstructured data is brought to the structured environment, it can be placed in a relational environment and accessed and analyzed by the BI technology that exists inside the organization.

Of course, the key to effective access and analyses is the unstructured database, discussed in Chapter 7, "The Unstructured Database."

7

The Unstructured Database

The foundation of textual analytics is the ability to access and analyze unstructured data in an unfettered manner. To achieve this state, an infrastructure suitable for analytical processing must be created. The heart of that environment is the unstructured database.

The term unstructured database/data warehouse is somewhat of an oxymoron in that it is a self-contradiction in terms. The term "unstructured" refers to the complete lack of discipline in the original creation of the unstructured text. The term "database" implies that the contents of the database are structured. Therefore, when one says unstructured database, it is like saying unstructured structured data. As contradictory as this seems, this is, in fact, exactly what an unstructured database/data warehouse is. An unstructured database/data warehouse is unstructured in that the content of the database is certainly unstructured. However, the structure and format of the database must be structured (as is the case with all databases).

Therefore, the very term unstructured database/data warehouse is a self-contradiction.

Previous chapters describe the source of the unstructured database/data warehouse and how data within the unstructured database/data warehouse must be integrated. This chapter addresses some of the specifics of database design and the actual implementation of the unstructured database/data warehouse.

The General Flow of Data

Figure 7-1 shows the general structure of where the data in an unstructured database/data warehouse comes from and where it goes. It shows that the source of an unstructured database/data warehouse database is unstructured data. The unstructured data passes through a layer of technology that integrates and preconditions the data. The resulting data then lands in a standard relational database such as Oracle, DB2, Teradata, or NT SQL Server. There are only a few differences between the final DBMS that the unstructured data lands in. Some DBMSs can handle large amounts of data, and others can handle smaller amounts of data. Some DBMSs are friendlier to analytical packages than others. However, for the most part, the DBMSs are very much the same in terms of capabilities and capacities.

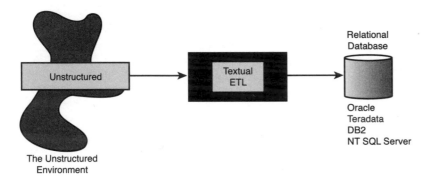

Figure 7-1   The unstructured database

Preventing a Blob of Unstructured Data

It is noteworthy that the data that passes through the integration and preconditioning layer does not end up in a blob, as shown in Figure 7-2. A blob of data is a construct used in DBMS in which whole masses of text are grouped together with no structure, editing, or organization. If all that was done was to put unstructured data in a blob and then place the blob in a database, there would be little analytical processing that could be done against the unstructured data. Instead, the data that enters the unstructured database/data warehouse is carefully integrated, edited, separated, and placed into a form that is suitable for analytical processing.

The notion that unstructured data is placed in a relational environment is, at first, a strange concept to many people. The idea takes some getting used to.

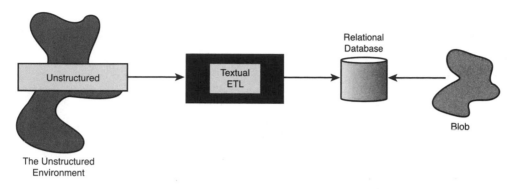

Figure 7-2 The unstructured data is not stored in a blob.

A Partial Relational Table

The relational format of unstructured data put into a relational table is depicted in Figure 7-3, which shows that the relational table contains fields/columns such as the following:

- Document ID
- Fullpath identification
- Size
- Date created
- Date modified
- Date last indexed

Figure 7-3 shows some of the fields/columns that go into a relational implementation of the unstructured data that has passed through the integration and preconditioning layer.

Document ID	Fullpath	Size	Date Created	Date Modified	Date Last Indexed			
{382CE20B-8E\\DSTNES		22016	7/11/2006 11:08	7/5/2006 13:22	7/11/2006 12:58	1	0	1{39A9575E-EFC2-45C
{A301EE5-D! \\DSTNES		135680	7/11/2006 11:08	7/5/2006 13:22	7/11/2006 12:58	1	0	1{39A9575E-EFC2-45C
{8DCE271C-D \\DSTNES		33792	7/11/2006 11:08	7/5/2006 13:22	7/11/2006 12:58	1	0	1{39A9575E-EFC2-45C
{D551D2CB-2 \\DSTNES		27136	7/11/2006 11:08	7/5/2006 13:22	7/11/2006 12:58	1	0	1{39A9575E-EFC2-45C
{B5BAC059-2 \\DSTNES		23040	7/11/2006 11:08	7/5/2006 13:22	7/11/2006 12:58	1	0	1{39A9575E-EFC2-45C

Figure 7-3 Part of a relational table that contains the words that have been extracted and integrated from the unstructured environment

Figure 7-3 does not show the entire contents of the relational table. Among other things not shown are the words and other relationships that are in the table.

A Document/Word Table

Figure 7-4 shows another simple way of depicting the contents of the relational table: The relational table can be thought of as a simple cross referencing of documents and words—the documents are the source of the unstructured data and the words are the actual words that come from the unstructured data. Through the relational table, the analyst can either look at the words by document or the document by words. Either manifestation is supported by the relational table.

```
Document/Word                           Word/Document
       /Word                                  /Document
       /Word                                  /Document
       /Word
                                         ....................
....................
                                         Word/Document
Document/Word                                 /Document
       /Word                                  /Document
       /Word          Or                      /Document
       /Word
       /Word                             ....................
                                         Word/Document
....................                     Word/Document
Document/Word                                 /Document
       /Word
                                         ....................
....................
```

Figure 7-4   A simplified way of thinking of the unstructured database

The Key of the Relational Table

What is the key of the unstructured database/data warehouse table? First, it is obvious that document and word are part of a compound key, which is a key structure containing two or more identifiers that concatenate together. Then there is the issue of whether the compound key is unique or nonunique. The answer is that it can be either way, depending on the needs of the end user. If the key is nonunique, there might be two or more words in the unstructured database/data warehouse that have the same document ID. This is almost always the case and is a natural assumption for the database designer to make.

The same word might be found in multiple documents, which is also normal; however, there might be a need for uniqueness, which can be forced by including the byte address within the document of the word. For example, suppose the word "fireman" appears twice in the document, "THE FIREMAN'S BALL." Suppose the first appearance is at byte 237 and the second appearance is at byte 1786. The key could include a byte address which would look like the following:

- THE FIREMAN'S BALL / fireman / 237
- THE FIREMAN'S BALL / fireman / 1786

By including a byte address, uniqueness of the compound key structure is forced; however, if there are occasions where uniqueness is not needed, a large number of index entries can be saved. By having nonunique compound keys, the designer can greatly reduce the size of the unstructured database/data warehouse. In the preceding case, there would be one key:

- THE FIREMAN'S BALL / fireman

When using this reference, it is not clear which occurrence of "fireman" is referenced in the document, but it is assumed that the database designer is aware of this limitation.

It might be useful to keep track of how many occurrences there are of the word in the document. In this case, the key would look like the following:

- THE FIREMAN'S BALL / fireman / 2

In this case, the number 2 is a reference to the number of times that "fireman" appears in the document "THE FIREMAN'S BALL."

Different Indexes

It is worthwhile to note that there are two types of indexes that are produced for the unstructured database/data warehouse. The simplest is the index that comes from editing unstructured data. As an example, take the phrase SOCIAL SECURITY NUMBER (SSNO). The index entry for SSNO would look like this:

- Document ABC, SSNO, byte 1289
- Document ABC, SSNO, byte 13776
- Document BCD, SSNO, byte 2
- Document DEF, SSNO, byte 1288

This is a simple index entry that tells all the places where SSNO is referenced.

Indexing Semistructured Data

Contrast this index entry with the one that is produced by reading and processing semistructured data. When semistructured data is read, the reference is not to the location of the word or phrase that is sought but to a specific value. For example, suppose semistructured data is indexed according to SSNO. The result might look like this:

SSNO Index

- Document ABC—667-89-9981
- Document BCD—128-88-2765
- Document DEF—unknown
- Document GHI—561-86-8871
- Document IJK—776-97-1184

When semistructured data is indexed, the result is the ability to search for specific values of a given field or column of data. When unstructured data is indexed, the result is the ability to search for the existence of a value of text, not the actual value of the text.

Indexes for Both Semistructured and Unstructured Data

An index can be created for documents that include both semistructured and unstructured data. The indexed tables can be joined to determine both kinds of values. As an example, consider two tables that have been created—one from unstructured data and one from semistructured data:

About a Cow

- Document ABC, brown, 2
- Document ABC, cow, 7
- Document ABC, ran, 13
- Document ABC, over, 19

And...

Cow's Name

- Document ABC, Elsie
- Document BCD, Daisy
- Document CDE, Ella Mae
- Document DEF, Bessie

A join can now be done on Document ABC to find the text and the specific reference.

Managing Large Volumes of Data

Although database design of the unstructured database/data warehouse is of great importance, that is not the only issue of database and system design that is of interest. Of great strategic interest is the relationship between the volume of unstructured versus unstructured data that can arrive in the database/data warehouse environment. Figure 7-5 shows what can happen if care is not taken.

Figure 7-5 If you are not careful, the structured data is overwhelmed by the unstructured data.

Figure 7-5 shows that if care is not taken the volume of data that comes from the unstructured data environment can completely overwhelm the volume of data in the structured data environment. It is conceivable that 95% or more of the data found in the database/data warehouse environment comes from the unstructured data environment. There is a problem when this happens.

When the volume of data changes dramatically for a database or a data warehouse environment, the entire subject of data management changes as well. When the volume of data is a manageable size, simple tasks such as loading, indexing, archiving, and accessing data are reasonable, manageable activities. However, in the face of significantly more data, these everyday tasks that must be done become problematic. Schedules are impacted, operating windows are stretched, and the long run times for certain jobs become intolerably longer. The structured data warehouse environment already has enough challenges; putting a much greater burden of tasks on the operations and management staff is not a welcome thing.

It is a little known fact that in most organizations there is much more unstructured data than there is structured data. This creates the potential of completely overwhelming the existing structured data environment when unstructured data is placed in the environment. This potential imbalance must carefully be considered by the systems programmers and analysts because unstructured data is brought over to the structured database/data warehouse environment.

There are several approaches to bringing unstructured data over to the structured database/warehouse environment. Depending on the total amount of unstructured data, one of these approaches will suffice.

Bring Everything into the Structured Environment

The first and simplest approach is simply to index everything in the unstructured data environment and bring that index over to the structured database/warehouse environment in the creation of the unstructured database/data warehouse environment, as shown in Figure 7-6.

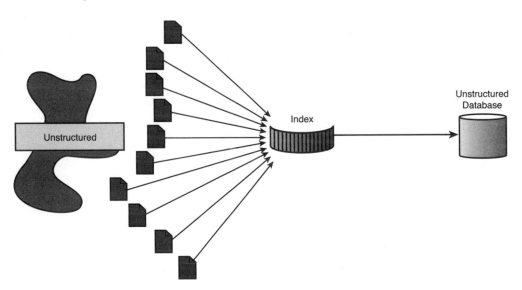

Figure 7-6   One approach is to index all text in the unstructured environment.

The approach shown in Figure 7-6 works well when there is not that much unstructured data to begin with and when all the unstructured data is important. However, there are cases where there is simply too much unstructured data to use this approach. There are other circumstances where there is a lot of "blather." Blather is textual data that is not relevant to the business of the corporation. For example, in a typical stream of emails, much of the emails will not relate to the business of the enterprise.

When there is a lot of blather, the approach of storing all the unstructured data in the unstructured database/data warehouse becomes unfeasible.

Selectively Storing Terms

A second approach is not to store all the words in the unstructured data environment. Instead, only certain words from the unstructured data environment are indexed. Some of the ways the words for indexing can be selected follow:

- Select only nonblather words.
- Select only words that are not stop words.
- Select words that can be indexed by semistructured data processing only.

There are many ways to select which words go into the index for the unstructured database/data warehouse when all words cannot be used. Figure 7-7 shows the selection of only certain unstructured text for inclusion in the unstructured database/data warehouse.

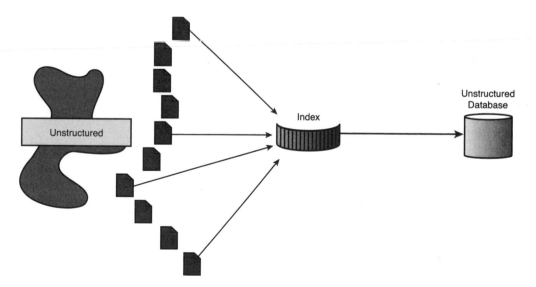

Figure 7-7 Another approach in bringing text into the structured environment is to index words selectively.

Simple Pointer

In many cases, a single index entry will represent its source document. This can be called a *simple pointer*, which looks like the construct found in Figure 7-8. There are three simple pieces of information in the index—the word that is pulled from the unstructured data environment, an identifier or name for the document, and the address or full path of where the document lies. These are the basic units of information that are used for the construction of the simple pointer.

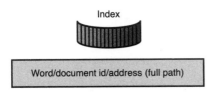

Figure 7-8   A simple pointer

From the basic information found in the simple pointer, much analytical and decision support processing can be done. This simple pointer is one of the fundamental building blocks that helps link the structured environment to the unstructured environment.

Moving the Underlying Document

Some limitations or issues are related to the usage of the simple pointer. One of those issues occurs when the document that is referenced is moved or deleted, as shown in Figure 7-9.

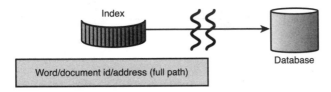

Figure 7-9   What happens when unstructured data is removed from its location

When someone tries to access the data in the original location using a simple pointer, the document will not be there. Depending on the document and the application, this might or might not matter. In some cases, all that matters is the reference to the document ID or name. In other cases, the document can be reconstructed by using the related words in the simple pointer index. If all data from the unstructured data environment has been captured, a reconstruction is possible. In a few cases, the unstructured data had been determined to be "hot."

When hot or sensitive data is encountered in the editing and integration of unstructured data and unstructured data passes to the unstructured database/data warehouse environment, the "hot" data is often taken whole cloth from the unstructured data environment.

In these circumstances, it does not matter when the document that has been referenced is moved or deleted from its original location. However, if all the words are not indexed and if the document is moved or deleted, there may be a loss of information.

Alternatives to Moved Documents

There are several alternatives when a document has been moved or deleted at its source and there are pointers or references back to the source of the document. One solution is to periodically examine the references and make sure the documents are still there. When there has been a change, either delete the simple pointer or make adjustments to the reference if the proper value for adjustment is known. Another alternative is not to periodically read and reference all the documents referenced in the simple pointer index but instead wait until the reference is made by a user and then tell the user of the condition. Depending on the uses of the simple pointer, either of these solutions might suffice.

The most extreme alternative is to create a separate unstructured data file when the simple pointer is created and copy the unstructured data to a separate file. This approach doubles the amount of unstructured data (which is almost never an acceptable solution). However, this approach absolutely mandates that an unstructured data document is never lost or misplaced.

The solution boils down to a business decision, not a technical decision. Ultimately, if an organization is willing to spend enough money to collect a vast amount of unstructured data, a perfect solution can be implemented. However, most organizations are not willing to do that, so something less than perfect must be implemented, and this involves tradeoffs and compromises.

Synonyms and Homographs

When the simple pointer index is created, one part of the index that can be created is the synonym and homograph resolutions that have occurred. Figure 7-10 shows the synonyms that have been created. If the synonym strategy has been replacement, the replacement synonym will be in place already. However, if the organization has chosen the synonym concatenation approach (which is the approach nearly all organizations take), the synonym concatenation as well as the original word is sent to the simple pointer index.

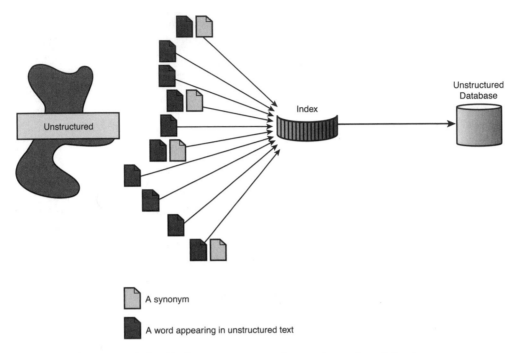

Figure 7-10   Synonyms are indexed in the same way as normally appearing words are indexed.

The same is true of the treatment of homographs. If homographs have been concatenated, both the original word and the homograph are sent to the simple pointer index.

Exactly how the simple pointer index is built depends on what options the organization has chosen.

External Categories

In a somewhat different category are the treatment of words in an external category. Words found in external categories might or might not be sent to the simple pointer index. There are advantages and disadvantages to whatever approach is used.

When external categories are resolved at the point of the creation of the simple pointer index, the external categories are "locked in" to the simple pointer database. This means that analytical activities against the unstructured database/data warehouse will be efficient and straightforward to execute, but it also means that the external categories are locked in and are inflexible. If an analyst wants to change his mind about the words found in an external category, he cannot do so easily after the words have been incorporated into a simple pointer index.

On the other hand, if an analyst wants to reserve the list of words found in an external category, the analyst might specify that the words in the external category NOT be placed in the simple pointer index. In this case, the analyst is free to alter the contents of the external index whenever he wants. However, the implication is that the external category will be used for the purpose of organizing and filtering data at the moment of access. In other words, when an analyst is getting ready to conduct an analysis, the external category can be used to select and filter the words that will be accessed. This is flexible but requires both machine resources and work by the analyst.

The basic tradeoff is between speed and simplicity of processing versus flexibility. By placing the external category words in the simple pointer index, the analyst achieves speed and simplicity. By not placing the words in the external category in the simple pointer index, the analyst achieves great flexibility, but at the expense of both speed and simplicity.

In the case of external categories, usually more than one exists. The analyst can place some, but not other, external categories in the simple pointer index. The analyst can choose to be selective as to which external categories are placed where. In any case, the decision needs to be thought out and made deliberately.

Figure 7-11 shows some external categories that have been placed in the simple pointer index.

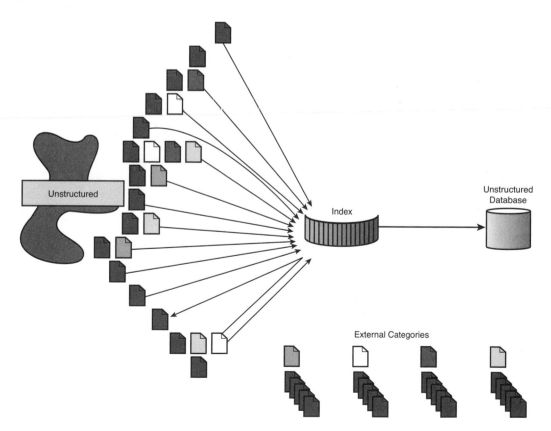

Figure 7-11 External categories can be indexed or can be applied at the moment of query.

Using the Unstructured Database for Analysis

After the simple pointer index has been created, the next step is to use the unstructured database/data warehouse for analysis. Figure 7-12 shows the unstructured database/data warehouse accessed and analyzed by the DSS analyst.

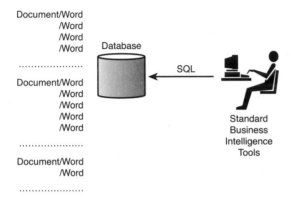

Figure 7-12 After the unstructured database is created, you can access the database and analyze with standard analytical tools.

After the unstructured database/data warehouse (that is, the simple pointer index) has been created, it is available for DSS analysis. Because the unstructured database/data warehouse is in the form of a relational database and is cast in the technology of relational technology (typically DB2, Oracle, Teradata, and NT SQL Server), it can be accessed by any analytical tools that can access these basic technologies.

Some of the more common technologies that can access standard relational technologies include Business Objects, Cognos, MicroStrategy, and Crystal Reports. There are, however, many other technologies other than those listed that are useful for accessing standard relational tables.

Access Through a Standard SQL Interface

The access to the unstructured database/data warehouse is through a standard SQL interface. There is nothing different or unusual about the SQL processing that is needed. There are no special SQL commands or unusual types of processing. The unstructured database/data warehouse is a basic relational table, and the SQL that is used to process against it is basic SQL.

The simplicity of the data and the SQL interface means that many technologies can be used for the access and analysis component of textual analytics.

The High Level Design

One of the major design issues before the analyst creating the textual analytics environment is that of the high level design of the unstructured database/data warehouse. There are essentially two basic approaches to the high level design of the unstructured database/data warehouse. One approach is that of creating a single large table and putting all simple pointers in the unstructured database/data warehouse. The other approach is to divide the unstructured database/data warehouse into a series of smaller tables. Each table contains simple pointers; however, the simple pointers can be grouped differently.

Some ways the simple pointers can be grouped is by type of document:

- Emails
- Reports
- Warranties

Another way the unstructured database/data warehouse data can be grouped is by geography:

- Unstructured data from the West coast
- Unstructured data from the East coast
- Overseas unstructured data

Yet another way the unstructured data can be grouped is by type of organization:

- Unstructured data from manufacturing
- Unstructured data from the legal department
- Unstructured data from sales

The approach for structuring the unstructured database/data warehouse when it is to be broken into several tables depends entirely on the organization and the usage of the unstructured data.

Accessing Multiple Tables

One downside to the creation of multiple unstructured database/data warehouse tables is that the SQL that will be accessing has to know to access multiple tables. If accessing multiple tables is not a serious imposition to the analyst, the creation of multiple tables presents little difficulty. Figure 7-13 illustrates the two basic approaches for the general structure of the unstructured database.

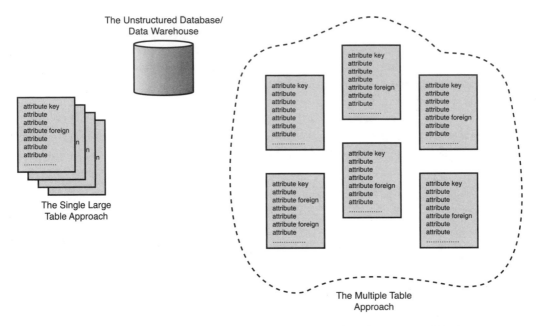

Figure 7-13   There are two distinct approaches to creating tables that constitute the unstructured database.

One consideration of creating and loading the unstructured database/data warehouse environment is the specific interface that is used to load the data.

There are two basic ways that data can be loaded into a DBMS—through a load utility or through an interface that is designed specifically for the DBMS. As a rule, it is much simpler to use a standard DBMS load utility. However, simple load utilities are usually slower in their loading. A customized interface for the DBMS is usually more efficient but requires more work for the developer of the integration and preconditioning program. In addition, on occasion, the DBMS vendor makes changes to the DBMS that affect the load interface. This means that periodically the developer must go into the customized interface and make changes based on the changes the DBMS vendor has made.

Figure 7-14 points out where the loading takes place.

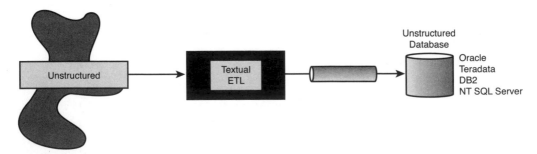

Figure 7-14   The loading interface can be customized or part of a load utility.

"Hot" Data

There is one special type of data found in the unstructured data environment that merits special attention. That data is "hot" data, which is data—text—that is sensitive or inflammatory and has the potential for harm, opportunity, or other immediate concern. Figure 7-15 shows some hot data in the unstructured data environment.

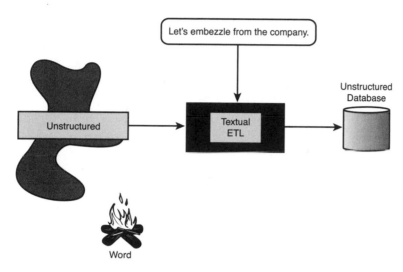

Figure 7-15   Upon encountering a "hot" word or a phrase, special handling is required.

Suppose that an email is found that says, "Let's embezzle from the company." Or, suppose that that there is a report on new technology that will change the entire fortune of a company.

Occasionally, there is textual data of a special nature. This textual data needs to be treated differently than other kinds of unstructured data. As a rule, the hot data is stored whole cloth in the unstructured database/data warehouse environment. In addition, any incidental information about the hot data is stored as well, such as the date the hot data was created and the specific people involved in the conversation.

Because there normally is not a lot of hot data, the considerations as to the volume of unstructured data stored in the unstructured database/data warehouse environment do not hold true.

Summary

The unstructured database/data warehouse is a structure that is filled with unstructured data and is built in standard relational technology, such as Oracle, DB2, Teradata, or NT SQL Server. One of the issues of the unstructured database/data warehouse is the volume of data that is consumed by the unstructured database/data warehouse. If care is not taken, the unstructured database/data warehouse will be significantly larger than the structured data warehouses.

One of the issues of the unstructured database/data warehouse environment is that of the uniqueness or nonuniqueness of the key found. The key is a compound key consisting of document ID and word. However, there might be other parts to the key such as byte address or number of occurrences in the document.

The unstructured database/data warehouse can be extended into multiple tables or can consist of a single, large table, depending on the needs of the end user.

After the unstructured data is integrated and placed into a structured environment, the stage is set for textual analytics, which is discussed in Chapter 8, "Analyzing a Combination of Unstructured Data and Structured Data."

8

Analyzing a Combination of Unstructured Data and Structured Data

The result of integrating unstructured data is the unstructured database. The unstructured database is unstructured data that has been refined into the form of an unstructured database. The unstructured database can be built from purely unstructured data or semistructured data, or both.

After the unstructured database is built, it can be queried and analyzed in a purely standalone manner. In this case, the queries and analysis look only at unstructured database data. There are, indeed, many useful analyses that can be done on purely unstructured database data.

Another type of analysis can be done: on a combination of unstructured and structured data. The ability to merge structured and unstructured data opens the door to many different and powerful kinds of analyses. Figure 8-1 shows that structured data and unstructured data can be analyzed at the same time.

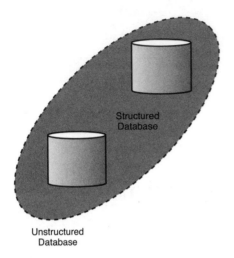

Figure 8-1 With an unstructured database, there is always the possibility of linking it with the structured data.

Intersecting Structured and Unstructured Data

To analyze unstructured and structured data in the same query, there needs to be some rational way to find the intersection of data. Unstructured and structured data with no intersection is simply uninteresting data. The real interest occurs when there is some intersection between the two environments.

Unstructured and structured data intersect in many ways. Perhaps the simplest way that they intersect is where pure unstructured data has been reduced to a relational table. In this case, one word or phrase can be used as a basis for a search of structured data, or one word or phrase from the unstructured data world can be used as a basis for the search against unstructured data. Although such a search is possible, and on occasion is quite useful, there normally is little data that intersects both the structured data world and the unstructured data world in this manner. If such a search is desired, it easy to set up a simple search against relational tables.

The interesting cases of intersection between the two environments occur when there is a much more reliable and repeating basis for intersection other than the occasional random word or phrase.

Linking Communications

One such reliable intersection between the two environments happens when there is a tagging of communications; then, a powerful and reliable form of linkage is possible. For example, there might be an email address or a telephone number that is common between the two environments. Figure 8-2 shows such an intersection.

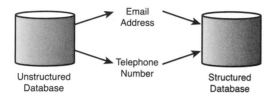

Figure 8-2 A simple form of linkage is by email address or telephone number.

In Figure 8-2, there are unstructured emails and telephone conversations. Each telephone conversation and each email has a moment in time and an address or telephone number associated with it. In the structured data environment, there is a reference from a customer or individual to an email address and a telephone number.

When these circumstances occur (which is common), the unstructured communications can be linked to the structured information about the customer or individual.

A Word of Caution—False Positives

There is a word of caution about these obvious links between the two environments. The two environments have an Achilles heel: false positives, which occur when there is a link established that is not representative of reality.

Figure 8-3 shows a false positive that occurred.

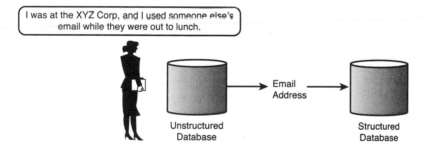

Figure 8-3 There is always the possibility of a false positive.

In Figure 8-3, a consultant is visiting a client. The client allows the consultant to get on the Internet using the client's computer. Now, a record is made between the client and the recipient of the email, even though it is the consultant that sends the message.

The same sort of complications arises with telephone conversations. For example, confusion is created when there is a record of a telephone conversation between A and B, even though C is using the telephone of A. In this case, the records reflect inaccurately that the owner of the telephone number is using the phone.

Notwithstanding these possibilities for a mix-up, there still is a solid link between the people participating in a communication.

Other Types of Linkages

Many other types of linkages exist between structured and unstructured data. When there is semistructured data, it is often possible to extract identifying fields of data from the semistructured data record. There are many possibilities of identifiers, such as the following:

- Social security number (SSN)
- Driver's license number
- Passport number
- Employee ID

Figure 8-4 shows that with semistructured data, you can extract identifiers.

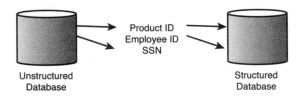

Product ID
Employee ID
SSN

Unstructured
Database

Structured
Database

Figure 8-4 Other potential links

After the identifiers are extracted from semistructured data, you can use the identifiers to link to the structured data, which often contains the same identifiers.

A Probabilistic Link

Another form of linkage can be made between unstructured and structured data. That type of linkage is a *probabilistic* link between structured and unstructured data.

A probabilistic link is different than other forms of linkages in that there is always a chance that the linkage is incorrect. (In actuality, there is always a chance that a linkage has not been formed properly with ANY form of linkage. However, with a probabilistic match, the odds of a mismatch are much higher than with other forms of linkage.)

A probabilistic match is made on more than one data element. Typical probabilistic matches are made on the following:

- First name
- Last name
- Address

- Occupation
- Education

Some of the challenges of a probabilistic match include the following:

- Matching on diminutive names, such as Bill/William, James/Jim, Scott/Scotty, Margaret/Peg
- Matching on close spellings, such as O'Neil/O'Neill/O'Neal/Oneal
- Matching on close misspellings
- Matching on common names

Then there is the issue of matching on address. Not only are there many permutations of the same address, but there also is always the possibility that the address is an old one.

As a rule, the more data that matches the better. A match on the name "Tom Smith" is weak because there are many Tom Smiths. However, a match on "Jerzy Zibilsky, 1865 Castle Butte Road, Castle, Rock, Colorado, 80109" has a high probability of being correct.

After the match is made, linkage between the structured environment and the unstructured environment can be made, as shown in Figure 8-5.

First Name
Last Name
Address

Unstructured
Database

Structured
Database

Figure 8-5   A probabilistic match is required for this kind of data.

Dynamic and Static Links

Linkages can take essentially one of two forms: dynamic or static links. Figure 8-6 shows the different kinds of links.

A dynamic link is made directly between the unstructured data and the structured data at the time that the unstructured and structured data are accessed. The dynamic linkage is made at the time of the query and uses both types of data. Because the link is made as a result of a query and is made at the time of the request, it is called a dynamic query.

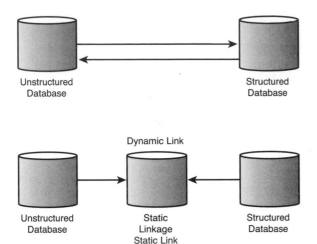

Figure 8-6 Two basic kinds of links

The other type of linkage is a static link, which is made by periodically reading the identifiers of unstructured data and seeking a match in structured data (or vice versa). When the linkage is established, a record is written. When a query is made against the system, the query looks at the static record that has been created. It is efficient to look for a single entry in the static link file that has been created. Also, the static link file can be queried independently.

Dynamic linkage is good for the cases where either the unstructured or structured data changes frequently. Static linkage is good for cases where the unstructured and structured data change infrequently or not at all.

Accessing Linkages

Accessing linkages—either dynamic or static—can be done in many different ways. One way access can be done is by looking for a specific linkage. For example, suppose there is a query: "Has Lynn Inmon made an email query on Tuesday, December 28?" In this case, there are browsing queries. A browsing query is one that is less than specific. Figure 8-7 suggests a browsing query. Some examples of browsing queries follow:

- Show me any emails made by customers in Texas.
- Show me any telephone calls made by Executive Premier customers from December 21 to December 26.
- Show me any queries that have come from people named Mary.

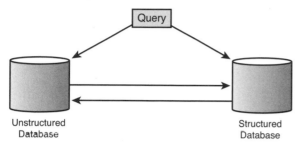

Figure 8-7 Browsing the relationships

In no small part, the success of a browsing query depends on the linkages that are formed between databases. The more powerful and meaningful the linkages, the greater the chance that the browsing query will lead somewhere meaningful.

One of the issues is that of adding and deleting linkages. Some linkages tend to be stable and others tend to be fluid. The issue of keeping linkages accurate is a challenge and is one of the considerations of the infrastructure. Figure 8-8 shows that adding and deleting linkages is an issue that must be considered, especially when dealing with static linkage.

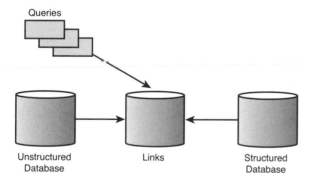

Figure 8-8 Adding and deleting links

Periodically Monitoring Linkage

Consideration must be given to the periodic monitoring of unstructured data and structured data to determine if the linkage is still valid. Figure 8-9 shows that, periodically, the different environments need to be monitored. It shows that the static link is read and then a reference is made to the unstructured environment and the structured environment to determine whether the link is still valid. Many things can happen to data in the unstructured environment and structured environment: Data can be deleted or changed; the physical storage location of data can be changed.

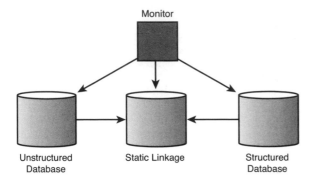

Figure 8-9   Monitoring linkages is an issue.

Independently Processing the Static Link

Occasions can arrive where the static index can be processed independently. Figure 8-10 shows this possibility.

Figure 8-10   Efficient processing of the static links

For example, a question can be asked: How many emails did we have from customers who made purchases in the last week? First, the query finds out which customers made purchases in the past week. Then, the static email link is examined to find out how many of those customers are on the static link.

A Join Based on the Link

One of the most useful things that can be done with unstructured and structured data when there is linkage is to join the data based on the linkage. Figure 8-11 shows the join that is created based on the intersection of unstructured and structured data.

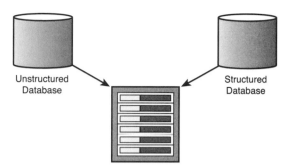

Figure 8-11   Data can be joined from the different sources.

Such a join has many uses, such as the following:

- What emails have been sent to customer Jane Smith and what have her replies been?
- What engineering changes have there been for all parts modified in the past six months?
- What contracts have there been for supplier ABC?

The two types of joins are one-to-many and many-to-many. A one-to-many join is one that joins a single unstructured record to many structured records or vice versa. Figure 8-12 shows a one-to-many join.

Figure 8-12   A one-to-many relationship

As a simple example of a one-to-many join, consider the join of Bill Inmon to all the emails that he sent.

The other type of join is a many-to-many join, in which any number of records can point to any other number of records and vice versa. Figure 8-13 shows a many-to-many join.

As a simple example of a many-to-many join, consider a query that looks at all contracts involving organizations that are both suppliers and consumers.

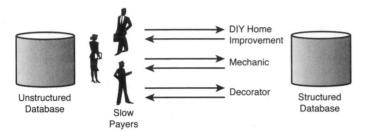

Figure 8-13 A many-to-many relationship

Submitting Real-Time Online Queries

Queries looking at linkages can be real-time, online queries, submitted directly from the consumer in an online mode where the expectation is that of online time—that is, response in a few seconds. Figure 8-14 shows an online query of linkages.

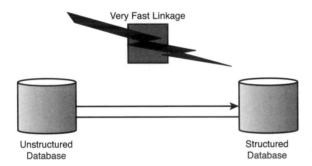

Figure 8-14 Online, high-performance access and analysis of links

In an ideal world, an online query of linkages is made against a static link. Good and consistent response time is a normal expectation, but occasionally an online query is made of dynamic links. If there aren't too many dynamic links, good response time can normally be achieved. However, when there are many unstructured and structured data references to be examined, it might not be possible to achieve good and consistent response time.

If enough hardware resources are thrown at a problem, performance can always be improved, but there reaches a point at which it is better to find alternatives.

Enhancing Performance Through Priority Ranking

One way to enhance performance is to qualify linkages based on predetermined criteria, as shown in Figure 8-15.

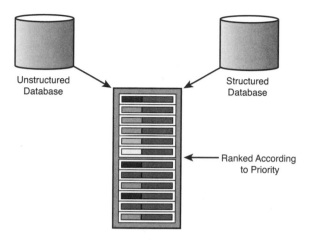

Figure 8-15   Qualifying the order of data based on criteria

In Figure 8-15, the linkages have been prioritized according to their capability to enhance performance. For example, suppose that there are many emails. The emails could be sorted by date on the assumption that the latest emails are the ones that have the highest probability of access.

Filtering Data Based on Probability of Access

Another related technique for the improvement of performance is to filter data based on probability of access. Instead of sorting emails by date, create a cutoff date where only emails of a certain date are indexed. The effect of this filtering is to ensure that the number of emails indexed is small and manageable.

Figure 8-16 shows the technique of filtering data based on the probability of access.

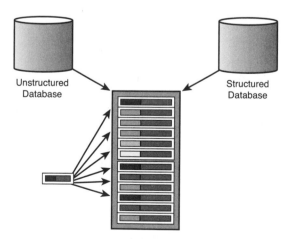

Figure 8-16   Qualifying the order of data based on criteria

Looking at Links Partially

A final technique worthy of attention looking at links partially. In a partial search of a link, a known part of the link is examined. (Note: This technique is sometimes called a wild card search.)

Suppose the analyst knows that a person's name sounds like "Inmon" but isn't sure of the spelling. The person enters a search for "Inm**." (Depending on the search done and the search engine, the person doing the query might enter either "INM" or "INM**.") The search will find such things as "Inmon," "Inman," "Inmar."

Figure 8-17 shows the support of a partial search of a link.

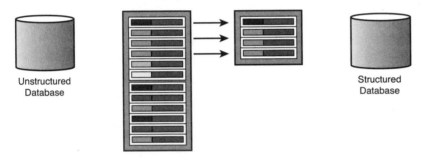

Unstructured
Database

Structured
Database

Figure 8-17   Filtering links can enhance performance.

Unstructured Text and Future Capabilities

The truth is that much of the promise of unstructured technology lies in front, not behind. The reality is that up to the present point in time, not many applications have been built using unstructured technology—but the future is full of opportunity. Some of those opportunities include the following

- **Customer relationship management (CRM) and customer data integration (CDI)**—CRM and CDI have a fixation on demographic information as a basis for getting to know a customer, but communications are as important as demographic information. In addition, communications are a form of unstructured data. The communications come in the form of email or other electronic messaging. The communications are broken down several ways—by the content of the communication, the tone of the communication, the criticality of the messaging. When the communication is broken down and analyzed, a new dimension of knowing a customer opens up.
- **Medicine and healthcare**—There are large amounts of textual information found in medicine and healthcare. Doctors have the habit of writing notes. It is said of doctors that they hate structured information until they have to find something. Unstructured

textual processing can be useful in many ways—in clinical day-to-day usage, in research, and other ways.

- **Contracts**—It is said that you can have a lawyer tell you what is in a given contract or several contracts. However, there is no lawyer alive that can tell you what is in ten thousand contracts. There are important pieces of information scattered over all sorts of places in contracts. The information is textual and unstructured. In the future, it will be possible to handle thousands of contracts as easily as one or two contracts are handled now.

- **Email**—Email is very catholic. There are benign emails, dicey emails, and important emails. There is email blather. There are emails that are time critical, and there is a large volume of emails. Sorting through emails is a big task. In the future, there will be applications that manage the large email bulk in a sophisticated manner.

- **Spreadsheets**—On an informal basis, the business of the organization first runs through spreadsheets before it is formalized. In the future, there will be a corporate vista of spreadsheets rather than the limited individual or departmental vista of spreadsheets that exists today.

There are more places where future applications will arise to address the challenges of textual analytics. There is HR, manufacturing warranties. and litigation support opportunities. Anywhere there is textual data, there are future opportunities.

Summary

You can analyze unstructured text in a standalone mode or unstructured data in conjunction with structured data.

The linkage between structured and unstructured data can be accomplished in several ways:

- By communications linkage
- By linkage of common keys, such as social security number, passport number, employee number, etc.
- By probabilistic matching of several data elements

Of these forms of linkage, the weakest linkage is the probabilistic variety.

You can create and manage links dynamically or statically. The joins of data from the two environments can be done based on the linkages used as a basis. If queries and linkages are important in query processing, even more important and potent are the opportunities that arise when textual information can be visualized. Chapter 9, "Analyzing Text Through Visualization," discusses some of those opportunities.

9

Analyzing Text Through Visualization

One of the most powerful forms of analytics is that of visualization. With visualization, information "pops out" that would not otherwise be obvious. Visualization makes obvious what would otherwise be difficult to discern.

Figure 9-1 shows a list of numbers. From the list of numbers is a visualization, which immediately brings out aspects of the list of numbers that would otherwise be difficult to see.

There are all sorts of visualizations: pie charts, Pareto charts, straight line point-to-point graphic depictions, scatter diagrams. Each type of visualizations has its advantages and disadvantages. Some types of visualizations are good for large amounts of data; some are good for large amounts of nonhomogeneous data; and some are good for showing percentages.

Analysts have long known about the inherent power of visualizations. For the most part, visualizations of an earlier day and age have been good for the visualization of numeric data. There is no question that numeric data is important and that visualization of numeric data is likewise important. However, numeric data is only part of the data that exists.

Another important form of data is textual data, which consists of text, which cannot be manipulated like numeric data. Text cannot be added, subtracted, multiplied, or divided. For this basic reason, textual data cannot be easily manipulated, but that does not mean that textual data cannot be graphically displayed.

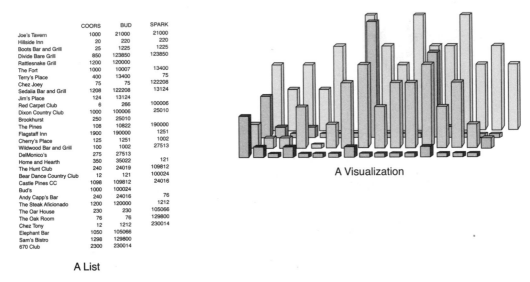

	COORS	BUD	SPARK
Joe's Tavern	1000	21000	21000
Hillside Inn	20	220	220
Boots Bar and Grill	25	1225	1225
Divide Bare Grill	850	123850	123850
Rattlesnake Grill	1200	120000	
The Fort	1000	10007	13400
Terry's Place	400	13400	75
Chez Joey	75	75	122208
Sedalia Bar and Grill	1208	122208	13124
Jim's Place	124	13124	
Red Carpet Club	6	266	100006
Dixon Country Club	1000	100006	25010
Brookhurst	250	25010	
The Pines	108	10822	190000
Flagstaff Inn	1900	190000	1251
Cherry's Place	125	1251	1002
Wildwood Bar and Grill	100	1002	27513
DelMonico's	275	27513	
Home and Hearth	350	35022	121
The Hunt Club	240	24019	109812
Bear Dance Country Club	12	121	100024
Castle Pines CC	1098	109812	24016
Bud's	1000	100024	
Andy Capp's Bar	240	24016	76
The Steak Aficionado	1200	120000	1212
The Oar House	230	230	105066
The Oak Room	76	76	129800
Chez Tony	12	1212	230014
Elephant Bar	1050	105066	
Sam's Bistro	1298	129800	
670 Club	2300	230014	

A List   A Visualization

Figure 9-1   Which of these portrayals is most meaningful?

Creating a Textual Visualization

Textual data can, indeed, be graphically displayed; however, the form is substantially different from the form in which numeric data is displayed.

To see one way that textual data can be graphically displayed, consider the following steps shown in Figure 9-2.

Selecting Homogeneous Data

The first step in the creation of a meaningful visualization of textual data is to select reasonably homogeneous data. To illustrate this point, consider two examples. Consider the selection of words in a Merriam Webster dictionary. This selection of words is non-homogeneous. The only thing they have in common is that they appear in a dictionary. Other than that fact, there is little homogeneity among the set of words. The visualization produced by looking at all the words in the dictionary would be questionable.

Now, consider the words that come from 10,000 patient records from a cardiology study. The records have been collected over a period of 25 years. The text is homogeneous in that all the text relates to the same general condition. When the text is gathered, the visualization can produce interesting and useful results.

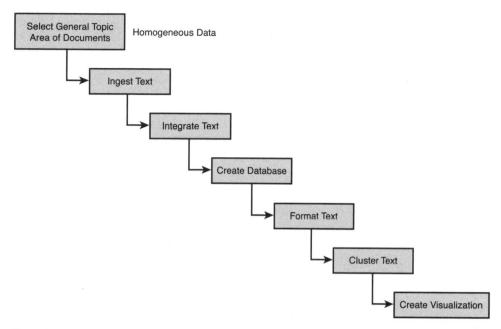

Figure 9-2 The steps to create a visualization

The first step in producing a useful visualization lies in the selection of the base text that goes into the visualization. An important consideration is the specification of the number of documents that will be read as input. As a general rule, the more documents, the better. Visualizations do not show anything particularly useful when there is only a small amount of data. Also, the greater the content of the documents, the better. For example, emails do not make a particularly good basis for a visualization because most emails have relatively little content.

Integrating the Text

Figure 9-2 shows that the next step after the base text has been selected is to ingest the textual data. Reading the text can be quite an adventure because there are many sources for textual data. When read, the textual data must be integrated. The steps of integration include the following:

- Resolution of synonyms
- Resolution of homographs
- Negativity exclusion
- Removal of stop words
- Grouping of words according to external categories

Note that if integration is not done, the results of visualization will be unorganized and confusing. Just as the selection of the base text is important, so the integration of the text is likewise important.

Creating a Database Format

After the text has been read and integrated, the next step is to place the text in a database format. Then, the text is clustered, based on the number of occurrences of words and the proximity of those words to each other. One way to cluster words is on a document-by-document basis. Another way is to gather the words from many documents together and create a common clustering based on the occurrence of all the words regardless of what document they came from.

Creating the Visualization

When the words have been clustered, the next step is to visualize them. Figure 9-3 shows a visualization.

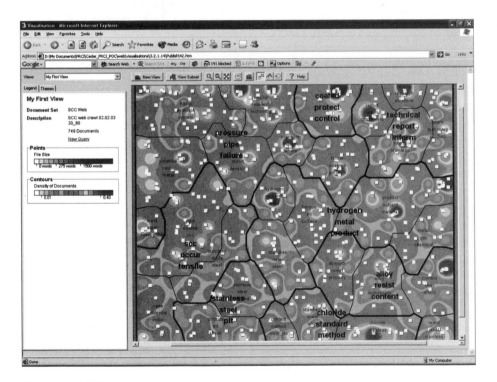

Figure 9-3   A SOM

The visualization shown in Figure 9-3 is produced by Compudigm. It is a "theme-based" visualization called a self-organizing map (SOM). (Note: SOM is pronounced like the book in the old testament—Psalm. However, there is nothing biblical about a SOM.) The only input into a SOM is raw text. There simply is no other input. The entire structure of a SOM is derived from the input.

Some of the features of the visualization—the SOM—done by Compudigm include the following:

- **Identification of major themes of the words that are visualized**—These major themes are shown in bold-faced type. The major themes are surrounded by a dark, black thick line. There is no overlap from one major theme to another.

- **Identification of minor themes**—These minor themes are shown in less than bold-faced type. There might be overlap of minor themes.

- **Density**—Where there is a density of information, the visualization grows darker.

- **Sparsity**—Where there is a sparsity of information, the visualization grows lighter.

- **Document designation**—The precise definition and placement of a document can be found on the visualization.

Other Types of SOMs

Although the visualization of unstructured data is important to the analyst, there are other types of visualizations. In particular, there is visualization of semistructured data. Although the end result of visualization looks the same, the basis on which the visualization is made is actually quite different. In the case of an unstructured SOM, there is no repeatability of data. Text can be grouped as having a relationship to other text based on proximity of text and number of occurrences. That is all there is to the relationship of text in creating a SOM from unstructured data. However, when it comes to semistructured data, there is repeatability of data types, and even more inferences can be made about the contents of semistructured data than can be made about the interrelationships of unstructured data.

Iterative Development of the Visualization

The nature of building visualizations—for unstructured or semistructured data—is iterative. It almost never happens that the steps of visualization are taken and the visualization turns out exactly as planned. In almost every case, visualizations are built iteratively. Each time a new visualization is made, refinements are made. Stop words, synonyms, and homonyms are added or deleted. All these refinements are made, and the next iteration of the visualization improves.

Analytical Activities

After the visualization is made, the analyst can do all sorts of analysis, such as the following:

- **Completeness**—One advantage of the SOM is that all the words are represented in their entirety and in proportion to the other words. The balance of completeness and proportionality is valuable in seeing the large picture painted by the text.
- **Correlative activities**—Where there are a lot of occurrences of words or themes, there is a correlation of text. There often occur multiple correlations to the central theme of the visualization. Upon selecting the text for the visualization and examining the correlations, it becomes obvious why a homogeneous selection of text at the outset makes a big difference.
- **Outliers**—Just as highly correlative text can be identified immediately when looking at a SOM, the reverse of high correlation is also obvious: outlying. An outlier is an occurrence of data that distinctly does not fit the pattern of all other occurrences of data. In a SOM, an outlier stands out in that it stands alone.
- **Drill-down processing**—When the analyst finds a point of interest in the SOM, the analyst can start to do what is termed drill-down processing. In drill-down processing, the analyst fixes the analysis on a particular place. Then, the analyst explores the location in lots of ways. Some of the ways that further information becomes available include the following:
  - Looking at the specific words that constitute the themes of the documents that exist at that particular location
  - Seeing what documents have been assigned to the location
  - Looking at the contents of the documents
- **Drill-across processing**—In drill-across processing, a word or phrase is entered, and all the locations (that is, documents) where the word or phrase exists are identified.

The specification of the location on the SOM that is of interest is indicated by a *lasso*. The lasso can be moved by a cursor or a mouse, expanded or shrunk as desired, and used for a "close up" of a location to be created. When the SOM has been created and produced properly, it can be stored for future analysis and reference.

Recasting a SOM Visualization

Another use of the SOM, when stabilized, is to add a whole new set of documents to the original set of documents and to "recast" the SOM. As an example of recasting, suppose the first SOM was for cardiologists and heart patients. Now, a different set of documents is added—records for patients who have diabetes. Another SOM is produced and the original relationships are recast. Such a recasting of documents is especially useful for the cases where there is an intersection of data. For example, if there is a relationship between heart patients and diabetics, it will show up prominently in the recast SOM.

Creating a SOM for Semistructured Data

As some examples of semistructured data, consider the following:

- **Human resource resumes**—Typically, resumes contain education, salary, last job, and training.

- **Medical records**—Medical records contain such things as blood pressure, pulse rate, age, and general condition.

- **Warranties**—Warranties contain such things as part numbers, defect description, injury or damage description, and date and location of mishap.

The semistructured data can be read and the recurring data elements extracted. Then, the semistructured data can be converted into a structured format and the resulting file or database can be visualized.

Figure 9-4 shows the creation of a SOM from semistructured data.

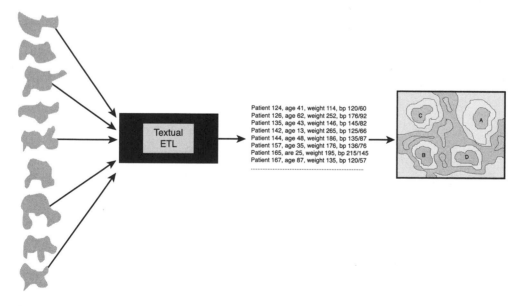

Figure 9-4 Creating the SOM from semistructured data

Summary

Numeric data can be visualized in many different ways—Pareto charts, bar graphs, pie charts, and many more. Numeric data is easy to manage because it can be added and subtracted, following a well-known set of rules.

Textual data is more difficult to manage. Textual data requires that it first be integrated. After integration, textual data is filtered for homogeneity. Next, textual data is used to produce SOMs (self-organizing maps). As a rule, the more points of data, the better.

SOMs can be created from semistructured data as well.

One of the most intriguing possibilities for visualization is in the commonly found forms of unstructured data—spreadsheets and email. Chapter 10, "Spreadsheets and Emails," discusses the issues associated with these specialized forms of textual data.

10

Spreadsheets and Email

Two forms of unstructured data are so pervasive and so unique that they deserve their own special treatment. Those forms of unstructured data are spreadsheets and email. Each has its own unique characteristics and considerations.

The Challenges of Spreadsheets

Spreadsheets are the lingua franca of the personal computer. Spreadsheets are as ubiquitous as grass in summer. They are used by financiers, accountants, secretaries, managers, planners, and practically everyone else. They are everywhere. Figure 10-1 shows the common spreadsheet.

You can use a spreadsheet for many purposes. Spreadsheets contain unstructured data, and there is no reason why that unstructured data cannot be accessed and managed like the other unstructured data found throughout the organization.

Spreadsheets are found all over the organization. A typical personal computer might have as many as one hundred spreadsheets on it. The first challenge in looking at corporate spreadsheets is that there are so many of them. Spreadsheets are constantly changing. Therefore, there needs to be a certain amount of selectivity in choosing which spreadsheets are fit for general scrutiny. Not all spreadsheets are fit for such analyses. As a rule, spreadsheets that are stable and have general interest around the organization make good candidates for general scrutiny.

Name	Addr	Zip	Phone	Sex	Ethnic	Salary	Nat'l
Jane							
Tom							
Jan							
Mary							
Jerry							
Mack							
Sue							
Bill							
June							
Terry							
Chris							
Judy							
Kevin							
Jeanne							
Carol							

Figure 10-1   A common spreadsheet

The second challenge is that the spreadsheets are not found in a single computer. So merely getting one's hands on all the spreadsheets that are of interest is a challenge. If the personal computers are networked, the spreadsheets can usually be accessed. If the personal computers are not networked, the spreadsheets are more difficult to access.

The first problem for the management of the unstructured data found on the spreadsheets is determining which spreadsheets are of interest and then finding and accessing them. Figure 10-2 shows the problem of the spreadsheets scattered all over the place.

Another problem with spreadsheets is that they change unpredictably. One user can create a spreadsheet and never change it. Another user might create a spreadsheet and update it daily. Another user might create a spreadsheet and alter it once or twice a year. There simply is no consistency among spreadsheet users when it comes to the mutability of the spreadsheet.

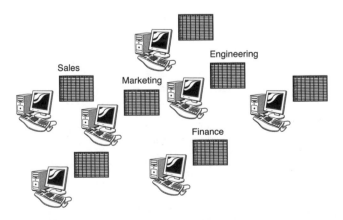

Figure 10-2   Spreadsheets are found all over the organization.

Another problem is that spreadsheet users can designate any column to be anything. There simply is no rhyme nor reason to the way spreadsheets are formatted or created.

Strategies for Access

The first thing the spreadsheet analyst needs to do is to determine which spreadsheets need to be looked at on a global basis. Not all spreadsheets meet this criteria. Then the analyst needs to determine the location of those spreadsheets and to determine how they can be accessed.

Several strategies for accessing the spreadsheets have been designated as globally accessible spreadsheets. One strategy is to leave the spreadsheets where they are, and every time there is a need to access a spreadsheet, go to the spreadsheet and access it.

The other strategy is to centralize the spreadsheets in a server. By centralizing the spreadsheets, several objectives are accomplished:

■ The spreadsheets are much easier to access, residing on a server. With centralized spreadsheets, otherwise unrelated spreadsheets can be examined at once.

■ The spreadsheets are "frozen." This means that the spreadsheets contain the version of the spreadsheets when they were copied to the server. In some cases, this "freezing" of the spreadsheets is advantageous.

Figure 10-3 shows that the spreadsheets are sent to a centralized server.

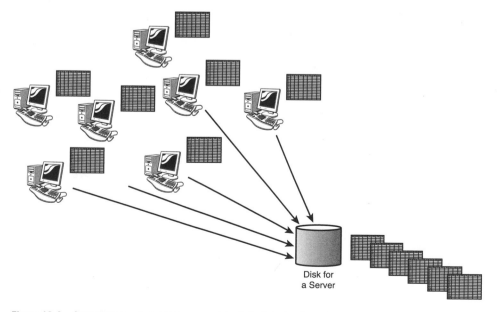

Figure 10-3 Centralizing and stabilizing spreadsheets by bringing them to a server

A Unique Spreadsheet Identifier

However the access to the spreadsheet is solved, one thing needs to be done. Each spreadsheet must be uniquely identified. There are lots of ways to achieve a unique identification—by the name assigned to the spreadsheet by the end user, by the moment in time the spreadsheet was loaded into the server, or by other means. However it is done, a unique name must be established for each spreadsheet.

Figure 10-4 shows that each spreadsheet must have or be assigned its own unique name and identifier.

Name	Addr	Zip	Phone	Sex	Ethnic	Salary	Nat'l
Jane							
Tom							
Jan							
Mary							
Jerry							
Mack							
Sue							
Bill							
June							
Terry							
Chris							
Judy							
Kevin							
Jeanne							
Carol							

Ssid.xxxxx

Figure 10-4   A spreadsheet ID must be established.

After the unique identifier—ssid—is assigned to the spreadsheet, the next step is to examine the types of unstructured data that reside in the spreadsheet.

Unstructured Data in the Spreadsheet

Figure 10-5 shows that certain cells in the spreadsheet contain unstructured data. However, the unstructured data found in Figure 10-5 is not of a normal variety. It has column headings and is properly called metadata. The implication is that the contents in the column are the same type and that the name (or acronym) of the column is specified in the first cell of the column.

Unfortunately, the column headings are not always in the first or top cells. Depending on the spreadsheet, the column headings can be found practically anywhere. So there needs to be a specification showing that a cell contains the unstructured metadata. One of the problems with specifying a given cell is that when the spreadsheet changes, the cell address might change as well. When the cell address changes, the specification of the cell to the ssid layout must also be modified. This is another reason why only a stable, selective spreadsheet needs to be specified for global analysis.

However, there is another kind of unstructured data that is found in a spreadsheet, in the cells that represent actual data values. Figure 10-6 shows that there are cells that contain textual data. These cells are part of a list.

Name	Addr	Zip	Phone	Sex	Ethnic	Salary	Nat'l
Jane							
Tom							
Jan							
Mary							
Jerry							
Mack							
Sue							
Bill							
June							
Terry							
Chris							
Judy							
Kevin							
Jeanne							
Carol							

Figure 10-5   Column headings are a form of unstructured metadata.

Name	Addr	Zip	Phone	Sex	Ethnic	Salary	Nat'l
Jane							
Tom							
Jan							
Mary							
Jerry							
Mack							
Sue							
Bill							
June							
Terry							
Chris							
Judy							
Kevin							
Jeanne							
Carol							

Figure 10-6   Cells that contain textual data are usually a form of semistructured data.

The cells shown in Figure 10-6 are part of a list and are unstructured data. In concept, they are a form of semi-semistructured data. They can be treated as semi-semistructured data the way that any other unstructured data in a list might be treated.

There are at least two types of unstructured data found in a spreadsheet—metadata (column headings) and list components (semistructured data).

Another type of data that can be found in a spreadsheet is numeric data. Figure 10-7 shows the many cells of a spreadsheet that have numeric data.

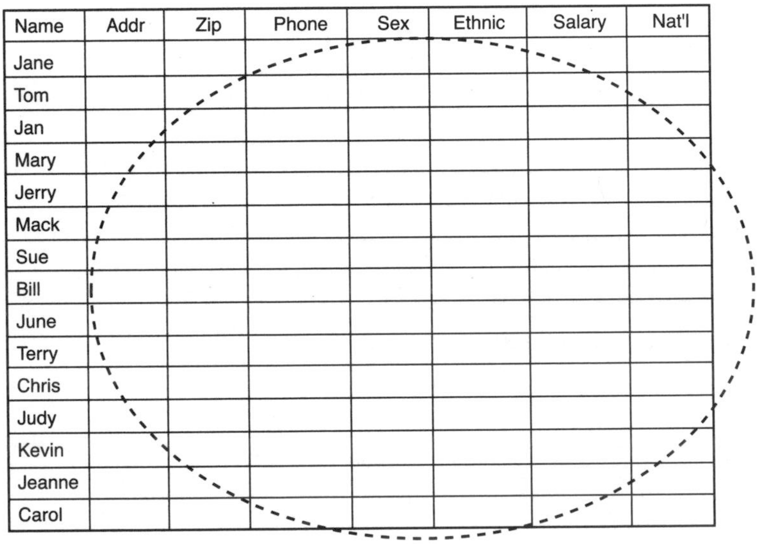

Name	Addr	Zip	Phone	Sex	Ethnic	Salary	Nat'l
Jane							
Tom							
Jan							
Mary							
Jerry							
Mack							
Sue							
Bill							
June							
Terry							
Chris							
Judy							
Kevin							
Jeanne							
Carol							

Figure 10-7 Certain cells contain numeric data.

Under normal circumstances, the numeric data in a spreadsheet is ignored. There is at least one exception and that is where the numeric data is recognizably another form of data. For example, when the system sees the pattern xxx-xx-xxxx, the system recognizes those numbers to be a social security number. Or, perhaps the system sees the numbers xxx-xxx-xxxx. The system recognizes those numbers to be a telephone number in the United States; but for the most part, numeric data in a spreadsheet is ignored.

Identifying Cells

The system needs to have the cells defined that will be part of the global spreadsheet analysis. This means that the cells for metadata and semistructured data need to be identified.

Figure 10-8 shows the need for the identification of cells of data.

Ssid.columns

Name	Addr	Zip	Phone	Sex	Ethnic	Salary	Nat'l
Jane							
Tom							
Jan							
Mary							
Jerry							
Mack							
Sue							
Bill							
June							
Terry							
Chris							
Judy							
Kevin							
Jeanne							
Carol							

Ssid.occurrences

Figure 10-8   The definitions that need to be made

Another kind of data relationship needs to be identified before the spreadsheet world becomes accessible on a global basis. This kind of relationship is the specification of different values having the same meaning across different spreadsheets. For example, spreadsheet A might have a value "total sales." Spreadsheet B has the value "grand total." Spreadsheet C has the value "total." Spreadsheet D has the value "tot." These different values mean the same thing.

Cross Equivalency

The system needs to know that there is cross-value equivalency between different spreadsheets. This is defined as a *common value*, as shown in Figure 10-9.

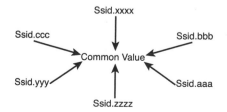

Figure 10-9   A metadata definition of how different search arguments relate to a common definition is built.

As an example of a common value being defined, suppose the common value were "annual total sales." The different spreadsheet values would be assigned.

There will be many such common values that need to be defined. Figure 10-10 shows that multiple common values need to be created.

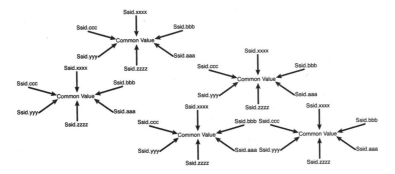

Figure 10-10   A directory of common values

Global Spreadsheet Analysis

When the multiple common values are created, the system is now ready to function for global spreadsheet analyses. Figure 10-11 shows that a query is created on a common value. The system then uses the link to the different spreadsheets to determine the values.

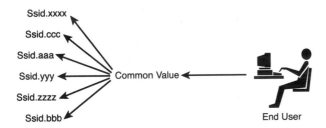

Figure 10-11   When a query is made, it is made on the common value that then accesses the ssid.

In such a manner, there is linkage to the different spreadsheets that are found in the organization. If the spreadsheets have been centralized on a server, they are easy to reach. If the spreadsheets have not been centralized but still reside on personal computers, the system might have to do more work to link the spreadsheet to the query.

Emails

Emails are the common form of communication that occurs in corporations and with individuals. Emails have long been used for all sorts of purposes:

- To send messages
- To send documents
- To integrate work efforts

Inside a corporation in a day, there might be millions of emails—from business person to business person and from business person to external customer or prospect.

Emails, depicted in Figure 10-12, are unstructured text; no one stands over the creator of an email dictating the form, substance, or language to go into the email. The epitome of unstructured data has to be email.

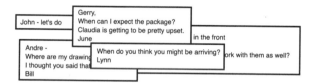

Figure 10-12 Emails are the lifeblood of communications in the organization.

As a class of documents, some common characteristics are associated with emails. As a rule, emails are voluminous (in terms of their total number) and short (in terms of their individual content), relative to other documents. Figure 10-13 illustrates a large volume of emails and the small size of each email.

Figure 10-13 Emails—Each is short, but a lot exist.

Emails tend to be archived—formally or informally—for a lengthy period of time. In some cases, the archival strategy is determined by the legal staff. In some cases, the legal staff wants to keep emails for a long time. In some cases, the archiving of emails is mandated legally.

In yet other cases, taking a contrarian position, the legal staff wants to get rid of emails as quickly as possible, thinking that emails represent a liability rather than an asset.

As a rule, there tends to be very little semistructured data found in an email. (In theory, it is possible that semistructured data be found in an email. However, in reality, little semistructured data is found there.)

Figure 10-14 shows that email records with semistructured data is a rarity.

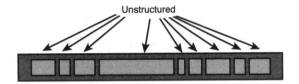

Figure 10-14   There tends to be little, if any, semistructured data in emails.

Screening Emails for Useful Data

Because of the freedom of creativity in the composition of emails, they contain all sorts of information. Some of the information is personal; some is related to the business. Because it is likely that there is a lot of data that doesn't relate to the business, it is a wise practice to screen the email, weeding out the unnecessary email.

The email that is weeded out is called *blather*. As an example of blather, consider the following email:

"Let's go out for pizza tonight."

There is no business content in that email.

The reason why blather needs to be separated from the regular email is that emails take up a lot of space. When blather is included, the volume of email grows unnecessarily larger. Figure 10-15 shows the screening of emails to remove blather.

Another interesting aspect of emails is that some emails are "hot." A hot email is one that holds sensitive information. The information can be sensitive for a variety of reasons. Some examples of sensitive emails are

- "Let's embezzle some money."
- "You look sexy today. How about a date tonight?"
- "You are fired."

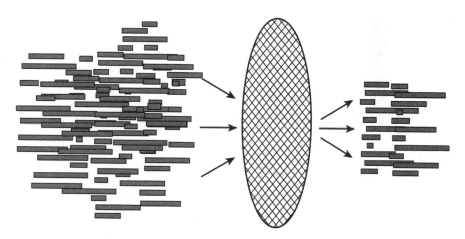

Figure 10-15 Emails need to be screened for business relevance.

All these emails—under the right circumstances—can be considered sensitive. As a rule, when an email is encountered that is sensitive, it should be captured and taken out of the control of the standard processing stream.

A hot email is one that contains corporate-sensitive information, such as, "Let's steal something," or, "Mary is taking off work and she isn't actually sick." Figure 10-16 shows that there are often hot emails.

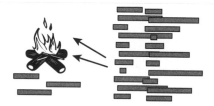

Figure 10-16 Some emails are "hot."

Collecting Customer Communications

After the emails are captured, they can be used for many purposes. One of the most obvious and important uses of the emails are as a collection of communications going to and from a customer.

There is a lot of talk about creating the 360-degree view of the customer. However, in most circles, the 360-degree view of the customer means that demographics about the customer are created. To create a true 360-degree view of the customer, it is necessary to include communications as well. Emails provide the basis of completing the 360-degree view of the customer, as shown in Figure 10-17.

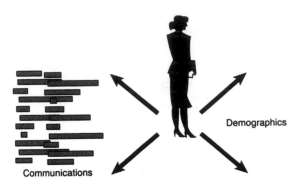

Demographics

Communications

Figure 10-17 Emails provide the completion of the 360-degree view of the customer.

Summary

Spreadsheets are a common form of analyses. Spreadsheets are found almost everywhere and contain unstructured data. There is the possibility of analysis of the different spreadsheets across the enterprise. The spreadsheets can reside on the personal computers that they originated on or can be placed on a centralized server. One of the issues of a spreadsheet is that there is the potential of change. For this reason only, selective spreadsheets need to be selected for global analysis.

There are two types of unstructured data found in a spreadsheet: metadata (column headings) and lists (semistructured data).

Query access is done on the basis of common values that then link to the actual spreadsheet.

Emails constitute an important and large part of unstructured data of the corporation. As a rule, there are many emails, and the emails are short (relative to other forms of unstructured data). Emails need to be screened because many emails do not relate to the business of the organization.

Some emails contain sensitive information. These emails are said to be "hot" and require special storage and handling.

Finding your way around the unstructured environment—whether with a spreadsheet, report, or email—is always a challenge. That challenge is greatly mitigated by the recognition and use of metadata.

II

Metadata in Unstructured Data

There is a level of abstraction sitting above all information processing, including that of unstructured data. That level of abstraction is commonly called *metadata*, which sits above unstructured data just as it sits on top of structured data. It is with metadata that we can see the "larger picture" of what is going on in the systems and components of information processing.

A simplistic definition of metadata is "data about data," which has been around for as long as there have been information systems. Although the definition gives a flavor of what metadata is, it is not a good definition. A somewhat better description of metadata is that metadata is an abstraction or a classification of data.

Metadata in the Unstructured Environment

In classical structured information systems, metadata included such things as the following:

- Attributes
- Entities
- Entity definitions

- Entity relationships
- Subject areas
- Tables
- Column definitions
- Indexes and identifiers

These characteristics of classical metadata enabled the analyst to understand what was happening with structured systems. There indeed is metadata in the unstructured environment; however, it takes on a different character.

To understand how metadata manifests itself in the unstructured environment, consider the diagram shown in Figure 11-1.

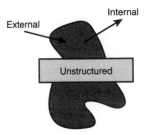

Figure 11-1 Two different kinds of metadata are relevant to the unstructured environment.

Figure 11-1 shows two distinct divisions of metadata in the unstructured data environment: internal and external metadata.

Internal Metadata

Internal metadata is metadata that is defined and is contained wholly within the domain of unstructured data. For example, suppose there were a body of unstructured data related to medicine. You would expect to find metadata structures internal to the unstructured data that related to such things as the following:

- Human body
- Medical treatments
- Medical diagnoses
- Pharmaceuticals

The internal unstructured metadata contains words and structures of words that are wholly contained within the boundaries of the unstructured documents. You would not expect to find the following in a body of work about medicine information:

- Batman
- The circus
- Monterey, California
- The Dallas Cowboys
- The stock market
- The dependence on foreign oil

Internal metadata is metadata that is wholly contained in the documents that constitute the unstructured data.

External Metadata

The other kind of metadata found in the unstructured data environment is external metadata, which is metadata found outside the body of knowledge represented in the unstructured data. External metadata is created outside the unstructured data and is mapped or superimposed over the unstructured data. As such, there might or might not be a close alliance between external metadata and the unstructured data. For example, one form of external metadata might relate to Sarbanes-Oxley. The Sarbanes-Oxley discipline or body of thought might have little or no mapping to medical unstructured data, but it might have a poignant mapping to financial data.

External metadata can represent anything and might or might not be relevant to the information found in the unstructured data environment.

One of the problems with unstructured data and external metadata is that there can be an almost infinite number of abstractions or classifications to consider. Take the external metadata classification—the word "boy." The word boy is representative of many people—for example, my nephew Kelsey, my young nephew Caleb, a child movie star. Or, take the word "house." The word house is representative of many, many locations found in cities and towns throughout the world.

When it comes to representations of external metadata, too many abstractions are possible. The challenge of dealing with external metadata and unstructured data is that there is too much metadata. The analyst must select which subset of external metadata is important and deal with that metadata. All other external metadata must be ignored or tabled.

The two distinct ways of looking at metadata are externally and internally. Both approaches are needed when managing the unstructured data environment.

Approaching Metadata Through the Data Model

A good way of approaching metadata—both internal and external—and the unstructured data environment is through the data model. A data model is merely another form of metadata. Figure 11-2 shows the external metadata.

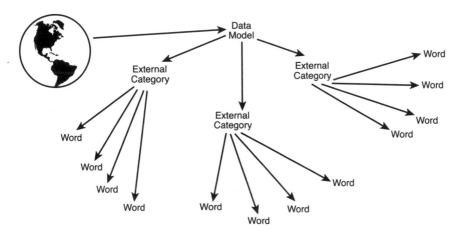

Figure 11-2 A data model is a good way to approach external metadata.

Figure 11-2 shows the world. An almost infinite number of things can be modeled in the world. The analyst selects the few things that are relevant to the unstructured data that is at hand. The data model is created for whatever the analyst has chosen. Then, the data model is used to produce *external categories* of data. An external category is a collection of words that relate to some common term. After the external categories are selected, they are used as a basis for selecting words and phrases that are relevant to the external category.

The Basis for the Data Model

As an example of the manifestation of Figure 11-2, suppose the analyst has chosen from the real world the following information on which to make a data model. The basis for the data models can be almost anything:

- Sarbanes-Oxley
- Genealogy of paint horses
- Actors who have portrayed James Bond
- Uniform code of military justice

First, the data model is created for the basis. Then, external categories of words are created. As an example of the words and phrases that might be created for Sarbanes-Oxley, consider the following:

Sarbanes–Oxley:

- Promise to deliver
- Revenue recognition
- Contingency sale
- Account
- Promise to pay

Each of the external categories has a relationship between the external category and the words that reside within its domain. For example, in the case of Sarbanes-Oxley, there is a "sensitivity" of Sarbanes-Oxley to each of the words. Each of the terms represents a business practice or condition to which Sarbanes-Oxley is sensitive.

Figure 11-3 shows that there is a relationship between the external category and each of the words or phrases that belongs to the category.

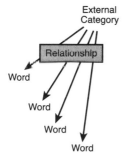

Figure 11-3 Every external category has a relationship to the words that reside in its domain.

Interestingly, there may be a different relationship between a word and the external category and another word and the external category in the same external category. There is no rule that all words in an external category must have the same relationship between the external category and the words that reside in the domain.

External metadata is one of the important factors in the handling and management of metadata and unstructured data; however, there is also internal metadata. Figure 11-4 shows some of the internal metadata that you can find in the unstructured data environment.

Not surprisingly, the internal metadata of a corporation relates mostly to text and different forms of literary constructs.

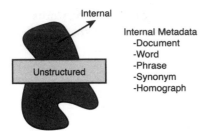

Figure 11-4   Some typical forms of internal metadata.

The Levels of the Data Model

Central to metadata and the unstructured data environment is the data model. There are two types of data models: an external data model and an internal data model. Figure 11-5 shows a data model along with some of its components.

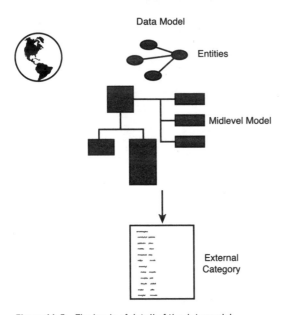

Figure 11-5   The levels of detail of the data model

There are basically three levels to a data model:

1. **Entities**—At the highest level of the data model exists the entity where the major subject areas of the corporation reside alongside the different relationships between the entities. Typical entities include customer, account, product, transaction, and shipment.

2. **Midlevel model**—Each entity is then "exploded" into its own midlevel data model (sometimes called the data item set [DIS]), where the major subject areas of the corporation reside along with the different relationships between the entities. The midlevel data model identifies specifics such as keys, attributes, multiply-occurring set of data, type of data, and relationship data.

3. **External categories**—The external categories are where the detailed text is found. The detailed text is based on the descriptions and associated words in the midlevel data model. The external categories can relate to either information in the data analyzed hand or from external sources of data.

These three levels of the data model work together to create a complete picture of the data that is considered. Figure 11.8 shows the symbiotic relationship of the parts of the data model.

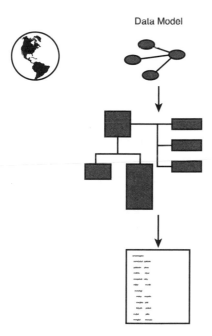

Data Model

Figure 11-6 How the levels of detail of the data model relate to each other

How the Components Relate—The Larger Perspective

There is another way to look at the data model. This perspective shows how the different components relate and the relative size of each part of the data model. In addition, the perspective shows the contrast in scope and levels of completeness. Figure 11-7 shows this perspective.

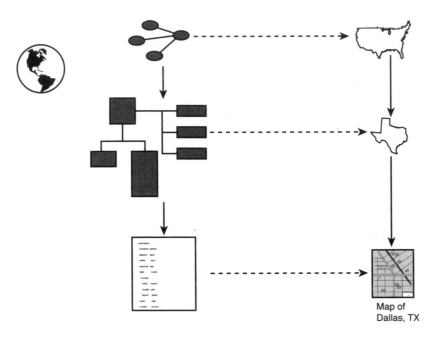

Figure 11-7   Analogically, the data model relates to a geographical map.

Figure 11-7 shows a map of the United States, a map of Texas, and a street map of Dallas, Texas. The U.S. map is large and comprehensive but with little detail. The Texas map is found in the U.S., but is only a part of the U.S.; however, the Texas map has much more detail than the U.S. map. For example, the Texas map shows how to get from Sanderson, Texas, to San Angelo, Texas. On the large U.S. map, it is doubtful that Sanderson is even on the map, much less the road used to get from Sanderson to San Angelo.

The map of Dallas, Texas, has a fine level of detail. Certainly, Dallas is found on a map of the state of Texas, but there is little if any detail about how to navigate through Dallas. However, the Dallas map has ample information to indicate how to get from Texas Stadium to Addison.

The perspective of Figure 11-7 shows how the different levels of the data model relate to each other. Also shown is that the broader the map, the less detail there is, and the more focused the map, the greater the level of detail.

Two Types of Data Model—External and Internal

In unstructured data, to organize text, you need to have two types of a data model. The internal data model is the one that looks inwardly—at the data that exists in and is described in the text. If the text is about combat, the internal model will contain information about weapons, deployment of weapons, training, and soldiers. If the text is about Wall Street, the internal model will contain information about stocks, bonds, traders, and exchanges.

The external data model can be about anything: birdwatching, Sarbanes-Oxley, bullfighting, cigars, and poker tournaments. In many cases, the text will have nothing to do with an external category that has been modeled. In other cases, the text analyzed will have a lot to say about a particular external subject. Stated differently, when an external category is measured against a body of text, there might be a large intersection, small intersection, or no intersection at all.

How Is the Internal Data Model Created?

So exactly how is the internal data model created? The basic steps to create internal data model are the collection of the topics found in the text, an analysis of their relevancy, and a grouping of their occurrences. In addition, word proximity might be used as a criterion for determining what a body of text is about. Figure 11-8 shows the basic steps.

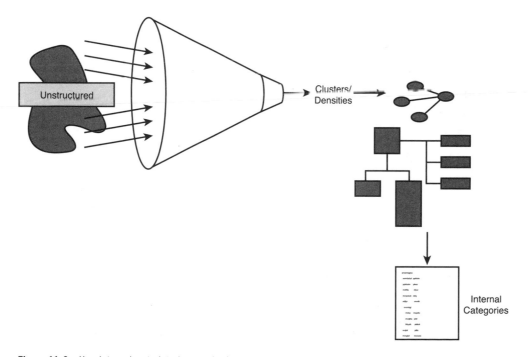

Figure 11-8 How internal metadata is organized

Figure 11-8 shows that unstructured text is collected and integrated. The effect of the integration is to create clusters or densities of text. Certain text clusters around other text. These clusters then become the basis for selecting the entities of the internal data model.

As in the case of external categories, internal categories also follow the pattern of having a relationship between the internal category and the words that exist within the domain of the internal category.

When the entities are selected, the lower level detail is added to the entities, creating the internal data model from the actual text that has been entered.

Creating the External Data Model

The external data model (or models) is created by selecting the major subjects that are to be examined. After the major subjects are chosen, the external data model is created. The sources for external data models come from a wide variety of sources. Each industry has its own methods for gathering and assimilating the sources for the external models.

Using Generic Data Models

In today's world, there are plenty of *generic* data models. Experienced consultants notice that when a data model has been created for one organization in an industry, the same companies in the industry will have similar (if not almost identical) data models. Therefore, when a data model has been generated for one company, it is only a little more work to create the data model for other companies in the same industry.

To this end, there are generic data models. (Visit the Web site www.inmoncif.com for a selection of generic data models or see Len Silverston's generic data models.) Only as a last resort should a company create its own data model because it is a good bet that there has already been a data model created for another company in the same industry that is readily available.

Figure 11-9 shows that there are two distinct types of data models: external and internal. The data models appear to be similar in construct. However, the content of the data models is different. Figure 11-10 shows that there are major differences between the different types of data models.

As an example of the difference between the two data models, suppose the unstructured text were for medicine and healthcare. The internal data models might include information about such things as cancer, pharmaceuticals, treatments, and patient outcomes. The external data models could be anything, such as a model for Sarbanes-Oxley, accounting practices, English grammar, or cultural practices relating to marriage.

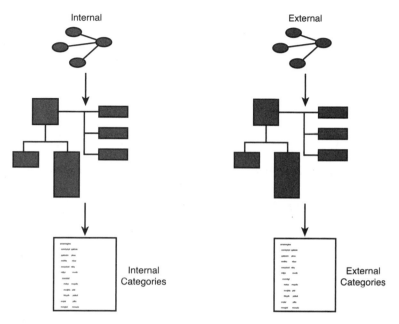

Figure 11-9 Two distinct data models

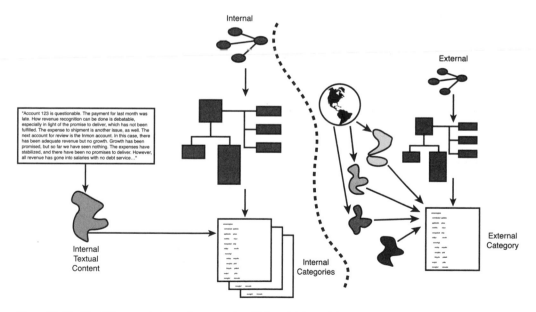

Figure 11-10 The differences between the external and internal data models

It is a mistake to think that these different data models need to be resolved; there is no resolution that is required. Instead, these data models become the intellectual foundation for the guidance of the different activities that surround the building and management of the unstructured data environment.

The Corporate Glossary

The internal categories that result from building the internal data model can be arranged in one of several ways. One way to arrange the output from the internal data modeling exercise is to create a corporate glossary. A *corporate glossary* is merely a list of words and definitions that are used in everyday language in the corporation.

Glossaries are simple in concept. There is only the need to collect and define the terms. No other data relationships are found in the glossary.

Figure 11-11 shows that a glossary can be created from the internal categories that are found in the internal data model.

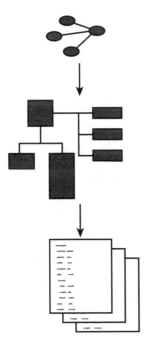

Figure 11-11   A glossary is one way to arrange the detailed data that comes from the model.

Corporate Taxonomy

Glossaries are not the only thing that can be built. Another structure that can be built from the output of the internal data model is a *taxonomy*, which is a classification of the components of the data model. Like the glossary, the taxonomy comes from the data model. However, building the taxonomy is a classification process, whereas the building of the glossary is a listing and compilation process. Figure 11.12 shows that a taxonomy can be used as input into the lower level of modeling.

A taxonomy is quite useful for understanding the different components of some subject. In many ways, the taxonomy is like an organization chart or a functional decomposition.

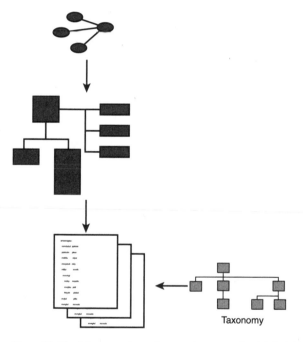

Taxonomy

Figure 11-12 A taxonomy is another way to arrange the detailed data that comes from the model.

Corporate Ontology

Similar to a taxonomy is an *ontology*, which is a classification or breakdown of a subject into its different components, where each component is then broken down into its different components. However, the breakdown of components in an ontology can be by any relationship, whereas the taxonomy usually has the breakdown of a component along the lines of the structuring of all other components.

In truth, there is just a shade of difference between a taxonomy and an ontology.

Figure 11-13 shows the creation of an ontology from the output of the internal data model.

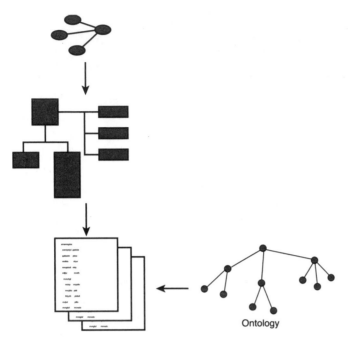

Figure 11-13   An ontology is another way to arrange detailed data.

The Role of the Data Model

A valid question is: What role (or roles) do the data model and metadata have in the building of the infrastructure based on unstructured data? The answer is that there are a lot of roles that the data model and metadata have in building the unstructured data infrastructure, such as:

- **Enabling the end user to see what is going on**—It is often difficult to see the larger picture when dealing with unstructured data. By understanding the data model and the metadata that are found in the unstructured data, the analyst has a chance discerning the larger picture of what transpires.

- **Seeing how things fit together**—Often, there are so many trees in the forest that it is difficult to see the larger patterns of how things fit together. With a data model and metadata, the general flow of events and the different outputs that are created start to form a larger picture.

- **Contracting practices**—Often, it is difficult to articulate what contracting services are to be performed. With a data model and with metadata, the organization stands a much better chance of specifying what activities the contractor is responsible for.

Data Quality in the Unstructured Environment

Data quality has long been one of the critical success factors in the structured environment. If data quality is high, the databases and data warehouses are usable. However, when data quality is low, the usefulness of the databases and data warehouses diminishes.

What is meant by data quality in the structured environment? Data completeness and data correctness are two attributes of data quality in the structured environment. For some examples of the lack of data quality in the structured environment, consider the following:

- An account balance that shows $100 when it should be showing $1,000
- Bill Inmon's name spelled as Bill Inman
- The month February spelled as Febuary

In some cases, these errors are an annoyance. In other cases, there are serious consequences for the lack of data quality in the structured environment. In the unstructured environment, the essence of what is an error is questionable. When people write emails and instant messaging, there is no such thing as a spelling error. People deliberately use acronyms and shorten names. Just because it is not spelled properly (or at least as the dictionary would have us think is proper) does not reflect the actual way the text was used, such as LOL (lots of laughs), thx (thanks), and Pls (please). There are many more language reductions.

The rules as to what is correct and incorrect have changed between the structured and the unstructured environment. In the unstructured environment, just because someone wrote what appears to be a misspelling does not mean that is it incorrect. Stated differently, correcting misspellings in the unstructured environment might be an entirely improper thing to do. In some cases, it can actually be illegal to make corrections. There is a legitimate case to be made for leaving text *exactly* as it is captured, with no corrections whatsoever.

However, leaving text alone might not help the case for analyses. When the analytical concerns are taken into consideration, it might be prudent to make corrections wherever they seem to be appropriate. However, there is a way to have your cake and eat it, too. Techniques of textual concatenation can be used (in much the same way that synonym concatenation is used).

As an example of textual concatenation used for error correction, suppose the name "Bill Inman" is encountered. It is known that the name should be "Bill Inmon." Rather than going back and changing "Inman" to "Inmon," concatenation can be used. Where the name "Inman" is found, the name "Inmon" is inserted. The result looks like "Inman

Inmon." Now when an analytical search is done for "Inmon," the search is satisfied. However, if someone wants to look for the original text, the term "Inman" is also found. In such a manner, data can be corrected without losing the original, literal text.

Summary

Metadata is found throughout the unstructured data environment, especially where the expanded definition of metadata is used. There are two basic kinds of metadata in the unstructured data environment: internal and external metadata. Internal metadata is wholly contained in the unstructured data environment. External metadata is modeled outside of the unstructured data environment and is then mapped on to the unstructured data environment.

Similarly, there are two types of data models that are associated with the unstructured data environment: external and internal. The external data model is created as a result of modeling some environment outside of the unstructured data environment. The internal data model is created as a result of collecting and analyzing the data found in the unstructured data environment. Clusters of text are found and then used as a basis for the major subject areas of the unstructured data environment.

The data models that are produced—external and internal—might or might not have any relationship or relevance to each other.

Other outputs from the data model process are glossaries, taxonomies, and ontologies.

12

A Methodology
for Textual Analytics

The first step in textual analytics is to create the proper integration of data on which to do textual analytic processing. Stated differently, unless the proper integration is built, it is not possible to do a good job of textual analytics. This chapter is a simple methodology that shows how all the different components that have been previously discussed should be blended to create the integration for textual analytics.

The bedrock of unstructured data is text, found in many places—articles, reports, email. The textual data is gathered and integrated and otherwise preconditioned to create the integration of textual analytics.

Preparing the Basic Components

Figure 12-1 shows the basic components needed to integrate and precondition of raw text in preparation for textual analytics.

The input is the unstructured text in an electronic format. The raw text is entered into the integration software where several kinds of editing are done against the data. In one kind of editing, stop-word editing, all stop words are removed from the stream of text. Another kind of editing is synonym editing, where synonyms can be either replaced or concatenated. It is in synonym editing that terminology differences are resolved. In the next type of editing, homographic editing, a word that has multiple meanings is broken into the different possibilities. The external categories are defined so that words can be grouped according to the categories.

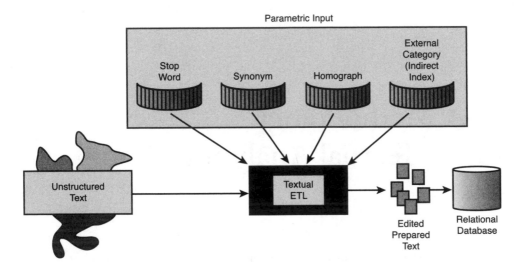

Figure 12-1 Basic processing of unstructured data for integration and preconditioning

Word stemming is also done. In word stemming, words are reduced to their Latin or Greek stems so that commonality of words can be recognized. Word stemming can be done parametrically or by means of a stemming algorithm.

The integration software is run and results are obtained. When the results are satisfactory, either the visualization is run or the unstructured database is created or both.

The different activities of creating the integration for textual analytics start with the definition of the stop words. Usually there is a starting list of words such as "a," "an," "the," and "to." But new words can be added or existing words can be deleted. For example, there might actually be a reason why an organization wants to see the word "the."

In any case, stop words need to be defined and refined before the base for textual analytics can be performed. Figure 12-2 shows how stop words are processed against raw text.

After stop words are in place, the next step is to define synonyms. The definition of synonyms can be as simple as defining a few popular words or can be as elaborate as accessing a glossary or ontology and pulling the entire (or even multiple!) set of words into the synonym list.

The synonym list consists of two components: the specific word and synonym. For example, there might be the word "rock." A synonym for rock might be "granite" or "limestone."

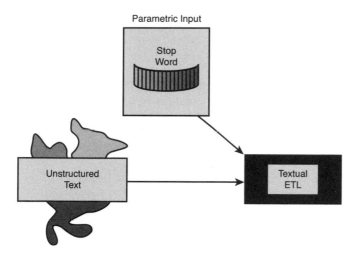

Figure 12-2 Make sure the stop words are ready and in place.

If multiple glossaries are used, it is usually not a good idea to mix the glossaries until they are placed in the synonym list. Also, if multiple glossaries are used and there is overlap, the analyst must determine which glossary takes precedence.

After the basic synonym list is created, the next step is to edit in (or out) the particular synonyms that might have special interest. Figure 12-3 shows how synonyms are processed against raw text.

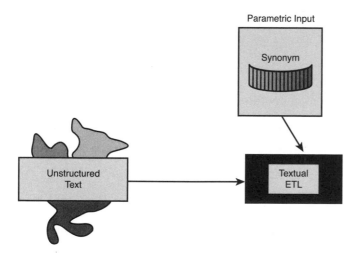

Figure 12-3 Make sure the synonyms are ready and in place.

An important aspect of the synonym list is the specification of whether the synonyms will be replaced or concatenated. In almost all cases, the synonym will be concatenated, but there are a few isolated cases where the synonyms will be replaced. The analyst needs to make this determination.

The homograph list is the next to be prepared, consisting of three components plus a default. The default is the value that is replaced in light of no other references. The specific word is the homograph that is to be replaced. And the homograph needs to have several words that help identify the context. As an example, the term "ha" might be a homograph. The term "heart attack" might be the replacement. And the context words might include "cardiologist," "blood pressure," "aorta," "valve," and "nitroglycerin."

As a rule, there are far fewer homographs than there are synonyms. Like synonyms and stop words, homographs are processed against raw text, as shown in Figure 12-4.

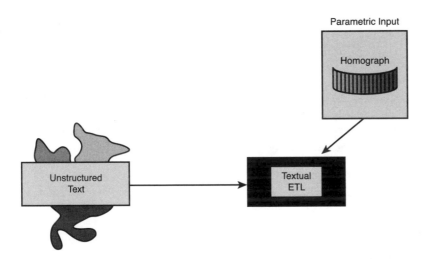

Figure 12-4 Make sure the homographs are ready and in place.

After the homographs are in place, the next step is to create the external categories that enable the textual analyst to do indirect searches. The external category can be based on any relationship between the operative word and the indirect word. For example, suppose that the operative word is "Sarbanes–Oxley." The indirect words might be "contingency sale," "promise to deliver," "revenue recognition," and "alternate contract."

As a rule, the software comes with a set of predetermined external categories. These categories can be used as is or can be modified—adding or deleting words from the category.

If business relevancy screening is to be done (as is typical on email), as many external categories should be entered as are useful. The screening process uses the external categories to determine if the email (or other text) is relevant to the business of the corporation. External categories are processed against raw text, as shown in Figure 12-5.

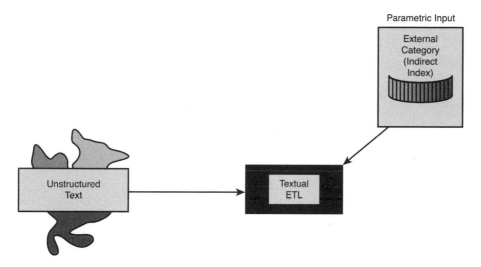

Figure 12-5   Make sure the external categories are ready and in place.

Stemming is done on an algorithmic basis. The raw text is read and determined if there is a Latin or Greek integration for the word. If there is, the word is reduced to its Latin or Greek integration so that all other forms of the word can be associated with it.

Specifying the Processing

After the stop words, synonyms, homographs, stems, and external categories have been defined, the next step is to tell the system what kind of processing needs to be done. Some of the parameters that the system needs to know about include the following:

- Whether visualizations will be produced
- Whether a database will be produced
- Whether a database will be produced; what DBMS the output is created in
- Whether relevancy screening will be done

Figure 12-6 shows many of the different kinds of processing that go against the raw text to integrate that text.

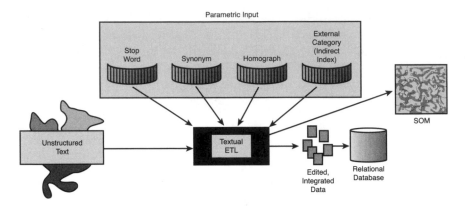

Figure 12-6 Determine what kind of output to generate.

Organizing the Source Data

The next major step is to make sure the source data is in order. If visualization is to be done, it usually is wise to limit the domain of the input to whatever topic will be addressed.

The first step in ensuring that the source data is in order is to select what kinds of data and which particular files of data will be used as input. If the source data has already been created in an electronic format, there is not much to do. However, if not, it needs to be converted into that format.

Figure 12-7 shows the considerations of the source of data that will be fed into the integration machine.

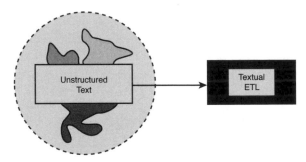

Figure 12-7 Determine what kind of source to input.

Figure 12-8 shows that there might be all sorts of input types (telephone, paper-based, HTML-based). Depending on the source input, these different types of input must be converted into an electronically readable format. Then, the system is ready to continue.

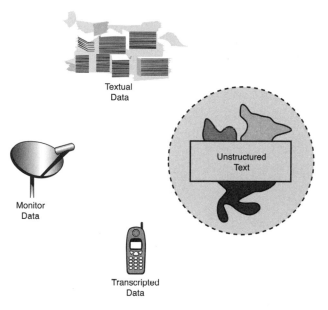

Figure 12-8 Make sure sources are available electronically.

Then the electronically readable text is teed up as input. Figure 12-9 shows this preparation.

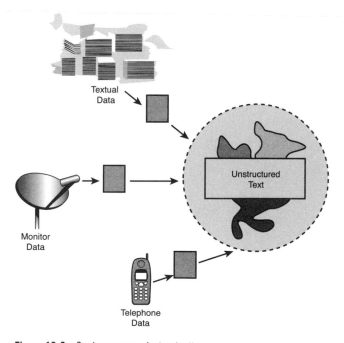

Figure 12-9 Capture source electronically.

Now the system is ready to operate. The next step is one last glance to make sure the system parameters are set properly and the textual analyst knows what kind of processing is to occur, as shown in Figure 12-10.

Figure 12-10 Make sure parameters are set properly.

After the last minute checks are in order, the system is ready to run. Figure 12-11 shows that raw text is ready to be processed.

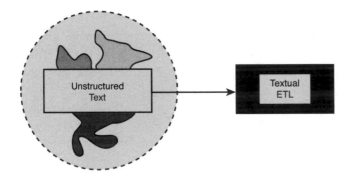

Figure 12-11 Read in source data and start to process.

Analyzing the Results

After the system has processed the input, the next step is to look at the results. The first time the system runs, it is almost guaranteed that there will be surprising results. Some results will please the analyst, and others will not. For example, when examining emails, the word "http" often appears. In fact, "http" is extraneous.

Figure 12-12 shows that results are analyzed as soon as they are available.

Based on the results, the analyst now goes back and "tweaks" the system: adding words to the stop word list, changing words on the synonym list, changing words on the homograph list, and adding external categories or adding or changing words already in the external category list.

The complete set of integration possibilities are shown in Figure 12-13.

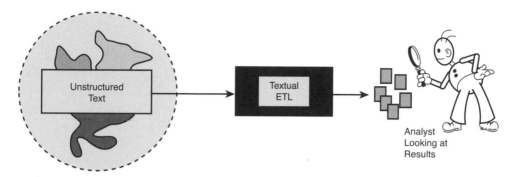

Figure 12-12 Take a look at results.

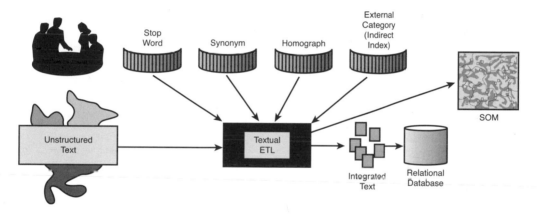

Figure 12-13 Go back and examine results and reset parameters.

After the tweaks are done, the analyst goes back and reruns the process. The rerun process continues in an iterative manner until the analyst is satisfied with the results.

These activities can be classified into several general groups. The first general group of activities is the setting of the word parameters, as shown in Figure 12-14.

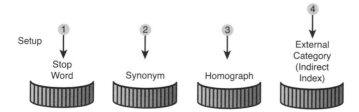

Figure 12-14 The steps of initial setup

The second general group of activities is the preparation of the input, as shown in Figure 12-15.

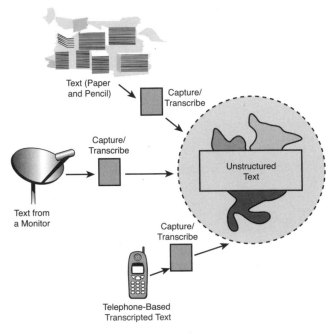

Figure 12-15   Electronically capture data.

The third general group is running the integration program. Figure 12-16 shows the execution of the integration program.

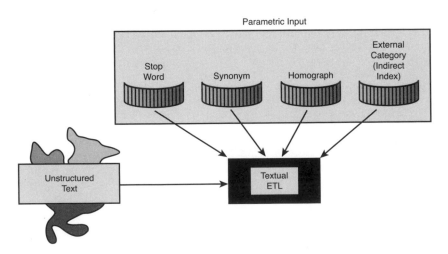

Figure 12-16   Run the integration program.

These activities can be shown as to how they interact as a methodology. Figure 12-17 illustrates these interactions.

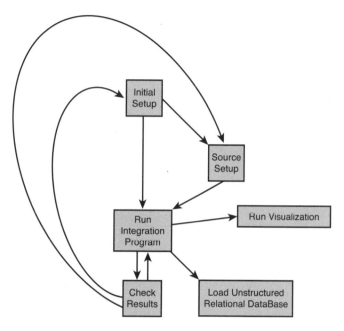

Figure 12-17   The basic steps in setting up and running an iteration of visualization or in the creation of a relational database full of unstructured data

The process seen in Figure 12-17 is essentially an iterative process used to create the integration of data needed to do textual analytics.

Summary

Textual analytics is created by editing and manipulating an integration of textual data. The raw textual data goes through a process of the following:

- Creating and modifying a list of stop words
- Creating a list of synonyms and determining whether synonym concatenation or replacement will be done
- Creating a list of homographs for homographic resolution
- Creating a list of external categories and their contents
- Stemming
- Selecting and filtering source data

After the data is prepared, an iterative process of development is followed. One primary output is the production of a visualization—a SOM (self-organizing map).

After processing and integrating has been done, the next step is to place the text in a database. An even more powerful possibility is the placement of the integrated text into a database which is part of a data warehouse. Chapter 13, "Merging Unstructured Databases into the Data Warehouse," addresses the implications of unstructured data and a data warehouse.

13

Merging Unstructured Databases into the Data Warehouse

The output of unstructured data integration is a database. The database can be either a database keyed on document/word or a database keyed on one or more identifiers. Figure 13-1 shows the output of unstructured data processing and the resulting databases.

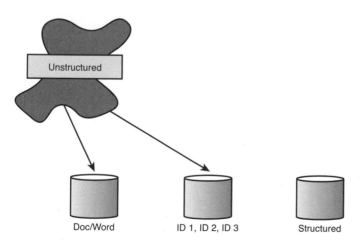

Figure 13-1 The two types of databases that can be created from structured and semistructured data

Of course, if the source is unstructured data, the database is likely to be a document/word database, and if the source is semistructured data, the database is likely to be an ID 1, ID 2, ID 3... database.

The question then becomes: Do the databases sit apart from other databases, and if the different types of databases can be integrated with structured data, do they form a data warehouse?

The Data Warehouse

In many ways, the unstructured databases have characteristics of a data warehouse. They contain detailed and integrated data that has date and time stamping as an integral part of the database. For these reasons, the unstructured databases are compatible with the structured data found in a data warehouse. The question then becomes: How can the unstructured databases be integrated with the structured databases? And more importantly, is there a business justification for merging or interfacing the two kinds of data?

The answers to those questions are determined on a case-by-case basis.

Linking Databases

Document/word databases can be linked with structured databases by means of a common word link, as shown in Figure 13-2.

Doc/Word   Structured

Figure 13-2   Linking the doc/word unstructured database to the structured database by means of a common value

In Figure 13-2, you can see that the linkage between the two types of databases is based on a common textual value. As a simple example, suppose there were an ÀJ 775-PT part. That part is referenced in several reports in the unstructured side of the equation. And that part is also found in the structured bill of materials and in the inventory catalog. A query can be made that uses the part number as a common reference to access data from both environments.

There is a problem with word linkages: The linkage might or might not reflect reality. In many cases, there will be a real-world connection between the structured and the unstructured data, but in other cases, there might be no real linkage at all.

As a case in point, suppose the term "GM" is found in the two types of databases. In the unstructured database, "GM" refers to General Mills. In the structured database,

"GM" refers to General Motors. Making a connection based on the mere coincidence of values might be a mistake. Because of this negative aspect of a word link, this is referred to as a *weak link*.

It is noteworthy that while linkages can be made from these two types of databases as depicted, that linkage is nonrepetitive. That is, the linkage does not happen with a great deal of frequency. When the linkage occurs, it can be quite useful. But there is nothing to say that the linkage can be made for many parts or made at all.

In such a manner, the linkage between the document/word database and the structured database can be made.

Communications-Based Linkage Between Unstructured and Structured Data

Another type of linkage that can be made from the structured to the unstructured environment is that of linkage-based communication. The most common forms of communication are email and the telephone. In the case of the telephone, the linkage is derived from transcripted conversations. When communications are made and captured electronically, they often can be linked to a structured database using the email address or the telephone number as a basis for linkage.

For example, suppose there is a customer in the structured environment with an email address of johnsmith@aol.com. The emails that use this email address—either sending emails to or receiving emails from this address—can be linked to the structured customer data. In doing so, the communications made by the customer can be linked to the customer.

Unlike the previous example where linkage was made on a random basis, the linkage of communications based on an email address or a telephone number is a frequently occurring, repeating type of linkage.

Furthermore, because the chance of a random email address just popping up out of nowhere is small, there usually is a basis for the existence of the data. For this reason, this form of linkage is strong (as opposed to the weak linkage made on words).

Figure 13-3 shows the regular and repeated linkage of communications to the structured world.

There is then the possibility of linkage of communications to the structured environment.

Figure 13-3 Linking the doc/word unstructured database to the structured database by means of an email address or a telephone number

Identifier-Based Linkage Between Unstructured and Structured Data

The third type of linkage that can be made from the structured environment to the unstructured environment is the case where there are frequently occurring common identifiers. In this case, semistructured data has been used as a source. The semistructured data is examined, and repeating identifiers are identified. A record is created for each document of the semistructured data that has been examined. An ID 1, ID 2, ID 3... database is created.

As an example, suppose there are 100 human resource resumes that are created. The system reads each resume and picks off commonly identified data elements from the resume. Typical resume data elements include the following:

- Name
- Address
- Telephone number
- Social security number
- College attended

When the record is created for each resume, the unstructured database is created. Then the unstructured record can be joined with the structured record based on one or more data elements. For example, a join can be made on "college." All people who attended Duke University can be joined with a description of the costs of tuition for attending Duke or the curriculum offered by Duke.

In this case, there are many repeating joins that can be made. Unlike the document/word case, in this case—the ID 1, ID 2, ID 3... to structured data case—it is common to have many matches between the data found in the unstructured and structured environments.

Figure 13-4 shows a linkage between ID 1, ID 2, ID 3... data and structured data.

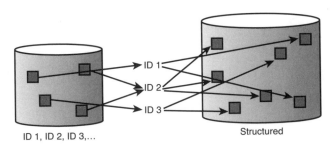

Figure 13-4   Linking the ID1, ID2, ID3... semistructured database to the structured database by means of common multiple identifiable data elements

An Integrated Data Warehouse

Because of the possibility of linkage and because of the basic nature of unstructured data as it resides in the databases, the unstructured and structured data can be considered together to form an integrated data warehouse, as shown in Figure 13-5.

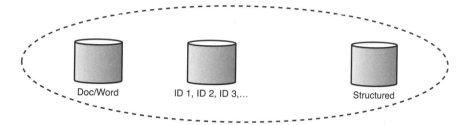

Figure 13-5 The integrated database containing both structured and unstructured data

The term *integrated data warehouse* is used because the warehouse contains both structured and unstructured data, and because the two types of data are linked.

Multi-Database Linkage

Although linking one unstructured database to the structured environment is a powerful thing to do, there is another even more powerful configuration, the multi-database link, as shown in Figure 13-6.

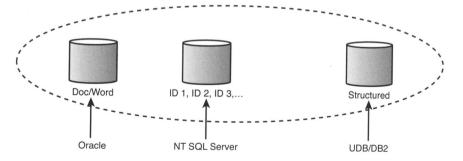

Figure 13-6 There is nothing to mandate that the different databases in the integrated database have to be managed under the same DBMS.

In Figure 13-6, a document/word database is linked with an ID 1, ID 2, ID 3… database. In turn, the ID 1, ID 2, ID 3… database is linked to the structured environment.

For example, suppose the document/word database is a human resource database having resume information residing on an Oracle foundation; the ID 1, ID 2, ID 3... database is one that has been extracted from the human resource database with common identifiers for the person residing in an NT SQL Server foundation; and a structured database for customers and employees residing in a DB2 foundation. Linkage to all three databases can be done by means of an identifier. It is noteworthy that the linkage does not depend on any given technology. The identifier can easily cross technologies, as shown in Figure 13-6. The record for Judy Jones is in the structured database.. The structured record for Judy Jones is matched to the ID 1, ID 2, ID 3... database and Judy is found there. Then the record for Judy Jones is found in the document/word database, too.

In such a manner, the linkage can be made through all the databases found in the unstructured data warehouse, and in doing so, massive amounts of new information are unlocked.

ETL for Unstructured Data

A standard part of the data warehouse environment—integrated or nonintegrated—is ETL (extract/transform/load). ETL allows for easy passageway into the data warehouse.

In the diagram shown in Figure 13-5, the data warehouse is integrated. The only difference between any other data warehouse and the one shown in the figure is that in the data warehouse there are some nontraditional sources of data. In a traditional data warehouse, the sources are legacy systems, which are structured. The legacy systems have their data pass through standard ETL processing.

In the data warehouse shown in the figure, the structured portion of the data warehouse has its data pass through ETL while the unstructured portion has its data pass through foundation software.

Other than that, the data warehouse shown in the figure is just like any other data warehouse.

Housing Databases in DBMS Technology

One of the issues of the integrated data warehouse is whether the different databases have to be housed in the same database management system (DBMS) technology. In Figure 13-7, you can see that three different technologies house the databases—DB2, Oracle, and NT SQL Server. There is absolutely nothing wrong with this scenario. There are some considerations to having a single technology house the databases versus having different DBMSs house the different databases. Some of the considerations follow:

- **Training**—Having multiple DBMSs means that there is multiple training needed for end users.

- **Software support**—With the different technologies, different types of support are required.

- **License costs**—Often the vendor makes the first license of the software the most expensive. With multiple software vendors, there are different, expensive, first-time licenses.

- **Analytical packages**—Most analytical packages access different kinds of software, but occasionally one analytical package works better with one DBMS than another analytical package.

Other reasons for having multiple DBMS technologies exist. From a technology standpoint, there is no reason why there cannot be different DBMSs housing the different types of databases within a data warehouse.

Figure 13-7 shows that different DBMSs can be used throughout the integrated data warehouse. As a rule, when different DBMS technology is used in the data warehouse, there is a need for a *federated query*. A federated query is one that can simultaneously access data from different DBMS technologies.

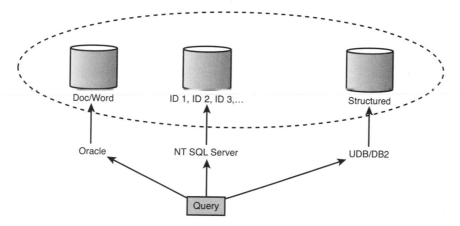

Figure 13-7   A federated query can access the different technologies at the same time.

Binding the Databases Together

The glue that binds the different databases together is not a particular brand of technology. Instead, it is the fact that the basic form of the packages is relational and that the data contained in the databases is integrated textual data. Other than that, there is no need for having a single technology house the different databases in the integrated data warehouse.

Figure 13-8 shows the unifying factors that bind the different databases inside the integrated data warehouse.

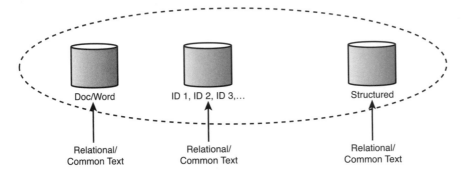

Relational/
Common Text
            Relational/
Common Text
            Relational/
Common Text

Figure 13-8   The unifying factors include having a relational foundation and having common text.

Federated Analytical Technology

Having different DBMSs that participate in the integrated data warehouse is mitigated by the usage of analytical technology that can federate data, in which data is looked at in one source and collected and then collected from another source that is housed in different technology.

Federated analytical technology works well with an integrated data warehouse because the data—the text—is integrated throughout the data warehouse. If the basic data—the text—were not uniform and integrated throughout the data warehouse, a federated analytical approach would not work.

Simple Queries

There are many different approaches to accessing and analyzing unstructured data in the integrated data warehouse. The simplest type of query is one that merely goes after data in the document/word database, as shown in Figure 13-9.

Doc/Word

Query

Figure 13-9   Queries can be written that access only the doc/word database.

In the query shown in Figure 13-9, the analysis is done strictly against data found in the document/word database. There is no reference to or join with any other data outside of the document/word database.

A simple example of this kind of query is the lookup of a word or phrase. For example, the analyst might look at the database and ask if there is any reference to "Bill Inmon." Or the query might look for "reindeer in Norway." The result of the query would be the locations where such data exists.

But the queries going against other databases can be much more sophisticated. For example, a join might be used to facilitate a query that goes against multiple types of databases. Figure 13-10 shows a query that spans more than one type of data.

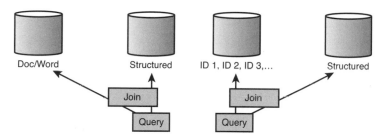

Figure 13-10   Queries can be written that access the ID1, ID2, ID3... database and the structured database by means of a join.

As an example of a query that spans document/word data (that is, communications related) and structured data, the query might ask what queries Judy Nesavich has written and is Judy a frequent customer, as shown in Figure 13-11. Or a query can be written using ID 1, ID 2, ID 3... data that is joined against structured data. Such a query might look like this: Show me the current engineering status of a product with the specifications for the change of the products.

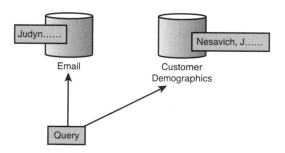

Figure 13-11   A query that spans multiple kinds of key structures across multiple kinds of databases

Summary

As the unstructured and semistructured databases are created, they can be combined with structured data to form an integrated data warehouse.

The data in the integrated data warehouse is joined in one of several ways:

- By random occurrences
- By communications reference
- By repeating identifiers

When the integrated data warehouse is produced, it can be accessed in several ways. One mode of access is by looking at data from only a single database. Another mode is to look at data from two or more databases by means of a join and technology that supports federated queries.

As important as database and data warehouse structures are, they are unimportant unless the data in them can be accessed in a common structure with a common language. SQL is the standard for query access in the industry. Chapter 14, "Using SQL to Analyze Text," shows that common SQL can be used to access and analyze unstructured data.

14

Using SQL to Analyze Text

For many people, the real payoff of textual analytics comes at the point of being able to formulate and execute queries. It is in writing queries that end users have full control of the ability to do textual analysis. In this way, they have full flexibility when writing the queries. Of course, the end users can execute prepackaged queries or generate reports. In addition, they can use technology that generates queries if that is what the end user wants to do.

In today's world, most analytical queries boil down to text in SQL. In some cases, the SQL is written by the programmer. In other cases, the SQL is written automatically by a front-end technology such as Business Objects or Cognos. However it is accomplished, SQL is the lingua franca of analytical technology. This chapter shows that SQL can be used as the basis for the query of textual data, after the textual data has been properly processed and integrated. It is noteworthy that if textual data has not been preprocessed and integrated, SQL is not useful. It is the preprocessing and integrating of text that sets the stage for effective use of SQL.

The ability to query data—textual data—is the ultimate objective of textual analytics. The queries that can be written can take many forms and do many things. The query can be as simple as looking for the occurrence of a word in one or more documents. Or the query can be sophisticated.

The following examples of queries are just a few of the possibilities. In truth, the possibilities are limited only by the imagination of the analyst. In the examples that follow, a query will be constructed that analyzes text. The text—for the purpose of this chapter—is an article I wrote titled "Honor Thy Father." The beginning and end of this article are shown here:

Honor Thy Father

By W. H. Inmon

In recent vintage there have been two curious vestiges of the same phenomenon. There has been the tendency for new technologies to have that attitude that previous technologies and business practices should be obliterated from the earth.

The first of these abasements of the "father" comes from the world of database design. For whatever reason, whenever a new style of database design becomes in vogue, the advocates declare that all previous forms of database design are invalid and incorrect and must be purged from the earth. This was true of the relational technologists who told database designers of a previous era that the relational database designers were right and that all database design that preceded relational design was incorrect. Then, a few years later the multidimensional star join advocates came along and said the same thing.

So trying to kill the father didn't work. There was a reason why technology and business practices of an earlier age were successful. And all the zealotry and all the venom in the world only made people mad and wasted a lot of people's retirement money.

Although this selection of text is useful, it is noteworthy that it could have been any text. The only thing outstanding about this text is that it was handy to access for the author.

The text has been put through the integration engine (textual ETL), and an unstructured database has been created. The database that has been created is typified by the partial database table shown in Figure 14-1.

In addition to the table that has been created to hold the text, other tables have been created. These tables hold information such as glossaries, synonyms, external categories, and homographs. Using this and other tables that are created to hold the text, the analyst is prepared to do textual analytics.

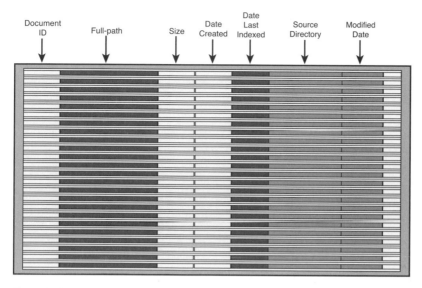

Figure 14-1   Some of the data elements in the table created to hold unstructured data

A Simple Query

As an example of a simple query against some of these tables, consider the example of specific word queries that list documents containing a specific word for a specific directory and the frequency with which that word appears.

This query functions as a query that

- Shows the document that a word is in
- Enables a search on a single word
- Shows the number of times a word appears in a document

NOTE

The code in this chapter uses a code-continuation arrow to indicate when a line has been manually broken to fit the printed page. When this arrow appears, the code should be entered on-screen as one line. For example, the broken lines

```
SELECT DISTINCT dbo.Themes.Word, COUNT(dbo.Themes.Word)
➥ AS Occurrences, dbo.Documents.Fullpath
```

should be entered as one line when actually programming.

```
SELECT DISTINCT dbo.Themes.Word, COUNT(dbo.Themes.Word)
➥ AS Occurrences, dbo.Documents.Fullpath
FROM           dbo.Themes INNER JOIN
                       dbo.Documents ON dbo.Themes.DocumentID =
➥ dbo.Documents.DocumentID INNER JOIN
                       dbo.MonitoredDirectories ON
➥dbo.Documents.SourceDirectoryID =
➥dbo.MonitoredDirectories.DirectoryID
WHERE      (dbo.Themes.Word = 'Term') AND
➥(dbo.MonitoredDirectories.DirectoryID =
                       (SELECT      DirectoryID
                        FROM            dbo.MonitoredDirectories AS
➥ MonitoredDirectories_1
                        WHERE       (Name = 'DirectoryName')))
GROUP BY dbo.Documents.Fullpath, dbo.Themes.Word
ORDER BY Occurrences DESC
```

The report results might look like Figure 14-2.

Word	Occurrences	Fullpath
term	320	\\IDSPOC02\DirectoryName\I.pdf
term	8	\\IDSPOC02\DirectoryName\j.pdf
term	8	\\IDSPOC02\DirectoryName\n.pdf
term	6	\\IDSPOC02\DirectoryName\b.pdf
term	3	\\IDSPOC02\DirectoryName\e.pdf
term	3	\\IDSPOC02\DirectoryName\f.pdf
term	2	\\IDSPOC02\DirectoryName\d.pdf
term	2	\\IDSPOC02\DirectoryName\m.pdf
term	1	\\IDSPOC02\DirectoryName\o.pdf
term	1	\\IDSPOC02\DirectoryName\t.pdf
term	1	\\IDSPOC02\DirectoryName\u.pdf
term	1	\\IDSPOC02\DirectoryName\w.pdf
term	1	\\IDSPOC02\DirectoryName\x.pdf
term	1	\\IDSPOC02\DirectoryName\y.pdf

Figure 14-2 Possible report results from a simple query

In this simple query, a search has been done against the text looking for the word "term" and is much like a simple query that could be created by Yahoo or Google, where the existence of a term is sought.

However, much more sophisticated queries are possible. What if the analyst wants to find not just the existence of a word or term? What if the analyst wants to find the text before and after a given term? In doing so, the analyst could determine the context of the word as it exists in the document.

The following query creates *snippets* of text. A snippet of text shows the text before and after the word that is sought. The snippet might or might not be for data that is edited by stop word removal.

```
CREATE VIEW dbo._DASD
AS
```

```
SELECT    TOP (100) PERCENT dbo.Themes.Word,
➥ dbo.Themes.WordLocation, dbo.Documents.Fullpath
FROM         dbo.Themes INNER JOIN
                     dbo.Documents ON dbo.Themes.DocumentID =
➥ dbo.Documents.DocumentID
WHERE      (dbo.Documents.Fullpath LIKE '\\IDSPOC02\NAME%')
➥AND (dbo.Themes.Word LIKE 'DASD') OR
                     (dbo.Themes.Word LIKE 'Disk storage')
ORDER BY dbo.Documents.Fullpath, dbo.Themes.WordLocation


SELECT DISTINCT TOP 100 PERCENT dbo.Themes.WordLocation,
➥ dbo.Themes.Word, dbo.Documents.Fullpath
FROM         dbo._DASD INNER JOIN
                     dbo.Documents ON dbo._DASD.Fullpath =
➥ dbo.Documents.Fullpath FULL OUTER JOIN
                     dbo.Themes ON dbo.Documents.DocumentID =
➥ dbo.Themes.DocumentID
WHERE      (dbo.Themes.WordLocation BETWEEN dbo._DASD.WordLocation
➥ - 140 AND dbo._DASD.WordLocation + 140)
ORDER BY dbo.Documents.Fullpath, dbo.Themes.WordLocation
```

The query produces a snippet of text 140 characters before and the 140 characters after the word in question. In addition, the query identifies the location of the snippet in the document.

Indirect Query

Perhaps the most sophisticated usage of the query facility is through the usage of external categories. It is with external categories that indirect queries can be done. An *indirect query* is one where you give the system a word or term and the system finds all occurrences of text that are related to the term. This is an extremely sophisticated and powerful capability.

As an example of the differences between a simple query and an indirect query, suppose that in a simple query the term "Sarbanes Oxley" is supplied to the query. In a simple query, the system looks for any reference to "Sarbanes Oxley." But in an indirect query, when the term "Sarbanes Oxley" is supplied to the system, the system finds all text related to "Sarbanes Oxley." The system would find references to "contingency sale," "promise to deliver," and "revenue recognition."

The way that the system links "Sarbanes Oxley" to the different text related to "Sarbanes Oxley" is by means of the creation of an external category.

In this example, suppose there was an entry to the external category table and a term—DASD—that was entered. Now the following terms are also entered into the external category table and are designated as related to DASD:

- Direct access
- Direct access storage
- Disk storage
- Direct access storage device
- Disk
- Fast storage
- Data farms
- Caching
- Cache
- Read/write arm
- Read arm
- Write arm

Now the external category can be used to search the text indirectly. The analyst enters the term DASD, and the query retrieves any place where any of the related terms appear. The following query shows such an analysis.

Query: Find all synonyms to DASD

```
SELECT DocumentCategorization.Term AS term,
   DocumentCategorization.TermLocation AS TermLocation ,
➥ Glossaries.Name AS
              GlossaryName
   Documents.Fullpath AS DocumentPath, Documents.[Size] AS
➥DocumentSize,
       Documents.CreatedDate AS DocumentCreatedDate,
       Documents.ModifiedDate AS DocumentModifiedDate
FROM   DocumentCategorization INNER JOIN
   Glossaries ON DocumentCategorization.GlossaryID =
➥ Glossaries.GlossaryID
INNER JOIN
   Documents ON DocumentCategorization.DocumentID =
➥ Documents.DocumentID
WHERE (DocumentCategorization.GlossaryID =
   (SELECT GlossaryID
    FROM Glossaries
    Where (Name = 'DASD'))
```

There are many other possibilities for the access and analysis of text after it is put in a database. Another such possibility is that of determining what words or phrases are the most popular by count of occurrence. This analysis can be done on a document-by-document basis or by a collection of words or phrases that have been collected from multiple documents.

Note that if the stop words haven't been eliminated by this point, they need to be edited out before the results are shown. Otherwise, the results show that the words "the," "a," "is," "was," and so forth are the most popular words. But stop words don't actually say anything about the content or meaning of the article "Honor Thy Father." One way or the other, they need to be eliminated: as the database is built or at the moment of query.

As an example of such a query, consider the next query that excludes these stop words by utilizing the NOT IN keyword.

Query: Find top occurring 50 words

```
SELECT TOP 100 PERCENT COUNT (dbo.themes.word) AS Occurrences,
    Dbo.Themes.Word
FROM  dbo.Themes INNER JOIN
    dbo.Documents ON dbo.Themes.DocumentID =
    dbo.Documents.DocumentID INNER JOIN
        dbo.MonitoredDirectories ON dbo.Documents.
➡SourceDirectoryID =
        dbo.monitoredDirectories.DirectoryID
WHERE (dbo.DocumentsSourceDirectoryID =
    (SELECT    dbo.MonitoredDirectories.DirectoryID
     FROM      dbo.MonitoredDirectories
     WHERE  dbo.MonitoredDirectories.Name - 'BLDGDW4TH')) AND
      (dbo.Themes.Word NOT IN
        (SELECT dbo.stopwords.word
         FROM dbo.stopwords))
GROUP BY dbo.Themes.Word
HAVING (Count(*)>=50)
ORDER BY Occurrences DESC
```

Proximity Search

Another useful type of query is a proximity search, which is done on the basis of whether two words are within n characters of each other in text. Of course, analysts can set n to be any value that makes sense. If analysts want only a close proximity, they can set n to 10 or 20. If they want to have only a general proximity analysis, they set n to be 200 or 250. The larger the value of n, the more general the search.

A proximity search can be conducted in many ways. One type of search is a word-to-word search. In this case, the query looks for a specific word occurring within n characters of another word. Another type of proximity search is a $1{:}n$ search. In this case, one word is compared for proximity to a list of words. And another type of proximity search is an $m{:}n$ search. In this case, two lists of words are compared to each other for proximity. In an $m{:}n$ search, any word in the first list is compared for proximity to any word in a second list.

The following query is one in which one word is compared to the proximity to another word (a 1:1 search) and utilizes a view that searches for both words at the beginning.

Query: Proximity searches—words

```
CREATE VIEW dbo_DSS.Loc
AS
SELECT   TOP 100 PERCENT dbo.Themes.Word,
    dbo.Themes.WordLocation, dbo.Documents.Fullpath
FROM    dbo.Themes.INNER JOIN
      dbo.Documents ON dbo.Themes.DocumentID =
    dbo.Documents.DocumentID
WHERE   (dbo.Themes.Word = 'DSS') AND
➡ (dbo.Documents.Fullpath LIKE
    '\\IDSPOC02\DiabTest$%')
ORDER BY dbo.Documents.Fullpath, dbo.Themes.WordLocation)


SELECT DISTINCT TOP 100 PERCENT dbo.Themes.WordLocation,
➡ dbo.Themes.Word,
    dbo.DocumentsFullpath
FROM    dbo.Documents INNER JOIN
   Dbo_historical.Fullpath INNER JOIN
      dbo_DSSLoc ON dbo.Documents.Fullpath
 dbo_DSSLoc.Fullpath RIGHT OUTER JOIN
      dbo.Themes ON dbo.Documents.DocumentID =
➡ dbo.Themes.DocumentID
WHERE   (dbo.Themes.WordLocation BETWEEN
➡dbo_DSSLoc.WordLocation - 200
         AND dbo_DSSLoc.WordLoaction + 200) AND
      (dbo.Themes.WordLocation BETWEEN
    dbo_historicLoc.WordLocation - 200 AND
➡dbo_DSSLoc.WordLocation + 200) AND
    (dbo.Documents.Fullpath LIKE '\\IDSPOOC02\Diabtest%')
ORDER BY dbo.documents.fullpath, dbo.Themes.WordLocation
```

All these query types can be combined into various combinations. The query in the following section is one where a snippet is produced when a 1:n proximity condition is satisfied.

Basic Word String Snippet Report

Basic Word String Snippet Reports can be used to see the surrounding text for instances of specific words without comparing them to other words. In this example, we ask SQL to show us word snippets of +/− 140 character spaces surrounding the word "extract processing" when "extract processing" is within n bytes of a list of words.

This is done in a two-step process:

Step 1

```
CREATE VIEW dbo._ProductivityLoc
AS
SELECT     TOP 100 PERCENT dbo.Themes.Word,
➡ dbo.Themes.WordLocation, dbo.Documents.Fullpath
FROM          dbo.Themes INNER JOIN
                    dbo.Documents ON dbo.Themes.DocumentID =
➡ dbo.Documents.DocumentID
WHERE     (dbo.Themes.Word = 'productivity') AND
➡ (dbo.Documents.Fullpath LIKE '\\IDSPOC02\DiabTest%')
ORDER BY dbo.Documents.Fullpath, dbo.Themes.WordLocation

CREATE VIEW dbo._organizationLoc
AS
SELECT DISTINCT dbo.CategorizationTerms.Term,
➡ dbo.Documents.Fullpath, dbo.Themes.WordLocation
FROM          dbo.Themes INNER JOIN
                    dbo.Documents ON dbo.Themes.DocumentID =
➡ dbo.Documents.DocumentID CROSS JOIN
                    dbo.Glossaries INNER JOIN
                    dbo.CategorizationTerms ON dbo.Glossaries.
➡GlossaryID = dbo.CategorizationTerms.GlossaryID
WHERE     (dbo.Documents.Fullpath LIKE '\\IDSPOC02\diab_Test%')
➡ AND (dbo.Glossaries.Name = 'GlossaryName')
```

Step 2

After you create your views that represent the areas of comparison you are interested in, you can use the following SQL to report against them and other tables in the database. (This query uses the two previous examples.)

```
SELECT DISTINCT TOP 100 PERCENT dbo.Themes.WordLocation,
➡ dbo.Themes.Word, dbo.Documents.Fullpath
FROM          dbo.Documents INNER JOIN
                    dbo._organizationLoc ON dbo.Documents.
➡Fullpath = dbo._organizationLoc.Fullpath INNER JOIN
                    dbo._productivityLoc ON dbo.Documents.
➡Fullpath = dbo._productivityLoc.Fullpath RIGHT OUTER JOIN
                    dbo.Themes ON dbo.Documents.DocumentID =
➡ dbo.Themes.DocumentID
WHERE     (dbo.Themes.WordLocation BETWEEN dbo._productivity.
➡WordLocation - 200 AND dbo._productvity.WordLocation
➡ + 200) AND
                    (dbo.Themes.WordLocation BETWEEN
➡ dbo._organizationLoc.WordLocation - 200 AND
➡ dbo._organizationLoc.WordLocation + 200) AND
                    (dbo.Documents.Fullpath LIKE
➡ '\\IDSPOC02\DiabTest%')
ORDER BY dbo.Documents.Fullpath, dbo.Themes.WordLocation
```

These examples show that when unstructured text is integrated and placed in a database, many different forms of textual analytics can be performed. The scope of textual analytics is strictly up to the analyst creating the query.

Summary

Textual analytics are best done when the end user creates the query. The query can be a raw SQL query, prepackaged query, or query generated by a BI tool such as Business Objects, Cognos, or MicroStrategy.

There are many different kinds of queries. Some of the basic queries follow:

- Simple search
- Search of snippets
- Search for synonyms found in an external category
- Proximity search

As interesting and as useful as discussion about unstructured textual analytics is, there is nothing that beats a good case study. The following chapters depict various ways in which textual analytics and unstructured data are used.

15

Case Study—Textual Analytics in Medical Research

The Alpha Omega Medical Research Foundation (a fictional organization) has a complete facility for patient healthcare. There are a series of related hospitals and an associated university. There is research and inpatient and outpatient healthcare.

The organization is run by committee. There are committees for many aspects of healthcare, and consensus is how decisions are made.

The organization has been treating patients in one capacity for more than 100 years. Research plays a big part in the long-term success of the foundation. The research organization gets grants from different organizations and institutions, including the government.

Medical Records

The Alpha Omega Medical Research Foundation keeps detailed patient records. The records have been created manually during each encounter with the foundation. For each patient, one record exists per encounter or episode of care. This means that when you look at the complete record for a patient over the life of the patient, you will have many records written by many physicians.

The records have been kept for a long time. From the earliest days, the records were kept manually, as each doctor wrote out the events that occurred during each encounter.

The manual records have been transcribed and sit in several sources. Some of the sources are electronic flat files, and some are integrated into an electronic record. In this case, there is an electronic record for each patient and encounter. In all cases, the information sits in an electronic text format, although there are many different forms of electronic text.

The organization can look at the records in several ways. One way the medical data can be examined is by patient. In this case, all the different encounters the patient had are grouped together so that you can see the complete history of a patient. Another way the electronic data can be organized is by physician. All the encounters in which the physician was involved can be grouped together. Another way the electronic data can be grouped is by disease or condition. In this case, all the data relating to a given condition can be grouped together. For example, there can be liver cancer data, cardiology data, neonatology data, and so on.

The Cardiology Study

The research organization has decided to study heart patients—cardiology. The organization is interested in looking at the effectiveness of heart treatments—how effective different treatments have been, the effects of certain medicines, the effect of practices, and so on. The organization wants to look at anything that will improve the effectiveness of heart survival and health. The conditions correlative to both good and bad heart outcomes are of great interest.

The Alpha Omega Medical Research Foundation knows that there is a wealth of information with the data that has been stored over the years; however, because the data is in a textual format, there is no easy way to get the data and prepare it for access and analyses.

The Challenge of Terminology

There are many challenges with the data, but perhaps the biggest challenge is that of terminology. The records have been collected over a period of years. Over time, medical terminology has changed. There are procedures today that weren't available ten years ago. There are medicines that exist and are effective now that were not available ten years ago. Doctors that practice now were trained under a different set of conditions and rules.

In addition, the medical records were created by a different set of employees: physicians, hospital administrators, nurses, and lab technicians. So there is a great diversity of people who originally created the text that finds its way into the medical records.

There is yet another challenge with terminology. Some of the doctors that created records were cardiologists, general practitioners, hematologists. Because of the diverse background of the different doctors, there was different terminology everywhere.

The Tower of Babel

It was recognized at the outset that terminology was going to be a large issue. If the raw textual data was dumped in a file, it would be like the Tower of Babel. Everyone would speak, but everyone would speak a different language, or at least a different dialect of the same language.

What was needed was the ability to look at data both generally and colloquially. A *general classification* of data looks at different classifications of diseases, medicines, and conditions. A *colloquial* term is used specifically by only one or two doctors to describe a condition, medicine, or practice. There is a need to access the information with both kinds of terminology.

Volumes of Data

Another challenge that was recognized was the volumes of data. Over the years, an impressive volume of data had accumulated.

Another important factor was the variable nature of the documents. For some patients, barely a page or two of information existed. Other patients had a long and well-documented history. These patients had up to several hundred pages of descriptive notes about their journey with the disease that was treated.

Throughout all these problems, it was recognized that there was a wealth of information in the records. The challenge was collecting, organizing, integrating, and then displaying all the information in a meaningful manner.

Revealing a Strategy

The first step was a planning session. At the planning session, a general strategy was proposed that consisted of first building a small test case to shake the system out. The second step was to take the records of only a hundred patients and use those records. The thought was that it would be simpler and more efficient to get the analytical system to the point where it was functioning in a viable manner and then to use the main body of data for the "real" analyses.

It was recognized from the outset that the process of doing meaningful analyses was not going to occur on the first or even second iteration of processing.

The First Iteration

The first iteration consisted of feeding the data from the different sources into the system. The first iteration was a test of the ability of the organization to access and gather the source data. It is significant that no changes were required to be made to the source data. The source data could be used "as is."

The source data came from a wide variety of sources. The records came from Microsoft-based files, embedded data elements in large record files, and servers where previous analyses had been performed on the data.

There were a few glitches when reading different formats of data. In some cases, there were system parameters that needed to be reset. In other cases, the sources were read without a problem.

After the data was entered into the system and "weaned" from the internal files, the next step was to integrate the data. The integration occurred primarily through the control of the system parameters—the external categories, synonyms, homographs, and stop words. In addition, the raw text was subjected to stemming algorithms that were buried in the text.

The initial system parameters were not set to anything special. The vendor supplied the initial sets of stop words, synonyms, homographs, and so on. There was little attempt on the first iteration to use anything other than what the vendor supplied. Again, on the first iteration, the emphasis was more on getting the system to work and to get through the "break in" issues than it was to try for a refined, final result.

After the data had run through the integration process, the next step was to produce the final output. A small database was produced along with a *self-organizing map* (SOM), probably the most useful form of output.

Upon examining the SOM, some words were obviously incorrect and other words required investigation. The system had interjected some words that had nothing to do with medicine but occurred frequently because of the source systems. These words were identified and added to the stop list.

Other words were curious, at best. Most of these words were acronyms or diminutives. The synonyms for these words were created so that it would be obvious what was being said. In addition, a few homonyms were identified, and the criteria for the resolution of the homonyms were added to the system.

The Second Iteration

After these "touch ups" were added, the system was rerun, and a new set of output was obtained. The second iteration of textual analysis was much more enlightening than the first. Nonsensical words disappeared. Acronyms were expanded into their original meaning. And now, new issues began to surface. The analysts could see the relationships of data that were developing. The major subject areas began to be obvious. The correlations of data started to appear.

The analysts now could see the larger picture much more clearly. The adjustments made in this iteration included more clarification of acronyms, more resolution of homographs and synonyms, and more additions and adjustments to the stop word list. The adjustments that were made in the second iteration of development were essentially the same as those in the first iteration; however, these adjustments were made with much more focus.

The Third Iteration

The adjustments were made, and the third iteration of analysis was initiated. Processing ensued, and the results from the third iteration of development were available. Note that because there was a relatively small amount of data run, rerunning an entire analysis was not a big deal. It didn't require a huge amount of machine resources, and it didn't take long.

After the results from the third iteration of analysis were available, they began to truly clarify themselves. There were still synonyms that needed to be clarified, homographs to be resolved, and stop words to be adjusted. However, the picture of what was developed began to make sense.

Now it was time to add the medical library to the picture. The organization had developed a glossary (taxonomy) of medical terms over the years. The terms were put in the form suitable to synonym resolution and served the purpose of resolving the terminology differences. The synonyms were resolved as concatenations. When a term was found that fit the now enlarged synonym list, the common term was concatenated with the colloquial term. For example, suppose the term "melanoma" was found coming from the source text. The synonym list would recognize the term "melanoma" as a cancer. Now the term "cancer" was concatenated with the term "melanoma" and "...melanoma cancer..." was found in the source text. This meant that anyone searching the data could look for melanoma or cancer. It was kind of like having your cake and eating it, too.

After more stop words were adjusted, more homographs resolved, and a few synonyms added to the organization-wide list of terms, another iteration of processing was ready to run.

At this point, the number of stop word, synonym, and homograph adjustments that were made were only a fraction of the same type of adjustments that were made in the first and second iterations of analyses. The big push in this case was the new, large list of synonyms that were added to resolve terminology differences between the different sources of data.

Fourth Iteration

The fourth iteration of analysis was executed. Now the output blossomed. One effect of adding the new glossary of terms for the purpose of resolution was that the major subject areas changed dramatically. Before the fourth iteration, there were terms such as "melanoma," "malignant tumor," "leukemia," "mammogram," "cervical," and "squamous cell" found in the SOM. When the concatenated synonyms were added, those terms all appeared under the generic term "cancer." It was now possible to look at information generically—under "cancer"—or specifically—under "melanoma" or "leukemia."

As in all iterations, a few stop words were added, and a few synonyms and homographs were adjusted.

Now the organization was set to process the entire library of machine-readable text. Previously, the organization had been processing only a small subset of text. Now that things appeared to be ready, it was time to process against the larger set of data.

Fifth Iteration

The fifth iteration of development was run. There were several breakdowns as the fifth iteration was executing. Some work areas were not large enough and had to be enlarged. Some processing parameters were set improperly and had to be adjusted for a much larger volume of data. But the biggest change was the amount of time the process took to run. What had occurred in a matter of minutes before, now was running a much longer time—in a matter of days.

While the analysts were waiting for their results, there was a discussion as to how to speed things up. There were essentially two choices—run the process on a larger machine or run the process in parallel (or both). Because of the length of time required for the process to run, it was decided to do both options.

A new and much larger machine was brought in, and several machines were allocated to run in tandem. Fortunately, the software was built so that a parallelization of the execution was no problem. Now that the process was running on much larger machines and on machines that were harnessed together in parallel, the process ran much, much faster.

The output was now ready from the fifth iteration.

Textual Analytics

It was at this point that the process took a different turn. Up to this point, the primary emphasis had been on getting the process to work. Now that the process was working, the emphasis was on doing textual analytic processing.

The analysts were turned loose on the results. Almost immediately, the analysts had some suggestions as to how to effectively use the data:

- One analyst wanted to add a blood pressure study to the mix of cardiology data to see what new information might be generated.

- Another analyst wanted to investigate subpopulations. The analyst wanted to look at heart disease for women, women who smoked, women over 50, women who had blue collar jobs, and women who were overweight. The analyst was interested in the contrast in outcomes for the different subpopulations.

- Yet another analyst wanted to remove some source data and see what the effect was. The analyst wanted to remove medication information and see what correlations there were based on other nonmedication factors.

The described process can be graphically depicted, as shown in Figure 15-1.

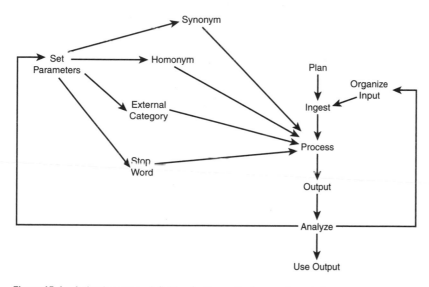

Figure 15-1 A simple process definition for the medical research analysis

One of the other outcomes of the processing was a relational database that was constructed as a result of the integration of data. The relational database was built from the source data and the steps of integration that occurred. The relational database was a classical document/word relational database.

Standard Analytical Tools

In addition to looking at SOMs for textual analysis, the analyst could now use standard analytical tools such as Business Objects, Cognos, Crystal Reports, and others for the purpose of analytical processing. The efficient thing about having a document/word relational database is that the analyst can use tools in an environment with which he is already familiar.

When the analyst has the ability to use tools in a manner that is normal, the analyst can do all sorts of spontaneous analyses.

16

Case Study—A Database
for Harmful Chemicals

Consider the Institute for Environmental Study (a fictional organization). This scientific organization monitors toxics, wastes, and other chemicals in the environment. The monitoring is done worldwide. The institution is funded by governments around the world as well as large philanthropic organizations. The institution has been in existence for a half a decade.

The institution makes a quarterly report that tracks certain well-known chemicals and makes an annual report for the environment in its entirety. The annual report makes news worldwide, and the quarterly reports are open to the public but do not receive as much scrutiny. In addition, the institution issues warnings when it senses that there is a condition the world needs to know about.

The Institution's Data on Harmful Chemicals

The institution tracks approximately 30 well-known harmful chemicals with regular monitors. The institution also tracks approximately 3,000 chemical compounds on a more relaxed basis. In addition, the institution keeps track of any new threats that might not have been noticed.

The institution makes its research available to any government and to its corporate sponsors. Two or three times a quarter, an agency of the government asks for a special study. In some cases, the study is as simple as searching a file, but often the request for a study requires new information to be gathered and integrated with the existing files.

The institution gathers its data from many sources. Many large corporations report data to the institution on a regular basis. This is done voluntarily because the large corporations want to have a good public image, and support of this scientific organization is one way to boost their image. Other governments from around the world periodically do studies that are relevant, such as soil testing, temperature recording, moisture recording, and so forth.

If needed, there is access to a wealth of other information relative to toxicity and waste. However, the main information and analyses come from the chemicals that are regularly traced.

An Abundance of Paper Reports

The monitored data is stored on a wide variety of technologies. However, the most basic reports are stored manually. The institution has more than 30 years worth of paper reports. At first, the collection of quarterly monitor reports stored on paper was a good idea. It was cheap and easy to do. And there were only a few numbers that were needed from each report. Also when the papers were first collected, there was little or no good technology for taking information from paper and storing it electronically.

However, times have changed. Today, technology can capture and analyze textual information. Paper is fragile. Over time, constant handling makes the paper brittle, and the reports begin to deteriorate. There is also a need for more information than what was originally collected on the paper reports. The monitor reports contained more information than the paper reports, but no one knew about the other information. In recent years, however, requests for information were included or would otherwise be enhanced by the information found on the monitor reports.

A Request for Analyses Leading to the Requirement for Storing Data Electronically

The institution received a request for information that was out of the ordinary and from a high-ranking official. To comply with the request for information, the institution hired 30 temporary workers to manually look through 30 years' worth of reports. Even after the reports had been scanned, the institution was not sure that it had gotten all the information that was requested. After the ordeal of having to look through 30 years' worth of reports manually, the institution vowed never again would it go through the same ordeal.

Putting Paper Data in an Electronic Format

The first step the institution took to make sure this never happened again was to capture all the paper documents and put them in an electronic format. This was a large undertaking. Optical character recognition (OCR) technology was used to capture a good percentage of the text written on the document. However, even in the best of circumstances, the institution had to have manual editing. There were many reasons why the OCR capture process was a less than perfect exercise:

- The font of the text on the paper was not one recognized by the scanning software.
- The paper was brittle and cracked before being subjected to OCR scans.
- The OCR recognized a word for something it wasn't.

Although the OCR process was a good start, there was still a considerable manual effort needed to convert the text on the papers to an accurate, complete electronic source of data.

Creating the Standard Set of Reference Tables

There were other challenges. The institution had no standard set of references for the chemicals that it operated on. The best it had was a narrative describing each chemical and each chemical compound.

There was a lengthy document that described the properties of each chemical. Some of the information found in the narrative included the following:

- Melting point
- Boiling point
- Atomic mass
- Molar mass
- Atomic number
- Valence

Although the institution had these numbers, it did not have them organized in a single table where they could be easily accessed. The chemicals were referenced by name in the narrative and were referenced by the Chemical Abstract Services (CAS) number assigned to each chemical compound.

After the OCR process was finished, the next step was to create a standard set of tables for chemical compound properties that was electronically accessible. This was done by treating the chemical description as a semistructured document. Using semistructured processing, the system looked—chemical by chemical—for properties of the chemical in the narrative. When the property was found, the chemical property, the chemical name, and CAS number were placed in a table that was highly structured and allowed the chemicals to be accessed in a structured manner.

After the semistructured data was accessed, analyzed, and placed in a table and after the quarterly reports were captured electronically, the organization was finally in position to do textual analytics.

Text Editing and Integration

Next, the stop words were edited to make sure that they were accurate. Synonym resolutions were specified as well as homograph resolution.

The electronically captured text was then entered in Foundation software. The software then integrated the text and produced an Oracle database. The database that was produced was a document/word type of database. Then another database was produced looking at the quarterly reports and using the semistructured facility. This database contained references to key words, such as date of the report and CAS numbers.

The document/word database contained data from the original quarterly reports that was integrated. This meant that

- Stop words were removed.
- Alternate spellings and common misspellings were recognized.
- Synonym processing occurred.
- Homograph processing occurred.
- Punctuation, case, and font were removed as considerations for searching.

After the textual data was integrated, the next step was to produce a database in Oracle that held the document/word data. Then the ID 1, ID 2, ID 3... database was built and put into Oracle. When the standard reference database, the textual document/word database, and the ID 1, ID 2, ID 3... databases were built, the organization was set for textual analytics.

The second database—an ID 1, ID 2, ID 3...—contained certain standard information about the quarterly reports that were filed.

By joining the two databases—the document/word and the ID 1, ID 2, ID 3... databases—on document number, sophisticated requests could be created.

Textual Analytics

The first textual analytics usage was to look for benzene and derivatives of benzene. A simple query was created that looked for benzene and derivative forms of benzene. This query showed the different documents that the word benzene and its derivatives were found in.

Next, a new set of queries was produced that looked at snippets related to benzene. In these queries, each reference to benzene had the words preceding the reference and the words following the reference displayed. This allowed the analyst to see the exact context in which the reference to benzene was made.

Then, an external category was created for dangerous chemicals. The external category for dangerous chemicals included the following:

- Hydrochloric acid
- Zinc compounds
- Arsenic
- Lead compounds
- Copper compounds
- Nitrate compounds
- Manganese compounds

After the dangerous chemicals external category was created, the next step was to do an indirect query on dangerous chemicals. The indirect query showed where all the references were to any of the dangerous chemicals.

Next, the institute created two more external categories. These external categories were created from the table of chemical properties that had been generated from the semistructured data. The first external category that was created was one for all chemical compounds whose melting point was greater than 120 degrees Celsius. The second external category was created for all chemical compounds whose melting point was greater than 100 degrees Celsius and whose boiling point was greater than 160 degrees Celsius.

Queries were generated for both external categories. The result was a reference to the many places where chemicals that had those properties were found. Finally, the institute generated proximity queries. The first query was for the words benzene and lead found in the same document within 200 bytes of each other. The result was a list of references that met these criteria.

The final query was done on a proximity search for the external category dangerous chemicals and melting point greater than 120 degrees. The result was a list of references for any documents containing any words from either list within 200 bytes of each other.

The institute now has a database that can be queried on an as-needed basis. The preparation time for a query is minimal compared to manually searching a large pile of papers.

Periodic Additions

Periodically, the database is enlarged as more data, more chemicals, and more external categories are added. As each new external query is added, a library of external categories is created so that querying the database indirectly becomes a normal and easy thing to do.

Figure 16-1 shows a high-level perspective of the activities of developing the three databases:

- Chemical properties database
- Unstructured database built around quarterly monitor reports
- Semistructured portion of the data found in the quarterly monitor reports

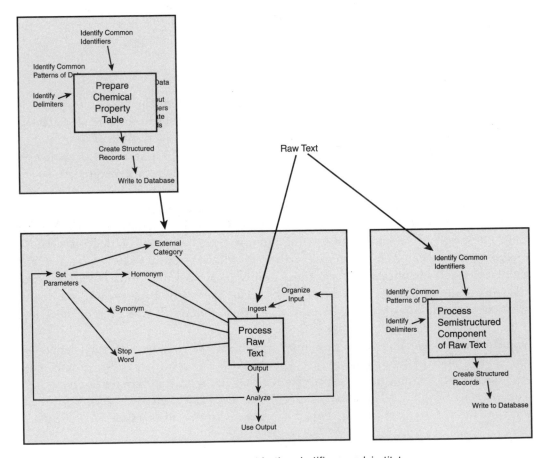

Figure 16-1 How the different databases were created for the scientific research institute

17

Case Study—Managing Contracts Through an Unstructured Database

The example company created for this chapter is the HTR Oil and Gas Company that has more than 10,000 contracts. These contracts have been collected over the years. The primary problem is that over the years companies have changed. HTR has been built from the merger of more than 10 companies over a 30-year period.

First, there was Flying Horse Petroleum that merged with SOHO in 1961. Then, Flying Horse merged with CalPetro in 1980, taking the name Jumbo Oil and Gas. CalPetro was the result of a merger with California Oil and Coastal Platforms. In 1991, Jumbo Oil and Gas merged with Station Time Gas and became HTR. In 1998, HTR acquired TexOil and all its subsidiaries. Furthermore, the companies that HTR deals with have a similar history of mergers and acquisitions.

A Hodgepodge of Contracts

Going back several decades, it is difficult to tell which company was dealing with which other company. Unfortunately, the lawyers of HTR cannot just throw up their hands. There are contracts between all those entities that have to be honored regardless of the confusion.

Part of the problem is that in some cases there are conflicting contracts, despite the best efforts of the management that has orchestrated the merger or acquisition. In most cases, when a merger or acquisition happens, it is clear how contract disputes are to be handled. However, in a few cases, it is not clear. The problem is that the differences of opinion inevitably lead to misunderstandings, and the misunderstandings often lead to litigation because the contracts are not honored as originally written. In addition, regardless of how the litigation is resolved, it is always expensive and time-consuming. HTR, along with many other companies, wants to avoid or mitigate as much litigation as possible, but trying to deal with the mass of contracts is difficult.

Over time, many of the contracts have expired, but that does not mean that there is not valuable information in those contracts. Past industry practices, an identification of what terms have been and how different companies live up to those terms, and industry knowledge of who has lived up to their agreements are all buried in the body of contracts.

Looking at a single contract or two contracts is not particularly difficult. Any good lawyer can do this type of an analysis. However, looking at 10,000 contracts is another matter entirely. No lawyer can look at that number of contracts and keep all the information that is stored in the contracts in mind. It simply is humanly impossible to do.

A Plan for Textual Analytics

It is clear that HTR needs to organize these contracts to make the most use of them and to prevent litigation. The first step is for the legal department to consult with the IT department to create a plan for the consolidation and analytical processing for the contracts. The first part of the plan is obvious; the contracts need to be gathered and consolidated into a single place. However, after that thought, the road becomes murky. The primary problem is that the contracts are in text. Standard database processing will not suffice because it depends on the repeatability of information and the fact that most information needs to be numeric to take advantage of standard analytical processing.

The IT and the legal department turn to textual analytic techniques to solve the problem of analyzing contracts.

The plan is to do the following:

- Consolidate the contracts into a single location.
- Ingest the contracts so that the text resides in a single technology.
- Read the text and integrate the text insofar as legal jargon can be integrated.
- Examine the data for external categories that are relevant and important.
- Create three databases.

The first database that will be created is one that takes the integrated unstructured text and produces a document/word relational database. The database will be produced in DB2. The only common identifier the document/word database will have is document ID, created by reading the contract and creating a unique, encrypted identifier.

The second database is created from the common information found in each contract and is an ID 1, ID 2, ID 3... style database as is normal with the treatment of semistructured data. One document ID is created for one contract. The semistructured capability of the product is used to find such data as effective dates, certain terms, rates, and agreeing parties. If the data is not found in the contract, a default is provided. The document ID that is created is the same as the one in the first database. By having consistent identifiers, the semistructured data can be linked with the document/word data.

The third database links different contracts together and allows the relationships between contracts to be identified. It is created using semistructured technology, creating an ID 1, ID 2, ID 3... database. However, in this case, the database is used for linking different contracts together. The primary identifier is the document ID that has been created for the contract that is accessed. The secondary identifiers are the contract IDs that are referenced or otherwise implicit in the contract. The purpose of the third database is to allow the relationships between contracts to be identified.

The next part of the analysis is the creation of external categories that reflect the changing ownership and corporate structure of the different companies. These external categories show how different companies were merged or acquired. Using the external categories, the analyst knows that the contract for Flying Horse petroleum in 1976 is for the company known as HTR today, even though the names are not the same.

The external categories are created not just for HTR, but also for the companies that HTR has done business with over the years. In some cases, the heritage of a company today is not known, and in some cases in the past, a company is thought to have disappeared when, in fact, the company was acquired.

These external companies are handled on a best-effort basis. As analysis is performed, these external categories are revised and refined over time.

Iterative Development

HTR goes through the standard database development that all people using unstructured text go through. There is iterative development. Some stop words are altered, deleted, and added. The synonym list and the homograph list are adjusted as well. The external categories are constantly undergoing adjustment.

Each contract is different. However, across most contracts is a commonality of information. Common to most contracts is a statement of the parties entering into the agreement, the effective dates of the contract, and a lot of legalese found in any contract—force majuere, for example. However, there are many differences in contracts, such as the terms, appendixes, rates, conditions, and expiration clauses.

The contracts have been captured electronically so that they do not have to be accessed by OCR technology. However, the contracts exist on a wide variety of technologies, such as .pdf files, .doc files, on IBM technology, and on Oracle technology. Indeed, one of the challenges of doing contract analysis is that of bringing together the many contracts into a single electronic place where the contracts can be analyzed.

As you might expect, the contracts are full of legal jargon. Because the contracts have been written over a number of years and by many different lawyers, the jargon, while similar, is not exactly the same.

The first iteration of the building of the databases operates on textual data that can only be defined as raw. The next iteration of building the databases operates on textual data that is more refined. Finally, after about four or five iterations of development, the databases are ready to use.

Analytical Processing

Now the work shifts from IT development to analytical processing. The analysts have a long list of questions that they have been waiting to look at.

Some of the questions follow:

- How many contracts has ABC been involved in over the years?

- How many contracts has ABC and its derivatives been involved in over the years?

- When mergers or acquisitions have occurred, how many contracts active at that time have overlapped?

- For overlapping contracts, has there been a conflict in rates? In terms? Other conflicts?

- What price ceilings/floors have been instituted in any contract?

- What contracts are in force today? How much longer will they be in force?

- What is the total exposure of the company according to all contracts that are in force to OPEC?

These and many more questions are what the first blush of analyses has addressed. However, after the first wave of analyses is done, a whole new wave of analyses is created. The answer to one analysis spawns another question.

After using the contracts databases for a while, the organization discovers that the data in the contracts is much more potent when combined with data found in the structured environment. When the analysts start to pry, they find that much of the data in the contracts database relates to other corporate data.

The first step to doing an analysis of both structured and unstructured data is to determine the linkage between the different environments. Fortunately, many of the structured data relate to contract ID. Using contract ID, the linkage is formed between the two environments. It is noted that this linkage is not perfect. There is some data in the structured environment that cannot be related to a contract. However, much of the structured data can be related back to contract ID.

Another linkage that is successful is that of company ID. Company ID appears in both the unstructured and the structured environments.

Using these linkages, the analysts discover that they can now tie unstructured data and structured data together, in many cases. Now it is possible to ask questions such as the following:

- From a delivery standpoint, how has company BCD performed over time and across multiple contracts?

- From a problem standpoint, what problems have occurred in a correlative fashion with which companies?

- Over the years, has performance gotten better or worse for the major companies that HTR does business with?

Figure 17-1 shows the first phase of development for the unstructured environment.

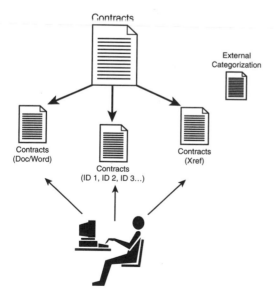

Figure 17-1 The analysis starts when the basic databases are built.

Figure 17-2 shows that, when the unstructured databases are built, the structured databases can be linked in one of several ways.

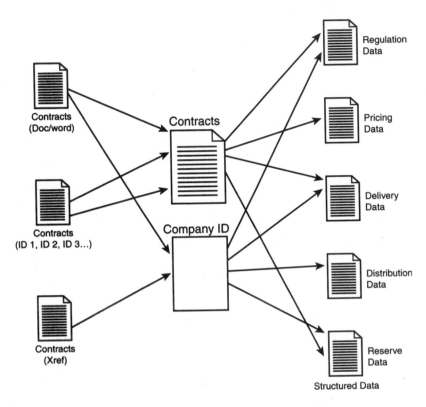

Figure 17-2 Unstructured data is linked to structured data in several ways.

18

Case Study—Creating a Corporate Taxonomy (Glossary)

The fictional Ark and Ladder Company has been in existence for more than 50 years. Ark and Ladder makes toys and books for children. In recent years, the company has expanded to children's clothing and eating utensils. The company started out small, but over the years has expanded to a surprisingly large size. The company has not had a national outreach until about a decade ago when it acquired an overseas competitor. Since then, through a series of mergers, the company has grown in size beyond anyone's imagination.

A Technological Jumble

The IT infrastructure has grown as well. Through the homegrown systems, acquisitions, and mergers, the IT function includes practically every known technology. There is IBM equipment, HP equipment, Microsoft technology, Oracle technology, CA technology, and so forth. When it comes to systems software, there is NT, MVS, NIX, Linux, and so on. In terms of database technology, there is Oracle, Teradata, IBM, Sybase, and NT SQL Server.

The applications technology is just as bad, with applications everywhere. Many of the applications have come from the acquisitions that have occurred. Some have come through software purchases. When an acquisition occurred, it was deemed too time-consuming and too expensive to bring the application into a corporate set of applications. Yet, over the long haul, just the opposite has been true. By keeping all the corporate data on separate systems, the result has been a maintenance bill that is high, constant, and never gets any better.

Data is kept all over the place at the company. Some of the data is on corporate systems, but a lot is found on personal systems, in the individual workstations found companywide.

Closing the books each month is a monumental task, but even more monumental is the fact that there are at least ten versions of the truth everywhere you look. No one really knows what has been sold, what has been shipped, what is being manufactured, and when deliveries are being made.

And taking corporate inventory is a nightmare. Over the years, it has taken longer and longer to do the annual inventory.

The IT Problem

Over the years, the management of the company has taken pride on how little was spent on IT. Traditionally, IT consumed less than 3% of the corporate budget. The corporate attitude has always been one of putting the money into marketing, new product development, sales, and so forth. However, recently it has been noticed that

- The IT budget has been growing despite the best efforts of management to minimize it.
- The company is starting to make costly decisions that could have been prevented had there been better information systems.

The company has hired a group of managers from companies that are well respected. Corporate management has listened to these new managers and has determined that a major upgrade of information systems is needed. Corporate management knows that it needs to do something about IT, but it doesn't know exactly what that means. The new IT management has pointed out the need for the following:

- Timely information
- Accurate information
- Believable information
- Information that can be used for analytical processing

Unfortunately, over time, the IT infrastructure that was built is well entrenched. For all the inadequacies of the IT infrastructure, the company does not part with what it knows well, despite the shortcomings. It takes a corporate mandate from the highest office to let people know that they will be supporting the IT modernization effort as part of their jobs.

The plan to modernize IT is to do several things:

- Standardize a single set of corporate systems to operate the mainline of the business.
- Build a data warehouse where integrated, historical data can be kept as a source for DSS processing.
- Centralize much processing that is now done on an ad hoc basis.

It is recognized that this modernization plan will take several years to implement.

The Issue of Terminology

As a central part of the plan, there is a need to standardize (or at least recognize) all the different terminology that exists within the company's data. One part of the organization refers to part numbers. Other parts refer to product numbers. Other people talk about SKUs. Still other people talk about P numbers.

The problem is that within the company's documents people refer to essentially the same thing without using the same words. In some cases, there are a few shades of difference, but for the most part, topics are known by ten different names.

The issue of fractured terminology applies to much more than a single term. There are terminology differences everywhere, which create all sorts of problems. The auditors have a hard time bringing the disparate data together; the finance people have a hard time making a consolidated balance sheet; management has a hard time understanding what is going on with the business because of the lack of concise communication.

Creating a Corporate Taxonomy (Glossary)

Out of the chaos, management decides to create a corporate taxonomy (or a corporate glossary). The output of the corporate taxonomy is the intellectual body of thought that acts as a corporate map of what data means throughout the corporation.

The many different colloquialisms will be captured, and a definition and grouping of the terms will be created. To this end, the textual ETL software is used to gather, integrate, and prepare the textual data for entry into an unstructured database.

One of the first steps is to find the corporate terms that exist everywhere: on personal computers, in corporate dictionaries and repositories, in the metadata assigned to a product, and in the reports and emails that are found everywhere in the corporation.

Furthermore, this corporate terminology exists in many different formats: Microsoft, IBM, Oracle, and Business Objects. It exists in emails, spreadsheets, reports, and filings.

As a general starting point, there is the process of the access and editing of these many sources. Textual ETL is used for that purpose. Then, the next step is weeding out words and terminology not central to the business of the corporation. The stop word facility is used for this purpose. It takes several iterations of gathering and editing the many sources of data to create the "master list" of terms.

Creating Definitions and Equivocations

After the master list is created, the next step is to create definitions and equivocations. The definitions are simply the statement of what the term means. Some definitions are created by hand, many come from the users, and still others are created by accessing glossaries online and then adapting the definition to suit the organization's needs.

Next is the equivocation process to assign terms general meanings similar to other terms. The external categorization is used for this purpose. For all the data found throughout the corporation, there are surprisingly few equivocations. Creating the equivocations by hand is not a large chore; although it is a chore that must be done carefully.

On occasion, there is an "imperfect equivocation." In this case, the equivocation is not complete or entirely accurate. When there is an imperfect equivocation, the external category facility is used to document the shades of differences that exist.

Using the Taxonomy

When the external categories have been created, they can then be used as part of the query process. For example, one DSS analyst can ask about "P numbers" or "part numbers," and the system knows that the person is referring to "SKU."

The other groups that have to deal with the company—auditors, financial analysts— now have a "Bible" that lays out the company wherever the contact is made. Now, a single corporate vocabulary is starting.

The taxonomy/glossary effort is done first for a few selected parts of the organization. However, after the first results appear, the effort is extended to other parts of the organization. In a year, almost all parts of the organization have been included, but occasionally an organization pops up that has been neglected or that the developers never knew existed. In that sense, the work is an ongoing effort.

Perhaps the organization that finds the taxonomy most useful is the redevelopment organization. As plans are made for modernizing the information systems of the company, the taxonomy/glossary is extremely valuable—for communications, for looking at old documentation, and for looking at different geographic locations.

19

Case Study—
Insurance Claims

The APEX Insurance Company (a fictional insurance company) has been selling casualty insurance for many years. APEX provides coverage for all sorts of casualties—fire, theft, flood, and so on.

The claims are settled by an adjustor. As part of the settlement process, the adjustor writes a report. Typically, the adjustor's report contains information such as the location of the claim, who was affected by the damage (which is often different than the person making the claim), police involvement, the time of year the loss occurred, the exact time of the loss, and the size of the loss.

A Collection of Inconsistent Claims

Of course, over the years, the claims have been written by many adjustors. Although a few adjustors have written many of the loss reports, as a whole, there have been many contributors. Each of the loss reports are dated and tagged with the policy or policies that are involved in the loss.

The loss reports vary in size considerably. Some loss reports are brief, consisting of about one page, and others are extensive, consisting of many pages.

The loss reports have been kept—in one form or the other—for at least 50 years. The loss reports were kept on paper for many years. But several years ago, the paper-based loss reports were put through an OCR process, and today the loss reports go directly to an electronic format. APEX now has a substantial file of loss reports.

Some coding of the information done on the loss reports has been attempted. Certain large and common items have been coded for things such as house, car, and building. Using the coding scheme, some analytical processing has been done on the loss report data. But merely encoding certain parameters gives only a rough idea of what the loss reports contain.

Because of the many sources that have contributed to the loss reports, there is a distinct variation in terminology. Many factors caused the difference in terminology:

- **Time**—Over time, the vocabulary for things changes. The APEX line of business changes. Competition changes. The customer demographics change over time.
- **Geography**—People in one region of the United States have a different word or phrase for an item than other people in the United States.
- **Educational background**—Based on the educational background, certain things are referred to by different terms.
- **Gender**—On occasion, there is a difference in terminology between men and women.

Complicating all these factors is the volume of data that has been collected. Had there been a small to modest amount of data to contend with, there might not have been a problem. But the APEX Insurance Company has been in business a long time, and a lot of loss report data has accumulated over those years. The large volume of data poses some challenges:

- Nothing can be done manually. There is simply too much data to even consider such an undertaking.
- Loading and reloading the data is a big challenge.
- Doing sequential searches electronically requires a lot of machine resources.
- Indexing the data requires resources.

A Wealth of Information

The APEX Insurance Company has a problem: There is a wealth of information that is locked up in the loss reports. But that information is simply not accessible. And there are plenty of potential uses for the information:

- Looking for a specific piece of information, especially an obscure piece of information
- Looking for patterns of information
- Looking for trends that are becoming more prevalent
- Looking for fraud or possible fraud
- Looking for the same person's or persons' involvement, even when the involvement is tangential
- Looking for defects
- Looking for tangible objects that correlate to losses

The management and the actuary community suspect that there is a wealth of information locked up in the loss report data that cannot be analyzed, primarily because the data is textual data. And the problem with textual data is that it traditionally cannot be analyzed by a computer.

Creating the Integrated Data Warehouse

At this point, the decision is made to organize the textual data into a data warehouse.

The first step is to define the stop words, synonyms, and homographs. In addition, the first attempt at defining external categories is made. The integration software APEX chose to use for this process provided a starter list of these parameters. But the data analysts from APEX Insurance Company modified the initial parameters that were provided.

The next step is to identify the sources of loss report data. There are surprisingly many different sources of textual data. Some textual data comes from PCs; some comes from mainframe technology; and some comes from the email collection.

There is so much source data that it is prudent to use only a representative subset of the source data for the first iteration of building the unstructured database.

The subset of the source data is fed into the integration engine that uses the stop words, synonyms, and homographs to integrate the data. In the creation of the synonyms, the differences in terminology are addressed. The differences in terminology implemented as synonym concatenations allow the end user to access and analyze data either by local, specific, or category reference.

First Iteration

The first iteration of the unstructured database is created. The analysts look at the results and find some immediate and obvious errors. They make adjustments to the stop word list, in addition to the synonym and homograph list. And a few external category adjustments are made. After these adjustments are in place, the insurance company reruns the subset of source data into the integration engine to reproduce the unstructured database.

The iterative process is repeated until such time as the unstructured database has no more obvious errors or omissions. Then, the large body of source data is run into the integration engine. A full set of data would have been produced had the run completed. But approximately 75% of the way through the load, the integration information ran out of space in the placement of the data.

The development team backs up and allocates more space. In addition, more processors and main memory are added. The source data is teed up for processing once again.

This time, the integration engine loads properly. The analysts notice a few errors and make some adjustments to the stop words, synonyms, and homographs so that those adjustments will be in place upon rerunning the load process.

Now, the development analysts load the full set of data once again. Preparations are made for the ongoing entry of new loss reports on a weekly basis.

The next step is to link the unstructured data to the structured data. The structured data environment has much information about customer and policy, among other topics. The linkage is made by means of a static link. A static link table is created. The linkage is then made by means of matching policy ID from the unstructured to the structured environment. The static link is to be updated weekly as new loss reports are entered into the system.

Periodically, an audit report is made to make sure that when a loss report points to a policy that the policy, in fact, exists. If the policy does not exist, a special audit report is created so that an analyst can determine what is happening and can make corrections.

After the databases are loaded, the analysts now need to create the external categories. It is in the construction of the external categories that much of the analytical capabilities' power is unleashed. Stated differently, without external categorization, the analysts are restricted to only the simplest form of analysis.

Some of the external categories that are loaded include the following:

- **Casualty type**—Fire, flood, theft
- **Tangible item type**—Expensive or inexpensive, marketable or unmarketable, unique or nonunique
- **Date of loss**—Year, month, day

The analysts create as many external categories as they want to organize data by. The external categories are loaded into the glossary maintained by the system.

When the unstructured data is loaded and the static linkage is created and loaded, the analysts can now start to access and analyze the unstructured database.

The analysts want two kinds of reports. One kind of report looks only at the unstructured database. The other kind of report needs to link unstructured with structured data.

The kinds of analysis that the analysts want to do vary from day to day. Some of the typical analyses include looking for patterns:

- Of loss by seasonality
- Of loss by expense of loss
- Of loss by items lost
- By similarity of loss

After the basic loss report data has been loaded into the claims database, the next step is to load other related and useful data. The intent of loading other related data is to allow the analytical processing the opportunity to look at many different facets of claim data.

Second Iteration

The second iteration of analyses captures and addresses condition reports, estimates, and a linkage to the insured.

The condition reports describe the condition of the loss. Usually, the condition report is made by the insurance adjustor. But occasionally, a condition report will be made by other individuals, such as the insurance agent or the insured. The condition report is primarily verbiage and is linked to the loss report by the claim number, which is common to both types of data.

The insured is the individual or corporation who actually has a policy in force where the policy covers the item that was lost, stolen, or damaged. The insured data resides in a structured database and is linked to the loss report data through a reference from the loss report to the identification of the insured.

The condition and the estimates data are added to the unstructured loss report data. In addition, a linkage is created to the insured database.

This data is the second iteration in the building of the unstructured data claims database.

Third Iteration

The third iteration takes into account a broad sweep of data. The third iteration of development for the unstructured claims database addresses settlement information, adjustor notes, emails, and other correspondence.

Settlement information resides in both a structured and an unstructured format. Each settlement note has several pieces of identifying information. There is a structured portion of settlement information where claim number, date of settlement note, and settlement reference number resides. Then there is other structured information, such as to whom the settlement was offered, the amount offered, and whether the settlement was accepted.

Then there is the unstructured component of settlement information. The unstructured component includes offers made, accepted, and rejected. The unstructured portion of settlement information is tied to the structured component by claim ID and settlement reference number. But the rest of the data is unstructured.

The unstructured settlement information is passed through the relevancy sieve to make sure that data that is not relevant to the claim is not entered into the claims database. The sieve consists of words relevant to a settlement and words that relate directly to a claim. All other information fails the relevancy test and is not entered into the unstructured claims information.

Adjustor notes are also entered into the claims database. The adjustor notes are tied to the other data through claim ID that is on every adjustor note.

Emails are entered into the database as well. They have to be passed through the relevancy screen (or sieve) to make sure that only relevant information is put into the unstructured claims database. Emails normally do not have a claim reference number. The linkage between the claims database and emails is by common textual reference points. A common textual reference point is one where the same word is found in both the email and the rest of the claims database. For example, the words "Ford 150" might be found in the claims database and the email that is added to the unstructured claims database.

There is little other correspondence among APEX employees other than emails. However, when there is other correspondence, it is converted to an electronic format and then processed in the same manner as an email.

This ends the third iteration of database development for the claims database for insurance processing.

Fourth Iteration

The fourth iteration of development for the unstructured claims database includes a wide variety of information, such as the following:

- Police reports
- Manufacturers' descriptions
- Warranty information

- Miscellaneous damage descriptions
- Other insurance information
- Witness reports

The inclusion of the miscellaneous type of information further extends the analytical possibilities of the unstructured claims database.

It is interesting to note that as each type of information is added, the possibilities for analyses of unstructured information increases while the complexity of the formulation of the query increases as well. In other words, when there are only one or two types of unstructured data in the unstructured claims database, formulating a query is fairly easy and straightforward. But as the different kinds of data are added to the unstructured claims database, the complexity of the query increases. This is because as the different type of data increases, the query needs to be specific about what data is needed for the purpose of satisfying the query.

Glossary

accuracy—A qualitative assessment of freedom from error, or a quantitative measure of the magnitude of error, expressed as a function of relative error.

ad hoc processing—One-time-only, casual access and manipulation of data on parameters never before used and usually done in a heuristic, iterative manner.

alternate storage—Storage other than disk-based storage used to hold bulk amounts of relatively inactive storage.

analytical processing—Using the computer to produce an analysis for a management decision that usually involves trend analysis, drill-down analysis, demographic analysis, and profiling.

application database—A collection of data organized to support a specific application.

attribute—A property that can assume values for entities or relationships. Entities can be assigned several attributes (for example, a tuple in a relationship consists of values). Some systems also allow relationships to have attributes.

backup—A file serving as a basis for the activity of backing up a database; usually a snapshot of a database as of some previous moment in time.

BI (business intelligence)—The activity of converting data into information.

blather—Text that is unrelated to business; text that is not useful in any way in the context of making business decisions.

blob—A format for holding unstructured data where there is nothing but raw text.

Boolean expression—An expression that designates items connected by an AND or an OR, or both.

clickstream data—Data generated in the Web environment that tracks the activity of the users of the Web site.

colloquialism—An expression intelligible to and used in a local geographic area.

column—A vertical table in which values are selected from the same domain. A row consists of one or more columns.

comments field—A data element in the structured environment used to gather text.

CPU (central processing unit)—One of the basic components of the computer, where logic is executed.

crawler—A program that accesses sites on the Internet and pulls data to an index for later reference.

CRM (customer relationship management)—A popular DSS application designed to streamline customer and corporate relationships.

database—A collection of interrelated data stored (often with controlled, limited redundancy) according to a schema. A database can serve single or multiple applications.

data element—(1) An attribute of an entity; (2) a uniquely named and well-defined category of data that consists of data items and that is included in a record of an activity.

data mart—A departmentalized structure of data feeding from the data warehouse where data is denormalized based on the department's need for information.

data model—(1) The logical data structures, including operations and constraints provided by a DBMS for effective database processing; (2) the system used for the representation of data (for example, the ERD or relational model).

data structure—A logical relationship among data elements that is designed to support specific data manipulation functions (trees, lists, and tables).

data warehouse—A collection of integrated, subject-oriented databases designed to support the DSS function, where each unit of data is relevant to some moment in time. The data warehouse contains atomic data and lightly summarized data.

DB2—A database management system by IBM.

decision support system (DSS)—A system used to support managerial decisions. Usually DSS involves the analysis of many units of data in a heuristic fashion. As a rule, DSS processing does not involve the update of data.

default value—A value designated when there is no other value.

DIS (data item set)—A grouping of data items, each of which directly relates to the key of the grouping of data in which the data items reside. The data item set is found in the midlevel model.

Documentum—A content management company.

DSS application—An application whose foundation of data is the data warehouse.

DW 2.0—An architectural specification for a modern definition of a data warehouse.

e-business—Commerce conducted based on Web interactions.

email—Electronic communications between two or more parties, often containing much blather.

entity—A person, place, or thing of interest to the data modeler at the highest level of abstraction.

ETL (extract/transform/load)—The process of taking data from one source—the source—and transforming it and loading it into another location—the target.

external categorization—The list of words created outside of and apart from another list of words or text.

external data—(1) Data originating from other than the operational systems of a corporation; (2) data residing outside the central processing complex.

external data model—A data model of data outside the boundaries of text that is held in a system.

federated query—A query made from multiple sources of data, usually dynamically.

glossary—A collection of words and their definitions. Glossaries are useful in preparing text for the treatment of terminology.

hit—A match between a list and a search argument.

homograph—Two or more words that are spelled the same but mean different things.

hot data—Data that contains especially sensitive contents.

ID 1, ID 2, ID 3, ... database—A database containing repeating identifiers.

index—The portion of the storage structure maintained to provide efficient access to a record when its index key item is known.

indirect search—A search of data related to a search argument, not the search argument itself.

integrated data warehouse—A data warehouse containing both structured and unstructured data. Usually, the structured data and the unstructured data are linked together.

internal data model—A data model created entirely from the contents of a document or collection of documents.

Internet—A network of users who have access to data and Web addresses around the world.

key—A data item or combination of data items used to identify or locate a record instance (or other similar data groups).

key, primary—A unique attribute used to identify a single record in a database.

key, secondary—A nonunique attribute used to identify a class of records in a database.

linkage—The means by which two databases can be related to each other.

loss of identity—The process of stripping data from its source or other identifying information. When data is brought in from an external source and the identity of the external source is discarded, loss of identity occurs. It is a common practice with microprocessor data.

Lotus—A system for managing email.

metadata—(1) Data about data; (2) the description of the structure, content, keys, and indexes of data.

MicroStrategy—A BI company that analyzes text using underlying SQL.

negativity exclusion—The act of not indexing a reference because of some form of negativity associated with the reference.

networked spreadsheets—Spreadsheets that are linked by one or more common values.

nontextual unstructured data—Unstructured data that does not contain text, usually graphic data.

Ontology—A taxonomy with internal structures.

Oracle—A popular database management system.

Outlook—A popular email system.

Pareto—A means of displaying numbers by relatively spaced bars.

prefacing value—A word or phrase that always precedes a value.

probabilistic match—A match made based on probability, not certainty.

proximity—Words that are close to each other within a predefined boundary.

query language—A language that enables an end user to interact directly with a DBMS to retrieve and possibly modify data held under the DBMS.

search argument—A value provided to a search engine to direct the search.

search engine—Software designed to look through an index based on a search argument.

semistructured—The environment in which unstructured data appears in a repeatable manner.

simple search—The act of looking for a word based on the search argument.

snippet—A string of words showing the words that occur before and after a word that is being searched.

SOM (self-organizing map)—A visualization for textual information.

spiral development—Iterative development, as opposed to waterfall development.

SQL—A relational query language; the standard query language for analytics.

strong match—In probabilistic matching, a match that is made where the probability of accuracy is high.

stemming—The activity of reducing words to their Latin or Greek roots.

stop word—A word that is useful for the flow of language but not for relating to the meaning of language.

synonym resolution—Replacement—the act of replacing one synonym with another; concatenation—the act of adding a synonym when a match is detected.

taxonomy—The articulation of the divisions and subdivisions of an entity.

terminology—The dialectic contents of a region or group of individuals.

textual analytics—The activity of analyzing text.

transcripted telephone conversation—A telephone conversation that has been formatted into an electronically recognizable form.

unstructured data—Text; textual data found in emails, reports, documents, medical records, spreadsheets. There is no format, structure, or repeatability to unstructured textual data.

unstructured database—A database whose contents consist of unstructured data.

Vb.net—A programming language supported by Microsoft that is useful for procedural execution.

weak match—A probabilistic match in which the probability of accuracy is low.

wild card—The specification of a search argument for which the argument contains letters that are unknown and are unspecified.

Index

Symbols

1:*n* proximity searches, 191
360-degree view of customer, 145-146

A

access integration, 66
  performance limitations, 66-68
access probability, filtering data based on, 123
accessibility of unstructured data, 9
accessing
  data linkages, 118-122
  multiple tables, 109-110
  spreadsheets, 137
  unstructured databases, 108
    in integrated data warehouses, 182-183
accuracy, degree in semistructured data, 78-79
alerts, 38
altering source text, 52
alternate spellings, 58
alternate terms, indirect searches of, 53
analysis
  global spreadsheet analysis, 142
  of structured and unstructured data, 113-114
    intersection of data, 115-118
  in textual analytics methodology, 170-173
  unstructured databases for, 108-111
  of visualizations, 132
analytical environment, 26-31
  in structured systems, 49
analytical processing. *See* textual analytics

applications, 17
  of integrated data, 61-65
archiving emails, 144
arguments in searches, 34, 38
  enhancements to, 42-43
attributes of records, 19

B

basic word string snippet reports, 192-194
BI (Business Intelligence) technology, 26-27
blather in emails, 144-145
blobs of data, preventing, 96-97
Boolean expressions, 43
browsing queries, 118
Business Intelligence (BI) technology, 26-27
business relevance, determining, 54

C

case studies
  contract management through unstructured
    database, 209-214
  corporate taxonomy (glossary) creation, 215-218
  database for harmful chemicals, 203-208
  insurance claims case study (data warehouse),
    219-225
  textual analytics in medical research, 195-202
case-sensitivity, removing, 58
categories, external, 60-61
  in simple pointers, 106-107
CDI, 124
cell identification in spreadsheets, 141

changing source text, 52

characteristics of unstructured data, 5-8

chemical reports (harmful chemicals) case study, 203-208

choosing. *See* selecting

cluster diagrams, 43-44

clustering text for visualizations, 130

colloquial terms, defined, 197

common data patterns in semistructured data, 75-76

common values in spreadsheets, 141-142

communication

  customer communications

    collecting, 145-146

    integration of, 62-64

  forms of

    corporate contracts, 25-26

    emails, 21-22

    legal information, 24-25

    medical records, 23-24

    spreadsheets, 22

    transcripted telephone conversations, 23

  linking, 114-115

  as unstructured data, 21, 124

communications-based linkages between structured and unstructured databases, 177

computers, components of, 16-17

concatenation

  synonym, 56

  textual, 161-162

conflicting values in semistructured data, 77-78

context of language, 44-45

contract management through unstructured database case study, 209-214

contracts

  corporate contracts, 25-26

  as unstructured data, 3, 125

corporate contracts, 25-26

corporate functions, unstructured data in, 3-4

corporate glossary, creating, 158

corporate ontology, creating, 159-160

corporate taxonomy, creating, 39-40, 159

  case study, 215-218

cost of unstructured data, 10

crawlers, 37

CRM (customer relationship management) systems, 62-63, 124

cross equivalency in spreadsheets, 141-142

customer communications

  collecting, 145-146

  integration of, 62-64

customer relationship management (CRM) systems, 62-63, 124

D

dangerous chemicals. *See* harmful chemicals case study

data flow in unstructured databases, 96-97

data integrity, need for, 86-87

data marts, 27-28

data models for metadata, 150

  basis for, 150-152

  corporate glossary, creating, 158

  corporate ontology, creating, 159-160

  corporate taxonomy, creating, 159

  external data model, 155-156

  generic data model, 156-158

  internal data model, 154-157

  levels of, 152-153

  relationships among components, 153-154

  role in building infrastructure, 160

data patterns, 75-76

data quality in unstructured environment, 161-162

data volume. *See* volume of data

data warehouses, 27, 86-87

  DW 2.0 architecture, 91-93

  insurance claims case study, 219-225

  integrated data warehouses, 179-180

    housing in DBMS, 180-182

    simple queries, 182-183

  unstructured databases as, 176

database management system (DBMS), 17-19

  housing integrated data warehouses, 180-182

databases, in harmful chemicals case study, 203-208. *See also* structured databases; unstructured databases

decision support data, 86

default values, in semistructured data, 77

definitions, creating for corporate taxonomy (glossary) creation case study, 218

degree of accuracy, in semistructured data, 78-79

departments, 3-4

document consolidation, 59

document/word databases. *See* unstructured databases

documents, moving in simple pointers, 104-105

DW 2.0 (data warehouse architecture), 91-93

dynamic links, 117-118

E

ECM (Enterprise Content Management), 44

editing, types of, 163

electronic format, transferring paper data to
    (harmful chemicals case study), 205
emails, 21-22
    archiving, 144
    characteristics of, 143-144
    for collecting customer communications, 145-146
    purpose of, 143
    screening, 144-145
    as unstructured data, 2
enhancements to search arguments, 42-43
Enterprise Content Management (ECM), 44
entities, in data model, 152
environments. *See* analytical environment;
    structured environment; unstructured
    environment
equivocations, creating for corporate taxonomy
    (glossary) creation case study, 218
ETL (extract/transform/load) processing, 180
external categories, 60-61, 150
    creating, 167
        contract management case study, 211
        harmful chemicals case study, 207
    in data model, 153
    in insurance claims case study, 222
    in simple pointers, 106-107
external data models, 155-156
external metadata, 149
    data models for, 150-151

F

false positives, avoiding, 115
federated analytical technology with integrated
    data warehouses, 182
federated queries, 41, 181
file types, selecting, 51-52
filtering data based on access probability,
    increasing performance with, 123
first generation textual analytics, 33, 89
    cluster diagrams, 43-44
    context of language, 44-45
    federated queries, 41
    hyperlinks, creating, 40
    index searches, 36-37
    integration of unstructured data, 41-42
    locations of unstructured data, 35-36
    multiple language searches, 39
    output of searches, 35
    pattern searches, 34-35
    schedulers, 38
    search argument enhancements, 42-43

search arguments, 38
simplicity of, 34
tagging source text, 38-39
taxonomies, creating, 39-40
flow of data in unstructured databases, 96-97
formatting hits (in searches), 35
    as hyperlinks, 40
    as taxonomies, 39-40
foundation integration, 66
    performance limitations, 66-68
future capabilities of unstructured databases,
    124-125

G–H

general classifications, defined, 197
generic data models, 156-158
global spreadsheet analysis, 142
glossaries (corporate), creating, 158
    case study, 215-218

harmful chemicals case study, 203-208
high-level design of unstructured databases, 109
hits (in searches), 34
    formatting, 35
        as hyperlinks, 40
        as taxonomies, 39-40
homogeneous data, selecting for visualizations,
    128-129
homograph resolution, 57
homographic editing, 164
homographs
    defining, 166
    in simple pointers, 105-106
hot data in unstructured databases, 111
hot emails, 144-145
hyperlinks, creating, 40

I

identifier-based linkages between structured and
    unstructured databases, 178
identifiers for spreadsheets, 138
increasing performance
    filtering based on access probability, 123
    with priority rankings, 122-123
indexes. *See also* external categories
    searching, 36-37
    in unstructured databases, 99-100
indexing
    all unstructured data, 102
    selective unstructured data, 103

semistructured data, 100
  with simple pointers, 104-107
indirect indexes. *See* external categories
indirect searches of alternate terms, 53
indirect searches of related terms, 53
indirect SQL queries, 189-191
industries, unstructured data in, 4-5
information systems
  DW 2.0 (data warehouse architecture), 91-93
  growth of, 83-87
    data integrity, 86-87
    online processing, 83-84
    personal computers, 85
  unstructured data, need for inclusion, 87-91
insurance claims case study (data warehouse),
      219-225
integrated data warehouses. *See* data warehouses
integration. *See also* methodology for textual
      analytics
  of text for visualizations, 129
  of unstructured and structured databases, 175-176
    communications-based linkages, 177
    housing in DBMS, 180-182
    identifier-based linkages, 178
    as integrated data warehouse, 179-180
    simple queries, 182-183
    word linkages, 176-177
  of unstructured data, 41-42, 49-50, 89-91
    external categorization, 60-61
    importance of, 53-54
    issues to address, 54-60
    reading raw text, 50-52
    selecting file type, 51-52
    selecting type of integration, 65-70
    usage examples, 61-65
integrity of data, 86-87
internal data models, 154-157
  corporate glossary, creating, 158
  corporate ontology, creating, 159-160
  corporate taxonomy, creating, 159
internal metadata, 148-149
  data models for, 152
intersecting structured and unstructured data,
      115-118. *See also* linking
iterative development
  contract management case study, 211-212
  of visualizations, 131

J-K-L

joining linkage data, 120-122

keys
  in records, 18
  for relational tables, 98-99
KPIs (key performance indicators), 26

languages
  context of, 44-45
  multiple languages, searching, 39
  in unstructured data, 10
lassos, 132
legal information, 24-25
linkages (of structured and unstructured data)
  accessing, 118-122
  monitoring, 119-120
  multi-database linkages, 179-180
  real-time online queries, 122-124
linking. *See also* intersecting structured and
      unstructured data
  communications, 114-115
  with dynamic links, 117-118
  with probabilistic links, 116-117
  with semistructured data, 116
  with static links, 117-118
  unstructured and structured databases
    communications-based linkages, 177
    identifier-based linkages, 178
    word linkages, 176-177
loading unstructured databases, 110

M

m:n proximity searches, 191
many-to-many joins, 121-122
medical field, unstructured data in, 124
medical records, 23-24
  as unstructured data, 3
medical research case study (textual analytics),
      195-202
metadata, 62
  data models for, 150
    basis for data model, 150-152
    corporate glossary, creating, 158
    corporate ontology, creating, 159-160
    corporate taxonomy, creating, 159
    external data model, 155-156
    generic data model, 156-158
    internal data model, 154-157
    levels of data model, 152-153
    relationships among components, 153-154
    role in building infrastructure, 160

definition of, 147
in spreadsheets, 138-139
in structured environment, 147-148
in unstructured environment, 148
  external metadata, 149
  internal metadata, 148-149
methodology for textual analytics, 163
analysis stage, 170-173
preparation stage, 163-167
processing stage, 167-168
source data organization stage, 168-170
mid-level data model, 153
misspellings, 58
monitoring linkages, 119-120
moving documents in simple pointers, 104-105
multi-database linkages, 179-180
multiple languages, searching, 39
multiple tables, accessing, 109-110

N–O

natural language processing (nlp), 44-45
negativity exclusion, 58
network managers, 16
non-textual unstructured data, 2
numeric data in spreadsheets, 140

OCR (optical character recognition), 50, 205
one-to-many joins, 121
online processing, 83-84
ontology, creating corporate ontology, 159-160
operating systems, 16
opportunities of unstructured data, 11-12
optical character recognition (OCR), 50, 205
organization of source data in textual analytics
    methodology, 168-170
organizational functions, 3-4
output of searches in first generation textual
    analytics, formatting, 35, 39-40
output types for preprocessing semistructured
    data, 80-81

P

paper, converting to electronic data, 50, 205
partial searches, 124
pattern searches, in first generation textual
    analytics, 34-35
patterns of data in semistructured data, 75-76
performance, increasing
  filtering based on access probability, 123
  with priority rankings, 122-123

performance limitations, access integration
    versus foundation integration, 66-68
permutations of words, 54
personal computers, 85
phrases, support for, 57
pointers, simple, 104-107
prefaced values in semistructured data, 76-77
preparation stage in textual analytics
    methodology, 163-167
preparation time for preprocessing
    semistructured data, 82
preprocessing semistructured data, 79-80
  preparation time for, 82
  variable output types for, 80-81
prioritization
  increasing performance with, 122-123
  of unstructured data, 10
probabilistic links, 116-117
processing stage in textual analytics methodology,
    167-168
proximity SQL queries, 191-192
punctuation, removing, 58

Q

quality of data in unstructured environment,
    161-162
queries. *See also* analysis
  browsing queries, 118
  federated queries, 41, 181
  real-time online queries, 122-124
  simple queries, 182-183
  SQL queries in textual analytics, 185-187
    basic word string snippet reports, 192-194
    indirect query example, 189-191
    proximity query example, 191-192
    simple query example, 187-189
  to unstructured and structured data
    simultaneously, 93

R

raw text, reading, 50-52
reading raw text, 50-52
real-time online queries, 122-124
recasting visualizations, 132
records in tables, 18-19
reducing words to stems, 55
related terms, indirect searches of, 53
relational tables in unstructured databases, 97-99
relevance, determining, 54

removing
case-sensitivity, 58
punctuation, 58
stop words, 54
retrieval of structured data, speed of, 19-20
rows in tables, 18-19

S

schedulers, 38
screening emails, 144-145
search arguments, 38
enhancements to, 42-43
search technologies, 33, 89
cluster diagrams, 43-44
context of language, 44-45
federated queries, 41
hyperlinks, creating, 40
index searches, 36-37
integration of unstructured data, 41-42
locations of unstructured data, 35-36
multiple language searches, 39
output of searches, 35
pattern searches, 34-35
schedulers, 38
search argument enhancements, 42-43
search arguments, 38
simplicity of, 34
tagging source text, 38-39
taxonomies, creating, 39-40
searchability of unstructured data, 10
searches
indirect searches, 53
partial (wild card) searches, 124
permutations of words, 54
simple searches, 53
second generation textual analytics, 50, 89-91
external categorization, 60-61
importance of integration, 53-54
issues to address, 54-60
reading raw text, 50-52
selecting file type, 51-52
selecting type of integration, 65-70
usage examples, 61-65
security of unstructured data, 10
selecting
file types, 51-52
homogeneous data for visualizations, 128-129
integration type, 65-70

self-organizing map (SOM), 130-131
analyzing, 132
recasting, 132
for semistructured data, 133
semantic processing, 44
semistructured data, 34-35, 73
common data patterns, 75-76
conflicting values, 77-78
default values, 77
degree of accuracy, 78-79
in emails, 144
examples of, 74-75
indexing, 100
linking with, 116
prefaced values, 76-77
preprocessing, 79-82
in spreadsheets, 140
visualizations of, 131-133
semistructured processing
harmful chemicals case study, 205-206
on unstructured data, 81
sensitive data, 111
simple pointers, 104-107
simple queries, 182-183, 187-189
simple searches, importance of integration, 53
simplicity of first generation textual analytics, 34
snippets of text, 188
basic word string snippet reports, 192-194
SOM (self-organizing map), 130-131
analyzing, 132
recasting, 132
for semistructured data, 133
source data organization stage in textual analytics
methodology, 168-170
source text
altering, 52
tagging, 38-39
spellings of words, 58
spreadsheets, 22, 135-137
accessing, 137
cell identification, 141
challenges of, 135-137
cross equivalency, 141-142
global spreadsheet analysis, 142
types of data in, 138-140
unique identification for, 138
as unstructured data, 125
SQL interface, accessing unstructured
databases, 108

SQL queries in textual analytics, 185-187
  basic word string snippet reports, 192-194
  indirect query example, 189-191
  proximity query example, 191-192
  simple query example, 187-189
static links, 117-118
  processing independently, 120
stemming, 55, 164, 167
stop words
  defining, 164
  removing, 54
stop-word editing, 163
storage of structured data, speed of, 19-20
structured data
  analyzing with unstructured data, 113-114
    accessing linkages, 118-122
    intersection of data, 115-118
    real-time online queries, 122-124
  explained, 1
  integration of unstructured data with, 90-91
  updating, 9
structured databases, integration with
    unstructured databases, 175-176
  communications-based linkages, 177
  housing in DBMS, 180-182
  identifier-based linkages, 178
  as integrated data warehouse, 179-180
  simple queries, 182-183
  word linkages, 176-177
structured environment, 15-16, 18-20
  bringing unstructured data into, 30-31
  computer components in, 16-17
  DBMS in, 17-19
  integration of unstructured environment with,
    49-50
    external categorization, 60-61
    importance of, 53-54
    issues to address, 54-60
    reading raw text, 50-52
    selecting file type, 51-52
    selecting type of integration, 65-70
    usage examples, 61-65
  metadata in, 147-148
  storage and retrieval, speed of, 19-20
  storing all unstructured data in, 102
  storing selective unstructured data in, 103
  textual analytics in, versus unstructured
    environment, 28-30
structured systems
  analytical environment in, 49
  unstructured systems versus, 47-49

synonym concatenation, 56
synonyms
  defining, 164-165
  editing, 163
  replacing, 56
  resolving, 56-57
  in simple pointers, 105-106

T

tables
  in databases, 18-19
  multiple tables, accessing, 109-110
  relational tables in unstructured databases, 97-99
tagging source text, 38-39
taxonomies, creating, 39-40, 159
  case study, 215-218
terminology
  in corporate taxonomy (glossary) creation case study,
    217-218
  in insurance claims case study (data warehouse), 220
  in medical research case study, 196-197
  in unstructured data, 9
text, visualizing. *See* visualizations
text clustering for visualizations, 130
text integration for visualizations, 129
textual analytics
  challenges for, 9-10
  contract management case study, 209-214
  first generation technologies, 33, 89
    cluster diagrams, 43-44
    context of language, 44-45
    federated queries, 41
    hyperlinks, creating, 40
    index searches, 36-37
    integration of unstructured data, 41-42
    locations of unstructured data, 35-36
    multiple language searches, 39
    output of searches, 35
    pattern searches, 34-35
    schedulers, 38
    search argument enhancements, 42-43
    search arguments, 38
    simplicity of, 34
    tagging source text, 38-39
    taxonomies, creating, 39-40
  harmful chemicals case study, 203-208
  medical research case study, 195-202
  methodology for, 163
    analysis stage, 170-173
    preparation stage, 163-167

processing stage, 167-168
source data organization stage, 168-170
second generation textual analytics, 50, 89-91
  external categorization, 60-61
  importance of integration, 53-54
  issues to addresss, 54-60
  reading raw text, 50-52
  selecting file type, 51-52
  selecting type of integration, 65-70
  usage examples, 61-65
SQL queries in, 185-187
  basic word string snippet reports, 192-194
  indirect query example, 189-191
  proximity query example, 191-192
  simple query example, 187-189
in unstructured environment versus structured
  environment, 28-30
visualizations, 127-128
  analyzing, 132
  creating, 128-131
  recasting, 132
  for semistructured data, 133
textual concatenation, 161-162
textual integration. *See* integration
textual unstructured data. *See* unstructured data
themes of data, 59
transaction processing data, 86
  unstructured data versus, 88
transcripted telephone conversations, 23

U

unique identification for spreadsheets, 138
unstructured data. *See also* textual analytics;
  unstructured databases; unstructured
  environment
  analyzing with structured data, 113-114
    accessing linkages, 118-122
    intersection of data, 115-118
    real-time online queries, 122-124
  bringing into structured environment, 30-31
  characteristics of, 5-8
  in corporate functions, 3-4
  in DW 2.0 (data warehouse architecture), 91-93
  emails. *See* emails
  explained, 2-3
  first generation textual analytics. *See* first generation
    textual analytics
  inclusion in information systems, need for, 87-91

in industries, 4-5
integration of, 41-42, 89-91
non-textual unstructured data, 2
opportunities of, 11-12
purpose of, 21
semistructured processing on, 81
spreadsheets. *See* spreadsheets
transaction processing data versus, 88
types of, 2-3
updating, lack of, 9
unstructured databases, 95. *See also* unstructured
  data; unstructured environment
accessing through SQL interface, 108
for analysis, 108-111
contract management case study, 209-214
as data warehouses, 176
flow of data, 96-97
future capabilities of, 124-125
high-level design of, 109
hot data in, 111
indexes, types of, 99-100
integration with structured databases, 175-176
  communications-based linkages, 177
  housing in DBMS, 180-182
  identifier-based linkages, 178
  as integrated data warehouse, 179-180
  simple queries, 182-183
  word linkages, 176-177
large volumes of data in, 101-102
multiple tables, accessing, 109-110
relational tables in, 97-99
simple pointers in, 104-107
storing all unstructured data in, 102
storing selective unstructured data in, 103
unstructured environment, 20-26. *See also*
  unstructured data; unstructured databases
communication, forms of
  corporate contracts, 25-26
  emails, 21-22
  legal information, 24-25
  medical records, 23-24
  spreadsheets, 22
  transcripted telephone conversations, 23
data quality in, 161-162
integration with structured environment, 49-50
  external categorization, 60-61
  importance of, 53-54
  issues to address, 54-60
  reading raw text, 50-52
  selecting file type, 51-52

selecting type of integration, 65-70
usage examples, 61-65
metadata in, 148
external metadata, 149
internal metadata, 148-149
textual analytics in, 28-30
unstructured systems, structured systems versus,
47-49
unstructured textual data. *See* unstructured data
updating structured/unstructured data, 9

V

VCR (voice character recognition), 51-52
visualizations, 43-44, 127-128
analyzing, 132
creating, 128
iterative development, 131
selecting homogeneous data, 128-129
as SOM(self-organizing map), 130-131
text clustering, 130
text integration, 129
recasting, 132
for semistructured data, 133
voice character recognition (VCR), 51-52
voice recordings, converting to electronic data,
51-52
volume of data, 10
in insurance claims case study, 220-225
in medical research case study, 197-198
in unstructured databases, 101-102

W–Z

weak links, 177
wild cards, 42-43, 124
word linkages between structured and
unstructured databases, 176-177
word permutations, 54
word stemming, 55, 164, 167
word-to-word proximity searches, 191
worksheets. *See* spreadsheets

THIS BOOK IS SAFARI ENABLED

INCLUDES FREE 45-DAY ACCESS TO THE ONLINE EDITION

The Safari® Enabled icon on the cover of your favorite technology book means the book is available through Safari Bookshelf. When you buy this book, you get free access to the online edition for 45 days.

Safari Bookshelf is an electronic reference library that lets you easily search thousands of technical books, find code samples, download chapters, and access technical information whenever and wherever you need it.

TO GAIN 45-DAY SAFARI ENABLED ACCESS TO THIS BOOK:

- Go to **http://www.prenhallprofessional.com/safarienabled**

- Complete the brief registration form

- Enter the coupon code found in the front of this book on the "Copyright" page

PRENTICE
HALL

87969155R00188

REVOLUTION IN ZANZIBAR

An American's Cold War Tale

Don Petterson

A Member of the Perseus Books Group

For JULIE, *again,*
and for
SUSAN, JULIANNE, JOHN, *and* BRIAN

Copyright © 2002 by Westview Press, A Member of the Perseus Books Group

Published in 2002 in the United States of America by Westview Press, 5500 Central Avenue, Boulder, Colorado 80301-2877, and in the United Kingdom by Westview Press, 12 Hid's Copse Road, Cumnor Hill, Oxford OX2 9JJ

Find us on the world wide web at www.westviewpress.com

Westview Press books are available at special discounts for bulk purchases in the United States by corporations, institutions, and other organizations. For more information, please contact the Special Markets Department at The Perseus Books Group, 11 Cambridge Center, Cambridge MA 02142, or call (617) 252-5298, (800) 255-1514 or email j.mccrary@perseusbooks.com

A Cataloging-in-Publication Data record is available at the Library of Congress.
ISBN 0-8133-4268-6 (paperback).

The paper used in this publication meets the requirements of the American National Standard for Permanence of Paper for Printed Library Materials Z39.48-1984.

10   9   8   7   6   5   4   3   2   1

Contents

List of Ilustrations   vii
Preface   ix
Acknowledgments   xi
List of Acronyms   xiii
Prologue   xv

PART 1: Revolution   **1**

  1 THE SPICE ISLAND   3

  2 BEFORE THE STORM   13

  3 ON THE EVE   33

  4 REVOLUTION: DAY ONE   47

  5 DAY TWO   71

  6 UNDER ARREST   91

  7 HOLDING THE FORT   105

  8 PEOPLE'S REPUBLIC   121

  9 OUT AND BACK   137

PART 2: The Cold War Comes to Zanzibar   **155**

  10 STARTING OVER   157

  11 RED TIDE RISING   171

  12 UNION   189

  13 UPS AND DOWNS   211

  14 DÉJÀ VU   237

  15 KWAHERI   255

Epilogue   265
Notes   273
Index   277

List of Illustrations

Maps

Zanzibar Island   2
East African Coast   5
Zanzibar Town   21
Zanzibar Town and environs   48

Photographs

Zanzibar Town skyline   6
Arab notables   10
House at Mtoni   18
American consulate/embassy   22
Abeid Amani Karume   35
Prerevolution Government of Zanzibar   40
Sultan Jamshid bin Abdulla   42
Sultan's palace, Zanzibar Town   57
House of Wonders   60
Field Marshal John Okello   70
Adam Mwakanjuki and rebel companion   77
Mohamed Abdulrahman Babu   109
Main Street, Stone Town   124
Author being expelled from Zanzibar   152
Frank Carlucci at hoeing ceremony   197
Presidents Karume and Nyerere   206
May Day–celebration effigies   212

Carlucci and Petterson (hidden by demonstrators)   234

Julie, Susan, and Julianne   238

Cartoon

"Greetings! I am the new comrade." (Bill Mauldin cartoon)   87

Preface

Like an unexpected comet, at the beginning of 1964 the fabled spice
island of Zanzibar came blazing into view, held the world's attention for
several days, then gradually faded back into obscurity.

On January 12, an armed uprising in the newly independent island
nation toppled the one-month-old government and in the space of a few
days took thousands of lives. Some sixty Americans living in Zanzibar
were caught up in the violent events of the revolution.

Capitalizing on the turmoil and the hesitancy of Western governments to recognize the new, apparently Marxist, revolutionary government that had come to power, the Soviet Union, Communist China, and
East Germany all quickly established an influential presence in Zanzibar.
The British and American governments saw Zanzibar as a Communist
cancer that could spread to mainland Africa and threaten their interests
there. For a time, the president of the United States and the prime minister of Great Britain themselves were preoccupied with the Zanzibar
issue.

The editors of *Time* magazine were going to make the Zanzibar revolution the lead international story, perhaps even the cover story, of their
January 17, 1964, issue. But an outbreak of violence in Panama, possibly
endangering the canal, pushed aside the attention given to the Zanzibar
story, and the intense interest in it began to wane not long afterward.

The only Western book wholly devoted to the revolution is *The
Zanzibar Revolution and Its Aftermath*, by Anthony Clayton.[1] Written from
a British standpoint and in general an excellent scholarly account, the

few remarks it makes about the Americans in Zanzibar contain factual errors or incorrect judgments. Until now, nothing at all has been published from an American perspective.

I am the only American who was in Zanzibar during a period that spanned the months leading up to independence, the revolution from its outbreak to its consolidation, and almost two years afterward. The story I tell in this book is one I have related in fragments over the years to family and friends. This is the first time, however, that I have told the tale in its entirety. I recount what happened in that time at that place from the vantage point of the handful of Americans who were caught up in the revolution's turbulence. I have also composed an account of the grave concern within the American and British governments about the events in Zanzibar in 1964 and 1965.

When my memory—leached as it is by the passing years—has needed help, I have drawn on published materials, the notes I took during my earliest months in Zanzibar, the diary I kept for a brief time, the letters my wife and I wrote from Zanzibar, interviews I have had with people who were there during the revolution, and declassified U.S. State Department documents.

The Zanzibar revolution is now only a footnote to the larger history of postcolonial Africa. Its effect on American diplomacy was ephemeral and is known to only a handful of people today. Yet I believe that what happened to the Americans in Zanzibar in 1963–1964 is a compelling tale, not only because of the human drama that was played out in a background of intrigue and violence but also because it provides a good example of how profoundly Cold War considerations affected U.S. foreign policy in Africa.

And with a return of political violence to Zanzibar in 2001, a look at the past provides a good reference for the present.

Don Petterson
Brentwood, N.H.

Acknowledgments

Of my nine assignments to African countries, the most tumultuous were the first, Zanzibar, and the penultimate, Sudan. The events of both, I came to believe, were stories worth telling. When I wrote *Inside Sudan* (Westview Press, 1999), I did not see a compelling need for the reminiscences of others to help flesh out my narrative. It was a different matter, however, when it came to the preparation of my manuscript about Zanzibar's revolution.

The recollections of some of my friends who were in Zanzibar during the era of the revolution have been of immeasurable help in putting together the following account. In interviews, these friends provided information that filled some gaps, corrected mistakes in my remembrances, or added some vitality to other source material. I am indebted to Brian Banks, James Bourn, Teresa Burch, Frank Carlucci, Richard Fox, Robert Hennemeyer, Jack Mower, Dale and Marilyn Povenmire, Carol Preece, and the late Rex Preece and Jim Ruchti, both of whom I talked to not long before they passed away in 2000.

I am also grateful to Brian Banks, Wolf Dourado, Jack Mower, the Povenmires, and Carol Preece for the comments they made after reading the manuscript.

Kelley Conway's thoughts on my first draft set me in the right direction in organizing and otherwise improving the text.

My thanks also to my wife, Julie, for helping me reconstruct certain events of the Zanzibar story.

D. P.

List of Acronyms

ASP	Afro-Shirazi Party
ASYL	Afro-Shirazi Youth League
CU	Bureau of Educational and Cultural Affairs
CCM	Chama Cha Mapinduzi
EAA	East African Airways
E&E	Emergency and Evacuation
FRG	Federal Republic of Germany
FRTU	Federation of Revolutionary Trade Unions
FSI	Foreign Service Institute
FSO	Foreign Service officer
GDR	German Democratic Republic
HMG	Her Majesty's Government
NASA	National Aeronautics and Space Agency
NCOs	Noncommissioned officers
PL	Public Law
TAA	Tanganyika African Association
TANU	Tanganyika African National Union
USAID	United States Agency for International Development
USIA	United States Information Agency
USIS	United States Information Service
ZPPP	Zanzibar and Pemba People's Party
ZNP	Zanzibar Nationalist Party

Prologue

Americans at the end of 1963 were still reeling from the assassination of John F. Kennedy in November and taking the measure of Lyndon Johnson in the White House.

The year had seen the march on Washington of 200,000 people demanding equality for blacks with whites, a march that culminated in Martin Luther King's "I Have a Dream" speech at the Lincoln Memorial.

In 1963, the number of U.S. military personnel in Vietnam would increase to 15,000.

In an eight-to-one decision, the United States Supreme Court ruled that laws requiring the recitation of the Lord's Prayer or Bible verses in public schools were unconstitutional.

Sydney Poitier became the first African American to win the Academy Award for best actor; *Tom Jones* won the Best Picture award.

The Feminine Mystique, *Silent Spring*, and *The Spy Who Came in from the Cold* were published.

The top pop song of the year was Jimmy Gilmer and the Fireballs's "Sugar Shack"; the Beatles were big in Britain, and Beatlemania in the United States was less than a year away.

The Los Angeles Dodgers, recently transplanted from Brooklyn, beat the New York Yankees in the World Series.

Charles de Gaulle blocked Britain's entry into the Common Market.

Nikita Khrushchev still presided in the Kremlin but, weakened by his mistakes during the Cuban missile crisis, would soon give way to Leonid Brezhnev.

The Cultural Revolution was in full flower in China.

In Africa, the transformation from colonialism to independence continued apace. In December, Great Britain granted independence to Kenya and Zanzibar.

A 1962 *Reader's Digest* article portrayed the British protectorate of Zanzibar as an island paradise inhabited by the least-threatening people imaginable:

> A languid sea, the color of purest emerald, surrounds the lovely island. A lazy surf laps softly against beaches of white sand. Day after day the island is bathed in golden equatorial sunshine. . . . Most Zanzibaris are plump, charming and exquisitely lazy. Spared by nature from the strain of the nine-to-five grind, they devote what energies they possess to cultivating the gentle life.

"Few places on earth are as idyllic," the *Digest* article said. "An independent Zanzibar, all agree, will not set the world on fire. But it may well teach the world a lesson in how to lead the lazy, and happy, life."[1]

The author of this shallow piece of fluff completely ignored the fact that beneath the island's beauty and apparent tranquility were ethnic and class hatreds that had existed for years and had occasionally led to bloodshed. Elections in 1961 for a preindependence government were accompanied by violence; sixty-eight people—sixty-five of whom were Arabs—were killed. The outcome of the elections was a stalemate that delayed self-government for Zanzibar. Under the watchful eye of British colonial troops, the next elections, in July 1963, were generally peaceful, but the overall result—an Arab-dominated coalition government that received a minority of the votes—did nothing to ease political and social tensions.

The unhappiness of Zanzibar's African majority grew over the five months between the elections and independence day. Now ruled by men who scorned their aspirations, the Africans referred to Zanzibar's impending independence as *uhuru wa waarabu tu,* freedom for just the Arabs.

The independence celebration took place on a hot, humid, moonless night, December 10, 1963. With not even a hint of wind, the air lay

heavy and still. Zanzibari and British colonial dignitaries, foreign guests, and diplomats gathered at a raised area at the cricket pitch next to the Cooper's Institute playing fields just south of Zanzibar Town. Sitting on chairs under a large tent that was open on all sides, they looked out onto the grassy expanse. Some fifteen yards in front of them was a large, white flagpole. Beyond it stood a crowd of several thousand people, some clearly visible within the arc of brightness projected by floodlights, others only dimly seen, many invisible in the darkness.

Queen Elizabeth's representative at the ceremony, Prince Philip, wore a tropical white naval uniform with gold braid, dress sword, and ribbons and medals. The sultan of Zanzibar was resplendent in a blue, red, and gold turban and a blue robe, the upper half diagonally bisected by a red-and-gold sash. The white dress uniform of the British resident (governor) was trimmed in red and gold; his white pith helmet featured white egret feathers. The prime minister and other cabinet ministers were dressed in Arab robes.

The Aga Khan, foreign delegations, and diplomats were among the honored guests. African political-opposition leaders were seated, but not in the front row. They watched impassively, obviously taking no pleasure in the ceremony.

As the police band played "God Save the Queen," the Union Jack was lowered at midnight. For a moment, the lights were turned off. When they went back on, the flag of Zanzibar was being raised. After three volleys fired by Scots Guards and a forty-one-gun salute from British naval vessels in the harbor, the anthem of the new nation was played.

From the gathered throng came shouts and applause, but the response was strangely muted. More ominous, the Africans in the crowd were silent.

The new flag, a green clove in a circle of yellow imposed on a field of red, was fated to fly over Zanzibar for only a month.

Part 1
REVOLUTION

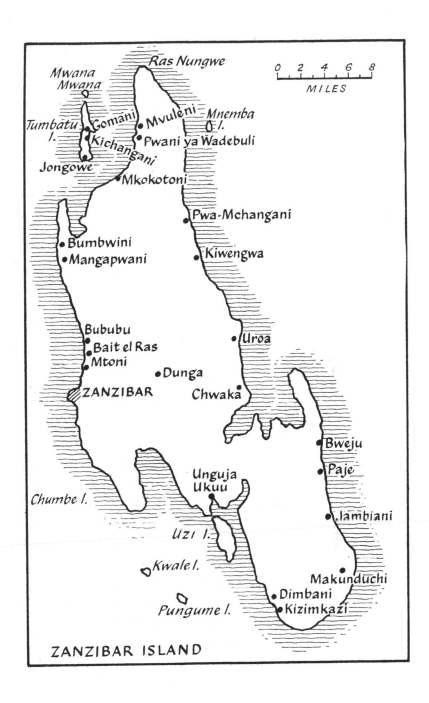

Mwana
Mwana

Ras Nungwe

Tumbatu
I.
Gomani
Kichangani
Jongowe

Mvuleni
Pwani ya Wadebuli

Mnemba
I.

Mkokotoni

Pwa-Mchangani

Bumbwini
Mangapwani

Kiwengwa

Bububu
Bait el Ras
Mtoni
ZANZIBAR

Uroa

Dunga
Chwaka

Bweju
Paje

Unguja
Ukuu

Chumbe I.

Jambiani

Uzi I.

Kwale I.

Makunduchi
Dimbani
Kizimkazi

Pungume I.

0 2 4 6 8
M I L E S

ZANZIBAR ISLAND

1

The Spice Island

Twenty-two American men, women, and children were inside the house, most of them crowded in the living room. The adults were in a state of disbelief that this could be happening in Zanzibar. With the doors closed and barred, the windows locked, and the shutters closed, it was stifling inside, as the tropical sun beat down on that hot and humid January day in 1964. The house sat in a rural area a few miles southeast of Zanzibar Town.

Those who peered through slats in the shutters could see African men furtively making their way through the trees of the surrounding area, heading for nearby houses, the homes of Arab families. The Africans were dressed for the most part in shorts and short-sleeve shirts and carried an assortment of weapons: sharp-bladed *panga*s (machetes), spears, and knives.

Momentarily, they passed from sight. Then, suddenly, the quiet was broken by shouts, and the armed men could be seen rushing the nearest neighboring house. The shouting was now joined by screams. The American onlookers saw a bearded Arab man dragged out of the doorway of the house. Struck by a *panga*, he fell to the ground, nearly decapitated. They saw no further violence, but the screaming within the house

continued for several minutes. Afterward, the attackers herded two disheveled women and three children, all five sobbing, from the house. The party moved toward another dwelling, only partially visible to the watching Americans. But all inside could hear the ensuing sounds of violence and terror, which were repeated several times in the minutes that followed as the armed men went about their grisly business.

Some of the American women began to cry, out of compassion for what was happening to the hapless Arabs and out of fear that the huddled Americans might be next. Most of the children were too young to understand what was happening, but they sensed the fear and clung to their mothers.

Zanzibar had known but little violence in most of the twentieth century. As for Americans on the island, in the 1830s commerce between New England and Zanzibar was so vigorous that the U.S. government established a consulate in Zanzibar Town in 1837. American ships, mainly from Salem, Massachusetts, came to trade cotton cloth, guns, and gunpowder for ivory and gum copal. But by the early 1900s, that commerce had dried up. In 1915, the consulate was closed and its functions moved to Mombasa, Kenya. Until 1961, there no longer was anything in Zanzibar to warrant the presence of Americans.

In the movie *Road to Zanzibar*, Bob Hope and Bing Crosby are lost, trying to find the island. A map appears on the screen, showing the two intrepid adventurers zigzagging and going around in circles in the middle of the African continent. Zanzibar in the late 1930s may have been a familiar name, but most Americans were probably as ignorant of its location as the makers of the film. And they knew even less about its history and its inhabitants.

Zanzibar lies six degrees south of the equator, about twenty-two miles off the east-central coast of Africa. A fabled land of spices, a vile center of slavery, a place of origin of expeditions into the vast, mysterious continent, the island was all these things during its heyday in the last half of the nineteenth century.

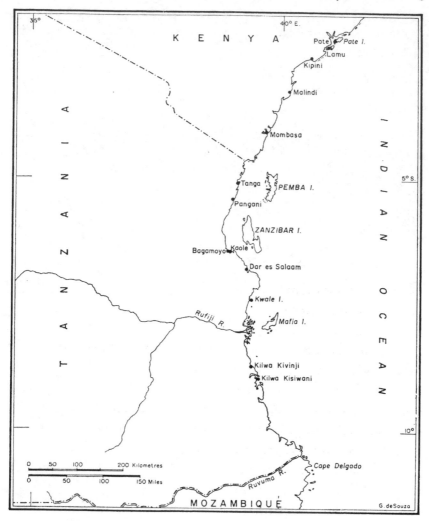

East African coast

Once a part of the mainland, a few million years ago the land that became Zanzibar Island was separated from the African continent by a shallow channel scoured out by the ocean. Its sister island of Pemba, thirty miles to the north-northeast, had been created by rift faulting millions of years earlier. Zanzibar's first known inhabitants were Bantu-speaking immigrants, people who had originated in west-central Africa and spread to the eastern and southern parts of the continent.

Zanzibar Town skyline

Swept in on the northeast trade wind, or monsoon, Arabs are known to have sailed to the eastern littoral of Africa as early as the eighth century B.C. Over the centuries, they established trading posts and then small coastal settlements. In Zanzibar, the racial mixing that blurred ethnic physical differences among many Zanzibaris began early, as Arab and other immigrants intermarried with the Africans.

The Portuguese became the dominant power of the East African coast in the sixteenth century, displacing the Arabs, whose control had grown as they expanded their slaving and other trading enterprises. In 1503, Zanzibar became a tributary of Portugal.

The two-century Portuguese era in East Africa had almost ended by 1698 when Omani Arabs captured Fort Jesus at Mombasa. After that, the whole of the coastal area, including the offshore islands, fell back into Arab hands. With its safe anchorage at Zanzibar Town and a plentiful supply of freshwater, by the early 1800s, Zanzibar had become a thriving entrepôt. By midcentury, after the sultan of Oman, Seyyid Said bin Sultan, the head of the Busaidi dynasty, transferred his capital from Muscat to Zanzibar in 1832, Zanzibar had become the most important trading center of the western Indian Ocean. It was also the hub of slav-

ing operations and the symbol of Arab oppression in East Africa. Sultan Seyyid Said's dominions included the islands of Zanzibar, Pemba, Lamu, and Mafia and the coastal areas of what are now Kenya and Tanzania. He claimed but did not control large expanses of territory extending inland.

Arab colonists now came to Zanzibar in large numbers. The new-comers, backed by the sultan's power, forced Africans to give up their land. Soon, the bulk of Zanzibar's and Pemba's most fertile lands belonged to Arabs.

Each year, hundreds of oceangoing dhows, sailing from as far as India's Malabar Coast, arrived with the monsoon's northeast winds, which began blowing in Zanzibar in November. The large, lateen-rigged boats brought cloth, iron, sugar, dates, and other trade goods. Leaving in March and April, after the monsoon winds had shifted to the southwest, the traders took with them slaves, ivory, tortoiseshell, copal, coir, coconuts, and rice.

Today's travelers to Zanzibar by boat view a scene that, from a dis-tance of a couple of miles, looks much the same as it did when explor-ers such as Sir Richard Burton, John Speke, and David Livingstone arrived there in the mid-1800s. Zanzibar Town's coral stone buildings, the sultan's palace, the minarets of mosques, the few dhows that still come to the island, and the polyglot population evoke images of the *Arabian Nights*. But whereas Zanzibar Town today is a pleasant place to visit, this was not the case a century and a half ago.

The unflattering descriptions of Zanzibar in that time emphasize the stench of the foreshore. Behind the beachfront facade of gleaming white buildings, Zanzibar Town's narrow, crooked lanes teemed with people, many of them slaves who roamed the streets in search of food. Venereal disease was rampant, as were cholera and malaria, which killed many of the Europeans who came to the island. The beaches were covered with garbage and sewage from the town. The corpses of animals added to the noisome atmosphere, and dead bodies of humans were not a rarity along the shore.

Burton, who with Speke came to Zanzibar in 1856 to mount an expe-dition to the mainland in search of the sources of the Nile, spoke lyri-cally of his first impression of the island as it appeared to him from the sea. "Earth, sea and sky, all seemed wrapped in a soft and sensuous

repose. . . . The sea of purist sapphire, which had not parted with its blue rays to the atmosphere . . . lay looking . . . under a blaze of sunshine which touched every object with a dull burnish of gold." But he quickly came to detest the place. So did Livingstone, who was in Zanzibar in 1866, preparing for his final exploration. He wrote in his diary: "The stench arising from a mile and a half or two square miles of exposed sea beach, which is the general depository of the filth of the town is quite horrible. . . . [I]t might be called Stinkabar rather than Zanzibar."[1]

Later in the century, the squalor was greatly reduced, and the town became much more livable. The change for the better coincided with abolition of the slave trade. Exports of slaves from Zanzibar ended in 1873. Britain, whose navy conducted antislaving patrols in East African waters, forced Sultan Seyyid Said's successor, Barghash, to put a stop to the practice and close the slave markets.

The possession of slaves was not outlawed, however. Cloves had been introduced into Zanzibar early in the nineteenth century. Seyyid Said encouraged Arabs to cultivate clove trees in both Zanzibar and Pemba, and the spice had become a valuable export commodity in the second half of the century. Because clove plantations relied on slave labor, the British believed that a sudden end to slavery would deal a fatal blow to Zanzibar's economy. But finally, in 1897, with Zanzibar by then a British protectorate, the legal status of slavery was abolished. Slaves were replaced by itinerant laborers, mainly Africans from the mainland, who were hired seasonally to pick the cloves.

A decade earlier, it had seemed likely that Zanzibar would become a German possession. One result of the European "scramble for Africa" was an Anglo-German agreement in 1886 that divided much of East Africa between the British and the Germans and stripped the sultan of most of his dominions. Britain took the area that now includes Uganda and Kenya, and Germany gained control of most of the territory that was later called Tanganyika.

Zanzibar was important to Britain for commercial reasons and because its location in the Indian Ocean figured in the British need to

protect the passage to India. But with Tanganyika under German sovereignty, from 1886 until 1890 it seemed likely that Zanzibar would fall
within the German sphere of influence. That year, however, British
prime minister Lord Salisbury offered the German kaiser the British-
held island of Helgoland, a few square miles of bare, red sandstone in the
North Sea off the coast of Schleswig-Holstein. In return, he asked for a
British protectorate over Zanzibar and for various territorial concessions
on the mainland. The Germans considered Helgoland of vital strategic
importance to Germany, and the kaiser readily agreed to the swap.

Although the concept of "protectorate" implied a limited governing
role by the protecting power, this was not the case in Zanzibar. There,
"through usage, agreement, and concession," the British were in firm
control.[2] As they often did in their colonial territories, they preferred to
rule indirectly, in Zanzibar's case through the sultan, while setting policy and retaining ultimate power. Exercise of that power in Zanzibar did
not bring prosperity to the island. Heavily dependent on clove exports
and vulnerable to fluctuations in the world price for the spice, Zanzibar's
economy was often depressed. The British did not invest nearly enough
resources and administrative talent in Zanzibar to overcome this condition by fostering a diversified and more robust economy.

Poverty among the masses and ethnic and class divisions antedated
British rule of Zanzibar. But British policies intensified the existing tensions, which smoldered over the years until, by the 1960s, they reached
a flash point.

The British colonial administration considered Zanzibar an Arab state
and, in the years leading up to independence, aimed to establish an Arab
constitutional monarchy. In various ways, British policy helped the Arabs
maintain "their hegemony into the postwar period."[3] The British provided the Arab community with educational opportunities and encouraged Arabs to become part of the colonial bureaucracy.

As for the Africans, the colonial authorities in Zanzibar paid little if
any heed to their political interests. By not reforming the educational
system, which very much favored the Arabs and Asians (people whose
origins were in the Indian subcontinent), the British helped ensure that

Arab notables

the Africans would not gain a more equal political footing with the Arabs.[4] The Asians had become focused on commercial activities and were generally indifferent to political activism.

British policy flew in the face of demographic facts. By the early 1960s, the estimated populations of Zanzibar and Pemba were 250,000 Africans, 50,000 Arabs, 20,000 Asians, and some 500 or 600 "Europeans" (as whites, including Americans, were termed), the bulk of them British.

Next after the British in Zanzibar's pecking order were those Arabs who belonged to the sultan's family, owned plantations, were in commerce, or held senior administrative positions in the bureaucracy. The Asians, who dominated the commercial sector but also held middle-level civil service jobs and were professionals, occupied the middle of the order. Rural Arab shopkeepers and peddlers were on the next rung. At the bottom level were the Africans, who were conscious of the scorn directed at them by many Arab and Asian Zanzibaris.

The African population was made up of three groups: people descended from the earliest inhabitants of the islands; descendants of freed slaves; and mainlanders who originally had come to work in the

plantations and the docks. Those in the first group called themselves Shirazis. Some Shirazis claimed descent from people who came from the Shiraz area of Persia to Zanzibar in about the tenth century A.D. and intermarried with indigenous Africans. Others "used the term simply to distinguish themselves, in terms of descent and length of residence," from more recently arrived mainlanders.[5] The Shirazis, who tended to be fishermen or farmers on private or communally held land, considered themselves a cut above the recently arrived mainland Africans, who for the most part were relegated to subsistence farming on land they did not own and to laboring jobs on the docks and the plantations and in the city.

After World War II, when it became clear that Great Britain would have to give up most or all of its colonial possessions, the British moved ahead with a policy of very slowly devolving governmental power in Zanzibar to the Zanzibaris, or, more accurately, to the Arabs. Before long, however, London shortened the timetable for independence. By the second half of the 1950s, Zanzibar's Arabs, driven by zeal to be the dominant political power after independence and aware that in time the Africans would gain political skills, were militantly nationalistic and demanded independence at the earliest possible time.

The British did not disagree. British colonial officials' political and social ties with Zanzibaris continued to be mainly with Arabs. The British in Zanzibar may have disliked certain Arab nationalists, but they could not conceive of a government in the hands of the African majority. Furthermore, by the 1960s, the British government was intent on Zanzibar becoming independent at about the same time as Kenya. Thus, the British were not inclined to heed the wish of Zanzibari African political leaders to have the independence process go more slowly.

By the early 1960s, most Africans— —Shirazis, descendants of freed slaves, and mainlanders alike—deeply resented the privileged economic, social, and political status of many of the Arabs and Asians. Setting aside their differences, the Africans on Zanzibar Island had joined together to form the Afro-Shirazi Party (ASP) in 1957 to oppose the Arab-dominated Zanzibar Nationalist Party (ZNP). On Pemba, Shirazis, who, unlike their counterparts on Zanzibar, lived in considerable harmony with Arabs and

wanted nothing to do with the mainlanders, generally refused to join the ASP and instead formed their own political organization, the Zanzibar and Pemba People's Party (ZPPP).

Bitter propagandizing by the political parties during the 1963 elections intensified an atmosphere increasingly marked by anxiety and anger. Fears that the violence of the 1961 elections (sixty-eight people, sixty-four of them Arabs, had been killed) would be repeated were not realized. Thanks in part to the presence of the Second Battalion of the Scots Guards, flown in by the British government to keep the peace, the elections were held without serious disturbances. The Afro-Shirazi Party won 54 percent of the popular vote, but took only thirteen of the thirty-one seats in the legislature. With twelve seats, the Arabs' Zanzibar Nationalist Party formed a coalition government with the Zanzibar and Pemba People's Party, which had won six. Not surprisingly, the ASP cried foul, but to no avail. The makeup of the constituencies was a factor, but crucial elements of the Africans' defeat were the bickering and infighting within the ranks of the ASP and the party leadership's poor organizational skills.

The new government wasted no time in adding to the Africans' grievances and fears. It decided to meet a budgetary deficit by cutting expenditures for schools, medical facilities, and housing and welfare projects. Those mainly affected by the cuts were the African poor. The government introduced legislation to provide censorship and political control of the press. It passed a law putting severe limitations on the activities of political-opposition groups. And it started placing Arabs in top civil service positions. In addition, the coalition government, led by ZNP ministers, made it clear that it intended to form close ties with the Arab world, not with black African countries, as desired by the ASP. Adding fuel to the Africans' sense of betrayal, humiliation, and rage, Arab leaders made no effort to hide their patronizing view of, or downright contempt for, their African countrymen.

The stage for revolution was set.

2

‒‒‒‒‒‒‒‒‒‒‒‒

Before the Storm

*In the narrow, tortuous streets are to be found representatives of almost
every Eastern race. The population . . . includes Arabs, Baluchis,
Comorians, Europeans, Indians from all parts of India and Pakistan,
Shirazis . . . and Africans from most of the Mainland tribes, and during
the northeast monsoon Arabs from the Persian Gulf, Shihiris and Somalis.*

—*A Guide to Zanzibar*

*I had a queer dream: someone talked to me, saying, "You will not die. God
has given you the power to redeem the prisoners and the slaves, and you
will make those who cannot understand to understand."*

—John Okello

My wife, our baby daughter, and I arrived in Zanzibar on a pitch-black night, July 13, 1963. Our journey there had begun, in a sense, a year earlier. I was in Mexico then, a recently minted Foreign Service officer (FSO) on my first assignment.

In 1960, I had passed the Foreign Service examination, saving myself from the dismal prospect of further studies at UCLA for a Ph.D. in political science. I had come to UCLA by way of the University of California, Santa Barbara (UCSB), where I enrolled after a hitch in the navy and

where I earned a B.A. in physical education and an M.A. in political science. At Santa Barbara, I had focused my master's degree work on Latin American affairs. But one day in 1959, while I was working for a year in Los Angeles after leaving UCSB and before taking up a teaching assistantship at UCLA, I chanced to read an issue of *Holiday* magazine that was devoted to Africa. Fascinated by its content, I decided to center my studies on Africa rather than Latin America.

Although I enjoyed my work at UCLA with Prof. James Coleman, one of America's premier Africanists, I was put off by the political science department's emphasis on a sociological approach to the discipline. To me, it was laden with mind-numbing jargon and irrelevant to what I wanted to learn about government, politics, and international relations. In addition to being unhappy with the Ph.D. program, I was getting tired of being a perennial student, scraping by at UCSB on money from the GI Bill, a small scholarship, and part-time jobs, and then at UCLA by means of a $250 teaching-assistant monthly stipend.

When, in April 1960, I was notified that I had been successful in the Foreign Service exam, my troubles seemed to be over. Not only was I going to leave the academic grind behind and start a career, but, even better, I was going to have a full-time job that would pay me almost $6,000 a year.

In the next few weeks, I took the medical and psychiatric examinations required by the State Department. The psychiatrist's main effort seemed to be to find out whether I was a homosexual, a disqualifying factor back then. That I was twenty-nine years old and unmarried may have raised a red flag in my file. Helping conduct my security check after I passed the oral exam, an FBI agent asked a former girlfriend of mine whether I was "normal." In another sign of those times, when some effects of McCarthyism still lingered, a State Department security officer asked me in an interview why I subscribed to "that pinko magazine," the *New Republic*.

In June, evidently adjudged to be heterosexual and neither a Communist nor a fellow traveler, I drove from California in my 1958 Volkswagen Beetle to Washington, D.C. For eight weeks, with nineteen other incoming officers, I took part in an orientation course at the State Department's Foreign Service Institute (FSI). At the end of the course,

after a personnel counselor had told me I would receive French language training and an assignment to the State Department, I was given intensive training in Spanish and assigned to Mexico. The last piece of advice I got from my counselor before I drove off for Mexico was to be sure not to marry a foreigner, for my career's sake.

I spent two years in Mexico, working in the consular section of the American embassy. I started out in the visa section. In late January 1961, I had been working on the visa line for a little more than a week. Looking at the latest set of passports and visa application forms given me by a clerk, I was transfixed by the picture of a beautiful young woman in one of the passports. The passport belonged to Julieta Rovirosa Argudin, age twenty-two. According to the application, she lived in Colonia Polanco, a middle- to upper-class neighborhood. She was a teacher and wanted to accompany an aunt on a shopping trip to Brownsville, Texas. Clearly, she qualified for a nonimmigrant visa. There was no need for an interview. But I wanted to see if she was as pretty as her picture. The ensuing interview turned out to be the first step in a fully chaperoned courtship that ended in our marriage eight months later. Pictures of the wedding show Julie, radiant in her white silk wedding gown, and me, somewhat bemused and awkward in a morning coat and striped pants (it was the only time I ever wore striped pants in my thirty-five years as a diplomat).

During my first year in Mexico, I had asked for Swahili language training after my assignment was completed. Early in the summer of 1962, the department notified me that I would start Swahili at the Foreign Service Institute in November with an onward assignment to the American consulate in Zanzibar. That November, with our infant daughter, Susan, in the backseat of the car, Julie and I drove in the VW Beetle from Mexico City to California for two weeks of leave, then across the country to Washington. There, while I studied Swahili, Julie took a course in English. Little more than a year earlier, she was a single young Mexican woman. Now she was married, an American citizen, a mother, away from her close-knit Mexican family for the first time, wrestling with a new language, and coping with a different culture.[1]

Immersed in the intensive language-training program at FSI, I wasn't much help to Julie in making the adjustment to her new life. Not that she needed that much help. I was to find then and many other times over the years of our nomadic existence that she adapted to new places and situations more smoothly and with less angst than I did.

Contrary to popular belief, Swahili is not a simple language. Spoken widely in the central part of eastern Africa—throughout Tanzania and Kenya, as far north as southern Somalia, as far west as the eastern part of the Congolese Republic, and as far south as northern Mozambique—the language becomes less complex and less grammatically pure the farther one goes from the Indian Ocean coast and Zanzibar, where the most sophisticated brand of Swahili is spoken.

FSI included Swahili among its "hard" languages, which were those whose degree of difficulty required more time to learn than the "world" languages, such as French and Spanish. When I had taken Spanish at the FSI two years earlier, the course lasted sixteen weeks. I would be enrolled in the Swahili course for twenty-six weeks.

As the time for our departure for Zanzibar drew closer, we began buying supplies of items we would not be able to get in Zanzibar or that would be prohibitively expensive there—diapers, for example. A two-year supply of toilet paper piled high in shopping carts drew some puzzled glances when one day we made a massive, for us, purchase of staples at a Safeway store near our Arlington, Virginia, apartment.

By the beginning of July, we had said good-bye to our families in Mexico and California and flown to New York, where we boarded the SS *Constitution* for a ten-day voyage to Genoa. After traveling to Rome by train, we flew to Nairobi. There we transferred to a twin-engine DC-3, the old workhorse transport aircraft of World War II, for the flight to Mombasa, Tanga, and Zanzibar, where we landed on a runway lighted only by kerosene lanterns.

Driving from the airport, we passed through checkpoints manned by British soldiers armed with rifles with fixed bayonets. The streets were deserted and dark that moonless night as we passed through Zanzibar Town to our house some three miles north along the shore of the Indian Ocean at a village called Mtoni. Any uneasiness we might have felt was

numbed by fatigue and overridden by exhilaration at having arrived at our exotic new post and begun the new chapter in our lives.

Alighting from the car at our house, Julie was momentarily alarmed when a man whose face was dimly illuminated by a lantern he was carrying approached us. When he got close, we saw that he had a spear in his other hand and that his front teeth had been filed to sharp points. The driver of the car who brought us told us that the man was Jacobo, the night watchman. Jacobo, we would find, was a kind and gentle Makonde from Mozambique.

We had a much more unsettling moment later that night, when we were jolted out of sleep by a piercing scream. Julie cried out, "The baby!" The interior of the house, which had been a stable, was narrow and long, about ten by eighty feet, with Susie's bedroom separated from ours by a fifty-five-foot-long living-dining room. Julie had a vision of some animal making its dinner of our little daughter. While I was still half asleep, Julie leaped out of bed and sped to her endangered baby, who was fast asleep and threatened only by the mosquitoes that were kept at bay by the mosquito net that enclosed her crib. In the morning, we learned that the source of the shriek was a bush baby, a tiny lemur noted for the bloodcurdling noise it can make.

When Julie opened the shuttered windows and the doors to the outside that morning, any qualms she may have had because of the previous night were instantly swept away. The eighty-foot length of the house ran from north to south. A door on the west side opened onto a porch, whose steps led down to a several-foot-wide band of grass that ended at the white sand of the beach. And about thirty yards from the porch, just beyond several tall coconut trees, lay the ocean, shimmering in the early-morning sunshine. Looking to the south, in the distance we could see the skyline of Zanzibar Town. We couldn't have asked for a more splendid location.

The house may not have been most Americans' idea of a model home. It was a low-ceilinged, whitewashed-coral structure, which was crumbling in some places on its outside surfaces. It had weathered, nondescript doors and windows without screens but whose shutters kept out most of the insects. The building was topped by a roof of thatch from

House at Mtoni

which bugs occasionally dropped onto the floor, furniture, or residents. The floor was made of mud covered with a thin layer of concrete that had been mixed with a deep-red paint and therefore reddened feet, shoes, baby, and whatever else came into contact with it. The light fixtures were naked bulbs dangling from a wire. None of this mattered to us, though. That morning, we were ecstatic. Who would not be happy living in a beach house on an exotic tropical island? For us, it was, I wrote in a letter, "a perfect place."

There is a myth that travelers to Zanzibar by boat can smell the aroma of cloves and other spices as they approach the island. Actually, the cloves on the trees have no odor. At the plantations, cloves are picked when ripe, then either dried in outdoor ovens or placed on mats to dry in the open air. Once dried, the cloves are bagged for shipment. The dried cloves do give off their familiar odor, but it does not carry far from the plantations.

Julie and I did find, though, the first time we drove into town and passed the dockside industrial area, that the scent of cloves was quite

strong at the clove-oil distillery. There, cloves and their stems were pressed into oil. On days when the wind was right and clove oil was at the port waiting to be exported, people on boats approaching the harbor might have caught a whiff of cloves.

Another myth was the kind in the *Reader's Digest* story, the idea that Zanzibaris are indolent, passive people who need only to pick fruit from trees to feed themselves. The only remote connection that this view has to truth is that years earlier, some of the Arab plantation owners were lazy and did lead lives centered around drinking, drugs, and sex. Mismanaging their plantations, they lost money, borrowed heavily, and in many instances sold or otherwise lost their property, often to Asians, who, like the Arabs, became targets of Africans' resentment.

One could see both in town and in the countryside how hardworking the Zanzibaris were. At the port, African laborers loaded huge sacks of imported grain or flour onto trucks and did other heavy labor. In the narrow streets of Zanzibar Town, men pulled enormous loads on two-wheeled wooden *hamali* carts. Driving into the countryside, Julie and I were struck by how neat and clean most villages were. The ground around huts was literally swept clean. The African villagers were subsistence farmers who worked hard on their small plots of ground to feed themselves and their children.

Zanzibar's roads were good, and it was easy to get around the island, which is about fifty miles long from north to south and twenty-four miles in breadth at its widest point. Its area is about half that of Rhode Island. In our early days there, we explored as much as we could before the birth of our second child, who was due to arrive in early September.

Adorned with groves of coconut and mango trees, palm forests, and orchards of clove trees, the western half of the island, which contained several ridges rising to more than two hundred feet, was gorgeous. There were lime, banana, casuarina, and other kinds of trees, along with a profusion of vines and various flowering bushes and shrubs. Nature was not nearly so prodigal with the rest of the island. The thinly populated eastern half was generally flat, less fertile, and not nearly so heavily wooded. Both coasts had long expanses of white-coral sand beaches and were dotted with fishing villages.

Zanzibar did have the look of a paradise. But for the majority of its inhabitants, reality was poverty, widespread diseases such as malaria, grossly inadequate educational opportunities, and what amounted to a caste system that had been perpetuated under British colonialism.

I had studied Zanzibar's history and politics and was aware of the political and social tensions on the island, but had no inkling, from the briefing material I had seen at the State Department, that revolution was in the air. Certainly, my new boss, Frederick P. "Fritz" Picard, the American consul, had communicated nothing of the sort to Washington. How could he? Neither the British authorities, the Zanzibar government, nor even most of the leaders of the African opposition were fully aware, if at all, of the imminence of what was coming. And the few Afro-Shirazi Party leaders who had an idea that violence was in the offing would not be in on the plot that actually hatched the revolution.

Fritz Picard was a tall, slender, darkly handsome thirty-eight-year-old Foreign Service officer from Nebraska. He was an extremely intelligent Africanist who, as a Fulbright scholar, had studied on a university fellowship in Australia and, like his wife, Shoana, at Tufts University's prestigious Fletcher School of Law and Diplomacy.

In Washington, I had been told that Fritz was a rising star in the Foreign Service who some thought was destined to go to the top of the profession. Possessed of a sharp wit, he could be engaging. There were some who considered him arrogant, and it was true that he had little patience for people who bored or annoyed him. But to many others, Fritz was a charmer and great fun. Once I got used to his barbed humor, I found that I liked Fritz and was comfortable working with him.

The American consulate was located at the western edge of Stone Town, near Shangani Point, the apex of the triangular peninsula where much of Zanzibar Town was located. Most of Stone Town—the old Arab and Asian part of the city that included the palace, post office, commercial buildings, shops, churches, and mosques—consisted of tall dwellings made of coral stone, red earth, lime mortar, and plaster. The

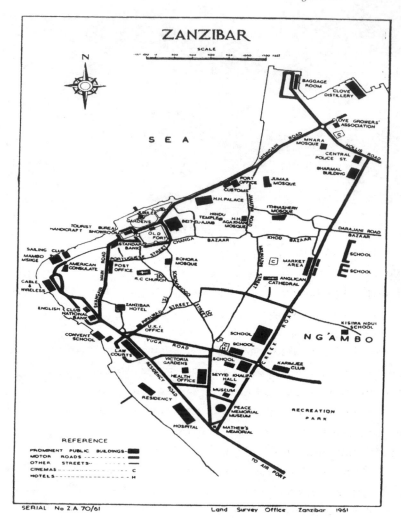

Zanzibar Town

houses were separated by narrow, winding streets and alleys, often so narrow that the high buildings blocked out all sunlight.

The approaching commencement of American-manned flights into outer space had given new life to an American diplomatic presence on the island, absent since 1915. In about 1960, National Aeronautics and Space Agency (NASA) scientists deemed Zanzibar an ideal location for one of the tracking stations needed for the U.S. space program. After the British and American governments signed an agreement providing

American consulate/embassy

for the establishment of a tracking station on Zanzibar, the United States reopened the consulate in 1961. The first flight of the Project Mercury series—the one-man orbital missions—took place on February 20, 1962, when John Glenn became the first American to orbit the earth.

The three-story consulate building had been the home of an Arab family. The ground floor housed the United States Information Service (USIS) library and office. The consulate's administrative office, staffed by three Zanzibaris, and consular office were on the next floor. The top floor included the offices of the consul and the vice consul, an outer office occupied by an American secretary, and a small vault containing classified files and a code machine. The outer office opened onto a veranda overlooking Kelele (Noisy) Square. Across the square was Cable and Wireless, where we took our official telegrams for transmission to Washington and elsewhere.

Dale Povenmire was the vice consul whom I was replacing. An overlap of more than a few days between a new officer's arrival and his predecessor's departure was unusual, but because Fritz was about to go on home leave in late August, Dale's departure was delayed until after Fritz

returned. As it turned out, Dale and I would work together for more than three months.

I found Dale to be Fritz's opposite in temperament. Quiet and unassuming, he was professorial in demeanor and, where Fritz tended to be elliptical, straightforward. His relationship with Fritz struck me as somewhat formal, and I sensed a distance between them.

Dale was a patient teacher, which was ideal for me since there was so much to learn. In Mexico, my work had been confined to consular matters. Here in Zanzibar, I was going to be the post's administrative officer, economic-commercial officer, consular officer, and labor reporting officer. The labor reporting, I hoped, would lead to wider political reporting. Never having handled finances beyond our own slim bank account, I was a little apprehensive about taking on the consulate's budget and fiscal work.

One of Julie's and my early explorations in town took us to the Cathedral Church of Christ, the Anglican cathedral, which was built on the site of the last slave market in Zanzibar. Its construction began in 1873, the same year that Zanzibar's slave markets were closed. "Basilican in design and a mixture of Gothic and Arabic in style," the cathedral was completed in 1879 and consecrated in 1903.[2] With a high-vaulted ceiling, marble pillars, and a large stained-glass window, its interior was of great beauty, offering a wonderful contrast to the ugliness of the trading in human beings that had taken place there for many years.

The Omani Arabs had brought to Zanzibar a culture of violence that, most commonly expressed through slavery, left an imprint on the psyche of the islands' people, even to the time of the revolution and its aftermath. Sultan Said, who moved his sultanate from Oman to Zanzibar, was no stranger to killing. He came to power when, at the age of sixteen, he assassinated his cousin Bedr, who had supplanted him as ruler of Oman two years earlier. After he came to Zanzibar, the Omanis solidified the primacy of their land expropriators and slave dealers.

Slaves were brought from the mainland in dhows. As many as possible were crammed into the boats. If winds were unfavorable, the trip could

take days, and many slaves never survived the passage. Describing a sale of slaves at Zanzibar's large slave market in 1811, the captain of an East India Company ship wrote that after they were cleaned and their skins burnished with coconut oil, they were ornamented with gold and silver bracelets and arranged in a line. Guarded by the slave owner's domestic slaves, who were armed with swords or spears, the men, women, and children were marched through the market and the town's principal streets. When someone showed interest, the procession was stopped, and the potential purchaser would closely examine slaves. The captain continued:

> The mouth and teeth are first inspected, and afterwards every part of the body in succession, not even excepting the breasts, etc., of the girls, many of whom I have seen examined in the most indecent manner in the public market by their purchasers. . . . The slave is then made to walk or run a little way to show that there is no defect about the feet; after which, if the price is agreed to, they are stripped of their finery and delivered over to their future master. I have frequently counted twenty or thirty of these files in the market at one time. . . . Women with children newly born hanging at their breasts and others so old they can scarcely walk, are sometimes seen dragged about in this manner. I observed they had in general a very dejected look; some groups appeared so ill fed that their bones seemed as if ready to penetrate the skin.[3]

Each year, thousands of Africans were enslaved in East Africa. Most had been seized in tribal warfare, then bartered to Arab and African slave traders. Others were kidnapped or forcibly captured by slave traders. The majority were brought to Zanzibar. Those who were not delivered dead or dying were sold—as many as 40,000 a year. About a third of those unfortunates were reserved for work on Zanzibar's and Pemba's plantations; the rest were exported to Arabia, Persia, Egypt, Turkey, and elsewhere. Of the male slaves who stayed to labor on the plantations, about 30 percent died of disease or malnutrition each year.[4]

Perhaps there was some truth to the assertion made in reports written by successive British consuls that the slaves who were kept in Zanzibar "were generally speaking not unkindly treated." However, there were "instances of shocking brutality."[5] And the high death rate of the

slaves spoke for itself. Moreover, all slaves certainly experienced the degradation that accompanied captivity and enslavement.

In 1963, there were ex-slaves still living in Zanzibar and Pemba. They and their children and grandchildren were passionate in their hatred of slavery and the Arab slavers. Numerous other Zanzibaris, especially those of mainland ancestry, shared that hatred, which many applied to all Arabs.

While Julie and I were getting acquainted with Zanzibar and I was scrambling to learn the ins and outs of my new job, a Ugandan who called himself John Okello was traveling around the island preaching revolution. Twenty-six years old, he was about five feet, nine inches tall and weighed about 170 well-muscled pounds. He might as well have been invisible to the British colonial police, for they were unaware of his presence, much less of what he was doing.

He was a strange but compelling man who said that he received in dreams messages from God, who he believed had chosen him to lead a revolution of the Africans in Zanzibar against those who oppressed them. Okello, who had come to Zanzibar Island from Pemba in February 1963, became the catalyst of the revolution. It was he, not the leaders of the African or radical Arab opposition, who would lead the ragtag force that killed thousands of Arabs, overthrew the Zanzibar government, and caused the sultan to flee into permanent exile.[6]

Okello was born in a village in Lango District, Uganda, in 1937. Baptized when he was two, he was christened Gideon. There is no record of when or why he changed his name to John, nor is it certain that Okello was his real surname. He was orphaned at eleven and lived with relatives until he was fifteen, when he left home to seek work. By that time, he had had less than four years of formal schooling.

He led a peripatetic life, moving frequently. He was seventeen when he went to Kenya, like Uganda still a British colony, where he worked at various unskilled jobs, such as house servant, office clerk, gardener, and laborer. In the process, he learned the masonry trade and acquired other building-construction skills. In Nairobi, he was arrested for what he later

termed "a sexual offense."[7] Two years in jail left him with an abiding hatred of colonial authorities. Once out of prison, he continued his wanderings, living in Mombasa and other towns in the Kenyan coastal area. In 1959, he went to Pemba to find work in the clove plantations.

Okello stayed in Pemba for almost four years. While there, he worked at making stone building blocks. In his autobiography, Okello did not claim to have been a policeman. However, his bearing, knowledge of police procedures and armories, and mode of dress gave rise to speculation after the revolution that he had been a police officer at some point, possibly while he was in Pemba.

Ex-policeman or not, Okello got involved in politics in Pemba, first joining the ZNP, then leaving it to join the ASP, even though he found it "weak and dispirited."[8] It is likely that he gained political experience by addressing ASP political gatherings, inveighing against colonialism, Arabs, and Asians. As a Ugandan, his Swahili must have been rough on Zanzibari ears, but Okello became adept at the language, and his strong personality and oratorical skills made up for his accent and unpolished grammar. With friends and acquaintances, including some mainland policemen in Pemba, he began discussing his ideas about wresting power from the Arabs.

While he was in Pemba, he continued to have dreams in which he received word from God. In one, he was told that God had anointed him to teach his African brothers "to unite . . . and struggle to free themselves in their own land." God would give him "wisdom, power and courage" to do this.[9] Aware that no revolution could succeed in Pemba alone, on February 4, 1963, he made his way to Zanzibar Island.

During his year in Zanzibar before the revolution, Okello developed contacts in the police, some of whom subsequently took part in his army of revolutionaries. He reconnoitered places that would be targets of his force's attacks: Zanzibar Town's police stations, the radio station, the prison, and the police armory (Zanzibar had no army). According to Okello, he developed a relationship with Seif Bakari, head of Zanzibar's Afro-Shirazi Youth League (ASYL). Bakari, in his early or midtwenties, about five feet tall, a round-faced, good-looking man, was a member of a small group of men who called themselves the Committee of Fourteen. They would play a prominent role in the revolt and its aftermath.

Okello became an official of the Zanzibar and Pemba Paint Workers Union. Union funds enabled him to travel around the island to speak about union issues, but more important to preach his doctrine of revolution, give instructions on making side arms, and raise money for axes, *pangas*, medical supplies, and transport. He recruited volunteers for a revolutionary force. Of the 330 men he said he had enlisted in the cause, most were mainlanders. He directed the men to follow a code of conduct that included abstinence from alcohol, sex, and cold food (a sensible precaution, for in a place like rural Zanzibar, unheated food could be loaded with harmful bacteria).

He told his men that when the fighting began, they were to kill all Arabs between the ages of eighteen and fifty-five. Young, old, and pregnant women were to be spared. Europeans, he ordered, were not to be attacked. Virgins and women whose husbands had been killed or detained should not be raped (all others, presumably, were fair game).

According to Okello, some of his followers wanted to start the fighting immediately after Zanzibar became independent. He dissuaded them, knowing that British troops would still be on the island and that there could be an adverse international reaction if foreign visitors to the independence celebrations were put in harm's way.

In the days following the December 10, 1963, handover of power, insensitive and foolish actions by the new government strengthened the resolve of Okello and others to rid Zanzibar of Arab rule. On January 4, 1964, Okello told his followers that the revolt would commence on or about the eleventh.

Although Okello had a relationship with the youth league's Seif Bakari, he was unknown to the leadership of the Afro-Shirazi Party. He had never met the ASP's head, Abeid Amani Karume.

There is reason to believe that others in the ASP besides Okello were getting ready for rebellion. Available evidence suggests that the Committee of Fourteen was either given or assumed on its own the task of preparing for and undertaking a violent overthrow of the government. This plan was to be implemented on January 20. It is unclear

just how Seif Bakari and the others of the Committee of Fourteen meshed with Okello, but it is certain that at some point they allied themselves with him and took part in the fighting that began on January 12.

Divisions and attendant backstabbing within the ASP leadership, as well as Okello's fear that his preparations for revolution would be leaked if ASP leaders were made aware of them, convinced him to keep his plans secret from all but his most trusted lieutenants. Although they were loyal members of the ASP, those members of the Committee of Fourteen who may have known about Okello's plot did not violate its secrecy. They probably agreed with him that word of the plot had to be held as tightly as possible. Whatever the case, Karume, as well as other ASP leaders, was kept in the dark.

Nevertheless, Karume somehow got wind that violence would break out on or about the eleventh or twelfth of January. Fearing that the authorities would put it down and that he would be accused of instigating it and punished accordingly, Karume told a British police officer what he had heard.[10] Subsequent events show that Karume was not taken seriously. The British and Zanzibar government authorities had only fragmentary indications that trouble might come soon and gave them little credence.

Zanzibar's Arabs were oblivious to the plots and preparations to oust them from power. They heard rumors of impending violence, but no one in the ZNP leadership took them seriously. Contemptuous of the Africans' abilities, the Arabs were blind to the possibility that the Africans could pose a real danger to their hold on political power.

Ali Muhsin typified the Zanzibari Arabs' self-confidence, some would say arrogance, and visible scorn for Africans. About fifty years old, short, and silver-haired, he belonged to a wealthy landowning family. The most powerful leader of the ZNP since its inception in 1955, he was an ardent nationalist, a fervent Muslim, and a friend of Egypt's Gamal Abdel Nasser. Muhsin greatly admired Nasser's pan-Arabism, and at times he echoed the Egyptian leader's anti-Western pronouncements. British and American concerns about this were mitigated by Muhsin's declared anti-communism.

Accounts written after the revolution alleged that the Americans knew it was coming. In the February 14, 1964, issue of *The Spectator,* Keith Kyle reported that by the evening of January 11, "American intelligence was aware that 'the balloon is going up tonight.'" In his book on the revolution, Anthony Clayton states: "Several officials of the U.S. Mission in Zanzibar were aware of trouble planned for the night of 11 January."[11] Both assertions are untrue. For one thing, the American officials in Zanzibar were only three in number: Picard, USIS public affairs officer Stuart Lillico, and me. And none of us knew what was coming. There was no reporting from the embassy indicating that big trouble would soon be in the offing.

On the night of January 11, Lillico heard from one of his USIS Zanzibari employees that the town was full of rumors that a fight was about to begin. Lillico passed this on to Picard who did nothing about it. That was it, a phone call about rumors of impending violence. None of us heard anything further until about three in the morning, when the same employee called Lillico and told him that shooting had begun.

In the half year leading up to the revolution, political reporting from the American consulate and then, after independence, from the American embassy (the consulate became an embassy when Zanzibar became independent) centered on Zanzibar's politics. Picard's messages paid special attention to the internal problems of the opposition Afro-Shirazi Party and to the activities of, and the Zanzibar government's opposition to, Zanzibari Marxists. Not one of the reports sent by telegram or in the diplomatic pouch referred to a possible uprising against the government.

Picard was well connected to British colonial authorities, leaders of the ZNP (particularly Ali Muhsin), and a few of the better-educated, more moderate members of the ASP. His reports to Washington reflected what his sources knew and did not know. He sent accurate information about the internal crisis within the ASP and the party's failure to get Mohammed Shamte and his Zanzibar and Pemba People's Party to join it in a coalition against the ZNP. And, later, he accurately chronicled the growing split in the ASP that had led to the January 3, 1964,

resignation from the party of some of its leaders who held Karume in disdain.

Not long before the July 1963 Zanzibar elections, Mischa Feinsilber, an Israeli who with his brother-in-law owned a firm in Dar es Salaam called Ocean Products, came to see Fritz. Feinsilber had cultivated Zanzibari politicians, especially the Africans. A few months after the revolution, Feinsilber told Marguerite Higgins, a renowned newspaper correspondent, that he had warned Picard the rule of the sultan and the Arabs was doomed. He said he had advised the American consul "to support or at least keep in contact with the Afro-Shirazi Party." He had suggested that "a few thousand dollars to help the Afro-Shirazi have a fighting chance against the Egypt-supported Arabs in the elections would bring him friendship and loyalty of the party." But Picard had "refused even to take up the matter with Washington," according to Feinsilber.[12] Even if Fritz had done so, and there is no record that he did, it is unlikely that the State Department would have favored getting too close to the ASP and possibly angering Ali Muhsin and his ZNP, by all accounts the man and the party that would lead the country after independence.

In keeping with the U.S. government's focus in those days, Picard paid a lot of attention to the goings on of the leader of Zanzibar's Marxists, Abdulrahman Mohamed Babu. Previously the general secretary of the ZNP, the thirty-nine-year-old Babu headed the pro-Communist Umma (Masses) Party, which he founded after breaking with Ali Muhsin and the ZNP leadership in June 1963. He had close ties to the Chinese Communists.

The relative handful of people in Washington who took an interest in Zanzibar were no doubt pleased when Picard reported on June 21 that no new support for Babu had developed after he left the ZNP. Ali Muhsin told Picard that, with the Communists now out of the party, "he wished to make it clear to 'all concerned' that Communist influence in [the] ZNP . . . [was] now completely gone." Picard recommended that the State Department exploit this "Communist setback" by getting the news

publicized in the press as widely as possible. Nothing came of his suggestion.

In August, the consulate reported that Ali Muhsin, who had made himself minister for home and legal affairs in the preindependence government, warned in a radio broadcast that anyone who attempted "to sabotage the march of freedom . . . must be regarded as an enemy of the people." He was referring to the Umma Party, which had become militantly and stridently opposed to the government. And he was referring to Babu when he said: "Those who having become devoid of any new political ideas with which to mislead the people now resort to the lure of liquor, hashish, and other worse forms of vices with which to ensnare the young and the gullible will soon find that this game is too hot for them."

A few days later, a bill was introduced in Parliament to enable the government to outlaw any organization deemed "prejudicial to the maintenance of peace, order, and good government." This was clearly aimed at Umma. About five months later, on January 6, Picard reported that the government had raided Umma headquarters two days earlier, "confiscating Communist-supplied office equipment and vehicles as well as party files." The party was banned. While a warrant for his arrest was being prepared, on January 8 Babu fled by canoe to Dar es Salaam.

Picard's last message to Washington before the onset of the revolution was sent on January 11. Once again, the subject was Babu and Umma. It was well known, Picard said, "that Babu and his *Umma* Party are bought and sold by Peking. Chicoms have furnished Babu with New China News Agency material, duplicating equipment, vehicles, propaganda material, tickets for tours and scholarships for [a] number of years."

It was apparent that the Zanzibar government, writing off the Africans as a threat, worried only about Babu and his followers. The British and Americans shared this focus and, like the Zanzibar government's leaders, were unaware of any other immediate threat to Zanzibar's peace and stability.

3

On the Eve

Those who make peaceful revolution impossible will make violent revolution inevitable.

—John F. Kennedy

It is impossible to predict the time and progress of revolution. It is governed by its own more or less mysterious laws.

—Vladimir I. Lenin

After the closure of the American consulate in 1915, Americans had been a rarity in Zanzibar. This changed with the advent of Project Mercury, which brought a relatively small but politically very visible bunch of Americans to Zanzibar. Of the approximately sixty Americans on the island, most were Project Mercury tracking-station employees and their wives and children. By the time Julie and I had been in Zanzibar a few weeks, we had met just about all of them. Only a few had ever lived in a Third World country before. They socialized mainly among themselves and with consulate personnel, British technicians, and low- to middle-level British civil servants. Of the people near or at the top of the British pecking order, a few accepted these Americans in

their midst; most just tolerated them. The rest of the Americans, apart from Julie, Susan, and me, consisted of two graduate students who were doing research; the wife and children of one of them; the Picard, Povenmire, and Lillico families; and Imelda Johnson, the consulate's American secretary.

Although the consulate's Americans saw a good deal of each other, I came to note that Fritz was not a social intimate of Dale or Stu. In part, this was because Fritz, who had pretty much reserved for himself the higher officials of the colonial authorities and the fledgling Zanzibar government, and political party leaders as well, traveled in different social circles from those of his more junior colleagues. In addition, Fritz's lifestyle contrasted markedly with theirs. A heavy drinker, he liked to party a lot and, as I learned later, to carouse in Zanzibar Town and its outskirts. I did not discover until after the revolution that the Picards' marriage was failing, that both he and Shoana were under great stress, and that, in addition, Fritz's drinking was symptomatic of an underlying psychological problem.

I was impatient to get to know Zanzibaris but had to content myself for a while with meeting Dale's contacts at social events. Outside of our African neighbors at Mtoni and the tradesmen there and in Zanzibar Town, the first African I met, at a dinner party given by Dale and his wife, Marilyn, was Adam Mwakanjuki, the head of the Zanzibar Dockworkers Union. Adam, a short, bearded man in his midtwenties, was pleasant, though inclined to be argumentative. The consulate had labeled him "a friend of the U.S." The inaccuracy of that characterization became startlingly evident the day after the revolution got under way.

As time went on, I met more Africans, as well as Arabs and Asians. I had a fifteen-minute talk with Karume at the Parliament building one day. He seemed pleased that I spoke Swahili. The British tended to be patronizing of the ASP leader, and the Arabs held him in contempt. I formed an entirely different impression of the man. He was friendly, open, and, it seemed to me, intelligent.

If Karume had been born in another place and time, he might have been a premier running back for an American football team. He looked the part when I knew him: about five feet, nine inches tall, weighing I'd

Abeid Amani Karume

guess about 220 pounds, with massive shoulders and thick thighs and neck.

Although some Zanzibaris claimed that he was born in Malawi, Karume said he was born of mainland immigrants in Pongwe, a village in west-central Zanzibar, in 1905. He attended primary school for a few years at Mwera, a larger nearby village. When he was sixteen, he became a merchant seaman. He quit the sea in 1943 to return for good to Zanzibar, where after World War II he founded a syndicate of small-boat owners. A well-known soccer player and founder of the popular African Dancing Club, since 1934 Karume was an official of the African Association, a precursor of the Afro-Shirazi Party.

In 1953, the British banned Zanzibari civil servants from participating in politics. Not wanting to give up their government careers, some relatively well-educated men ceased their political activities. This left the road open to Karume to rise to the top of the association. He was elected its leader that year and continued as its head when in 1959, by then called the Afro-Shirazi Union, it became the Afro-Shirazi Party.

A blunt, strong-minded, and stubborn man, as the leader of his party, Karume made up for his rudimentary education and lack of sophistica-

tion by his rough but powerful oratorical ability, which greatly appealed to the average Zanzibari African. But his style of leadership did not set well with other ambitious men in the ASP. One of them, Othman Sharif, denounced Karume as "an utter failure" and called on him to resign. Sharif, a forty-seven-year-old Shirazi from Pemba who was a civil servant in the Agriculture Department, saw himself as a better-qualified political leader. Unable to oust Karume, Sharif and other well-educated, moderate ASP leaders resigned from the party on January 2, 1964, ten days before the revolution.

The British colonialists had found a class and caste system in Zanzibar, and they did nothing to discourage it during their years in power. Their own class and hierarchical proclivities were strong factors within the British community. Some colonial government officials displayed a distinctly pukka-sahib attitude. Because I was a junior American official, Julie and I were not welcomed into the social circle of the British upper crust in Zanzibar. But we met and made friends with other Britons.

Among the British officials were some talented administrators and specialists. For example, Sir George Mooring, the British resident, could see the destructive potential in the hardening racial divisions and worked strenuously to bring the different communities to a political accommodation. He had warned the British government that Zanzibar was not ready for self-government.

On the whole, though, the British colonials in Zanzibar were less than impressive. According to some of the British we met, other people in Zanzibar, and British officials with whom I talked in Dar es Salaam, the British colonial administration in Zanzibar was composed to a certain extent of some of the least-able members of the colonial service. Although this characterization may have been overdrawn, it had a basis in fact. Clayton wrote: "Although honest and reasonably efficient, the British administrators were often unimaginative; service in Zanzibar was in any case not attractive to the more ambitious colonial officials."[1]

The isolation of living on an island and the exclusionist nature of their ways also contributed to what, by the 1960s, had become a somewhat inbred, and in some cases odd, collection of colonial officials and staff. There was a lot of sexual—both heterosexual and homosexual—hanky-panky going on. Live and Let Live seemed to be the order of the day. For example, the predilection of one high official and some of his friends for Zanzibari boys was an open secret that elicited ribald comments but no official censure and little condemnation among the British community.

We continued to be happy in our house at Mtoni. An abundance of cockroaches and even an infestation of bedbugs did not dampen our enthusiasm. The bedbugs' headquarters seemed to be on my side of the mattress or in the part of the mosquito net over my head, since I got most of the bites. A first spraying had no effect, but a more thorough second effort wiped them out.

Our African neighbors, who made their living fishing or farming, were friendly and came to our front yard to use the water tap, the only one in the area. Demonstrating our acceptability, or figuring I was a soft touch, the man who sold us fish and fruit came by one day for some medicine for an illness. He coughed vigorously to show how severe it was. He also hit me up for several shillings, justifying the request only on the grounds that I was a *bwana mkubwa* (important man). Naturally, I couldn't refuse him.

I didn't have much time off to enjoy our lovely surroundings of sand, sea, and coconut palms at Mtoni. Pressing to learn the myriad details of the responsibilities I would inherit from Dale and having to fly to Dar es Salaam every Sunday to meet the courier bringing the consulate's diplomatic pouch, for a while I was working seven days a week.[2]

A little after midnight on September 3, seven weeks after our arrival, Julie woke me up to let me know it was time to go to the hospital. At 8:45 that morning, Julianne was born, only the second American child ever born in Zanzibar (Marilyn Povenmire had had a baby daughter several months earlier). After Julie and the baby returned home from the

hospital to the house in Mtoni, we remained there for a few more weeks until the Povenmires left for their next assignment, Paraguay.

Dale and I had worked closely together while Fritz was on home leave, and he and Marilyn had helped us a lot while Julie was in the hospital. We were sorry to see them go, but I was happy to assume full charge of my various duties. The Povenmires seemed relieved to be departing. One night, Dale told me, with a note of bitterness in his voice, that he hoped Julie and I would have a better tour of duty than he and Marilyn had had in Zanzibar.

Dale and I had the post in good shape for the Foreign Service inspectors, who arrived on October 6, the same day that Fritz returned. The inspectors gave us good marks, but puzzled me by asking some pointed questions about Fritz's lifestyle. Since I knew hardly anything about his private life then, I spoke of Fritz in positive terms.

From the beginning, the Project Mercury tracking station had been a target of political attacks. In June 1960, four months before the United States and Britain signed the agreement on the tracking station, Zanzibari leftists voiced opposition to its establishment. Babu and his followers kept up the campaign against the station from then on, first within the ZNP, then later as the breakaway Umma Party. They charged that the station was an American rocket base and "a center of imperialist aggressions in East Africa." In time, Zanzibar's two labor federations joined in the attack.

When it seemed likely that ZNP and ZPPP moderates and conservatives would favor continuation of the station, which had created jobs and was a source of foreign exchange, the issue became a political football. To try to squelch the opposition to Mercury, the United States agreed to a proposal for a neutral observer to inspect the facility and issue a report. The observer, a Swede, made his inspection in mid-August 1963 and left a report with the government giving a clean bill of health to the project. Prime Minister Mohammed Shamte told Picard that the report was "very favorable."

This did not end the matter, however. Karume issued a statement objecting to "the continuation or establishment of any foreign bases." At Fritz's invitation, Karume and other leading figures in the ASP came to the consulate to discuss the Mercury question. One member of the delegation was Abdulla Kassim Hanga, the ASP's deputy general secretary. A declared Marxist, the thirty-one-year-old Hanga had a year of university training in the Soviet Union, visited there several times afterward, and married the daughter of American Marxist expatriates in Moscow. He was vocally anti-Arab, anticolonial, and anti-American.

Karume's English was not bad at all, but he preferred to speak to Fritz in Swahili, which I translated. It bothered me that Fritz handled Karume in a somewhat patronizing manner. After some initial evasiveness, Karume said his statement had been aimed not at Project Mercury but at the British. The objective was to dissuade them from maintaining security forces in Zanzibar to protect the government after independence. Hanga said nothing, but his hostility toward us was palpable. Karume told Picard that he would call a meeting of the ASP leadership and "take care of everything." Nothing positive came of his assurances, however.

The ASP's opposition to Project Mercury was a cause of mild concern in Washington. More important, however, was the positive attitude shown by the Zanzibar government. There seemed to be no reason to expect that the Mercury operations would not be able to continue for the life of the manned space program.

Ali Muhsin, Prime Minister Shamte, and their colleagues in the government seemed intent on pouring salt into the wounds of injured African pride. After the election, Shamte had responded to ASP negotiations for some cabinet posts by telling Karume and the others that they could enter the government only if they dissolved their party and applied for membership in the ZPPP. The splits within the ASP, culminated by the resignation of Othman Sharif and others of the leadership, reinforced the Arabs' perception that the Africans were no match for them.

Prerevolution Government of Zanzibar. (On the sofa, left to right, Ali Muhsin, Prime Minister Mohammed Shamte, Minister of Finance Juma Aley)

As noted earlier, the preindependence government responded to its budget deficit by cutting spending on schools and social services. The Africans, who were the population group most affected by this, were also experiencing high unemployment, a rare occurrence in Zanzibar.

The government turned a deaf ear to an ASP request for land reform, an issue of great importance to the largely landless Africans. Instead, the ZNP-ZPPP coalition proposed that the Parliament approve creation of a land bank whose loans would be restricted to people who already owned land. Those who would benefit the most were the large-plantation owners: Arabs and Asians.

The banning of the Umma Party and raids upon its headquarters and Babu's house did no harm to the ASP. But it fed Africans' fears that the ASP was next in line to be banned and added to the belief of some that the forcible overthrow of the government was the only way to salvation. This belief was fueled by rumors, widely believed by the Africans, that the government was secretly arming the "Manga" Arabs, whom the Africans feared and hated.

The Manga were relatively recent arrivals in Zanzibar, most coming to the island after the 1920s. Many were petty traders, and most lived in the countryside, where they monopolized the commerce of selling food items and other necessities to the rural population. Africans despised the Manga for their sharp trading practices, including price gouging, and for the disdain they openly showed for Africans. Fear of the Manga grew out of previous political violence, in which they had gained a reputation for ferocity and cruelty.

Arabs in general, not just the Manga, persisted in displaying their contempt for African aims and political leaders. In Parliament, Minister of Finance Juma Aley referred disparagingly to Karume as "the boatman." And he expressed contempt for the abilities of Africans.

Shortly after independence day, Ali Muhsin, now minister of external affairs, made two trips to Cairo, emphasizing the government's desire for a close association with the United Arab Republic (as Egypt was called in those days) in particular and Arab countries in general. This was yet another slap in the face for the Africans, who continued to want Zanzibar to have its closest relations with black African countries.

The height of the government's stupidity, though, stemming from the Arabs' hubris and their low regard for Africans, related to security. Three decisions made a successful revolt decidedly more achievable. First, intent on having a close relationship with Nasser's United Arab Republic, the Shamte government, again, guided by Ali Muhsin, abjured future military cooperation with Britain. Their scorn for the Africans must have led them to conclude that there would be no need to have a British garrison stationed in Zanzibar or to enter into any other form of security arrangement with London.

Second, the government did nothing to keep retiring British police officers from leaving before or after independence. Twenty out of twenty-six British policemen departed and were not replaced before the revolution occurred. The government planned to strengthen the Police Mobile Force and ensure its loyalty by a heavy infusion of Arabs but, complacent, saw no urgency in getting this done.

Sultan Jamshid bin Abdullah

And third, not only higher-level police officials but also inspectors and noncommissioned officers (NCOs) were dismissed from the force. All of them were mainland Africans, whose loyalty the government doubted. Almost guaranteeing an available supply of disgruntled ex-policemen for the revolutionaries, in its most myopic move, the government refused to pay the dismissed policemen's travel expenses back to the mainland. A good number of them (Okello said forty-two) were enlisted into Okello's ranks. They brought with them both their paramilitary skills and their knowledge of the armory system.

Perhaps if Sultan Seyyid Khalifa bin Harub had still been alive, the revolution might not have been virtually certain to take place. He had been enormously respected by the Africans as well as by other ethnic groups throughout the forty-nine years of his reign, which ended with his death in 1960. His son, Abdulla, took the throne, but was infirm and died in July 1963, just a week before the elections. Abdulla was seen as supporting the ZNP, and so, too, was the new sultan, Abdulla's son Jamshid.

The thirty-three-year-old Jamshid enjoyed nothing of the kind of respect that had been given to his grandfather. Jamshid's sympathy for the views of Ali Muhsin and the ZNP was well known and alienated him

from the Africans, whose needs were of little interest to him. Even Arabs who strongly backed continuation of the sultanate did not hold Jamshid in high regard. In general, islanders viewed the sultan as a feckless playboy, a man best known for his passion for sports cars and speedboat racing. John Okello regarded him as an Arab colonialist who would have to be killed or forced into exile.

Julie, the two little girls, and I moved into our new two-storied house not long after the Povenmires left Zanzibar. Located in an area called Mnazi Mmoja (One Coconut Tree), it was an attractive, much more substantial, and larger house than the Mtoni place. The spacious living-dining room, cooled by ceiling fans, opened onto a terrazzo porch and a yard of spotty grass and luxuriant tall trees. Our next-door neighbor was Ali Muhsin, who had us over for tea soon after we moved in.

The comparatively mild weather of the southwest monsoon had ended by early November with the onset of the short rains, and we were happy to be in the new house, with its ceiling fans. The rains tapered off by the end of December, when the hot northeast monsoon began to blow.

I continued to work long hours, even after courier service to Zanzibar was resumed in November. This ended the requirement for me to fly to Dar es Salaam every Sunday. Dar is only forty miles from Zanzibar Town, but air service between the two was limited to a morning and a late-afternoon flight, which ate up the whole day for me.

I wrote a survey report on the labor situation and another on Zanzibar's economy. Fritz and I put in many hours of (uncompensated) overtime, making preparations first for a mid-November visit by a U.S. trade delegation and then for the U.S. delegation to the Uhuru (freedom, or independence) celebration.

The government received the Americans and other Western and African delegations to the celebration cordially but paid much greater attention to the Egyptian and other Arab delegations. In doing so, it signaled again that Zanzibar intended to align itself with the Arab world.

The ranking State Department member of the U.S. delegation was Assistant Secretary of State for African Affairs G. Mennan "Soapy"

Williams, former governor of Michigan. He could see that the Africans were decidedly unenthusiastic about Zanzibar's approaching independence. He asked Fritz whether he was sure that, as Fritz's reporting indicated, the minority Arab government could rule over the long haul. Fritz replied that it could. He cited what he viewed as the political skills of the ZNP leadership, said the party was multiracially based, and pointed to the divisions among the Africans.

After Julianne was born, Julie and I had resumed an active social life, which for better or worse was part and parcel of a career in diplomacy. We both developed an aversion to cocktail parties, and I began to develop skills in how to talk to everyone I needed to and then leave unobtrusively as early as possible.

I took time to start playing golf at the island's short nine-hole course, which was close to our house. Grazing cattle helped keep the fairways mowed but caused a small problem: the course rules provided that if a ball landed in a cow pie, it could be dropped a club length away with no penalty. Putting had to be done quickly. Large red ants, which had a sharp bite, swarmed over the greens and began crawling up the putter's legs as soon as he got in place to putt.

American cargo ships called at Zanzibar about every three months. Their arrivals were like a holiday for us, since they brought our surface mail, which meant books, presents, magazines, food, and clothing from mail-order houses, as well as other welcome items unavailable in Zanzibar. In early December, a freighter came into port bringing Christmas packages.

Two days before Christmas, the official mourning period for President Kennedy ended. All of us had been emotionally affected by his assassination. We were touched by the expressions of sympathy and condolence shown by many Zanzibaris in letters and visits to the consulate. The Parliament passed a resolution of condolence to be sent to the U.S. government and the family of the slain president. Marring the occasion, Hanga and another young parliamentarian, Hassan Nasser Moyo, who, sponsored by the consulate, had accepted a grant to visit the United

States in 1962, had walked out of the session to show their disapproval of the resolution.

The sadness of that November was eased by the happiness of Christmas and the diversion of New Year's Eve. My job, though busy, was no longer hectic. I was concentrating on carrying out my responsibilities for a United States Agency for International Development (USAID) project in Zanzibar. Julie and I made new friends and were enjoying our assignment more and more.

As the new year began, the exodus of colonial officials was well under way. One of them, a high-ranking police officer, told Fritz and me that there would be serious trouble in Zanzibar, but not for six months or so.

Many of the British officials intended to remain until the government was able to implement its plan to replace them with Egyptians. The approximately 130 who stayed after independence and their families, along with businesspeople and others in the British community, looked forward to continuing their pleasant way of life in Zanzibar. They, like the Americans, were blissfully ignorant of what lay just around the corner.

4

※

Revolution: Day One

*You [the sultan] are allowed twenty minutes to kill your children and
wives and then to kill yourself. I do not want to see your face and request
you to save me in this way from an unpleasant duty. If I find you I shall
kill you and all your dependents, and then burn your remains with a fierce
and hungry fire.*

— **John Okello**

*The United States was hopeful today that developments in Zanzibar
would portend no international dangers, but it was fearful that the
Western political and strategic position in East Africa would be severely
impaired.*

— *New York Times,* **January 14, 1964**

The western part of the triangle encompassing Zanzibar Town was
bisected by Creek Road, which ran one mile, southwest to northeast. The apex of the triangle, at the sea, lay some five hundred yards
due west of the midpoint of Creek Road. Stone Town, government
offices, banks, other commercial firms, and the port facilities were in
the area west of Creek Road. At its northern end, Creek Road intersected the main road leading from the city to the northern part of the

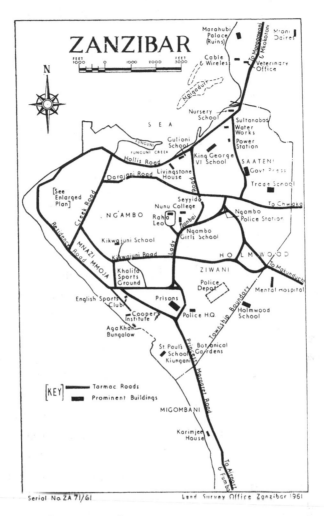

ZANZIBAR

Zanzibar Town and environs

island. Zanzibar Town's police station was a stone's throw west of this intersection, in the area known as Malindi. About four miles out on the northern road, at Mtoni, just past our first house, was the Police Mobile Force's headquarters and armory. Ng'ambo, the populous African quarter, extended for more than a mile to the east of Creek Road. The Raha Leo Community Center and the Sauti ya Unguja (Voice of Zanzibar) radio station were located near the eastern limits of Ng'ambo.

Creek Road's southern end met the road running southeast to the airport. It passed by our house at Mnazi Mmoja. Less than a quarter mile
beyond the house, toward the airport, the road went by the prison and
just beyond it the Ziwani police headquarters and armory. The police
headquarters at Ziwani, the prison, the Police Mobile Force at Mtoni,
and the radio station at Raha Leo were John Okello's initial main targets.
The Malindi police station would be attacked later.

At ten o'clock on Saturday night, January 11, some eight hundred
men gathered at the Mwembe section of Ng'ambo to get their orders
from Okello. They had filtered in from an African *ngoma* (dance) festival
near Mnazi Mmoja, carrying their weapons: spears, *pangas*, knives,
sticks, tire irons, stones, and bows and arrows. No one had a firearm.

Okello, Seif Bakari, and their lieutenants divided the men into four
groups, one for each target. Shortly after midnight, the largest unit,
about three hundred men, headed off to Mtoni. The others moved out at
the same time. Okello himself led the group that was to attack the
Ziwani police headquarters.

The attacks began at three o'clock on Sunday morning. The effects of
the dismissals of experienced officers and NCOs and of the low morale
of the police became readily apparent. There was little resistance at the
Police Mobile Force station at Mtoni, and it fell quickly to the rebels.
The armory there yielded two hundred rifles, twenty-five semiautomatic
carbines, two Bren machine guns, some pistols, and ammunition.

At Ziwani, Okello and his men waited quietly until the time for
attack. They cut the barbed wire fence surrounding the compound, then
rushed the main building. The armory was downstairs, the sleeping quarters upstairs. As Okello had expected, there were only a few guards.
One of them spied the attackers and shot and killed two of them, but he
and the other sentries were quickly overwhelmed. Okello bayoneted a
sentry with the man's own rifle.

In the melee that followed, the police threw tear gas down the stairs,
but were kept at bay by the attackers, who used bows and arrows. The
rebels battered the door open and began distributing arms. They were
not needed immediately, however, for by then the fight had ended as the
surviving policemen surrendered. A Police Mobile Force unit counter-

attacked at four-thirty, but was easily defeated. By five-thirty, the Ziwani station was secure.

It was around four o'clock that morning when Julie heard the telephone ringing. We had had an enjoyable Saturday. It had been a clear day that became hot as it wore on. I went out for a session of flailing away on the golf course, then took a bike ride with Julie after our *ayah* (nanny), Agnes, arrived to look after the girls.

That night, we went to a party at Mtoni given by Teresa and George Burch. George was the chief of party of the Bendix Corporation technicians who manned the tracking station. About thirty-five years old, he was soft-spoken and retiring. Teresa, a Spaniard, was quite the opposite: an outgoing, gregarious young woman who loved to talk. Unlike some of the Project Mercury people, the wives in particular, she liked to get out and around. Teresa once told me that when she and George went to the Pigalle, one of Zanzibar Town's two small hotels, she often encountered Babu drinking at the bar. The fiery, anti-American radical political leader was always friendly and seemed to enjoy having long conversations with her.

We got back home from the Burches' at eleven-thirty, and I took Agnes to her house in Ng'ambo. Returning to Mnazi Mmoja, I could faintly hear the sounds at the *ngoma* but neither heard nor saw anything unusual. Because the nights were now so hot, we had started using the air-conditioning window unit upstairs in the children's bedroom. By closing the door to the hall and keeping open the one between our bedroom and the children's, we could cool both bedrooms. The loud whirring of the air conditioner muffled outside noises.

When Julie told me the phone was ringing, I got up and went out into the hall to answer it. Before picking it up, I could hear popping sounds outside the house. As they continued, I realized I was hearing gunfire. Fritz was on the line. He said that some of Babu's people were trying to take the Ziwani police station. We agreed that I would alert the Americans, including the several tourists who were in town, while he continued to call around to find out what was going on.

Some of the firing was right by the house. I later learned that revolutionaries, armed with weapons seized at the Ziwani station, had fired on Ali Muhsin's house next door to us in an attempt to capture him. However, he had already fled.

Although the more distant firing was in the area of the Ziwani police station and the prison, it sounded as if it might also be coming from the part of Ng'ambo closest to our place. Julie worried about the safety of Agnes, Jacobo, and our other domestic helper, Omari, all of whom lived in that part of Ng'ambo. I assured her that if the government was being attacked, they, as Africans, would be all right. In a later phone call, Fritz told her the same.

The shooting at Ali Muhsin's was on the other side of the house from our bedroom, so I believed we were safe where we were and told Julie that for now, she and the girls should stay in the bedrooms. I continued using the phone in the hallway, calling all the Americans I could reach.

By five o'clock, the shooting by our house had ended. I took a shower and shaved. After Julie had bathed and dressed, she nursed Julianne. Susie was awake by then, and we took her downstairs with us when we went for breakfast. Fritz had called again to inform me that apparently the government could not cope with the rebellion and had asked for outside help. He had been talking to the British high commissioner, Timothy Crosthwait, and to one or two of the British officials who had remained in their jobs after independence. Fritz, like Crosthwait, had been unable to get in touch with either Zanzibar government officials or Karume and other politicians.

The rebels had not yet moved into Stone Town and the adjacent area to the west. Telephone service, international as well as local, was open, as was the office of Cable and Wireless. It would remain out of Okello's control until about nine-thirty that morning. With international communications open, at 6:10 A.M. Fritz was able to call American ambassador William Leonhart in Dar es Salaam. In a brief cable to Washington, Leonhart reported: "Picard phoned 0610 hours mobs have seized police arms. Fighting has broken out. Prime Minister has requested British Hicom bring in troops and aircraft from Kenya to restore order. Picard recommends we urge British do so and requests immediate evacuation

of dependents." Shortly afterward, Fritz called Cable and Wireless and dictated a similar message to the State Department. In it, he added that the Zanzibar government had also asked for help from the Tanganyikan government.

The rebels had seized the radio station with little if any resistance. They pressed a BBC technician into service to operate the transmitter. With the police at Ziwani and Mtoni defeated and no sign of effective resistance elsewhere, Okello went to Raha Leo at seven to make his first broadcast. Possession of the radio station gave him a powerful tool to gain support from the African masses and to confuse and terrify his opponents. Reflecting his hatred for the Arabs who ruled Zanzibar and his tendency to use flamboyant, Old Testament-like language, Okello's radio messages often included some bloodcurdling passages. His first broadcasts, however, were somewhat restrained. In one of them, he announced:

> I am the field marshal. Wake up, you imperialists; there is no longer an
> imperialist government on this island. This is now the government of the
> freedom fighters. Wake up, you black men. Let every one of you take a
> gun and ammunition and start to fight against any remnants of imperial-
> ism on this island. Never, never relent, if you want this island to be yours.

Despite the absence of any grisly threats, non-African Zanzibari listeners must have been chilled by the realization that the government had lost control of the radio station. It was also alarming that the unknown man calling himself field marshal spoke Swahili with the accent of a mainland African. Okello did not divulge his name on the radio until the next day.

After breakfast, Julie went upstairs to pack. Because Fritz had told me about a possible evacuation, I had told her that we might have to leave the house. While she was packing, I made ready to take a ride on my bicycle to see what was going on. We could still hear gunfire in the direction of Ziwani, although it was less intense now. Fearful that I would get my head blown off, Julie urged me not to go. I told her not to worry and

joked that I was so thin nobody would notice me. She was not reassured. I left the house at about six o'clock.

Riding out our driveway onto the short street leading to the road to town and the airport, I saw no activity at Ali Muhsin's house and found nobody at all. I headed west toward town. Seeing no one on that stretch of the road, I turned north, taking a street toward Ng'ambo, where I could see there was some activity. The first few people I met knew very little about what was happening. But they all said the situation was dangerous and warned me to get out of the area. Realizing I was not going to get any useful information in this manner, I rode back home.

When I called Fritz again, he told me it was too risky for me to be out and about and said I should stay put. This probably was sound advice. Small bands of rebels had come into town, and some had engaged in mindless shooting. A family of adults and children on their way to the Catholic church for Sunday morning mass had been massacred.

Stu Lillico lived less than a mile from the airport. Well after the fighting at Ziwani had begun and his employee had alerted him, he could hear no sounds of firing. Throughout the morning, he stayed in contact with Picard by telephone. His closest neighbor, a New Zealander named Bill Belcher, who was a Clove Glowers' Association official and reserve police officer, dropped by. Belcher said he had been told to report for duty at the Malindi police station in town and to bring a weapon if he had one, for the police were low on weapons.

Belcher made his way in the darkness to Malindi, running into no trouble in town on his way there. The police station's contingent, headed by J. M. Sullivan, commissioner of police for Zanzibar and Pemba, consisted of several police reservists and some seventy-five Zanzibari policemen. Belcher found that the men were reasonably well armed but grievously short of ammunition. Several hours passed before a series of attacks on Malindi began.

It was still dark when George Burch got a call from Fritz telling him that that fighting had broken out. Picard asked him to go to the nearby house of John Cameron, a South African architect who with his wife,

Lorna, had lived on the island for several years. Burch was to pass a message to Cameron to report to the Malindi station, after which George and Teresa were to sit tight at home.

George and Teresa drove to the Camerons' and delivered the message to John and Lorna's house servant. They then followed Fritz's advice to return to their house, but as the darkness was giving way to daylight, George decided to drive to the Project Mercury station. He wanted to communicate by radio from there to the Mercury operation at Lagos, Nigeria, to get word to NASA and the Bendix Corporation about the disturbing events in Zanzibar.

He and Teresa got in their car and headed for the station, which was located at Tunguu, about ten miles east of Zanzibar Town. Fearing the dangers that might await them if they went into town to pick up the road leading most directly to Tunguu, they drove north to take a series of roads that would get them to the station. Approaching the sultan's summer palace at Kibweni, less than a mile from their house, they heard shots. As they continued, the shots got louder. It seemed to George that the firing was being directed at them. He did a fast U-turn and sped back to their house, where they waited inside for further word.

As noted earlier, Afro-Shirazi Party leader Abeid Karume may have been aware that something was going to happen that weekend, but he was not privy to Okello's plans. In the early hours of the morning, some of Okello's men awakened Karume. Okello apparently was concerned for Karume's safety. The men took him first to Raha Leo, which had become the revolutionaries' headquarters, then to the harbor, where he boarded a dhow that took him to Dar es Salaam.

The ASP's deputy leader, Abdulla Kassim Hanga, also went to Dar in those early-morning hours of January 12, but under different circumstances. Believing, with good reason, that Hanga was planning to displace Karume as ASP leader, Okello strongly disliked him. It is said that Hanga was on a list Okello had made of people to be killed. In any event, once aware that the revolution had started and afraid for his life, Hanga fled to Dar.

Othman Sharif, having broken with Karume and resigned from the ASP, may have believed he was in danger. Okello did not intend to harm him, however. As had happened to Karume, some of Okello's men aroused Sharif from his sleep. They were armed and told him that he was in protective custody and would have to remain out of sight for several hours.

Babu had been in Dar since January 8. Like the other politicians, he was taken by surprise when word reached him the morning of the twelfth that a revolution was under way. Late that morning, he told Tanganyikan president Julius Nyerere, who had called him into his office, that although he had expected trouble, he had no knowledge of the timing or character of the revolt. On the outside looking in, he nevertheless had a great asset that would soon make him a powerful figure in the revolutionary government. Among his followers were young men who had recently returned to East Africa from Cuba, where they had received training, including military instruction. They had stashed automatic rifles, either on the mainland or in Zanzibar. Coincidentally returning to Zanzibar on the night before the onset of the revolution, they joined in the fighting. Because of the superior firepower of their weapons, they became a force to be reckoned with in the aftermath of the revolution and were an important factor in Babu's position of power in the new government.

Rex Preece was a graduate student from Johns Hopkins University who had come to Zanzibar in 1962 to do research for his dissertation on Zanzibar's constitutional development. Picard, and others as well, suspected that either Preece or Michael Lofchie, another graduate researcher in Zanzibar, might be working for the CIA.[2] Lofchie definitely was not. Years later, Rex told me that he had been associated with the CIA while he was in Zanzibar.

Picard was not happy with Preece's presence on the island and, according to Preece's wife, Carol, went out of his way to make that clear to Rex. Fritz, who did not want any nonembassy Americans reporting on Zanzibar to the U.S. government, had demanded to know

if a U.S. agent was on the island. Subsequently, he learned about Rex's status. He was annoyed and did not establish a cooperative relationship with Rex.

By late 1963, Preece's research in Zanzibar was done, and he was ready to return to the United States. He and Carol had completed their travel arrangements when, as he later told me, his arrangement with the CIA caused him to delay his departure for a couple of months. Accordingly, Carol and their three children left before him.

In 1998, Rex told me that he had not received any advance notice of Okello's revolution. His reporting did, however, indicate that trouble might be in the offing. In November 1963, Dennis Pitcher, who had become the head of the police in the Zanzibar District, second only to the commissioner of police for both Zanzibar and Pemba, related to Preece a conversation he had had with Ahmed Qullatein, one of Babu's lieutenants. Qullatein told Pitcher that there would be a revolution at some unspecified time after independence. Many years after the revolution, Pitcher told Dale Povenmire that the plot had been revealed in advance to the British police. Pitcher, who was in England when the revolution took place, said he had been told the exact date of its commencement. But if the British and Zanzibar government authorities were as informed as Pitcher says, why did they get caught, as they did, with their pants completely down? Other British colonial officials said the revolution took them by surprise.

The night before the revolution, Rex had a terrible headache. It would prove to be caused by cerebral malaria, which over the days ahead almost killed him.

The disinclination of the rebels to quickly move in force into Stone Town enabled the sultan to escape with his life. Mindful that the Arabs' grip on power might not last, Jamshid and his advisers had made a plan to flee to safety in the event of an uprising. A few hours after daybreak, he, his wife

Sultan's palace, Zanzibar Town

and children, his siblings and their families, and others close to him bundled into three well-guarded cars and made the less than a half-mile drive from the palace, which fronted the sea, to a boat landing at the harbor. From there, they went to the *Salama,* one of the government's two steamers, which was anchored in the harbor. That afternoon, Jamshid and his party transferred to a larger and better-appointed steamer, the *Seyyid Khalifa,* which had been called back from the Tanganyikan port of Tanga.

Okello remained at the radio station until shortly after ten in the morning. Before leaving, he broadcast that he was about to join the attack on the prison. He warned that resisters would be shot, and he said the commissioner of prisons should leave the prison and hide somewhere. The commissioner would be better off killing himself than encountering Okello, the field marshal declared.

The attackers at the prison had been unable to defeat its defenders and seize it. With well-armed reinforcements, Okello arrived at 10:10. Not long afterward, the defending fire ceased, and Okello's force occupied the buildings of the prison compound. The defenders had fled from the rear of the compound.

Back at our house, I had continued to keep in contact with Americans by telephone. Each time I talked with Fritz, I suggested that it could be useful for me to go into town to see what was occurring there. And each time he turned me down, saying it was too dangerous. Fritz kept in touch with High Commissioner Crosthwait and with various British colonial officials. He had also been able to talk to Prime Minister Shamte. Based on what he had heard from these sources, he judged the situation hazardous enough to warrant evacuation of the American community.

Fritz had already begun implementing the embassy's Emergency and Evacuation (E&E) plan. Before midmorning, the Americans residing in houses along the airport road had gone to the E&E gathering point, the Lillicos' house, close to the airport. The Americans living on the northern side of Zanzibar Town began gathering at George and Teresa's place.

It was not until shortly before ten o'clock, however, that Fritz called to say that my family and I should drive to the Lillicos'. We had already packed, and Julie hurried down to the kitchen to get some milk, baby food, cereal, and cookies for the children. She ran back upstairs to find Susan's favorite doll. I put the bags and food in the car, then helped Julie carry the girls downstairs and into the VW. Wanting to keep the girls as close to her as possible, Julie put Susie on her lap and placed Julianne in a basket at her feet in the front seat. I drove out to the road and turned right.

The prison was close to the left side of the road, a couple of hundred yards down the road. Unknowingly, we approached it at the time the attack was intensifying. Suddenly, we saw just ahead on the right side of the road a group of twenty or thirty men. They had been shielded from our vision by the thick foliage along the road. Armed with rocks, bows and arrows, *pangas*, and some rifles, as soon as they saw us coming their way, they turned toward us, brandishing their weapons and pointing the rifles at us. Julie believed they were going to kill us. She embraced Susie and prayed for deliverance. I recall that it happened so fast that I had no time to think, and I simply stopped the car. Once the men saw we were whites, however, they lowered their weapons and told us to drive on.

As we passed them, I could hear firing coming from the prison. Some fifty yards farther on, the road bent to the right, hiding whatever was around the curve. No sooner had we passed the bend than we came upon another band of armed men. They had blocked the road with a couple of coconut trees that they had chopped down. Once again, weapons were leveled at us but fortunately not fired. Here, the firing from both sides was more intense and the atmosphere somewhat frenzied. Within seconds, some of the attackers motioned us to drive off the road around the right side of the roadblock. Bullets were whizzing over the car, and we could hear some smack into nearby trees. As we got around the roadblock, the men directing us frantically urged us to drive on. Maybe a quarter of a mile farther, clear of the danger, it dawned on me what a close call we had had. Stunned for a moment, I slowed the car, took a deep breath, and drove on. Julie was as shaken as I was, and Susie was crying.

Most of the people who were supposed to be at the Lillicos' were there. Counting the four of us, there were twenty-two adults and children. Rex Preece and another family arrived soon afterward. The Picards were still at their place a half mile away, so I drove there to see how they were doing. I gladly accepted Fritz's offer to join them for a beer. After downing it, at their request I took their three children, along with their *ayah* and her daughter, to the Lillicos', then returned to their house, where Shoana was finishing packing.

It was clear by this time that the Zanzibar government existed in name only. We had learned that cabinet members and lesser officials were in hiding. Fritz's most reliable source that morning was M. V. Smithyman, permanent secretary in the prime minister's office, the highest-ranking British colonial officer in postindependence Zanzibar. Until eight that morning, Smithyman had worked from his office at the Beit el-Ajaib (House of Wonders), the large government office building on the waterfront, about one hundred yards south of the sultan's palace. Judging the situation in the area increasingly unsafe, he left the Beit el-Ajaib and swam out to the *Salama*. He had been communicating by telephone with government ministers, urging them to take refuge on the *Salama,* from where they could safely negotiate with the rebels.

House of Wonders

Before leaving the Beit el-Ajaib, Smithyman turned his authority over to Henry Hawker, the permanent secretary for finance, who continued to advise the ministers to go to the ship. For reasons that are not entirely clear, Prime Minister Shamte refused, and his colleagues followed suit. Some seemed to believe they could better negotiate with the rebels from town. Others were simply afraid to leave wherever they had holed up.

Hawker, Smithyman, and other colonial holdover officials were doing what they could to be useful in the chaotic situation that day. All had been surprised and alarmed by the turn of events. As Zanzibar's attorney general, Jack Rumbold, told American embassy officials in Dar es Salaam three days later, British officials and the Zanzibar government were "taken completely by surprise and had no intimation of the coming revolt."

At noon, Fritz, Shoana, and I left their house and drove to the Lillicos', where we joined the others for lunch. Fritz's best means of communicating with the embassy in Dar had been through the British air-traffic controllers at the airport tower. He decided that he and I should go to the airport to send a message and at the same time see

what the prospects were for an evacuation by aircraft. We got into his official car, a medium-size black Ford, and, with a small U.S. flag attached to a staff on the front fender whipping in the breeze, we headed for the airport. Slowing down as we approached it, we spied a car parked on the right side of the road. Several men were inside it. Just as we began passing it, we saw a long barrel of a huge rifle of some kind emerging from the side nearest us. It let off a loud boom and emitted a cloud of black smoke. I had no idea what kind of firearm it was, but I could have sworn it was a blunderbuss. The car's occupants intended to scare, not harm, us. They succeeded, but nevertheless we continued on to the terminal.

Once there, we got out of the car and yelled to the two Brits in the tower. They told us to come up. In the tower, they pointed out the few groups of armed rebels who were standing about in the tall grass just beyond the periphery of the airfield. They told us it was far too dangerous now for any airplane to land.

The control tower had been relaying messages from British officials, including the ranking police officers. Earlier in the morning, the police sent a message asking for a supply of weapons from the police in Pemba. Through the tower, arrangements were made for the regular Dar es Salaam–Zanzibar-Pemba-Tanga flight to pick up the arms and fly them to Zanzibar. The aircraft used for this run was a 1929 De Haviland. It was a canvas-covered biplane with an enclosed cockpit and passenger area, which could accommodate a maximum of six people. Both the luggage and the passengers had to be weighed before boarding. The plane was affectionately called the *Bamboo Bomber.*

The *Bomber*'s ETA that morning was 10:10. East African Airways (EAA), however, refused to let the airplane return to Pemba until after it had gone to Tanga and disembarked those passengers who were going to that mainland town. This meant a delay of a least an hour, which turned out to be decisive: by the time the plane neared the Zanzibar airport, it was no longer safe to land there.

After the two air-traffic controllers had related this to us, Fritz got on the line to the embassy in Dar es Salaam, which relayed a message from him to the State Department. In it, he reported that the government of

Zanzibar had collapsed and that there were a "considerable number of fatalities, primarily among Arabs." He noted that the aircraft flying arms in from Pemba had been waved off and that Cable and Wireless was "in insurgent hands."

At some point in his earlier calls, Fritz had backed away from calling for an evacuation. But now, in this latest communication, he asked that the "USS *Manley* proceed Zanzibar for possible evacuation and embassy Dar es Salaam attempt charter DC-3 from EAA on standby basis as alternate means evacuation dependents." In the course of his talks with Dar, Fritz had learned that the *Manley*, a naval destroyer making goodwill calls at East African ports, was in Mombasa. In the cable relaying Fritz's message to Washington, the embassy in Dar es Salaam commented that Picard would notify it by telephone if he decided to call for the evacuation.

The two men in the tower told us they expected the terminal and tower to be soon seized by rebels. With nothing more that we could do at the airport, Fritz and I drove back to his house. By three o'clock, the airport was in the hands of the rebels.

The first communications from Dar es Salaam and Zanzibar that fighting had broken out reached the State Department at about midnight in Washington. The African Bureau's duty officer was informed, and he in turn passed the word on to appropriate department officials. There was little anyone could do in those early hours of the morning except wait for more Information from Zanzibar and Dar es Salaam.

It was a different matter in London. With only a three-hour time difference between the UK and the East African coast, as opposed to the eight-hour span between Washington and the area, the Commonwealth and Colonial Office was well manned not long after word of the trouble in Zanzibar was received. Prime Minister Shamte's request for British military intervention to restore order was considered, but because the Zanzibar government had no military agreement with the UK, the request was quickly rejected.

At noon in London, the American embassy there sent a cable with information it had obtained from the British government. A British rush

to judgment that Babu was behind the revolution was evident. The cable began by stating: "Riots and revolt led by Babu and Communists, with new govt reportedly now in existence. Afro-Shirazi Party not . . . involved." It went on to note that because the UK high commissioner in Zanzibar had reported no immediate threat to British nationals or property, Her Majesty's Government (HMG) had decided there was no need for a British evacuation. The embassy's message also reported that "HMG has just telegraphed UK reps in Kenya, Tanganyika and Uganda instructing them inform govts that inasmuch as Zanzibar independent country and as revolt an internal matter HMG does not consider it appropriate that UK troops intervene."

Although the British had concluded that they would not intervene to restore order in Zanzibar, they made preparations to take action if British nationals were endangered by the violence there. The government of Kenyan prime minister Jomo Kenyatta had signed an agreement with Britain providing that some units of the British armed forces would remain in Kenya after it became independent. Two battalions of those forces were alerted, and steps were taken to transport them by air to Zanzibar, if that became necessary. A Royal Navy marine survey ship, the *Owen,* was sent from Mombasa to Zanzibar to stand by for a possible evacuation. A British frigate, the *Rhyl,* accompanied by an auxiliary, the *Hebe,* set sail from Aden later. A company of British army infantrymen was aboard the *Rhyl.*

The Kenyan and Ugandan governments had quickly decided not to agree to Shamte's request for military intervention. In Dar es Salaam, Tanganyikan president Julius Nyerere was unsure what to do. During a meeting with Ambassador Leonhart and British High Commissioner Stephen Miles on the morning of the twelfth, Nyerere told them there was no precedent for dispatching Tanganyikan troops abroad. With it unclear whether the revolt was political in nature or a mob action, the mission of an intervention force could not be defined. If there was uncontrolled mob action leading to heavy loss of life, his government would do its part to restore order, Nyerere said. If, however, the fighting in Zanzibar was politically based, any use of Tanganyikan troops to support the Zanzibar government against African rebels would raise a

clamor in Tanganyika and throughout sub-Saharan Africa. That afternoon, in another meeting with Leonhart and Miles, Nyerere told the diplomats that he was virtually certain there would be no East African military deployment to Zanzibar.

With all his primary targets save Malindi captured, Okello devoted more attention to the Manga Arabs. Hearing that the Manga were killing or wounding rebel attackers in the rural areas where the bulk of the Manga lived, Okello sent some of his men and a supply of weapons to help the attackers. Manga resistance was fiercest at Bububu, a couple miles north of Mtoni; Mangapwani, another eight miles up the coast; Bumbwini, just north of Mangapwani; and Ras Nungwe, at the northern tip of the island. This northwest part of the island became the revolution's major killing field. According to Okello, there also was a great deal of bloodshed at Paje and Makunduchi in the southeastern part of the island.

The Manga were armed not by the government, as the Africans believed, but with their own personal hunting and sporting guns. Once their attackers got better armed, the tide swung against the Manga. Hundreds of them and other Arabs were shot dead, stabbed, clubbed or hacked to death, or burned alive when their huts or shops were set on fire. Some drowned trying to reach boats in the sea.

Arab resistance persisted in rural areas that night; by the end of the next day, it had mostly ended, although some killings and other violence against Arabs, and Asians as well, continued. In the days that followed, hundreds of rural and urban Arabs and lesser numbers of Asians were rounded up and put into detention camps.

At the Malindi police station, attacks had been little more than half-hearted attempts by small groups of rebels who melted away when the police fired back at them. Seif Bakari and another rebel were captured during one abortive attack. During questioning, Bakari said the ASP was carrying out the rebellion, but lied when he said Babu had returned and organized it (Babu did not get back to Zanzibar until early the next day). Commissioner Sullivan duly reported what Bakari had said, which added

to the misapprehension that Babu and his men were the movers and shakers of the revolution. Bakari and the other man were released to carry a request to their superiors to enter into talks. They reported to Okello at Raha Leo. Infuriated, he got on the radio to send a warning to Sullivan:

> Unless you, as commissioner, instruct your men to surrender unconditionally, I shall be obliged to come there myself. In such an event, things will be worse than a living creature can bear. I will fight to the end, and order my soldiers to kill every living thing there, and their blood will be on your head. I warn you imperialists, if I come there myself I shall kill all of you, even Asians and Europeans, whom I promised not to kill. . . . Surrender or we shall have no alternative but to extinguish you from the face of the earth and destroy whoever or whatever we find.

By midafternoon, having failed in a telephone call to Raha Leo to get agreement for a cease-fire and running out of ammunition, Sullivan decided to abandon the Malindi station. During a lull in the attacks, he marched all his men—none had been killed or wounded—to the wharf, where they were taken out to the *Salama*. Resistance at other, smaller police stations was also at an end. At one, the deputy police commissioner, an Arab named Sketi, was hacked to pieces. Some of his body parts were displayed on the hood of a car.

Looting, which had begun in town at a place called Darajani, an area of Arab and Asian shops and homes between Ng'ambo and Stone Town, would last throughout the day and well into the night. At the same time, the rebels in town continued to kill Arab men and rape Arab and Asian women. But most of the killing that took place in town was over, now that there no longer was any organized resistance to the rebels.

This was the season the Zanzibaris called the Tangabili (Two Sails), the time between the monsoons when the winds died down so much that fishing boats needed to use two sails instead of the customary one. It was the hottest time of the year. Holed up in the Lillicos' house, with the doors closed and barred, the more than two dozen Americans were

sweltering. Some of us watched though slits in the closed shutters as a group of armed Africans attacked nearby houses, killing or savagely mistreating the Arab inhabitants. All of us heard the shouts and screams, and some feared that we too would be victims.

We had no idea that Okello had ordered his people not to harm Europeans. Nor did we know that no European had been killed. Some had come close to death, but generally because of proximity to shooting directed at others or in an encounter with ill-disciplined, drunken rebel soldiers.

John and Lorna Cameron had not received the message relayed from Fritz for John to report to the Malindi station. They had gotten up early that morning and, unaware of what had been happening, driven north from their home at Mtoni to go fishing. Rebels stopped them near the Police Mobile Force armory. The men who seized them threatened to kill them, struck John several times, tied them up, and took them to Raha Leo. Still tied up, they were taken inside and left there until Karume, who was about to leave for the mainland, heard about them, went to them, and ordered their release.

At the Lillicos', ill-informed as we were, we could not rule out that we might become targets for violence or be caught in a crossfire. Fritz had been trying all day to reach Karume and other ASP leaders but, like British high commissioner Crosthwait, had had no success. He wanted to hear from the leaders of the rebellion before making a decision about evacuation. Discussing the situation with Stu Lillico and me, he decided that, since the airport was no longer an option, we should not stay where we were; instead, we should gather the Americans at the English Club in town in case an evacuation by sea became necessary. The English Club was located on the waterfront about two hundred yards southeast of the tip of the Zanzibar Town triangle and looked out on a sandy beach suitable for boats to land.

Was it safe to drive into town? Someone would have to find out, and Fritz suggested that Irv Zolo, the oldest of the Project Mercury employees and probably the steadiest among them, and I do the reconnoitering. We got into the VW, and I headed the car down the road. As we got closer to town, we passed cars that had been riddled with bullets.

Not knowing whether there would be roadblocks manned by nervous armed rebels, we were apprehensive as we rounded each curve in the road. Sweat was pouring off my body, and not just because of the heat. The road was deserted. We got into town, turned around, and went back to the Lillicos'.

It was about five o'clock when we returned. People got their things together, and all of us, except for Rex Preece, whom Fritz had asked to remain to monitor the telephone in case calls came in from Dar es Salaam, set off in a convoy of about seven cars. Before we left, Fritz called George Burch and told him that the Americans at Mtoni should meet us at the English Club. Our trip into town passed without incident.

The Americans living to the north of town had been gathered for the past several hours at George and Teresa Burch's house. That morning, seeing carloads of armed men driving by the house, George and Teresa had covered the windows with sheets, thinking that the rebels might want to come in if they saw people inside the house. After Fritz called to tell them to go to the English Club, the Burches and the others loaded themselves and their belongings into three cars and started off for town. They hadn't gone far when a band of men, dressed for the most part in rags and armed with rifles and *pangas*, stopped them. One of the women was almost pulled from her car by a man who was obviously drunk. The drunk jabbed at one of the male passengers with a bayonet. Another rebel took a woman's wallet.

Things seemed to be getting out of hand when, angered because the children in the cars began crying, a rebel yelled at a small child and said he would kill him if he did not stop crying. At this, Teresa, infuriated, jumped out of her car and began hollering at them, cursing them in English and Swahili. They seemed taken aback, and eased off a bit, but continued their harassment. After taking the several cartons of cigarettes in the Burches' car, they told George to open his trunk. Just then, an African friend of George and Teresa arrived on the scene and tongue-lashed the rebel band. The molestation ended, and the Americans were allowed to proceed. Whenever other rebels accosted them, George, driving the lead car, simply sped up and passed them.

The enormity of what had been happening that day became graphically apparent to them. They saw the bloody bodies of men lying by the side of the road. Some had been mutilated, their genitals stuffed into their mouths. The three-car convoy entered the town and made it from there to the English Club at about half past six without further trouble.

We settled in for the night. Except for a few of us who set up a guard post in the anteroom by the club's main entrance, everyone found space in rooms upstairs. There was a telephone, a desk, and four chairs in the anteroom. I took the first watch, accompanied by a couple of the other men. Fritz came down occasionally to use the phone. He continued to have no luck in getting hold of anyone in authority among the rebels and was unable to make further calls to Dar es Salaam.

The narrow, winding street in front of the club was in total darkness. As the night wore on, an occasional lone armed rebel silently walked by. Now and then, shooting broke out. Then we began hearing sounds of people breaking into dwellings. Fritz came down to use the phone. He reached a nearby house where he had learned that Maulidi Mshangama, one of the government ministers, and other members of his family were holed up.

One of Mshangama's relatives in the house was Fathiya, a young woman who was Stu Lillico's secretary. Of mixed ancestry—like so many Zanzibaris—Fathiya was extraordinarily beautiful, and I remember her as being the most sensual-looking woman I had ever seen. A member of the Busaidi family, she was a distant relative of the sultan. Her husband was a pro-Communist political activist. Fritz, I was to learn later, had been having an affair with her for many months.

Soon afterward, now after midnight, as the sounds of nearby violence persisted, Fritz became frantic. To my deep consternation, he stepped out into the street and began making a racket. He was trying to divert rebels who might be preparing to go into the house where Fathiya was. I was appalled, fearing that he would attract rebels who might demand to enter the club and possibly put our people in danger. I yelled, "For Christ's sake, Fritz, shut up and get back inside," but he paid no attention. Sure enough, a rebel patrol came down the street. The patrol's leader angrily demanded to know what Fritz was doing. Fritz said we

were having a party inside. The rebel told him to get back inside and quiet down. Once Fritz was inside, the patrol walked off.

Fritz went back upstairs. I said nothing further to him, but I was churning inside with anger. Later that night, after Fritz had phoned her again, Fathiya, with her two children and her mother, slipped inside the front door of the club. Fritz was there to meet them and hide them away somewhere inside. By this time, there was neither sight nor sound of rebels, and I figured Fathiya and her family's arrival did not jeopardize us. I made no objection to giving them refuge.

Because of all that had been going on, having lost confidence in Fritz's judgment, and not knowing what might occur next, I decided to man the guard post all night.

The ministers of the deposed government remained in hiding. Some of them had sought refuge in the British high commission but were turned away. Apparently, none had fully understood the gravity of their situation until it was too late to escape from the island. At one point that Sunday, Ali Muhsin and Juma Aley, the former finance minister who was much hated by the Africans, had come by the Malindi police station. Finding no succor there, as the day wore on they must have begun to see that neither the British nor the mainland African governments would intervene on behalf of the Zanzibar government. As night fell, whatever opportunity they had to flee vanished.

By the end of the day, Okello had broadcast an appeal to Karume to return to Zanzibar. He named himself minister of defense and broadcasting and leader of the revolutionary government. Karume was president, Hanga prime minister (changed to vice president a few days later), Babu minister of external affairs, and Othman Sharif minister of education. Perhaps acting in concert with Seif Bakari, Okello had decided to end the divisions in the ASP and the rift between the ASP and the Umma Party by bringing the leaders of the various factions together in the new government.

Washington and London still had no clear idea who was running the show. Telegrams received in both capitals late in the night signed "John

Field Marshal John Okello

Okello, Field Marshal of the Zanzibar Republic" and asking for recognition only added to the mystery.

5

Day Two

An air of weird unreality hung over the sleepy, sun-baked capital of the world's newest "people's republic." Cuban-trained "freedom fighters" sporting Fidelista beards and berets stalked the narrow twisting streets. Carloads of whooping blacks careened through the Arab and Indian quarters, looting and shooting. Radios blared ominous messages of doom and death. From the hood of one car dangled a grisly trophy: the testicles of a murdered Arab.

—*Time*, January 24, 1964

The sounds of violence lessened as the night wore on. Periods of silence were interrupted now and then by bursts of gunfire. Just before daybreak on Monday, we heard a few shots nearby, followed by the sound of a heavy door being broken down. We never found out whether rebels had captured or killed the people they were hunting in the area close to the English Club. But we did see evidence of looting. The Bata shoe store just down the street, for example, had been broken into and stripped of its goods.

I had been alone during one stretch of time, but Stu Lillico was with me when predawn light washed over Zanzibar Town at about five

o'clock. I felt great relief that the long night was over. Fritz came down shortly after six. He was a bit haggard but seemed calm and self-assured.

While Fritz was on the telephone trying again to reach Karume and other ASP leaders, I went upstairs to see how Julie and the girls were doing. Julie looked tired, but otherwise she was all right. She had awakened earlier to nurse Julianne and was about to go to the dining room to see if she could get something to eat for herself and Susie. The English Club's kitchen staff had somehow rustled up enough food to feed everyone, and I had breakfast with Julie and Susie before going back downstairs.

Either earlier in the morning or after failing again to contact anyone in the revolutionary government, Fritz had concluded that an evacuation was called for. Neither Lillico, George Burch, nor I saw reason to disagree with him. Long-distance phone service, which had not been available that night, was restored, and at half past seven, Fritz called Ambassador Leonhart. He told Leonhart that the situation was very dangerous and that he wanted to evacuate all the Americans, except himself and me. He explained that the two of us should stay to secure the embassy's files and cryptographic materials. Leonhart reported the conversation in a cable to the State Department, and several hours later (at 4:10 A.M., Washington time) managed to telephone the information to Jesse MacKnight, director of the African Bureau's Office of East African Affairs.

Two hours later, State, the White House, and the Defense Department had agreed to go ahead with the evacuation. Instructions were sent to Picard, via Leonhart, to try to get the revolutionary government to give approval for the evacuation. If the government refused, Picard was to seek further instructions from Washington. The *Manley*, which had been steaming in the area but, as instructed, keeping clear of Zanzibar, was ordered to proceed to the island to undertake the evacuation.

It was quiet in town. For a while after sunrise, the streets were deserted, except for small bands of rebels roaming around. Okello had declared a curfew starting at seven Sunday night, and on Monday morning, few people were willing to test whether it was still in effect. But by nine o'clock, an occasional car was seen moving about, and now and

then some Britons slipped in and out of the club to exchange information with us.

Once made aware of the decision to evacuate, the Americans in the English Club were overjoyed. Knowing little about what was happening in town and next to nothing about the rest of the country, some of them having seen gruesome results of the violence or been stopped by undisciplined, antagonistic rebels, and fearing that something awful could happen at any time, they quite understandably wanted to get away from Zanzibar. Almost all, excluding those who had to look after the small children among us, congregated on the club's large second-floor terrace overlooking the sea. Although everyone was hoping to catch sight of the *Manley,* most had come there simply out of a desire to cluster together with friends and acquaintances.

A few of the armed men who were in the vicinity of the club that day were young, light-skinned, and dressed in battle fatigues. Some had beards. Believing they were Latinos, Julie and Teresa called out to one in Spanish. When he seemed to understand them and even said a word or two in Spanish in reply, they concluded from the way he accented the words that he was Cuban. They were mistaken. No Cuban, he was one of Babu's Cuban-trained Arab or Afro-Arab followers. Not knowing this, however, Julie and Teresa told some of the assembled Americans that they had seen a Cuban. In this manner, the first seed of the story about Cuban involvement in the Zanzibar revolution was sown.

Later, another man in fatigues was seen patrolling the area. Olive-skinned but clean-shaven, he looked the part of a Latin American. Intrigued, I ventured out into the deserted street in front of the club and in a few minutes met him as he was passing. I greeted him in Spanish. This and other comments I made in Spanish drew a look of puzzlement, so I switched to English. Keeping his revolver leveled at me, he responded in English that it was dangerous to be out in the street and that I should go back into the club. Once back inside, I told the Americans that the man was not a Cuban. But their first impression was the one that stuck with at least some of them.

Several European tourists, some of them women, had been staying at the club, and we readily agreed to their request to be included among

the evacuees. This led to an unseemly incident. We had made it known that children and women would precede adult males in getting out to the *Manley*. Two Project Mercury employees piped up to demand that Americans should go before all others, females included. Fritz was not there at the time, but Stu and I angrily told the two men that they and all the other men would bloody well wait until the last of the women was in a boat and ready to go out to the ship. The rest of the men firmly supported us.

Karume, Babu, and Hanga got together in Dar es Salaam sometime on Sunday after Okello had broadcast his appeal for Karume to return to Zanzibar and named all three to important posts in the government. They arranged with Israeli businessman Mischa Feinsilber to take them back to the island in his boat. With Feinsilber at the helm, they left Dar late that night. Arriving Monday morning at the fishing village of Fumba, twelve miles south of Zanzibar Town, they made their way to Raha Leo and, for the first time, met John Okello.

It must have been a heady moment for the Ugandan. Unknown to Zanzibar's leading political figures and a figure of virtually no political consequence, he was now the man in charge. And, for the time being, Karume and the others acknowledged this fact. They did not know what to make of him, but they knew enough to be in fear of him.

The outside world also continued to know nothing about the background and nature of John Okello. This did not prevent some "authoritative" biographical sketches on Okello from appearing in the press or in intelligence reports. The Kenyan newspaper the *Daily Nation* printed a story on Okello that included erroneous information that he had joined the Zanzibar police force in 1957, was awarded a scholarship by the ZNP to study military and science courses at the University of Havana, stayed in Havana from June 1961 until December 10, 1963, and turned against the ZNP when it reneged on a job offer it had promised him.

The embassy in Dar es Salaam passed on to Washington information it had gotten from the British Security Service, MI5, that Okello was an ex-constable who had been dismissed from the Zanzibar police force two

years earlier and was a protégé of Kenyan left-wing politician Oginga Odinga. MI5 also reported Okello had gone to Cuba and, adding to its concoction of misinformation, speculated that he had been a member of the Mau Mau movement in Kenya. The American embassy in Uganda also submitted a similarly flawed report on Okello.

The misreporting on Okello was a good example of the fallibility of intelligence agencies. Apparently, MI5 uncritically accepted as fact certain information it had received from Tanganyikan or Kenyan sources. Washington, influenced by MI5's good reputation in intelligence circles, would have been inclined to accept, at least initially, the information contained in the report on Okello. It was a case, however, of "garbage in, garbage out."

Julius Nyerere told Leonhart that Okello was a Luo from Kenya; Mischa Feinsilber believed that Okello had a Leopoldville accent; the British passed on to the American embassy in London that Okello was a Luo who not only went to Cuba, but also "spent some time in the United States."

At a news conference four days after the outbreak of the revolution, Okello denied having received any training abroad and said he had never traveled to Cuba or Communist China. No evidence was ever produced to prove the contrary, and there is no reason not to take what he said at face value. He told the reporters at the press conference that he had learned his revolutionary tactics from the Bible: "Everything can be learned from the Bible." No doubt adding to the fears in Washington and London about Communist influences in Zanzibar, Okello also told the reporters that he had sent personal greetings to Soviet premier Nikita Khrushchev. He said he agreed with Khrushchev that capitalism, colonialism, and imperialism should be buried. "The grave," he added, "is ready for them."[1]

Although untrained in the art of propaganda, the field marshal made effective use of radio to demonstrate his control of events and instill fear in the hearts of his enemies. In broadcasts that Monday, the thirteenth, he stated that the ZNP and ZPPP were banned. He said the previous government was one of "hypocrites and robbers, cursed and wicked people who do not respect humanity."

Okello warned that anyone possessing membership cards or other items of the banned political parties or pictures of the sultan would be killed or detained indefinitely. If all the weapons belonging to ZNP youths were not turned in, a thousand of those youths would lose their lives. Any of them found to be in possession of arms would be hanged or shot. Anyone resisting the revolutionary government's forces faced "complete extermination." He declared that if his orders were disobeyed, "I will take measures eighty-eight times stronger than at present."[2]

In Zanzibar Town on the thirteenth, the large-scale pillaging tapered off. What had been indiscriminate searching and ransacking of houses became an organized search, primarily for enemies and arms. More Arab and Asian women were raped. There were additional killings, but by now they were few in number.

In the rural areas, however, the slaughter continued. There, more homes and other Arab property were burned—as before, sometimes with the occupants inside. Pitched battles continued to take place in some locales, and whole families were massacred. The day before, enraged by what he said was evidence that the Arabs at Bumbwini had been storing ammunition and arms and conspiring to use them to kill Africans, Okello ordered his men to "fire in all directions and to kill whatever came before them—men, women, children, disabled persons, even chickens and goats."[3] This may have led to a belief among some of his men that the license to kill that he had given them during prerevolution training sessions was now open-ended. The killing lasted throughout the day and into the night.

Late that morning, intent on getting in touch with rebel leaders, Fritz made a foray along the beach in front of and extending to the northwest of the English Club. I went with him. Possibly trying to show the rebels that he trusted they would do him no harm and that his intentions were open and aboveboard, Fritz insisted on bringing his six-year-old son with him. For reasons that still elude me, he carried a mug of beer in his hand.

Up the beach near the Cable and Wireless building, which was some one hundred yards from the club, we encountered our labor union

Adam Mwakanjuki and rebel companion

friend Adam Mwakanjuki and several other men. All were armed; Adam held a revolver in his hand. Fritz began to bait him. Adam bristled, and his latent or hidden hostility toward Fritz began to spill out. "You son of a bitch, Picard," he cried, and he began brandishing the revolver in Fritz's face. Worried that Fritz was going to get himself killed, I said something to cool them down and got Fritz to agree to return to the club.

At noon, the *Manley* appeared, at first hull down, then soon in full view, definitely heading our way. Its officers and crew were intent on rescuing the Americans in Zanzibar. Jim Ruchti, the head of the political section at the American embassy in Nairobi, was aboard. Two days earlier, he had gone to Mombasa to greet the *Manley* when it arrived at the Kenyan port. When he heard on the radio about the trouble in Zanzibar, he recalled having reviewed Zanzibar's Emergency and Evacuation plan, and called the chargé d'affaires in Nairobi to suggest that the *Manley* be employed to evacuate the Americans on Zanzibar if an evacuation became necessary. The chargé agreed and passed the suggestion on to Washington. Before long, the Joint Chiefs of Staff authorized the *Manley* to head for Zanzibar. Permission also came for Ruchti, whom the ship's captain wanted to have aboard, to make the trip.

Before the *Manley* got under way, Ruchti, who did not speak Swahili, convinced the taxi driver who had driven him to the port, a Kenyan named Alexander, to come along as a translator. The *Manley* had no up-to-date chart of Zanzibar's waters. But as luck would have it, a British naval officer stationed in Mombasa, still there even though Kenya had gotten its independence a month earlier, had a 1950 chart on hand.

After the *Manley* sailed from Mombasa, it received its instructions to stay out of sight of Zanzibar and remain in midchannel between the island and the mainland. It was still the twelfth, and the decision to evacuate had not yet been made. While the ship was waiting for orders to proceed to Zanzibar, the captain called for volunteers to make up a landing party. Every man on the ship volunteered, although Ruchti had stressed that the landing could be highly dangerous. The ship had two boats: the captain's gig and a larger whaleboat. The gig was chosen; its forward part could be covered with a tarpaulin, under which Alexander, whose translating services would be needed, could be hidden. The captain insisted that the landing party be armed. Ruchti didn't like the idea, but went along with it when the captain agreed that the weapons would be stashed under the tarp.

As the hours passed and no word came from Washington, the *Manley*'s crew, their adrenaline flowing at the prospect of rescuing Americans, began to fret that the *Rhyl,* the British frigate that had left Mombasa about the same time as the *Manley,* would complete the evacuation before the American ship got to Zanzibar. They needn't have worried; the British government had opted not to evacuate British nationals for the time being. The men aboard the *Manley,* however, were unaware of this and had little knowledge about the current state of affairs in Zanzibar. They did not even know where the Americans were. The embassy in Dar es Salaam, which knew the Americans' location, had no way of communicating directly with the vessel.[4]

The *Manley* did have two helpful sources of information. The communications center at the embassy in Nairobi was picking up transmissions from the Zanzibar airport tower. Okello had mandated that one of the two British air controllers should return to the airport and man

the tower. For the most part, he was left to his own devices, and he continued to pass situation reports to Dar es Salaam. The *Manley*'s second source was Alexander, who monitored Radio Zanzibar and passed the gist of broadcasts along to the captain, the ship's executive officer, and Ruchti. One particularly important piece of information Alexander heard was that all the foreign civilians were now in Zanzibar Town.

The destroyer's captain, uncertain about the accuracy of the chart, but knowing that the channel into the harbor was tricky, edged his ship in slowly and cautiously. Finally getting into the harbor, the *Manley* dropped anchor. From the bridge, through binoculars, the Americans could be seen gathered on the terrace of a building. The gig was lowered into the water, but the captain needed more information before sending it to shore. He and Ruchti soon got what they needed from Ray Speight, former head of the Police Special Branch who had swum out to the *Salama* and later been transferred to the *Owen*.[5] Informed of his presence by the *Owen*'s captain, the *Manley*'s skipper invited him over. Once aboard, Speight filled the Americans in as well as he could on what had happened and what the current situation was. They also found out that the British had made no decision to evacuate civilians. Upon learning this, and now in communication with the Americans at the club, the captain, after conferring with Ruchti, ordered the landing party to proceed to the shore. The ship's executive officer was in charge. Ruchti went with them.

At the club, we had no transmitter for radioing out to the *Manley*. But the embassy in Dar had given us the ship's radio frequencies, and, using them, we were able to hear its transmissions on a Zenith portable radio that someone had brought to the club. More important, we had come up with a way to communicate with the ship. Irv Zolo, who was a retired United States Navy chief petty officer, stood on a table on the terrace and sent and received messages by semaphore. He acknowledged a message that the captain was sending a boat ashore. We could see that a small boat had gotten under way.

By this time, armed men were on the beach, close to the club. As the boat neared, a rebel carrying an automatic weapon warned it off, and the

boat stopped its approach and began circling. It was abundantly clear that we were going to have to get permission for the evacuation from whoever was in charge of the revolutionary government. Fritz went down to talk to the man with the automatic weapon. He told him of the intention to evacuate the American civilians. With no orders on how to handle this matter, the Zanzibari said we could not go ahead with an evacuation.

Fritz then went with him to Cable and Wireless, which, we had observed, had become a headquarters for the revolutionaries in the area. The leader of the men there was dressed in the khaki uniform of a police NCO. Fritz explained who was at the club and why the *Manley* had come. The group did not fully buy the story, and the policeman asked to inspect the club. Fritz agreed, and they walked there, accompanied by the man with the automatic weapon. After making his inspection, the policeman asked Fritz and me to return with him to Cable and Wireless. Further discussion there produced a decision to allow the boat to land but no progress on the evacuation question.

I went back to the club to tell the people there what was going on. Fritz walked out to the beach again. He signaled the boat to come to shore. In the boat, the executive officer and Ruchti saw Picard waving his arms at them, which they took to mean the boat could go in. Just short of the beach, Ruchti got out and waded to shore. Fritz told him the boat could land, but, except for Ruchti and the executive officer, the landing party would have to stay with it.

While Fritz and I had been in Cable and Wireless, Stu Lillico took a call from the embassy in Dar es Salaam. In brief terms, he related what had happened, adding that all the Americans in Zanzibar were safe (Rox Preece, by now seriously ill and suffering from an almost incapacitating headache, had arrived at the club in midmorning). Lillico was told to pass on to Picard and me a message from the State Department that we could stay in Zanzibar but were not to put our lives in danger for the sake of the cryptographic materials.

Soon after this call, just as I came back to the club, an Arab acquaintance of Stu telephoned to report that Juma Aley would come to the club momentarily. Lillico and I could see that several other ousted ministers were huddled about a hundred feet away, out of sight of the rebels at

Cable and Wireless. We signaled them to move around to the front side of the club. They did so and, meeting us at the door, told us they had heard a radio broadcast ordering them to assemble at the English Club for transportation to a meeting with the new government's leaders. The ministers had been in hiding for two days. Dispirited and fearful, by now they knew they had no choice but to surrender.

That morning, Henry Hawker, after a meeting with rebel leaders at Raha Leo, agreed to ask Prime Minister Shamte, whose whereabouts he knew, to go on the radio to announce his resignation and appeal for an end to the fighting. Shamte signed a formal letter of resignation, and Ali Muhsin, still in hiding, made a tape for use on the radio. In it, he informed listeners that all the ministers had resigned. He said further resistance would bring only "more loss and hatred to the country." He concluded by appealing for a restoration of peace.

As Stu and I were talking to the ministers, a car bearing Ali Muhsin and Juma Aley pulled up. Like the other ministers, they appeared tired and frightened. After a short argument, the group decided that Ali Muhsin would be the first to go, by himself, to Raha Leo. The strongman of the former government, looking totally dejected, left in the car. The others stepped inside the club entrance to wait. No sooner had they done so than Fritz came to the club with the policeman and his group from Cable and Wireless.

Fearing that, if known, the ministers' presence could jeopardize our effort to evacuate our people, Stu and I bundled the ministers into a nearby small office and closed the door. They remained there, "mystified, a trifle scared and very hot," as Lillico later wrote. After several minutes, Fritz and the rebels went back to Cable and Wireless. Stu and I opened the office door and led the ministers to the doorway leading out into the street. Ali Muhsin's car had not returned, nor did it show up later. We asked a passing policeman to take the ministers to Cable and Wireless, where they could get the transportation they needed to get to Raha Leo.

At half past four, Aboud Jumbe, a former teacher and ASP back-bencher whom Okello had appointed minister of health and welfare, called. He said he wanted to talk to Picard. Told that Fritz was not there, Jumbe said we should inform him that the Revolutionary Council, a thirty-

one-man body that Okello had formed that day, wanted to meet with the American chargé d'affaires. An escort would be provided to take him to Raha Leo.

Shortly afterward, Fritz, Ruchti, and the *Manley*'s executive officer came up from the beach to the terrace, and we waited for the escort. It was not long in coming. An open Land Rover pulled into an area between the club and Cable and Wireless. In it were Aboud Jumbe—who was armed with a tear gas gun and a pistol—a couple of other armed men, and a driver. Fritz, Ruchti, the exec, and I climbed into the back, and off we went.

It took us just a few minutes to reach Raha Leo. The sides of the road leading up to the community center building were jammed with people, and hundreds were crowded into the area immediately in front of it. Many were armed. Their weapons included sticks, spears, and bows and arrows; we saw several old Enfield rifles. Chanting and yelling, the crowd made an awful din. The atmosphere was electric. The recent arrival of Ali Muhsin, we learned a bit later, had put the throng into an ugly mood.

Highly agitated, dozens near us began to surge around the Land Rover, waving their weapons. Jumbe stood up and bellowed in Swahili, "Get back or I'll shoot!" They quieted down and backed away enough for us to be able to get out of the Land Rover. Someone went inside to give notice of our arrival, and we stood waiting. The late-afternoon sun dyed the cinnamon-colored stucco structure a deep orange. Items of loot were piled in front of it, and dirty, forlorn-looking Arab prisoners, some of them bloodied, sat or lay disconsolately nearby.

Fifteen minutes passed with no word from inside the building. While we waited, the bodies of several dead Africans, evidently revolutionaries who had been killed in the fighting, were carried out on rude stretchers. This added to the angry mood of the crowd. After another ten minutes or so, several men emerged. One was dressed in khaki shorts, tan kneesocks, a dark-blue shirt, and a peaked cap. Ironically, an American naval petty officer's stripes, with a yeoman's badge, were attached to his shirt. He had a pistol in his belt. The man walked up to us, drew out his pistol, and stuck it into the executive officer's chest. "How do you do?"

he said. "I am John Okello." The exec was understandably startled, and the crowed roared with laughter. Okello holstered his pistol, then said, "Let's have some pistol shots, before we go inside," adding that he had some available targets in back of the building. It was clear he was referring to some of the many Arab prisoners who were being held at Raha Leo. We demurred. He showed disappointment, whether feigned or real we had no way of knowing, and led us inside the building.

Some Arabs, who showed the marks of having been beaten, lay inside the entrance. There was blood on the walls. We followed Okello up the stairs. At the next floor, the stairway opened into a hall extending to the right and left along which were several doorways. He beckoned us to wait and went into a room at the top of the stairs. Before the door closed behind Okello, we caught a glimpse of British high commissioner Timothy Crosthwait. He had come to Raha Leo seeking assurances about the safety of British subjects. Our wait stretched into almost a half-hour, and we began to worry that, with the day drawing to a close, we would not have sufficient time to carry out the evacuation. Finally, Crosthwait came out, and we were ushered inside.

Okello was sitting at a small table, flanked by Karume and Babu. Other members of the Revolutionary Council were sitting behind them, cramped into the smallish room. Okello made a show of taking his pistol out of his belt and laying it on the table with the barrel pointing at Picard. After a moment, Fritz said, "We did not come here to negotiate at gunpoint." Okello said nothing, but put the pistol back in his belt. Fritz then explained clearly and succinctly what we wished to do. He emphasized that the *Manley* had come only to evacuate the Americans and said the decision for an evacuation was made because of the uncertainty regarding security. He noted that he and I would remain on the island. And he told the council that we wanted their assistance in ensuring that there would be no hindrance in moving the evacuees from the English Club to the destroyer.

Okello remained silent as Karume and Babu criticized the American decision to evacuate. Babu, especially, seemed angry. (In a cable sent that night from Dar es Salaam, Leonhart reported that President Nyerere had told him that Babu had telephoned at four o'clock—shortly before our

meeting at Raha Leo—to ask his opinion on the American request for the evacuation. Babu said most of the council were opposed on the grounds that an evacuation would have an adverse effect on outside opinion of the new government. Nyerere replied that the impact would be far worse if the request were denied.)

Despite their obvious displeasure, Karume and Babu said they would not oppose our request. Karume then turned to Okello and said the decision was his to make. The field marshal shrugged and said he agreed with them. Karume and Okello told Aboud Jumbe to continue to liaise with us and to see to it that no one interfered. With that, we took our leave.

Approaching a landing halfway down the stairs, we saw Ali Muhsin standing there with several armed men. He had been struck in the face and was bleeding from a gash. Fritz made a point of stopping so he could nod to him in a way that indicated respect and sympathy. Muhsin nodded back, and we made our way down the stairs. Outside, the crowd was still in a high state of excitement but watched in silence as we climbed back into the Land Rover and were driven back to the club.

With daylight fast fading, we got word to the *Manley* that permission had been granted and to send in the whaleboat. The executive officer and Ruchti took charge of getting the evacuees into the boats and out to the ship. Because of the limited capacity of the gig, not all the mothers with children could be accommodated on the first trip. This produced some anguish, but Ruchti explained that to get as many children as possible out right away, it was necessary for a few mothers to be temporarily separated from their kids.

As soon as we returned to the club, Fritz and I got into his car to drive the short distance to the Zanzibar Hotel and the Pigalle to let the tourists know what was happening. Except for an occasional short burst of gunfire, the city was quiet. All the tourists wanted to be evacuated and were ready to go. Several non-American tourists asked if they could come along, and we said sure. There were cars available at the hotels, and in a few minutes we all were at the club.

The gig, bearing most of the landing party and the first load of children, had gone, and the whaleboat had just arrived. I met with Julie and the girls on the terrace. They were to be among those to go out on this

trip. Julie nestled Julianne in her arms, and I carried Susie as we walked down to the beach. The area where the boats landed was bathed in yellow light from a couple of portable floodlights brought in from the ship. I kissed them good-bye, sailors helped Julie and the baby into the whaleboat, and I handed Susie to her. With the boat now filled, I stood back as it was pushed off and got under way. Dusk had almost completely turned to darkness; quickly, the boat faded from sight, its movement discernible only by a light on its stern.

In the boat Julie was distraught, and looking back at me as the boat pulled away, she thought she would never see me again.

Rex Preece's condition had worsened, and by now he was in terrible shape. He had stayed in bed since he arrived that morning, lapsing in and out of consciousness. Fortunately, someone remembered he was upstairs, and he was helped downstairs and taken to a boat. He remembers almost nothing of the passage and of his subsequent admittance to a hospital in Dar es Salaam. Had he not left Zanzibar when he did, he would have died. He would not have survived, either, had it not been for the round-the-clock skilled care he received from the Peace Corps doctor in Dar before he was flown to London.

It took several more trips to get all the passengers out to the *Manley*. Around half past seven, a patrol of armed men approached us on the beach and demanded that we stop the operation. When we explained we had the Revolutionary Council's permission, they said they had received no instructions about us. Obviously, Aboud Jumbe, who had never shown up, had not done his job. However, one of the band was the man who had waved off the gig that afternoon. Upon seeing Picard and Ruchti, he said we could proceed with what we were doing.

Except for the cone of light given off by the floodlights, it was totally dark when the last batch of passengers came down from the club to get in the boats. Fritz was escorting four people: Fathiya, her two children, and her mother. He had kept them hidden inside until now. He told Ruchti that Fathiya was Lillico's secretary, and, because she was related to one of the deposed ministers, her life would be in danger if she remained on the island. It was not until the next day that any of the passengers knew of her presence on the *Manley*.

Fritz and I waited at the club until we knew the ship was under way. As we left, we met the young, olive-skinned man wearing fatigues whom I had encountered in front of the club several hours earlier. We talked to him and learned that he was a Shirazi who had previously been a steward on the *Seyyid Khalifa*. We could not get him to admit he had been to Cuba. Although it is likely that he had gone there for training, it was again obvious to me that he was no more a Cuban than we were.

I followed Fritz as he drove the several miles to his house. After he got two cans of beer from the refrigerator, we reviewed what we had seen and heard that day and discussed what we should do the next day, Tuesday. We did not know whether we would be permitted to travel around freely or reopen the embassy. Fritz seemed to be in a mood to drink more beer and talk at length, but after one beer, all I wanted to do was go home and sleep; by then, I had been awake for forty-two hours.

Back home, all was quiet and dark. There were two armed guards at Ali Muhsin's place. As I pulled into my driveway, I saw a man carrying a battered-looking bolt-action rifle. He said he had been told to guard the house. That was fine with me until, just as I was falling asleep, I heard a gunshot, followed by the sound of voices. Then, nothing but silence, and soon I was fast asleep. The next morning, I learned that my guard had nodded off and accidentally fired his weapon. A few nights later, a guard at a nearby property was killed in a similar mishap.

The ship's officers and men were kindness itself to the evacuees, giving up their sleeping quarters and most of the remaining food on board. Unable to enter Dar es Salaam harbor at night because of its narrow, winding entrance, the *Manley* did not disembark its passengers until the next morning. Reporters were at the dock to interview the evacuees. Stu Lillico and some of the tourists said they had seen Cubans carrying weapons and wearing fatigue uniforms. The international press picked this up, and the myth of Cuban involvement was spread far and wide.

"GREETINGS! I AM THE NEW COMRADE."

"Greetings! I am the new comrade." Bill Mauldin, Reprinted with special permission from the Chicago-Sun Times Inc. 2001.

The record does not show if Ambassador Leonhart, a highly competent diplomat who was well respected in Washington, put any stock in the story of Cuban involvement. However, in one of his messages to Washington, he did use the "Zanzibar as the Cuba of Africa" analogy that

had been carried in the U.S. press. In what Leonhart's deputy chief of mission, Bob Hennemeyer, regarded as "an unwise cable," the ambassador referred to revolutionary Zanzibar in that manner, spoke of its use as a base for subversion on the mainland, and called for U.S. military intervention.

Embassy personnel met the evacuees, assisted everyone in finding accommodations, arranged for onward travel, and provided whatever other help the evacuees needed. Julie and the girls were housed at the unoccupied deputy chief of mission's house (the Hennemeyers were living in another house at that time), which was situated in a nice part of town close to the beach at Oyster Bay.

Was the evacuation necessary? Probably not. Despite the obvious dangers in and around Zanzibar Town, the revolutionaries had not targeted foreigners, and no Americans were killed. However, unable to contact any rebel leaders at all, we were totally in the dark as to the rebels' intentions. We knew the United States had been the target of vitriolic attacks by radicals in the ASP and by the Umma Party. Violence in town may have begun to subside, but it was still rampant, and the American civilians were deeply afraid and wanted off the island. In retrospect not necessary, then, but under the existing circumstances, Fritz's decision to evacuate was the right one.

British critics of the American evacuation compared it to the British decision not to evacuate, and some labeled the American action "panicky."[6] The situation of the British was different from ours, however. They had been criticized by the ASP and Umma but not, like the Americans, vilified. British officials and technicians still occupied key positions in the government, and at least the moderates in the ASP valued their continued expertise and assistance. And the large number of potential British evacuees, close to 500, meant that an operation to evacuate them would have been a complex and difficult task, possibly requiring more resources than the British had available in Zanzibar at the time.

Despite all this, the British authorities did not definitively rule out an evacuation. On the morning of the fourteenth, Crosthwait told Picard that he was still considering one. That afternoon, he opted for a partial rather than a full evacuation. On January 17, the evacuation of 159 British nationals—women, children, and men not working for the government of Zanzibar—commenced.

6

⌘

Under Arrest

WASHINGTON. Zanzibar's new President and his pro-Communist Foreign Minister arrested the last two remaining American diplomats in the East-African island yesterday, a report received here said. . . . So far as is known here, the two American diplomats' arrest was the first time any United States officials abroad ever were taken into custody by the president of the country to which they were assigned.

—*New York Herald Tribune*, January 17, 1964

Tuesday, January 14, was another hot and humid day. After breakfast, I drove to the Picards' house. Fritz learned that we would need permission from the Revolutionary Council to go to the embassy. In the course of the day, he was able to telephone Dar and, through the embassy there, send four messages to Washington. He reported that the new government was in control and that essential services were being maintained. The city was calm, he said, and he knew of no damage to American property. In fact, though, we had been unable to get permission to go where we needed to check on the security of the houses where Americans had resided. We were relying on third-hand information about their condition.

In the afternoon, someone from the government told Fritz that we could go to the embassy to prepare a short telegram for transmission by Cable and Wireless. We could not, however, send encrypted communications. I had gone home. Fritz phoned me and dictated a brief message. I went to the embassy, typed the message, and walked across Kelele Square to the Cable and Wireless building, which was guarded by several armed men. The British manager, B. P. Hampton, came out to greet me and took me inside to see the Zanzibari censor. The censor was not at all friendly but cleared the text after reading it. It was obviously harmless: "Embassy now able send and receive censored unclassified traffic only. Request Dept keep cables at essential minimum."

Outwardly, Fritz appeared to be in command of himself. He contin ued to drink too much, but not to the point that he showed any noticeable effects. The turmoil inside him, however, continued to surface at times. It was apparent in two of his phone calls to Dar es Salaam that day. In one, he said (as reported by the embassy): "Would like to know my options if I wish to leave. Would [the Tanganyikan government] send its plane to evacuate me?" Two hours later, at half past seven, telephoning again from his house, he put the number of casualties at an estimated 5,000, then said: "No cause for flap. Would like USS *Manley* be requested stand by on alert for evacuation." Fritz had made no mention to me about any threat to our safety, and I knew nothing about the content of his messages. He may well have had good cause to be worried; if nothing else, he knew that some of the radical left-wingers in the new government did not like him. But his manner of expressing his concern in the messages was odd.

Between midnight and 3:40 A.M. on Wednesday, the fifteenth, Fritz made more calls to Dar, drawing on information he had received from various sources, mainly Britons who had been with the colonial service. He had been unable to get together with Crosthwait, who kept fending off Fritz's requests that they meet. The high commissioner seemed to be taking pains not to associate with the Americans.

Some, but not all, of the information Fritz got from his sources was accurate. He reported that Zanzibar Town continued to be quiet, although occasional looting persisted (true); whereas ASP adherents

were being "encouraged to attack Arabs and loot stores," Babu and his followers were "quietly consolidating their position" (partially true); food supplies were running low (true); there was a "more sophisticated approach now in evidence in GOZ [government of Zanzibar] with trained and experienced foreign elements moving behind scenes to consolidate control" (incorrect).

We kept busy reopening the embassy and making contact with government officials. Two of the embassy's several Zanzibari employees dropped by. They were happy to find that the embassy was undamaged and, especially, that they still had their jobs. They said they would return to work as soon as it was safe to do so.

Fritz and I still could not travel the north road to Mtoni, but late in the morning, we managed to inspect the homes of the evacuated Americans along the airport road and found all of them intact and unlooted.

As we were driving in his car back to the embassy, my knowledge of Swahili saved us from possible grief. As we went past a group of armed men, I heard one of them shout, "Simama!" I yelled, "Stop!" to Fritz, who had not understood the Swahili command to stop. Looking back at the men, we saw that they had their weapons trained on us. In a distinctly unfriendly mood, they came up to the car. I greeted them, explained who we were, and said we had not realized that they were manning a checkpoint. Mollified, they let us proceed.

Back at the embassy, in a phone conversation with Ambassador Leonhart, Fritz learned that the message I had taken to Cable and Wireless on Tuesday had been received and that messages from the State Department would be sent to Dar es Salaam for relay to us by telephone. Leonhart said the Office of East African Affairs director, Jesse MacKnight, had sent a telegram to Fritz expressing the department's confidence in him. Leonhart also said a Tanganyikan government or charter aircraft would be available for an evacuation if one became necessary. Fritz replied that he did not wish to leave at that point.

International Red Cross officials, who had flown in from Dar es Salaam, asked Fritz if the United States could supply blood plasma and food. In midafternoon, he drove to Raha Leo to meet with Prime

Minister Hanga. He asked Hanga whether the Zanzibar government would be interested in an offer of Public Law (PL) 480, surplus U.S. food. Hanga welcomed the idea but said it would have to be cleared with Karume. He provided Fritz with an armed escort to take him to Karume's house. Karume said he would be happy to have any assistance, particularly in the form of blood plasma and wheat. Fritz stressed that he had no formal authority to supply anything. Karume understood this but repeated that an offer of U.S. help would be welcome. Fritz said the question of recognition did not enter into the picture, inasmuch as the assistance would be of a strictly humanitarian nature.

At Fritz's request, Karume called Cable and Wireless and ordered that the American chargé d'affaires be given full use of cable facilities. In the cable he sent to Washington that evening recounting his talks with Hanga and Karume, Fritz asked if the Defense Department would authorize the *Manley* to take on bulgar wheat, edible oils, or other PL 480 food in Mombasa or Dar and proceed to Zanzibar as soon as possible. He also asked whether the crew would be prepared to donate blood.

The worst of the killings in rural Zanzibar were over, but Okello went on with his reign of terror. The Zanzibar Africans' hatred of Arabs had exploded during the revolution. *Genocide* was not a term that was in vogue then, as it came to be later, but it is fair to say that in parts of Zanzibar, the killing of Arabs was genocide, pure and simple. By further inflaming passions, Okello's actions and his radio broadcasts directly contributed to the slaughter. ASP moderates were fearful of Okello and horrified by his excesses.

It was clear that, though he may have initially desired to let Karume and others run the country, Okello's success as the field marshal had given him a taste for power. However, his chances of achieving his new-found political ambition were fatally flawed. Ninety-five percent of Zanzibaris were Muslim, and Okello was a Christian; he had alarmed Nyerere and other East African leaders to the point that none would provide him with support; and his followers in Zanzibar numbered at most

a few hundred unskilled, unsophisticated Africans. For the time being, though, ultimate power continued to reside in his hands.

In the days immediately following the events of January 12–13, Okello made frequent use of Radio Zanzibar's transmitter. He warned that those who resisted him would be killed or imprisoned. On the fourteenth, in a broadcast that deeply disturbed President Nyerere, Okello declared that Juma Aley and two other prominent men had been sentenced to be hanged; another man was sentenced to be shot or burned to death. Okello said a well-known Arab in the village of Dole should "kill all his children by slashing them" and then hang himself. He ordered that when he visited Mungi District the next day, all the people would have to kneel when he passed and sing "God Bless Africa." Okello told listeners that he was capable of making "not less than five hundred guns per day" and that he could construct "a bomb that can destroy an area of three square miles."

That night, Nyerere told Leonhart that Kenya and Uganda had decided to recognize the new Zanzibar government without delay. Kenya's Jomo Kenyatta and Uganda's Milton Obote had asked Nyerere to do the same, but he had declined, even though he was an adherent of East African unity. Nyerere and his cabinet were highly sympathetic to the new regime, but it had forcibly overthrown a constitutional government. Tanganyika had previously withheld recognition from Togo and Congo Brazzaville revolutionaries after they had taken power in their respective countries. The Tanganyikans declared that first the new governments had to demonstrate popular support and the capacity to maintain law and order. Nyerere felt that the same had to apply to the revolutionaries in Zanzibar. They would have to vindicate their claim to be the government by restoring the rule of law. Nyerere told Leonhart and High Commissioner Miles that his government would almost certainly recognize the new government "after a while." In the meantime, he hoped this cautious approach would encourage restraint by the revolutionaries and a more rapid return of order.

Neither the American nor the British government was in any hurry to act on Zanzibar's request for diplomatic recognition. Speaking in the House of Commons on the fourteenth, Commonwealth and Colonial

secretary Duncan Sandys said the status of the authorities who had seized power in Zanzibar was still obscure, and Her Majesty's Government could not consider recognition until the situation was much clearer. Another factor, which he did not mention, was that the Conservative government was reluctant to recognize a regime that had all the earmarks of being radically leftist and had come to power by means of violence. Washington was similarly not ready to move speedily toward recognition, if for no other reason than the existing American policy of following the lead of former colonial powers in African matters. There were limits to this policy, though, as Assistant Secretary of State G. Mennan Williams pointed out to Under Secretary of State George Ball.

Ball, having read Picard's cable regarding food aid to Zanzibar and heard "a radio report that the new government is proposing some rather imaginative executions," told Williams in a memorandum on January 16 that "this is one situation we should leave to the British." He said: "I can formulate my attitude toward this kind of problem quite simply. God, I am reliably informed, marks every sparrow that may fall. I do not believe we should try to compete in that league."

Williams replied four days later. He said, "It has been and will be US policy to give the UK the lead in solving problems [in Zanzibar]." He added, however, "that 'leaving it to the British' may not completely protect American interests there." He then went on to speak in terms reflective of the foreign policy of the United States at that stage of the Cold War:

> The Zanzibar situation, furthermore, is probably not the problem of Communist penetration in one small insular country alone but the poten tial cumulative deterioration of American interests in a number of African countries. In these circumstances, a policy of withdrawal or inaction seemed to me less than what the situation called for. It is my assumption that the President, the Secretary and the American people have a vital interest that no country fall to the Communists. I therefore conceive it my duty to take appropriate measures to prevent any African country, large or small, from falling or tending to fall to the Communists.

A State Department press briefing did not overplay the notion of Communist involvement in the revolution. Reporting by U.S. newspa-

pers reflected what was said in the briefing. For example, though noting U.S. concerns about Babu and the tracking station, a front-page article in the *New York Times* reported that although it was unclear who was the dominant power in Zanzibar, the new government included Afro-Shirazi Party moderates, as well as ASP and Umma radicals. Radio and television coverage, on the other hand, stressed the Communist angle. Probably driven by their appetite for sound bites, they highlighted such terms as "Communist-dominated" and "Cuban-type" when characterizing the revolution.

By Thursday, the embassy was just about fully operational. We could send classified telegrams, our doors were open (though apparently no Zanzibaris dared to come in), and we expected that the restrictions on our travel would soon end, enabling us to go to the tracking station at Tunguu and to inspect the rest of the American property.

Fritz was in fine fettle that morning. Evidently, he had had a good night's sleep. He looked well, was good-humored, and appeared to be as sharp as ever. Before Fritz arrived at the embassy, I had taken a call from Leonhart. I told him that the situation in town was much improved but that fighting continued to be reported in rural areas. Although shops remained closed, some food, mainly bananas, was reappearing in African markets.

Fritz had been in the embassy a few minutes when Crosthwait called. He told Fritz that several American journalists ("some of your people") who had sailed into the harbor were being detained at the waterfront. Crosthwait said their action was a source of "grave embarrassment" to him. Fritz told me to check it out. I took the Land Rover and drove to the port.

At the approach to the boat landing, I got out of the car and walked over to several armed men who were gathered at the top of a concrete seawall from which steps led down to the water. A couple of British colonial port officials also were there. I could see the top of a dhow's mast. I explained who I was and why I had come. The Zanzibaris grudgingly allowed me to go to the edge of the seawall and have a look.

There were seven men in the dhow. I told them who I was and joked that they had picked a nice time to arrive. They were American, British, and Canadian newspapermen and an Indian photographer for *Life* magazine. They had sailed in the dhow from Bagamoyo on the mainland, arrived in Zanzibar the night before, spent that night aboard the *Owen* at the invitation of its captain, gone into Zanzibar on the dhow early in the morning, and been held at the wharf since then.

They began asking me questions about what was happening in Zanzibar, and, unwisely, I answered. After a minute or so, an Arab-African, one of Babu's men, who was armed with an automatic weapon, shouted at me, "Stop talking to the imperialists!" The newsmen were made to hand in their notebooks and cameras. The armed men were getting agitated, calling the journalists spies. When I tried to calm things down, one of them pointed a rifle at my face and snarled, "You shut up!" I did. About then, a battered Land Rover drove up, and the newsmen and I were ordered to get into it.

We were driven to Raha Leo. In front of the community center building, hundreds of Africans milled around. At the door, two women waved guns and knives at us. Next door, scores of Arabs, many with fear etched on their faces, were still being detained. We were marched into the building and taken to a large meeting room. My request that I be taken to someone in charge was unavailing. We sat and waited. I learned that my companions were Bill Smith of *Time;* Robert Conley of the *New York Times;* John Nugent of *Newsweek;* Peter Rand, a stringer for the *New York Herald Tribune;* Clyde Sanger of the *Manchester Guardian,* Robert Miller of the *Toronto Globe and Mail;* and Pryan Ramracha of *Time-Life.*

At the embassy, Fritz called Dar es Salaam to report that Karume, Hanga, and Babu were flying there that morning and would return in the afternoon. He said four American reporters had been arrested for trying to enter Zanzibar illegally. He was trying to get their names.

Having heard nothing from me for a couple of hours, Fritz began making phone calls and soon learned that the seven journalists and I were being held at Raha Leo. He got in touch with Aboud Jumbe and arranged to meet with him. After the two men had met, Jumbe gave an

order permitting the newsmen and me to be released. It is not known whether he called Karume in Dar to clear this.

Fritz came over to Raha Leo and told the journalists they were free to go about their business. After helping transport the newsmen into town, Fritz and I went off to his house for a late lunch, then returned to the embassy.

The journalists spent the afternoon looking for stories. At one point, an armed patrol stopped some of them and examined their papers. The Americans among the reporters showed the patrol their Defense Department press passes. This and Bob Conley's last name gave rise to a rumor that the journalists were CIA agents and that one or more of them was a colonel. This misinformation filtered back to the revolutionary leaders and added to the increasingly strong current of anti-American feelings.

It was late in the day, just after sunset, when Fritz finished writing a fairly long cable describing the events of the day. He gave it to me to encode and type up for transmission by Cable and Wireless while he went over to the Zanzibar Hotel, where the journalists had assembled, to see how they were getting along. At the hotel, Fritz found the reporters and Othman Sharif. He joined them and others for drinks. The atmosphere was cordial.

In the meantime, Karume, Hanga, and Babu returned from Dar es Salaam, where they had met with Tanganyikan government ministers and made requests for police advisers, airport-communications experts, and medical personnel and supplies. After they arrived back in Zanzibar, they learned of unfavorable comments contained in the reporters' notebooks, which had been examined while the reporters and I were in custody at Raha Leo. Karume was furious and, being told that the foreign journalists were at the Zanzibar Hotel, ordered that he be taken there immediately.

At about eight-thirty, he stormed into the hotel lobby, where Picard, Sharif, and the others were sitting, and upbraided the newsmen for preparing to tell lies about Zanzibar. When Fritz tried to intervene, Karume accused him of supplying the journalists with false information. He might have also been angered to see Fritz sitting there with Sharif,

his enemy in the ASP. Continuing to shout at Fritz, he cried, "Why don't you recognize us?"

According to another reporter who was there, Dennis Neald, a British stringer for the Associated Press, Karume hammered his fist into the palm of his hand and yelled, "You have interfered with our government!" Neald reported that Babu chimed in, "Why waste time with these Americans? We have nothing to do with them." Karume told Picard he was under house arrest and would be deported the next day. With a Sten gun in his back, Fritz was escorted out of the hotel and driven to his house, where he was kept under heavy guard.

Ignorant of all this, I was laboriously encrypting Fritz's message to Washington. I had never used the code machine—a device about the size of a breadbasket; as I recall, it had been out of order for months. Because of that, we used one-time pads for encrypting and decrypting classified messages. The essence of the one-time pad system was random substitution of numbers for letters. For each day of the year, sender and receiver would have a pad containing the letters of the alphabet and their corresponding numbers, which changed randomly each time they were used. The number given to a letter would not follow any pattern; for example, the fifteen letters in the words *Zanzibar Embassy* could read 37894 24701 63602. The next time the same two words would be encrypted, the numbers would be randomly different, such as 79255 10894 02750.[1] It was slow, painstaking work to transcribe each letter in the message into the correct random letter corresponding to it in the pad. It must have been nine or nine-thirty when I finally had the message in shape for Cable and Wireless. I locked up the embassy and, message in hand, began to walk across Kelele Square. It was very dark, and not until I was about halfway across the square, when the lights of Cable and Wireless cut into the gloom, did I see that some people were between the building and me. Coming up to them, I saw that they were Karume, Babu, and a bunch of armed men.

"What are you doing?" Karume asked.

"I'm going to Cable and Wireless to send a telegram."

"No, you cannot. It is not possible now." Picard, he said, had done something bad and would be expelled from Zanzibar. I would have to be

placed under arrest. Nothing was said about whether I would be expelled with Fritz.

Neither Karume nor Babu appeared angry with me personally. There wasn't anything I could think to say except to ask them where I would be taken. "To Picard's house," Karume replied. They and their men escorted me back to the front of the embassy, where my car was parked. Four men armed with rifles got in the VW with me, and we drove off. It was a tight squeeze, and I was nervously conscious that the tip of the rifle barrel of one of the three men in the rear seat occasionally poked the back of my head. I doubted that I was being taken for a last ride, but I wondered whether the three knew what a safety was.

Fritz was in his living room when I entered the house. We sat talking and drinking beer for two or three hours. International telephone service had been cut off, so we were unable to communicate with Dar that night. Weariness eventually overcame me, and I went upstairs to sleep.

The next morning, armed guards still surrounded the house. After breakfast, Fritz and I sat outside the house on a patio overlooking the ocean. Fritz's British neighbors dropped by to see him and wish him well. Despite what had happened, he was in a good humor. About mid-morning, an official from the Ministry of External Affairs came by to reaffirm to Fritz that he was persona non grata. The official told me that if I wished, I could remain in Zanzibar.

In Dar es Salaam, Leonhart, like Fritz, had had a long night. He met first with the Tanganyikan vice president at ten-thirty and then with the foreign minister at three in the morning to discuss the arrests. A Tanganyikan offer to bring Picard, the newsmen, and me out on a government aircraft fell through, so the embassy booked a charter flight on a standby basis. Leonhart cabled the State Department that "unless hear from you to contrary, assume both Picard and Petterson and newsmen should be evacuated HMS *Owen* to Mombasa. Believe Petterson should not be left Zanzibar unless Dept expects replace Picard."

The journalists had spent the night at the Zanzibar Hotel, where they remained under house arrest the next morning. Some of them reported later that they were taken outside to the hotel's courtyard and made to stand against a wall. At least one of them, John Nugent of *Newsweek*,

believed they were going to be shot. Some of the revolutionaries pointed their weapons at the newsmen, only to lower them again and laugh as an Asian with a camera appeared and snapped some pictures. That afternoon, the seven and a few other visiting journalists were driven to the wharf and ferried out to the *Owen,* which took them and British evacuees to Mombasa.

Telephone service to Dar es Salaam was restored to Fritz's house. In the early afternoon, Fritz talked to Leonhart, who told him a small Cessna had been chartered and would be coming to pick him up. Leonhart asked to talk with me. I told him that I had not been ordered to go. He asked me what I would do, and I said I wanted to stay.

At about four o'clock, the official from External Affairs arrived to tell us the plane had landed. Fritz and I loaded his baggage and the Lillicos' dog, Bronca, into the Ford and drove to the airport, preceded and followed by armed escorts. Once there, we hardly had time to say farewell. Fritz was led directly to the single-engine Cessna, he and the dog boarded, the bags were loaded, and the plane taxied away and took off.

My feeling was one of relief. For the past several days, I had worried that Fritz might come to some harm. His antics on the beach during the day of the evacuation, the confrontation with Adam Mwakanjuki, the risk he ran to get Fathiya into the English Club, and his persistent heavy drinking had led me to wonder whether he would commit another reckless act.

Turning to go back to the car, I saw Babu and several other officials emerge from some cars parked on the tarmac. Babu came over to me, and we talked for a few minutes. I told him I was going to the embassy and then later to my house. He said that would be fine, but I should not stay out after dark. We agreed to meet the next day.

At the embassy, I typed a short message to Washington on a Cable and Wireless form, took it across the square, and cleared it with a censor. In it, I reported that Fritz had departed for Dar, and I listed the American and non-American reporters who were leaving aboard the *Owen.* Then I said, "I am staying."

The State Department replied: "Received your [message]. Delighted receive direct report successful evacuation Picard and newsmen.

Department lauds your decision remain and will give you all possible support." I sent a second telegram to inform Washington that I could send and receive only unclassified messages, all of which would be reviewed by a government official.

Despite Babu's warning, I was unable to get home before dark. There was nothing to eat, but fortunately two of my British neighbors, Bill and Monica Hall, took me over to their apartment and fed me. They would do this often over the next several weeks.

Back in my house, my adrenaline now flowing at a normal level, I mused on the day's events that had left me, a junior officer, in charge of an embassy. Perhaps because by now I had learned the basics of running the post, and also because this latest business was just one of a series of numerous unusual happenings over the past six days, I more or less took it in stride. I remember looking to the days ahead with anticipation rather than apprehension. Had I known the extent of high-level attention in Washington to the Zanzibar saga, I probably would not have been so untroubled.

7

Holding the Fort

Suddenly the world has run amok and left you alone and sane behind.

—Wole Soyinka

You have to expect things of yourself before you can do them.

—Michael Jordan

Sultan Jamshid bin Abdulla, his family, his retainers, and British and Zanzibari officials, including the police who had defended the Malindi station, had sailed on the *Seyyid Khalifa* for Mombasa on the twelfth, arriving there the next day. Okello announced on the radio that the sultan was banished from Zanzibar for life: "His foot may never touch our soil again." More bad news for Jamshid came from the Kenyan government, which refused to allow him to land. Tanganyika's Nyerere decided to permit him to come to Dar es Salaam, but only so he could take a flight from there to London.

On the fifteenth, the *Seyyid Khalifa* steamed into Dar es Salaam harbor and dropped anchor. A crowd of several hundred people jeered the deposed sultan. Jamshid and his people were provided accommodations for the few days they remained in Dar. On the morning of the nine-

teenth, Jamshid and the forty-four people in his retinue were driven to the airport, where more than one hundred armed police and soldiers had cordoned off the airplane that had been chartered for the flight to London. That night, the duke of Devonshire, minister of state for Commonwealth and Colonial Relations, met Jamshid and his party at the London airport. With a pension from the British government, the former sultan began his new life of obscurity in a foreign land.

On April 6, Jamshid, accompanied by his brother Mohamed (a much overweight, arrogant man whom some of the Americans and Britons in Zanzibar had dubbed, not with affection, "Porky Pig"), called at the American embassy in London. Jamshid said each day that went by meant increased Communist control of Zanzibar and greater potential for subversion of the East African mainland. He said the only course of action now available was an armed invasion. He could get the men to do the job but needed money to finance it, and he appealed for U.S. financial help.

The embassy officer who received Jamshid and Mohamed told them that U.S. policy was not to interfere in the affairs of any state. He agreed to transmit the sultan's views to the Department of State, however. In his cable reporting the meeting, the officer said he "took care to discourage any anticipation on [Jamshid's] part" that the U.S. government "would in any way respond to his appeal for financial assistance."

Over the years, Jamshid, seemingly unwilling to accept that the Busaidi dynasty was finished and that he would never be restored to the throne of the Zanzibar sultanate, would make additional fruitless appeals for help to overthrow the Zanzibar government.

Despite Okello's threats, none of the ministers of the former government was hanged or otherwise executed. All, however, were imprisoned. Because of the Nyerere government's concern for their safety, most were transferred to a mainland prison later in 1964. One, Ibuni Salah, died there in 1968. The few who were kept in Zanzibar were released that year, rearrested, then later released again. Ali Muhsin, Juma Aley, and the others in jail on the mainland were not set free until 1974.

By the end of the first week following the outbreak of the fighting, more than 2,000 Arabs were confined to various detention camps in and

close by Zanzibar Town. Initially, conditions in the camps were appalling, and some detainees died. However, the situation of the detainees soon improved, thanks largely to the efforts of the Red Cross and British nationals still working for the Zanzibar government.

Many Arabs fled in dhows and small boats. As they reached the mainland and began telling stories of massacres, it became increasingly clear that the death toll was much higher than had been imagined. My own estimate, which I made some weeks later, after I had been able to talk to public health officials and others who had been involved in mass burials, was that about 5,000 people had died in the Zanzibar revolution.

In the years to come, there would be worse pogroms in Africa; in some countries, tens of thousands of people would be killed. But under any circumstances, the slaughter of 5,000 human beings in the space of a few days is an awful thing. The preponderance of the dead were Arabs; about one of every ten Arabs in Zanzibar was killed, and as many as one of every three of those who survived was injured.

Monica and Bill Hall continued to feed me supper most nights. This was a lifesaver, since there was precious little food to be found in the markets and shops remained closed. The suppers were light—good, healthy food and plenty for most people. But I was cursed, or blessed as the case may be, with a high rate of metabolism. I had to eat a lot just to maintain my weight. The cook that Julie and I had hired had not came back, and I didn't find much in our pantry to make meals. In the weeks ahead, I would lose a lot of weight, and I had none to spare to begin with. The nutritional deficiencies and weight loss didn't hamper me while I was alone in Zanzibar, but would catch up with me later.

It was quiet at the embassy while I was working on Saturday, the eighteenth. No Zanzibari would risk coming there yet, for it was well understood that the government would detain any visitors to the American embassy. I prepared a telegram and carried it out onto the sun-drenched square and over to Cable and Wireless. Because of the continued prohibition against sending encrypted messages and the requirement that communications be approved by a censor, in this cable and the others I

would send during the coming weeks, I had to choose my words with care.

Okello had been on the radio again the previous night. I reported the field marshal had announced that the United States was welcome to continue relations with Zanzibar as long as it did not interfere in the country's internal affairs. Okello had asked the troops under his command to turn in their weapons. I also reported that the *Owen* and the *Hebe* had departed with the British evacuees aboard them. Mail service had not been resumed, and only Zanzibar government officials could make overseas telephone calls.

That evening, I met with Babu. High Commissioner Crosthwait was just leaving Babu's office when I arrived. Wolf Dourado, the permanent secretary in Babu's Ministry of External Affairs, had been in the meeting with Crosthwait and sat in on the one between Babu and me. Babu greeted me warmly and was affable throughout our conversation, the first of any substance I had had with him. Of Somali-Arab parentage, Babu was born in Zanzibar in 1924. He went to London in 1951 to study journalism at the Regent Street Polytechnic, attending evening classes. According to some who knew of his stay in London, Babu had invested considerable time in pub hopping and chasing women. His Marxist leanings were honed during his six-year sojourn in Britain through his association with "left-wing, Communist, and Communist-front organizations."[1] He denied having joined the Communist Party, insisting that "if anything, I was closer to the anarchists than to the Communists."

Far from handsome—he had a bad complexion and wore a scraggly mustache—Babu had a magnetic personality. He never lacked female companionship. He was highly intelligent and learned the journalism trade well enough to become the ZNP's principal propagandist after he returned to Zanzibar in 1957. He established and edited a daily broadsheet for the party. Later, after he broke from the ZNP, he founded his own newspaper.

By 1959, Babu had risen in the ZNP to the position of general secretary. In that capacity, he established an office in Cairo that became a conduit for sending young Zanzibaris to Communist countries on scholarships. Not long afterward, he set up a ZNP office in London and one in

Abdulrahman Mohamed Babu

Havana, where a number of his young followers went for training. Ironically, as it turned out, it was the ZNP leadership, frightened by the rioting and killing during the 1961 elections, that had chosen to send groups of the party's youth wing to Cuba for military training. Babu himself had traveled to the Soviet Union, Communist China, and East Germany in 1960. He formed a close tie with the Chinese and in 1961 became the East African correspondent for the New China News Agency.

Babu did not confine his revolutionary Marxism to words. In June 1962, he fomented the burning of the British Information Office and was accused of other acts of sabotage. He was convicted of sedition and spent fifteen months in jail. It was believed that he was behind an arson attempt against the American consulate in August 1961.

At the outset of our conversation, Babu insisted that Zanzibar had no quarrel with the United States and wanted the friendship of the U.S. government. Zanzibar, he said, did not wish to be involved in "Cold War propaganda or activities." Its foreign policy would be an African policy whose ultimate goal was African unity. Its domestic objective would be the elimination of poverty; to achieve this end, he said, Zanzibar had to

become a socialist state, for it did not have the time that the United States and Britain had to develop their economies.

"What about the tracking station?" I asked.

"We have not yet made a decision about it. When we do, we'll let you know."

I voiced my concern about the Americans' houses. "I have to be able to go see all the properties to be sure they're okay."

"You will have to wait another two days," he said. "We can't provide you with a police escort until then."

"But I really need to see them right away," I argued.

"We do not have enough policemen available now. You'll just have to wait."

I kept insisting that it was imperative for me to inspect the properties immediately, not two days later, but he was adamant. I told him that my ability to send and receive diplomatic communications freely was an important factor in how Washington regarded the new government.

Babu said, "Look, I can appreciate what you want to do, but you have to understand our position. Because of the atmosphere that comes with revolution, some people could misunderstand the purpose of coded messages and become upset."

"Well, at least let me place overseas calls."

He indicated that this might be possible, and said, "I'll ask the cabinet for a decision."

After the meeting, I wrote a cable reporting my talk with Babu, and took it over to Cable and Wireless. There was a telegram from the State Department for me. It instructed me to "acknowledge orally" to an appropriate official that the U.S. government had received the Zanzibar government's messages to President Johnson and Secretary of State Dean Rusk, messages that I assumed had requested diplomatic recognition of the new government. The department also told me to remind the Zanzibaris that their contact with the U.S. government could be effective only if official communication channels were open to me in a normal manner.

It was getting late, but on the off chance that I might catch him, I called Dourado. Wolf was a member of Zanzibar's Goan community. There were only about 250 Goans living in Zanzibar, making them the

least populous of the islands' ethnic groups. The Goans were Catholics whose forebears had come to Zanzibar in the nineteenth century from the Portuguese enclave that lay on the west coast of India, about 250 miles south of Bombay. The first Goan to arrive in Zanzibar, in 1865, opened a small grocery store. In 1964, the Goan community included merchants, skilled artisans, and professional people.

Wolf was a lawyer who had trained in Britain. Now a civil servant, he gave his loyalty to the government in power. But not his soul. Short, slender, outspoken—at times to the point of indiscretion—he was a man whose abilities and honesty were so prized that the revolutionary government did not fire him. Eventually, he rose to become Zanzibar's attorney general. Dourado often disagreed with government actions and policies and did not hesitate to express his disagreement. More than once, this would lead to his imprisonment in the years ahead.

That night I was able to reach him by phone. After I had told him the substance of Washington's message, he said he would notify Karume and Babu the following morning. When I called Dourado the next morning, Sunday, he said he had talked to Karume on the telephone but was unsure that the import of the message had been understood. We agreed that I would drop by his house and leave a copy of the State Department cable, which he would take to Karume.

After I had given him the cable and his wife, Yvonne, had served us coffee, I brought up a couple of issues. "Wolf," I said, "it's really important that I be able to make overseas calls and that I be allowed to send and receive encrypted telegrams. Washington is insisting that if Zanzibar wants better relations, these things have got to be given to me."

"I understand that, Don," he said, puffing on his pipe, "and I hope normal diplomatic privileges will be granted soon. But it's not going to happen right away. Nobody, including Crosthwait, is permitted to send or receive coded messages. You've got to be patient."

I vented some of my frustration at not being able to inspect all the American property. I said I felt a strong obligation to do everything possible to protect the belongings of the evacuated Americans. I told Dourado, "I must inspect U.S. property this morning; I just cannot wait until tomorrow."

"Don, I understand your feelings, but wait until I can arrange for a police escort."

"Okay, I'll wait, but if they don't show after one hour, I'm going to make the inspection."

I went to the embassy, where I waited for a little more than an hour. When no escort showed up, I drove out of town toward the airport and stopped at four homes of Americans who had lived along the road. They were locked up and showed no sign of forcible entry. I returned to the embassy and wrote a cable reporting what I had found. I also recounted my conversation with Dourado and said that I intended to inspect the remaining American properties "with or without escort."

As received in the State Department, the reporting cable's last paragraph read: "GOZ has provided guards for embassy building and my home. I am being treated courteously. I am in no danger." A passage between "courteously" and the last sentence was excised by the censor, who had angrily and peremptorily red-penciled, "and since my release have been stopped only three times by irresponsible individuals who do not like to see U.S. flag flying from flag staff of automobile."

Responding to the cables reporting my talks with Babu and Dourado, the State Department said: "Good work. At same time would like emphasize Dept does not wish or expect you to place yourself in jeopardy in any way. You in the best position to judge and should act accordingly." As far as I was aware, nobody had been shot and killed by patrols in the past few days, and I knew that Okello had ordered his men not to kill Europeans. Consequently, I did not believe I would be in much danger by driving to the American properties.

That afternoon, I set out for Mtoni and Beit el Ras, a mile beyond Mtoni, where the Burches' and four other American houses were located. I found, to my anger and distress, that all five houses had been broken into and looted. Shortly after I arrived at the last one, a police car and a truck carrying some policemen drove up. Eddington Kisassi, the new police commissioner, got out of the car, came up to me, and asked what I was doing. I told him.

A mild-mannered, well-intentioned man, Kisassi did not bridle at this, and merely said it would have been more prudent for me to have

waited until I had been given a proper escort. I responded that the government's delay had contributed to the looting. Later, however, after I had talked to people in the area, I concluded that the ransacking had occurred during the second or third day of the revolution.

Kisassi stationed men to guard each house. He told me that permission had been granted for me to inspect the tracking station the following day. Back at the embassy, I wrote a cable letting the State Department know this and also that Karume, whom I had just called, had given me permission to make phone calls to Dar es Salaam beginning the next day. I also reported that Red Cross officials had asked me to repeat their earlier request for U.S. assistance. In Washington, this request would sit unanswered, superseded by the recognition issue and the growing concern about Communist influence in the Zanzibar government.

The willingness finally to provide police guards for the American property had come about because of the arrival on the island of Tanganyikan police. Nyerere, appalled by the violent excesses of Okello and his men, had decided to send policemen to help restore law and order and in the process strengthen the hand of Karume, the ASP, and their Umma allies. On the afternoon of the seventeenth, at about the same time Fritz was expelled, forty Tanganyikan Field Force police boarded a DC-3 and flew to Zanzibar. Over the next few days, another ninety joined them.

On Monday, the twentieth, accompanied by a police escort, Ernest Clark of the Electricity Board, who had a contractual arrangement with the Bendix Corporation and now was responsible for looking after the Project Mercury facilities, drove with me first to the main site at Tunguu. From there, we went to the East Coast village of Chwaka, where one small Mercury building was located. Along the way, we passed many destroyed Arab dwellings and shops. We found that there was no damage to the buildings or equipment at either Tunguu or Chwaka. After checking the amount of fuel oil available, Clark estimated that there was enough to keep the generators operating for several weeks. This meant that the air conditioners in the buildings could oper-

ate to protect the communications equipment from corrosion or other ill effects of the high heat and humidity.

I went back to the embassy to write a message describing what Clark and I had found. When I took it to Cable and Wireless, I learned that all communications with the mainland had been cut. Details were sketchy, but apparently there was some serious trouble in Dar el Salaam involving the Tanganyikan army.

Suffering from a sore throat, John Okello had left Zanzibar for Dar on the night of the eighteenth for what was announced as a few days' rest. The next day, Leonhart went over to State House to talk with Nyerere. The room in which Leonhart and Nyerere met looked out onto a terrace. Okello and a few other Zanzibaris were sitting there, drinking beer with most of the Tanganyikan cabinet ministers. Leonhart asked Nyerere whether Okello was sane. "Yes," Nyerere replied, then quickly added, "The man has no depth."

During their discussion, Leonhart commented that the United States looked to Britain and to East African governments to take the lead in dealing with the Zanzibar situation. Nyerere said quietly that Washington should not count too much on the British. Nyerere confided to Leonhart that he was going to recognize Zanzibar very soon. He said he believed efforts to restore law and order and to end racial violence were sufficiently well in hand for him to extend recognition.

London, however, continued to dither on the recognition issue, and Washington followed suit.

Deputy Assistant Secretary of State for African Affairs William Trimble cabled to the State Department an account of a meeting he had in Nairobi with the governor-general of Kenya, Sir Malcolm MacDonald, and British high commissioner Geoffrey De Freitas. Trimble stressed that the American government considered the Zanzibar problem primarily a British responsibility. MacDonald and De Freitas urged the United States to maintain a presence in Zanzibar. De Freitas emphasized that the UK had to stay in Zanzibar at all costs. He said Britain's lifeblood was foreign trade and presence abroad and that if the British

were compelled to leave Zanzibar, their position would progressively erode elsewhere.

Despite this kind of concern, London was not yet disposed to recognize the revolutionary government; in fact, Her Majesty's Government would soon be giving more consideration to military intervention than to recognition.

In Washington, in a memorandum dated January 23, Jesse MacKnight advised Soapy Williams that it would be in the interest of the United States to recognize Zanzibar. He pointed out that Tanganyika had recognized Zanzibar, as had Israel. Even though NASA had indicated it would not use the Zanzibar tracking station for future manned space flights, MacKnight said its presence "places Zanzibar in a special category." He wondered how long I would be permitted to remain in Zanzibar without U.S. recognition. And he said the United States would "be in a better position to nurture and support" Nyerere's constructive influence on the situation in Zanzibar by recognizing Zanzibar.

This was good advice, and Williams agreed with it. However, two factors stood in the way of a decision by the Johnson administration to recognize Zanzibar: the slowness of the British to grant recognition and an escalation of concern that Zanzibar was sliding into the Communist orbit.

On the twentieth, Julie, Susan, and Julianne had been in the deputy chief of mission's house for a week and were very grateful for the kindness that embassy people had shown them. That morning seemed to promise another agreeable, peaceful day, the norm in pleasant Dar es Salaam (in later years, Dar es Salaam would degenerate into an overpopulated, dilapidated, crime-ridden city). But shortly after she was up and about, Julie heard what to her now well-trained ears was the sound of gunfire. Looking outside into the front yard, which ended at a road paralleling the beach, she saw Tanganyikan soldiers taking up positions in the yard and shooting at something or someone outside her line of vision. Alarmed, she paused for a moment, wondering what was going on; then she hurried to alert the others in the house to stay indoors.

At one-thirty that morning, at Colito Barracks, some ten miles north of the city, soldiers of the Tanganyikan Rifles had mutinied. Bitter about their pay levels, rate of promotion, and continued subordination to British officers, about forty men—most of them noncommissioned officers—sparked an uprising by the full contingent of soldiers at Colito. They arrested all the British officers, except for the commanding officer, Brig. Patrick Sholto Douglas, who had fled with his wife and daughter to Dar es Salaam. Dividing into several groups, the mutineers boarded trucks and drove to the city.

Once he was in Dar, Douglas got on the telephone to sound the alarm. When Nyerere was alerted, his advisers prevailed on him to go into hiding. Reluctantly, he complied, thereby avoiding what could have become the overthrow of his government and possibly the end of his life.

The soldiers quickly seized key points in the city. In a meeting with the leaders of the mutiny, External Affairs and Defense Minister Oscar Kambona listened to their grievances; accepted their choice, a second lieutenant, to replace Douglas; and acceded to their demand to remove the British officers. He arranged air transport to fly the officers to Nairobi. By noon, all the soldiers had returned to Colito Barracks. That afternoon, Kambona called some of the soldiers back to the city to put down rioting by mobs that had taken advantage of the mutiny to loot and destroy several blocks of largely Asian-owned stores and businesses. Seventeen people were killed in the rioting and the military action employed to quell it.

On Wednesday morning, Nyerere emerged from hiding and toured all sections of the city. By Friday, negotiations with the army were failing, and the soldiers were becoming defiantly insubordinate. That evening, Nyerere requested British military assistance. At six-thirty the next morning, led by Brigadier Douglas, British commandos aboard a carrier, HMS *Centaur*, which had sailed from Aden to Dar, were flown in helicopters to a playing field at Colito. Firing airbursts and exploding harmless but noisy charges, they stormed the barracks. When the Tanganyikans did not respond to Douglas's order to come out, the commandos launched a 3.5-inch bazooka rocket into a guardhouse, killing

three soldiers and wounding twenty others. With that, the mutineers either surrendered or fled.

Coincidentally, that same day, answering a request by Milton Obote and Jomo Kenyatta, British forces put down mutinies that had broken out in both Uganda and Kenya. There was much speculation that the three mutinies were linked and that somehow Zanzibar had something to do with them. *Time* magazine wrote, histrionically, "The chain of army mutinies that rocked East Africa like an earthquake had its epicenter in Zanzibar, where bloody revolution sent shock waves rumbling up and down the Great Rift." No evidence was ever found, however, to show that the mutinies were in any way coordinated. As for the influence of Zanzibar, the success of the armed revolutionaries there could well have influenced mainland soldiers to mutiny. But neither Okello, Babu, nor any other Zanzibari leader had anything at all to do with what happened in Tanganyika, Uganda, and Kenya.

Two days after the mutiny in Dar es Salaam, Fritz went to see Julie. He told her Ambassador Leonhart had decided that in view of the uncertainty about security in the Tanganyikan capital, she and the children, along with Shoana and the Picard children, would be flown to Nairobi the next day. In a letter to me, Julie said she felt the same way as the ambassador, "after the small revolution we had last Monday." During the several weeks that she would be in Nairobi, Julie would teach Spanish, help some African women learn to sew, make new friends, take a course to learn to drive, and, of course, look after our two little girls.

Fritz was on the airplane to Nairobi with Shoana; Julie; the children; Stu Lillico's wife, Helen; and Imelda Johnson, the American secretary of the embassy in Zanzibar. Fritz had been staying in Dar es Salaam to provide information to Ambassador Leonhart and his staff about Zanzibar and to send reports to Washington on his experiences and observations. Some peculiar things he had said and done led Leonhart, Deputy Chief of Mission Bob Hennemeyer, and Jim Ruchti, who had stayed in Dar to help the embassy report on the Zanzibar situation, to conclude that Fritz needed medical treatment. When the violence had broken out in Dar, he had become agitated and seemed to be reliving the Zanzibar experience.

Leonhart asked the State Department to authorize Fritz's return to the United States. The department agreed.

Some of the evacuees had complained to the embassy about Fritz's eccentric behavior at the English Club. This and some second-guessing about the need for the evacuation cast a shadow over Fritz's career prospects. In his favor, however, the newsmen whom the Zanzibar government had expelled gave Fritz high praise for his courage and efforts on their behalf. Several British nationals who had witnessed the event in the Zanzibar Hotel joined in the praise. Governments of the non-Americans who had been evacuated expressed gratitude for what had been done to help their nationals.

In a cable to Washington, Leonhart wrote that in arranging for the safe evacuation at a critical and unstable time when the United States and Fritz had "very little leverage in Zanzibar," Picard had made the "right decisions at the right time." Leonhart said a key element in the negotiations for the evacuation was Fritz's decision to remain in Zanzibar, "despite very real personal danger." This had convinced Okello, Karume, and Babu that the United States was "not fearful of the situation and not abandoning representation." Leonhart told Washington that "under most difficult circumstances," Fritz had done an outstanding job.

Leonhart's remarks may have helped Fritz in the short run. However, the Foreign Service promotion system tends to be unforgiving. Officers are rated every year and within each grade compete for promotion to the next-higher grade. Only a portion of them get promoted. It is a highly competitive "up or out" system, similar to that of the officer corps of the U.S. military. Any negative comments about an FSO's performance put that individual at a distinct disadvantage. Fritz would never again be promoted.

I was out of contact with the outside world again. When news of the trouble in Tanganyika had reached Zanzibar, the government had immediately banned all means of communicating overseas and closed the port.

On the morning of the twenty-first, I went to see Karume. He brought up U.S. recognition. I told him Washington was considering it

but wanted me to tell him that my ability to communicate freely would be a major element in its decision. After we had talked some more about this, Karume said he would see to it that I could resume overseas telephone calls and send cables, although still unclassified only.

Life had taken another good turn for me at the beginning of that day: Mfaume, our cook, showed up. He said he wanted to work, but only during daylight hours; he was afraid to be outside after dark. I readily agreed, happy at the prospect of having cooking better than my own.

Things were also getting better at the embassy. Some of the Zanzibari employees had returned to work, making it much easier for me to get things typed, mail or other cargo at the port picked up, homes for the pets of evacuated Americans found, the doors of homes that had been broken into repaired, and a thousand and one other quotidian administrative tasks done.

In the afternoon, I was able to get out a cable reporting the gist of my conversation with Karume. At first, the censor at Cable and Wireless said I could not send anything out, and Mr. Hampton told me that no word had arrived from President Karume. So I returned to the embassy and, called Wolf Dourado, who said he would call Karume. Forty minutes later, Wolf phoned to say that everything was now arranged. At Cable and Wireless, the censor released my message but, annoyed by my actions, deleted a sentence in which I had noted that the cabinet had been unavailable all day and that Babu and Hanga had gone to Kenya for discussions with Kenyan officials.

President Karume had also ended the prohibition on international phone calls. I called the embassy in Dar es Salaam, reported the item about the cabinet and Babu and Hanga, described the inspection of the Mercury sites, and gave a rundown of what was happening in Zanzibar. Then I called Timothy Crosthwait to tell him about the lifting of the ban on communicating with the outside world.

The next morning, I inspected the American houses at Mtoni again. They were totally unprotected, not a guard in sight at any of them. Angered, I took a letter over to the Ministry of External Affairs. In it, I referred to an earlier protest I had made and renewed my request for the government to provide adequate protection for the American property.

Wolf Dourado was sympathetic, but he and I knew that the fledgling government of Zanzibar could not be counted on to carry out its responsibilities as laid down by normal diplomatic practices.

My inexperience caught up with me in the telegram I sent reporting on what I had done. I said I had "delivered a note" to the ministry. In the world of diplomacy, a note means a formal written document from one government to another. Implicit in this is that the two governments have diplomatic relations with each other. A diplomatic note could be construed as a sign of recognition. Making my faux pas appear even worse, a cable from Dar reporting on my latest phone call said I had "sent [a] *formal* note to GOZ today requesting protection American property" (italics added).

The State Department sent a quick reaction back to Dar asking for an explanation. The embassy in Dar passed this message on to me in a phone call the next morning and relayed my response to Washington that the communication I had sent to the Zanzibar government was in the form of a letter, not a diplomatic note. In my own short cable to the department, I asked to be excused for using "poor terminology" and explained what I had done.

Because I was alone and was learning as I went along, inevitably I made other mistakes. However, they were minor things, such as forgetting to put a title on an airgram[2] or assigning an incorrect number to an outgoing cable. Nothing of consequence, at least not until I almost destroyed the embassy a few weeks later.

8

❦

People's Republic

And by the end of the week there was scant doubt that the revolt in tiny Zanzibar represented the first Communist take-over in an African country.

—*Newsweek*, **January 27, 1964**

A revolution with ties to Russia, Cuba, Red China and black Africa toppled the Government of Zanzibar January 12. From the first, the rebel regime showed leanings toward both Communism and comic opera.

—**U.S. News and World Report, January 27, 1964**

It is generally only when the White House is confronted by a crisis situation in Africa that a formerly obscure country becomes the focus of the President and his closest advisers.

—**Peter Schraeder, United States Foreign Policy Toward Africa**

John Okello returned to Zanzibar from Dar on January 23. He left almost immediately for Pemba. Accompanied by a contingent of his men, all well armed, he traveled there on the *Seyyid Khalifa*. The wholesale killings in Zanzibar were not repeated in Pemba, but what did occur was enough to add to Okello's fearsome reputation. Some Arabs were publicly executed, women and girls were raped, Arab and Asian homes

were looted, and men were publicly flogged. To humiliate Arab and Asian men, their heads were shaved; Arabs' beards were shorn. Some Pemban Africans, especially some Makonde tribesmen, joined Okello's men in committing the atrocities.

The sea separating Zanzibar from Pemba, along with the Zanzibar government's strict censorship, kept the truth of what happened in Pemba a secret from the outside world. In Zanzibar, all that was heard were vague rumors, nothing concrete enough to report as fact. Even when reliable information began to filter in from Pemba, people had to be careful about repeating it. For fear of being expelled from Zanzibar, Joan Pasco, who had been the British resident's secretary and was a free-lance journalist, dared not write about Pemba when she filed stories with Dar es Salaam's *Tanganyika Standard.*

Knowing that my telephone calls to the embassy in Dar were proba-bly monitored, I was in somewhat the same boat as Joan. When I had sen-sitive information whose source might be revealed and thereby endan-gered if the wrong people heard me relate what I had learned, I simply could not report it. Even when I was angry or frustrated over my inabil-ity to communicate freely with Dar es Salaam and Washington, if I believed there was any chance that a source could be jeopardized, I would not disclose what I had picked up.

Sometimes, the need to protect a source was not the problem; it was the information itself. It was possible that the rebels would be so dis-pleased by what I was going to reveal that they would cut off my ability to communicate. Usually I decided to risk it and reported what I had learned. Perhaps the Zanzibari authorities did not listen all the time, or perhaps they did not want to reveal that my telephone conversations were being monitored. Be that as it may, I never got in trouble after I had said something on the phone that was bound to have annoyed or angered the Zanzibar government.

More than three weeks would pass before I was able to report any-thing of substance about Pemba. In a telephone conversation with the embassy in Dar on January 28, I said the situation on Pemba was unclear, for no hard facts were available. But finally, on February 14, after Okello had made another trip there, I got some word out in an airgram that

Crosthwait had agreed to put into the high commission's diplomatic pouch. In the airgram, I reported about the executions, public floggings, and rapes.

I enjoyed a good relationship with Timothy Crosthwait and his staff, particularly Brian Banks and Harry McBrinn, highly capable officers who were about my age. The high commissioner, who was forty-eight, had entered the Indian Civil Service in 1938 and joined the Commonwealth Relations Office in 1955. He came to Zanzibar from Ceylon, where he had been deputy high commissioner. The revolution, which took place only weeks after he arrived, was a rough introduction to Africa, and some in the British community believed Crosthwait was having difficulty adjusting to the turbulence of the situation in Zanzibar. In Dar es Salaam, former colonial officials who went there from Zanzibar were critical of his performance. This was, in my view, unfair. I believe that under the circumstances he found himself in, he did a creditable job. During the uncertainty and chaos of the first two or three days of the revolution, he comported himself with courage and dignity. He was handicapped by London's extreme slowness in realizing that there was a cost to pay for not recognizing the new government. For my part, I found Crosthwait approachable, and he was more than cooperative with me during the time I was the lone American in Zanzibar.

By late January, I had developed some reliable sources of information. One was a well-placed government official. When we met in his office, we usually were alone. Nevertheless, he generally spoke guardedly, aware that if he divulged certain information, it could lead back to him, with a fatal consequence.

An Asian businessman was another source. His office was in the rabbit warren of the old part of Stone Town. To get there, I walked from the embassy through a couple of alleys to Stone Town's main thoroughfare, Main Street. Crossing Main Street, I entered Portuguese Street, which extended back into the densely packed area of multistoried houses and shops. It was more a long alley than a street. Cut off from the sun by the height of the buildings and so narrow that two bicyclists meeting would have barely enough room to pass, Portuguese Street was a bustling, friend-ly place. There were a lot of passersby, and shopkeepers sat in front or

Main Street, Stone Town

stood in the doorways of their shops. Other narrow streets intersected Portuguese Street at various points along its length.

It would be easy, I believed, to keep an eye out for a tail. Each time I went to see my source, I would stop to browse at a shop now and then, glance back the way I had come, and routinely go off on side streets and double back. Two or three times, I spotted a surveillant, or at least someone who seemed like a surveillant to me. When this happened, I wandered through the streets for a while, then made my way back to the embassy. Insofar as I knew, my businessman friend was never compromised, for he was never interrogated or arrested in connection with our meetings.

In February, another good source of information came my way. After a friend had suggested that it would be a good idea for me to meet with a certain young man, and I had agreed, he said he would arrange it. Once he had done that, he instructed me on what I should do on the night chosen for the meeting. I slipped out of my house around ten at night,

walked the thirty or so yards to the airport road, proceeded along it toward the airport for a few minutes, then stopped, concealing myself in roadside foliage. In a few minutes, a car came slowly down the road. I figured it had to be my prospective new source, and shortly before the car reached me, I stepped out to where I could be seen. Now committed, and knowing I was taking a risk, I was a bit apprehensive as the car stopped and the passenger-side door opened. Inside was the young man I had been told about, and no one else. We drove around for a while, sizing each other up. Satisfied with what we saw and heard, we agreed to continue to meet. He drove back to where he had picked me up. I got out, walked back home, and slipped back into the side of the house. As he had been when I left, the government guard was still sleeping near the driveway entrance to the house.

I knew it was possible that this source could have been a double agent, but neither I nor others in the embassy later had any reason to believe that this was the case. Certainly, as time went on, his information proved accurate and useful. Officials in the State Department would not have approved of the clandestine manner in which I met with him, but I decided that the intelligence I was collecting was worth the minor deception and that what the State Department didn't know wouldn't hurt me.

Mfaume's return to the house in mid-January had freed me from having to do household chores and given me more time each day to work at my job. Preparing breakfast and lunch for me took little of his time, so he was easily able to wash clothes and keep the house clean.

Much of my time at work was devoted to looking after American property. I got approval from Karume and Babu for the air-conditioning to be turned on at the Project Mercury site. After some Zanzibar government bureaucratic inefficiency, this was done, and Zanzibari watchmen were permitted to return to the site. I gathered together the Americans' cars in one place where they could be better protected. And I continued to visit the houses just about every day.

On January 23, I reported that the Revolutionary Council, chaired by Karume, was now the supreme body in Zanzibar. Interestingly, John Okello was only number twelve on the announced list of thirty-one

members, which included only one of his close associates. I tried to send a cable reporting the arrival of the Chinese chargé d'affaires and three other Chinese embassy officers, but the censor refused to clear it. So I reported the information by phone to Bob Hennemeyer at the embassy in Dar es Salaam.

Since I now was the only American on the island and had gained some notoriety as a result of my arrest and other recent events, my social calendar, such as it was, had become fuller. Zanzibaris did not dare invite me to their homes, but the British in town had no such qualms. With long days at work and now fairly frequent social events, even if I had been inclined to brood about being alone, I would not have had the time to do so.

Two weeks after the armed revolt, Okello's power seemed undiminished. Still dreaded by many, Okello was seen by Karume, others in the ASP, and Babu as not only a threat to their political fortunes, but also an embarrassment because of his extremely violent behavior and his wild pronouncements. He had to go. Karume and the others, however, had to bide their time before making any moves against him.

On January 28, Jim Ruchti left Dar es Salaam to return to Nairobi via Zanzibar. By prearrangement, I was at the Zanzibar airport when his plane landed for a fifteen-minute stop to pick up passengers. Despite some suspicious looks from armed guards, we were able to have a private conversation on the tarmac near the waiting airplane. I told him a struggle for leadership of the Zanzibar government was in play and involved three groups: Okello and his lieutenants, Karume and ASP moderates, and Babu and ASP and Umma radicals. I said Okello, still an enigma, remained the strongman of Zanzibar. Karume was strong-minded and had popular support, but was not as intelligent as Babu. The approximately forty well-armed, Cuban-trained Babu loyalists gave Babu and his supporters a disproportionate amount of power within the triumvirate.

Commenting at the end of his cable reporting on our meeting, Ruchti said, "Conversation itself, points Petterson made, presence armed

guards at airport, and behavior officials all conveyed clearly that basic elements of fear and uncertainty pervade Zanzibar." He added that "further slippage toward instability and eventual overt Communist takeover appears certain unless something done to stop it."

Late that night in Dar es Salaam, Ambassador Leonhart sent a long, analytical cable to Washington. His message was a call for action. He said Okello's presence prolonged instability and added to the threat to Karume from "Communist ambitions." An "active and armed minority in Zanzibar" would pose a danger to East African heads of state. Resultant instability in East Africa would jeopardize British interests to the point that British communities would leave. This, in turn, would have a devastating effect on the future of Kenya, Tanganyika, and Uganda and on "Britain's position in central Africa."

As for U.S. interests, Leonhart said, "A Communist Zanzibar would serve [the Communists] as a base for subversive and insurgency operations against the mainland from Kenya to the Cape." For southern Africa, Zanzibar would provide an example of the eradication of "an unpopular racial and economic minority," lead to a Communist takeover of southern African liberation movements, hasten the advent of war in Mozambique and violence in Southern Rhodesia, further the spread of communism in South Africa, and bring about "Communist lodgment on [the] western reaches of the Indian Ocean." Leonhart recommended that Washington "urge the British to persuade East African governments" to cooperate with Britain to bring about military intervention to assist Karume in disarming and confining the "Sten-gun slingers" who were supporting "Communist operations [in] Zanzibar." Crucial to this would be to get Karume to make a request for help.

Leonhart's cable resonated well in Washington. It is easy, from the perspective of almost four decades later, to take issue with Leonhart's analysis, to scoff at his assumptions. But to those who were involved in it, the Cold War was very real and the Soviet threat very compelling.

In the early 1960s, communism seemed to be winning successes, whereas democracy was viewed as in retreat. The USSR had developed the hydrogen bomb much earlier than expected, was exceeding the U.S. rate of industrial growth, and had supported successful revolutions in

Algeria, Cuba, and North Vietnam. The policy of stopping the spread of communism and containing perceived Soviet and Chinese expansionism had solid support from the public, politicians, and policymakers. Only fourteen months before the Zanzibar revolution, the Cuban missile crisis had underscored for Americans the danger the Soviet Union posed to the security of the United States.

President Kennedy believed that the most crucial arena of conflict between the West and its Communist adversaries would be the fight for the soul of the developing nations of Africa, Asia, and Latin America. He saw Africa as particularly important. In 1962, Kennedy signed a policy paper that stated: "What we do—or fail to do—in Africa in the next year or two will have a profound effect for many years. We see Africa as probably the greatest open field of maneuver in the worldwide competition between the [Communist] bloc and the non-Communist world."[1]

The record does not show whether Leonhart's January 28 cable energized the State Department or if its contents merely accorded with what the department had already decided to do. In any event, the next day a cable approved by Under Secretary of State Averill Harriman, an ardent proponent of aggressive containment of communism, went to London. It instructed Ambassador David Bruce to get the British assessment of the Zanzibar political situation and, if it was consistent with Washington's, to ask the British to consider extracting a request from Karume for military assistance to shore up his position.

Responding to Bruce, the British indicated agreement with the American assessment and the need for prompt action. On February 1, Bruce received another urgent message from the State Department. Its opening sentence showed how big an issue Zanzibar had become: "The President is concerned about the Zanzibar situation and does not wish it to deteriorate." The ambassador was told to see Duncan Sandys and tell him of the level of concern in Washington. Bruce was also to make it clear that although the United States continued to recognize Britain's primary responsibility for handling the Zanzibar problem, Washington was prepared to support, short of military assistance, British efforts.

After hearing this message, Sandys said the British government was worried about Zanzibar. However, he poured some cold water on the

American ideas about intervention. He said cabinet ministers had dis-cussed intervention but had found no satisfactory pretext to justify it. Ministers were agreed that the "UK could go in and would go in . . . if the lives of UK citizens are endangered." He noted, however, that British lives were not in danger. Moreover, it would be difficult to get Karume to make a request for intervention. Still, Sandys kept the door open to British action. He said it would be a different matter if Nyerere could be convinced "to ask Karume to invite British landings." Assurances of sup-port from East African governments would be highly important.

Picking up on this, the State Department instructed Leonhart to sound out Nyerere. He did so, on the third of February. Nyerere, he found, was almost totally preoccupied with his domestic affairs in the wake of the British military action in response to his cry for help.

The Tanganyikan president enjoyed considerable goodwill among the Americans and the British, although some in the British government were not enthusiastic about their erstwhile colonial subject. Nyerere, forty-one, was given the name Kambarage when he was born in Butiama, a town southeast of Lake Victoria. He adopted the name Julius when, at age twenty, he was baptized a Catholic. Nyerere's father was one of eight chiefs of the Zanaki, one of the smallest of Tanganyika's 126 tribes. Because of the boy's obvious intelligence, he was sent away to pri-mary school when he was twelve and still spoke only the Zanaki lan-guage. Later, he attended the prestigious secondary school in Tabora in western Tanganyika and then Makerere College in Uganda. Graduating in 1945, Nyerere taught history and biology at St. Mary's College, a Catholic secondary school in Tabora. A skilled debater, he had an instinct for politics and became active in the Tanganyika African Association (TAA).

With a grant from St. Mary's and a colonial government scholar-ship, Nyerere went to the University of Edinburgh in 1949 for three years' study of history and economics. In 1953, he resumed teaching, taking a position at St. Francis College, a secondary school twelve miles from Dar es Salaam. Within three months, he was elected presi-dent of the TAA. In 1954, he and colleagues established the Tanganyika African National Union (TANU), and Nyerere became its elected

leader. Committed to working for Tanganyika's independence from Britain, Nyerere was compelled by the British governor to choose between his teaching job and politics. He resigned from St. Francis. With the advent of independence in December 1961, Nyerere became the new country's prime minister. After only six weeks in office, he resigned to rebuild TANU into a strong political organization, which he said was needed to lead the country in a struggle against poverty, ignorance, and disease. During the year of his absence from government, Tanganyika became a republic, and in 1962 Nyerere returned to power as its president.

In his February 3 conversation with Leonhart, when Nyerere finally focused on Zanzibar, he said Babu and Karume needed each other, and he deprecated the notion of a Communist takeover of Zanzibar. As for outside intervention, Nyerere said that if Karume needed help, the Zanzibari would have to ask for it. He said it was the British, not he, who should speak with Karume: "He is still in the Commonwealth, and the British are there."

The Americans persisted in trying to get Her Majesty's Government to act. On the fifth, President Johnson sent a message to British prime minister Sir Alec Douglas-Home. Zanzibar, he said, had "many of the earmarks of a Communist operation in which they are walking lightly until they get their position solid." Now was the time to act, and only the British government had the "necessary position and influence in Zanzibar and in the nearby African states." The president said the United States would give whatever support it could usefully give, "because I think we would both pay a heavy price for any entrenched Communist position in Zanzibar."

At a meeting at the White House a week later, on February 12, Douglas-Home, repeating what Sandys had said to Bruce, told Johnson that Britain would "go in" if British nationals were endangered or if Karume invited them. But, he said, neither condition obtained. Soon afterward in British-American deliberations on Zanzibar, possible intervention would give way to the issue of recognition.

I was totally unaware of the discussions about Zanzibar within the U.S. government or between Washington and Dar es Salaam, Leonhart and Nyerere, and the Americans and the British. I had no idea whatsoever that Zanzibar was an issue of concern to the American president and British prime minister. Cut off from classified information, I was out of the loop and would remain so throughout my solo stint in Zanzibar.

Had I known of the thinking behind the U.S. policy toward Zanzibar, I would have most likely agreed with it. I had joined the navy during the Soviet blockage of Berlin in 1948, served in Korea in 1950, and been deeply influenced by events of the East-West struggle since then. I had been fully in accord with the essentials of the foreign policy of the Kennedy administration. Yet I was increasingly unhappy with the failure of Washington to recognize the government of Zanzibar. It seemed clear to me that our delay was unnecessarily angering Karume and increasing the Communists' influence.

Zanzibar Town presented a semblance of normality in late January. With more goods becoming available, fair numbers of people were seen in the markets. Car traffic was now almost back to its prerevolution level, the flow controlled where necessary by traffic policemen. The courts began functioning again; a British colonial jurist was named acting chief justice. Mail service was resumed. Nevertheless, the situation in town was ugly at times. Armed groups of Okello's men roamed the streets, apparently beyond the control of the Tanganyikan and regular Zanzibari police. Harassment was common; arbitrary detentions, interrogations, and beatings were not unusual occurrences.

On January 27, I met with Babu again. "What about my communications?" I asked, noting that a couple of days earlier, the British high commission had been given permission to send and receive encrypted messages.

Babu replied, "We gave the British this favor, but only because of our interest in remaining in the Commonwealth." He said he would present to the cabinet the question of whether I should be granted the use of "all official channels of communication." But, he added, "There's a risk that

people might not understand the motive behind sending messages in code."

I wrote a telegram reporting this conversation, but the censor would not permit it to be sent. He objected to my direct quotations of some of Babu's remarks. I retyped it—same message but no quotation marks—and he said it could be sent.

The next day, the cabinet granted my request to allow Project Mercury's Bendix Corporation project manager, George Burch, and NASA official Tom Spencer to return to Zanzibar from Dar es Salaam temporarily to have a look at conditions at the Mercury sites at Tunguu and Chwaka. But the cabinet deferred a decision on my use of encrypted communications.

Burch was not in Dar, but Spencer was, and he came over to Zanzibar for a couple of days at the beginning of February. He and I went out to the Mercury sites, and we devised a plan to place all the Americans' household goods in a central place under the supervision of Ernest Clark.

Over the next few days, I reported on continuing attacks on the United States in the Zanzibar press (*Kweupe*, the government's newspaper, and *Zanews*, Babu's Umma Party propaganda sheet), an announcement by Karume that Zanzibar was now a one-party state, and the entry into and possible looting of another American house. I continued my daily rounds of American property, and when I found no guard at a house, I managed to convince police officials to provide one right away.

I believed danger to foreigners was minimal now and suggested to Washington that two young American men who had been teaching at a Zanzibar school and were on leave when the revolution broke out, be allowed to return. Washington turned me down, sending me a message through the British that reached me several days later. The message, from the State Department, said: "Until our position regarding new regime clearer Dept does not . . . believe it advisable for additional non-official Americans . . . to return Zanzibar, with exception periodic visits selected NASA station personnel." It was a polite turndown, softened even more by praise for my work ("We are pleased and proud of job you are doing"). But why, I continued to wonder, was Washington taking so long to recognize the Zanzibar government?

The department would not have been pleased and proud to know of a stupid mistake I made not long afterward. I had been calling Dar es Salaam regularly every morning and afternoon but one day simply forgot to make the afternoon call. That day, I had already reported in during the morning, checked on American property, and sent a cable or two. Government offices were closed, and there wasn't anything else useful I could do in the afternoon. So I went out into the afternoon heat, when I would have the golf course all to myself, and played a round. That evening at home, I got a call from Dar. They had been frantic with worry that something awful had happened to me, I was told. I took the coward's way out and told the officer who called me that there had been both technical difficulties with the phone lines and inefficiency at the Zanzibar telephone exchange.

At the beginning of February, the Revolutionary Council denied my request for full access to diplomatic communications. The negative decision was tied to the lack of U.S. recognition. Wolf Dourado told me on February 5 that an anti-American, anti-British statement by Karume in a recent radio interview was a result of nonrecognition.

Four days later, I bicycled out the airport road to inspect the American houses adjacent to it. I took the bike instead of the car so that I could approach the houses quietly. This paid off, for I surprised three young men carting things away from one of the houses. I saw red and, without thinking whether or not they had weapons, charged them on the bike, yelling at them to drop the stuff and stand where they were. They threw down what they were carrying and took off, running down a path through waist-high grass. Coming close to the slowest of the three, I jumped off the bike, sprinted after him, and tackled him. He cowered, terrified; my pent-up rage at all the looting of American families' possessions must have given me a furious look, and I was cursing a blue streak. But when I saw that he was just a teenager, I calmed down. I knew that if I turned him in, he would probably be executed. Only two days earlier, in fact, several Shirazi Africans charged with looting had been flogged to death. The looters had been given a sentence of sixty-five lashes and thirty years' imprisonment, and several had not survived the lashing. So I let the youth go, warning him never to do any looting

again and advising him to tell all his friends that Okello would kill any-one stealing foreigners' property.

I turned my angry thoughts to the failure, once again, of the Zanzibar authorities to provide adequate protection for American property, de-spite my many and repeated appeals. After reporting the looting to one of Kisassi's deputy commissioners, I went to the embassy and wrote a short telegram: "Am moving American property from residences to safer central storage place. This action prompted by inadequate police protection, continued looting, and govt seizure apartment formerly occupied by American." Not surprisingly, the censor did not let the cable go out.

The contents of my censored telegram were passed to Babu. On the tenth, I was informed that he wanted to discuss the matter with me. I phoned the embassy in Dar es Salaam that I thought Babu wanted to sug-gest changes to soften the tone of the message.

I went to Babu's office that evening. Our previous talks had all been cordial. He told a mutual friend that I was open and honest and that he liked me. This time there was no cordiality. "What are you trying to do—make it seem as if the government is weak?" he asked angrily. He accused me of painting an inaccurate picture of the situation and said what I had done was grounds for expulsion from Zanzibar. Hot under the collar myself, I recounted the repeated pillaging of Americans' possessions and my many requests for better protection. I acknowledged that I had been irate when I wrote the cable but said I had a right to be angry.

After we argued some more, Babu said he would take the matter up with Karume. In a letter I wrote to my parents, I said Babu and I had had "a dispute, a rather bitter dispute," over a cable I had not been permitted to send. I said that when I had later received a phone call from President Karume, "I figured he was going to tell me to pack my bags. However, he just called to ask me if I would be so kind as to escort two visiting Congolese dignitaries on a tour of the Project Mercury site."

The recognition issue was a constant in my dealings with Babu and Karume. The failure of the United States and Britain to recognize their

government embittered them, especially Karume. It made it easier for the Communist countries to gain influence and harder for Karume to resist a growing leftward orientation within the government. In his January 23 memorandum to Soapy Williams, Jesse MacKnight had rightly said: "The U.S. will be in a much stronger position to be helpful if it recognizes the new government and supports the more desirable elements than if it retires to the sidelines." London, however, still vacillated.

The emphasis that the Zanzibari leadership placed on recognition came through in my reporting. On January 24, Babu, after telling me that power generation at the Mercury sites could be resumed, said: "It's difficult to discuss any other matters because as far as you [the U.S. government] are concerned, we do not exist; you have not recognized Zanzibar." He insisted that nonrecognition was the reason my ability to communicate was restricted and added, "We have been recognized by most nations of Africa—why not the United States?"

A week later, he repeated that because of the lack of recognition, I was not permitted to use all official channels of communication. Catch-22: Washington stipulated that my ability to communicate was a factor in a U.S. decision on recognition; Zanzibar said that without recognition, I could not communicate freely.

Babu also told me: "The U.S. has put us in an awkward position. People are asking why the American embassy is allowed to stay open if the U.S. government has not recognized the government of Zanzibar." He said the anti-American feelings of some Zanzibaris, including members of the Revolutionary Council, would "become more confirmed the longer recognition is delayed."

"This anti-American campaign in the press," I said, "isn't helping matters."

"It's not the government that's doing this," he replied. "Commentators are permitted to write what they please, without censorship."

"Like hell," I thought but didn't say, keeping a straight face. No sense in saying something that would not change the situation but would make my life more difficult.

On February 13, Nyerere asked Leonhart to come over to State House for a talk. When they were alone in his office, Nyerere said the

situation in Zanzibar had taken a turn for the worse. Karume was losing out, and it was doubtful, because of Western unwillingness to have anything to do with Zanzibar, that the Zanzibar government would remain non-Communist. Nyerere had told the British that time was running out. He had hoped the British would grant recognition to Zanzibar but had heard nothing further from them. He asked Leonhart to convey to Washington his view that there now was an urgent need for early Western recognition.

Later that day in Washington, President Johnson, Prime Minster Douglas-Home, and some of their advisers met for a follow-up session to the one they had had the day before. Sir Alec said the UK could recognize Zanzibar, but the country had no constitution and its leaders "were an odd lot." He noted that West Germany had recognized Zanzibar. Sir Alec's foreign minister, R. A. Butler, said diplomatic recognition was "about the best thing under the circumstances." Secretary of State Rusk said the best bet would be to support Karume and "have Nyerere preach moderation to him." Averill Harriman remarked that if the UK recognized Zanzibar, then the United States should follow suit "in order to prevent our man from being thrown out" and to keep in step with the British government. Douglas-Home said he would send a telegram to Duncan Sandys suggesting that, unless Sandys had objections, the UK recognize Zanzibar.

While the machinery at Whitehall and Foggy Bottom was ponderously grinding out a final decision, events in Zanzibar were moving swiftly to a different kind of decision.

9

❦

Out and Back

The passive policy of "control of whatever situation may arise" as described by Sandys is inadequate. In our view [the] British clearly have the responsibility for developing an action program for Zanzibar. . . . While [the] British are understandably preoccupied with Cyprus, neither we nor they can afford to neglect Zanzibar with its serious Communist implications for East Africa as well as Central and South Africa.

—Under Secretary of State Averill Harriman

Karume and Okello had a confrontation at the end of January when, while Okello was in Pemba, his men in Zanzibar arrested some Tanganyikan police. Karume responded by ordering Okello's men off the streets.

After returning to Zanzibar, Okello was furious when he learned what had happened and also found out that Karume was trying to take over command of the military. He went to Radio Zanzibar and broadcast a speech in which he complained bitterly that the Revolutionary Council had passed laws during his absence, bypassing him and ignoring his authority. At about this time, during a Revolutionary Council meeting, Karume ordered Okello to put his pistols at a place out of reach on the table.

Karume may have won that round, but he knew he was not strong enough for a showdown with Okello. He had succeeded in clipping Okello's wings a bit, but the Ugandan was still far too powerful to be trifled with. Karume must have set about to ease the tension and mollify Okello, because two days following Okello's radio broadcast, Karume, Babu, and Okello all spoke on the radio stating that the previous misunderstanding no longer existed.

Thomas Franck, a young Canadian professor of constitutional law and international law at New York University, was in Zanzibar for a few days to advise the Zanzibar government on legal and constitutional matters. Franck, a close friend of Karume, had been legal adviser to the Afro-Shirazi Party. He witnessed the confrontation between Karume and Okello and told me he continued to believe Karume would come out on top in the three-way struggle for power. He feared there would be more violence, however, because too many arms were in too many mutually hostile hands.

Franck told me he had advised Karume and his cabinet not to attempt to draw up a constitution in a short time. Instead, he had counseled them to rule by decree until the situation became more stable. He said he had emphasized to them that their decrees would have to be designed to establish a responsible democratic government and could be incorporated into the future constitution. He had faith that Karume and the moderates in the ASP would prevail. He would not, he told me, allow himself to be involved with a government that would try to do away with democratic principles. This hope, unfortunately, would not be fulfilled.

Franck, like Nyerere, knew that Karume and other ASP leaders were being subjected to incessant Communist propaganda, but the young professor seemed to believe they would withstand it. Nyerere told Leonhart that Karume's advisers, egged on by the Communist diplomats in Zanzibar, were urging Karume to close down the British and American diplomatic missions in the absence of recognition.

Despite the signals coming from Zanzibar, Duncan Sandys still seemed in no hurry to confer recognition on the Zanzibaris. He held Karume in low regard. He told David Bruce that Karume was "not a very respectable character," was extremely left wing, and was once drunk in

Sandys's presence. It is unclear which of these sins Sandys considered the more disgraceful.

Nyerere's appeal to the British to give immediate recognition to Zanzibar did not stir Sandys into action. Apparently, he was not someone to take advice from the likes of Julius Nyerere. According to Nyerere, he had warned Sandys in London in the fall of 1963 that an explosion was bound to occur if the British persisted in their plan to keep the sultan in power and deal only with an Arab-dominated government. Nyerere told Sandys that instability was inevitable when a majority of the people lived and worked in conditions of feudal poverty on lands owned by a minority of a different race. Sandys, Nyerere later told Ambassador Leonhart, had not seemed to think there was much in what Nyerere had told him. And now he was not heeding Nyerere's appeal for speedy recognition of Zanzibar. Sandys's response to Douglas-Home's recommendation for recognition was to continue consulting with Commonwealth countries.

The Zanzibaris warned Crosthwait that unless recognition was granted, they would order the high commission closed. The British asked Nyerere to intervene, and he called Karume on about February 6 to request that the British be given a little more time. Karume agreed. When, after several more days, the British still did not act, Nyerere told High Commissioner Stephen Miles on the eleventh that time was running out. He heard nothing further from the British.

The Americans, unlike Duncan Sandys, understood the need for prompt action but could not seem to move with anything but deliberate speed. On February 14, the day after Johnson and Douglas-Home's second meeting on the Zanzibar issue, the State Department sent a long cable to Dar es Salaam with detailed instructions for an approach to Nyerere. The department said, "UK and US now thinking seriously early recognition Zanzibar. Dept desires coordinate US action closely with British . . . [who] we believe . . . should take lead in announcing recognition." This, of course, virtually guaranteed more delay.

The department's plan was for Leonhart to get Nyerere to organize a quiet meeting in Dar es Salaam between Leonhart and Karume for a "preliminary discussion." If this went well, Leonhart would go to Zanzibar to

talk to Karume and his advisers on the recognition problem, the Project Mercury station, the arrival of a new U.S. representative to Zanzibar, and possible U.S. food and medical aid. Leonhart would stress to Karume that U.S. recognition could not be a condition for the meetings.

The department was not in touch with reality. Karume was in no position politically to leave the island at this point to go off to Dar for a quiet tête-à-tête with the American ambassador. Showing a partial awareness of this, the department said Nyerere would have to develop "an excuse to have Karume come to Dar."

While noting that "direct dialogue with Karume should be initiated soonest," the department's instructions mentioned that the preliminary talk between him and Leonhart should take place "in a few days' time." Events in Zanzibar were moving much too fast for the department's inexplicably unhurried timetable.

Leonhart met with Nyerere on the sixteenth. The ambassador made the case for a meeting with Karume, which, he said, in view of the deteriorating situation in Zanzibar, should take place within the next few days.

The Zanzibar situation, Nyerere said, was becoming more critical. Unless the West could move swiftly and find some way to help, Zanzibar would become "another Congo." He said the armed men loyal to Karume had not been paid since the revolt. Karume had given each of them fifty shillings out of his own pocket but could not continue to do this. Nyerere said the people who had guns were hungry. Karume was being driven to the Communists. Nyerere told Leonhart he would contact Karume and try to arrange a meeting in Dar.

Karume had other things on his mind than meeting with an American emissary. Id el Fitr, the Muslim holiday marking the end of the fasting month of Ramadan, was about to begin, and rumors abounded that an outbreak of violence was imminent. Karume went on the air to tell Zanzibaris that fear of post-Ramadan trouble was unfounded. He appealed for calm and said policemen would be in the streets to see that law and order were maintained.

On the fifteenth, Karume and Okello had addressed a crowd of about 20,000 that had marched in a procession organized by the government

to pledge support for the revolution. Placards featured in the march condemned the United States and Britain, imperialism, and capitalism. To the cheers of the crowd, Karume proclaimed that in Zanzibar everyone would be equal and that the government pledged to raise the standard of living of the masses. He warned the people of the danger of being divided by foreigners who were interested in sowing seeds of discord. Okello said the sultan was the devil and so were imperialists and capitalists.

After the procession and the speeches, Zanzibar Town was quiet that weekend of the Id. Tom Spencer and George Burch came over from Dar es Salaam on the seventeenth to do some work at the site and begin packing up the personal effects of Project Mercury employees. I spent some time with them, lending a hand until they left for Dar on the afternoon of the next day.

At home that evening, I caught the tail end of a Radio Zanzibar broadcast. Okello was speaking, and I heard him say something about the American consul coming to the palace. I called a Zanzibari friend. He had heard the broadcast. Okello had declared: "The American consul must listen; even if he is in his grave, he must listen. He must come to the palace before ten tomorrow morning or immediately leave Zanzibar." Okello said I was guilty of spying.

I was in a quandary. On the one hand, I wondered what Okello had in mind and did not want to miss a chance to talk to him, especially at the palace (which had been renamed the People's Palace). On the other hand, should I, the representative of the U.S. government, respond to a publicly delivered threat by doing what Okello told me to do?

The next morning, I called Wolf Dourado to get his advice. He said to come over to his office at the Beit el-Ajaib. I drove the quarter mile through Suicide Alley, down Main Street, and just past the Portuguese Fort to Zanzibar's then largest building, a squarish, several-storied structure topped by a clock tower and surrounded by tiers of pillars and balconies. Built in 1883 as a ceremonial palace for Sultan Barghash, the Beit el-Ajaib was heavily damaged in 1896 by a British naval bombardment

during a brief battle between the British and a pretender to a recently deceased sultan's throne.

I walked past the two sixteenth-century bronze cannons standing at the entrance. An armed guard nodded at me as I went inside. The front part of the interior was cavernous and featured an ornate elevator cage that rose at a snail's pace. I went up to Dourado's office, but he was nowhere to be seen.

Looking for Dourado in other offices, I ran into Abdul Azziz Twala, a member of the Revolutionary Council and a junior minister in the government. Probably in his late twenties, Twala, like Hanga, was an ideological soul mate of Babu, but a Karume loyalist. Dour, a true believer in Marxism, he despised the United States and made no effort to hide it. Gazing at me stonily, Twala asked what I wanted. I explained that in a radio broadcast, Okello had summoned me to the palace. With neither explanation nor apology, Twala said I should ignore the summons, and he walked away.

Still uncertain what to do, I set out again to find Dourado. As I walked down a hall, Okello and Hanga came out of a room. I stopped, they stopped, and Okello glared at me. After a moment, I asked Okello in Swahili what he had meant in his radio announcement. Placing his hand on his holstered pistol, he angrily replied that he had met me the day before and that I was engaging in subversive activity. *Subversive* was not a word I had added to my Swahili vocabulary, so Hanga translated it for me.

"I didn't see you yesterday," I said, "and I don't know what you are talking about. This is a serious charge; tell me just what I am supposed to have done."

"The United States gave weapons to the old regime, and I have proof."

"That's untrue. I would like to know which of my present activities you consider to be bad."

Okello thought a moment, then told me I did not have to leave Zanzibar. Then he said: "The United States is not God. Zanzibar does not need recognition from the United States, and it does not fear the United States."

I said no one needed fear the United States since it was striving only for peace.

Not buying that at all, Okello said: "The Soviet Union is strong for peace, while the United States is trying to dominate the world. The United States has evil policies and should get out of Zanzibar."

Seeing that this was leading nowhere, I said I was in Zanzibar only to represent my government and obtain protection for American property.

"No American has been killed," Okello interjected, "and property has been protected."

"That's not true; six American houses have been looted."

Okello paused, then said, "I did not know that. And you know? Some things have been taken from my house." With that, he nodded, and he and Hanga went their way.

I finally found Dourado, told him what had happened, and said I would like clarification from the Ministry of External Affairs. Wolf and I grinned at each other, knowing full well that I might as well have been asking for the moon.

I had no knowledge of the state of play on recognition. The cables going to and from Washington, London, and Dar es Salaam were highly classified, and none of the information in them could be passed on to me over an open telephone line. But I certainly was getting the drift of the Zanzibar government's growing displeasure over what the Zanzibaris regarded as inexplicable delaying tactics of the UK and the United States. About the second week in February, I started burning classified papers.

If some American embassies had shredders in those days, Zanzibar was not among them. Our modern tool to get rid of classified files was a small potbellied stove. A hand crank on the side was employed to suck some air into the stove to help the combustion process. The little stove could handle only a few sheets of paper at a time. Each afternoon, I took a load of files to the stove and began burning, cranking away for an hour or two at a time. By mid-February I was working longer hours at the burning but still had many files to go.

Karume spoke again on February 18. Addressing a crowd at Zanzibar's Public Hall, he stressed the theme of equality, unity, and erasing racial disharmony. Except for a throwaway line or two warning about imperialism and neocolonialism, he had nothing negative to say about the West. He said nothing about recognition.

It was much on his mind the next morning, however. I opened the embassy as usual at seven-thirty and was working at my desk about midmorning when I got a phone call telling me President Karume wanted to see me. Karume's presidential office was in the building known as State House, just outside Stone Town on the road leading out of Zanzibar Town to the airport. The seat of the colonial government, the elegant, gleaming-white building had housed the residence and office of the British resident, intending to go there, I was told that because the United States had not recognized the Zanzibar government, Karume would not receive me at State House; instead, the meeting was to be at Raha Leo. When I got there, I saw Crosthwait's car, with the Union Jack on its flagstaff. I met him inside, and we were escorted into a room where Karume, flanked by Babu and Hanga, was sitting with his cabinet.

Getting right to the point, Karume said the people of Zanzibar had put pressure on him and the cabinet to oust the British and American representatives because Britain and the United States had not recognized the Zanzibar government. He said, "I am sorry, but I am forced to ask you to leave." If he did not, there would be dissension, and "the people could rise up and commit violent acts." I wasn't sure whether he meant the violence would be aimed at us or at the government.

Karume said British and American official and personal property would be protected. In answer to a question from me, he gave his assurance that the Mercury station would be kept inviolate. Local personnel could continue to maintain the station, but no American personnel could return until U.S. recognition was granted. Crosthwait asked how much time we had. "Twenty-four hours," Karume replied.

Reporting to the British embassy in Dar es Salaam, Crosthwait said he believed the decision was irrevocable. High Commissioner Miles in Dar told Leonhart that he did not plan to ask Nyerere to intervene. Crosthwait and his staff would be coming out the next morning.

Back at the embassy, I got a call through to Dar to inform Leonhart and Washington what had happened. In a cable to Washington, after reporting what I had told him, Leonhart said he would "concert departure arrangements with Petterson and advise Department. Believe he fully understands destruct procedures."

After talking to Leonhart, I spent most of the afternoon burning papers.

In Dar es Salaam, Leonhart had been exchanging messages with the State Department. He now knew that the slow train to recognition was finally about to arrive. On the strength of this, he went to Nyerere to ask him to urge Karume to delay my expulsion for as much as another forty-eight hours. Nyerere insisted it would be impossible for him to intervene again. But Leonhart pressed him, telling him that recognition was imminent, that much-needed emergency aid would be given to Zanzibar, that there was no protecting power in Zanzibar to look after U.S. interests, and that Tanganyika and the United States had a common interest in avoiding a severance in relations between the United States and Zanzibar.

Leonhart thought the Tanganyikan president was wavering, but then Nyerere left the room to take a phone call from Duncan Sandys. When he returned, he was furious. Sandys, presumably in a high-handed manner, had suggested that Nyerere ask Karume to hold off on the expulsion of Crosthwait for ten days. By then, Sandys would be in East Africa and, he said to Nyerere, "willing to discuss the problem with Karume" if Karume would come to Dar for a meeting. Nyerere told Sandys that he could ask his high commissioner in Zanzibar to tell this to Karume if he wished, but Nyerere could not help on this matter.

Thoroughly put out by his talk with Sandys, Nyerere told Leonhart he was sorry, but there was nothing he could do. With that, he excused himself, leaving Leonhart no option but to return to the embassy.

Once there, he called me, reaching me at home early in the evening. He said I should try to see Karume, ask that my expulsion be held off for another twenty-four to forty-eight hours, and tell him a U.S. official had just arrived in Dar es Salaam and could come to the island the next day for a discussion of recognition and emergency aid. If Karume preferred,

Leonhart could come for an initial talk and bring the official with him. This was the first I had heard that recognition might be at hand and that someone from Washington was waiting in Dar to come over to Zanzibar. Leonhart spoke briefly about an emergency aid package but obviously did not want to go into details about that or anything else over the open phone line.

I called State House and managed to be put through to Karume. He said to come over right away. Without taking time to change out of my sport shirt, Bermuda shorts, and sandals, I drove to State House. Word had been received at the gate to let me pass, and after I parked, I was escorted upstairs to Karume's office. Karume had shown before that he liked me, and he greeted me warmly that night. As always when we were together, we spoke in Swahili. When he saw how I was dressed, he laughed, pointed at my sandals, and said, "Now you are a *sheikh.*"

I delivered the message that Leonhart had given to me. After hearing me out, Karume said: "You can stay if the American representative, whether from Washington or the ambassador himself, is coming tomorrow, not to consult but to make the announcement of recognition." This was necessary, he said, because his government had announced that I was going, and the people would not understand otherwise. Given the revolutionary atmosphere in Zanzibar, he would be unable to say an American diplomat was coming just for consultations; a visit would have to be to announce recognition. If not, I would have to go.

I said I would get back to him as soon as I had further clarification. Back home, I called Leonhart, who at ten o'clock sent a flash message to Washington informing the State Department of what I had told him.

The Johnson administration did not want to announce recognition unless the British were ready to do so, and the British were continuing to hesitate. After news of the decision to expel Crosthwait reached Britain, Sandys told the House of Commons that consultations with Commonwealth countries were taking a long time.

Trying to temporize, at 5:20 that afternoon in Washington—1:20 A.M., January 20, in Dar es Salaam and Zanzibar—the White House sent a message from President Johnson to President Karume. The embassy in Dar reached me by phone at about seven in the morning. An embassy

officer read the text slowly so I could write it down verbatim. Then Leonhart got on the phone to urge me to see Karume as soon as I could. I assured him I would. After typing the message on a piece of paper, I called Karume and told him I had received a communication for him from President Johnson. He told me to come to State House. The message from Johnson, which I read slowly in English to Karume, stated:

> I have just learned of your instruction to Mr. Petterson. I am sure the diplomatic relations between our two countries can be established with advantages to the government and people of both our countries. I have great personal sympathy for the national aspirations of the people of Zanzibar, and I am most hopeful that by the early establishment of diplomatic relations it may be possible for this country to be friendly with you. On the other hand if our representative is required to leave your country, it will inevitably be more difficult for you and for me to have the friendly and effective relations which I am sure we both desire.

Karume indicated he understood what I had read, and I gave him the typed copy. After thinking a moment, he said the American representative, and the ambassador if he wished, could come to Zanzibar that morning to meet with him and his cabinet. I thanked him, went home, and called Leonhart. He told me that he and Frank Carlucci, the representative, would fly over in a chartered plane.

Frank C. Carlucci III, I was to learn, was a highly regarded Foreign Service officer my age, thirty-three. His previous two assignments had been in South Africa and the Congo. At the embassy in Leopoldville (now Kinshasa), Frank had gained renown for his exploits in making monthly trips into hostile territory to bring back firsthand reports of what was happening in that turbulent country. Those reports were highly valuable to the embassy and to Washington for the insights they provided about the Congo situation.

A risk taker, he believed that you could not understand a country without understanding its people and that, as he once told a reporter, to know people, you had to "get out and shake their hands and talk to them."[1] Although that might seem self-evident, it was not the style of

many diplomats and certainly not easy to do in a land wracked by the violence of internal struggles for political power. While he was in the Congo, he had been challenged at bayonet point by Congolese soldiers, threatened with arrest in Stanleyville by the breakaway leftist regime of Antoine Gizenga, and stabbed in the back by a member of an angry mob.[2]

It was midmorning when the four-place Cessna bearing Carlucci and Leonhart arrived at the Zanzibar airport. Not long afterward, Tim Crosthwait and his British staff left the island. When I got to the airport that morning, I was placed under guard. The armed men guarding me refused to let me join the two Americans as they debarked from their airplane. Spying Dourado and Babu, I got them to intercede and was able to follow the government car that took Carlucci and Leonhart into town. At State House, I greeted them and went with them into the meeting with Karume, Okello, and the cabinet.

Karume listened stoically as Leonhart repeated the substance of President Johnson's message. Leonhart and Carlucci made it clear that recognition was coming shortly, and they urged Karume not to cut communications between Zanzibar and the United States by expelling me.

Karume said he could not do as they wished. Pressures had built up among the people against the presence of representatives of two countries that had not recognized the government of Zanzibar. To resist these pressures would imperil the government and put Crosthwait and me in grave danger. He said his government regretted having to take this action. It would safeguard American property. He repeated that he could not withdraw the expulsion order. Some of the others joined him in expressing hope for early U.S. recognition.

The meeting went on for more than two hours. Finally, there was nothing more to say. As we were preparing to leave, Carlucci said he hoped to be returning with me very soon. Karume smiled and said that when we came back, we would be greeted with a parade of welcome.

I accompanied Frank and the ambassador to the airport, said goodbye, and drove back to the embassy to continue burning documents. I told the three Zanzibari employees in the embassy the gist of what had taken place and asked them to go home. Skipping lunch for the time

being, I began gathering up the remaining classified materials. Hearing a pounding on the embassy's heavy wooden door, I went downstairs and opened it.

There at the door was Ali Mafoudh, dressed in his Cuban combat fatigues. Mafoudh, an Arab disciple of Babu, had received military and ideological training in Cuba. At one time, he was head of the ZNP office in Havana. He was one of those who returned to Zanzibar shortly before the revolution. Conspicuous ever since, sporting a Castro-type beard, Mafoudh seemed to delight in playing the role of a revolutionary military figure. He was, in fact, intelligent and well trained. Just days earlier, a special police force was set up with Mafoudh as its head.

He said he wanted to come in and have a look around. When I stepped outside, I could see that there were armed men at the front and sides of the building. I closed the door behind me and said no, the embassy was U.S. territory and I would not allow it to be entered. He didn't argue the point but said he would have to take me into custody. I got into Mafoudh's Land Rover, and we drove to State House. There, Salim Rashid, the clerk of the Revolutionary Council, told Mafoudh to take me back to the embassy and let me go about my business.

After another half hour of burning papers, I went home for lunch. When I returned to the embassy, the officer in charge of the troops surrounding the building said I could not go back in. When I protested, he said, "You must come with us," explaining that a government official wanted to talk to me. Reminding him that no one was to enter the premises, I made sure the door was still locked and got into a waiting Land Rover in which three men with automatic weapons were seated. We drove to the Beit el-Ajaib, and I was escorted into Twala's office. Several men were with him. Some of them looked uneasy as he asked me what I had been doing. I explained that I was securing the embassy and burning some papers before locking up and going to my house. Twala listened passively, then told me to finish up, go home, and stay there until late in the afternoon, when I would leave Zanzibar.

Years later, Mohammed Ali Foum, who had been one of Babu's close associates, gave me his version of what had happened. Foum was a high-ranking diplomat with the Tanzanian mission to the United Nations

when I talked with him. He told me that he been with the others in Twala's office that day I was brought in. Some of his companions had been inflamed by Okello's accusation that I was a spy and said I should be shot. While I was being sent for, Foum said, he argued that it would be a dangerous mistake to kill an American diplomat. By the time I was brought in, the plan to kill me had been scrapped.

With my escort, I returned to the embassy, reentered, locked the door, and went back upstairs. It was now obvious to me that I would never finish burning the files using the stove. Before turning to that problem, I took an ax, went into the vault, and proceeded to pound the code machine into rubble. Satisfied that the mangled remains would be of no use to anyone, I took the consulate's emergency supply of five hundred Maria Theresa taler coins from the safe. The coins were acceptable specie in East Africa. I also gathered up a few personal papers and a picture that John F. Kennedy had inscribed for me when I worked on his 1962 state visit to Mexico. Then I got all the rest of the classified papers together.

In a storeroom near the vault were two emergency destruction kits. Each was a cylindrically shaped heavy cardboard drum, roughly three feet high and two feet in diameter, about the size of a large garbage can. Inside were several bags of inflammable chemical granules and a hand grenade-like magnesium igniter with a lever that was held closed by a pin.

I dragged one of the drums over to the vault, took out the chair next to the now destroyed code machine to make enough space for the drum and me, and pushed the drum inside. Following the directions printed on part of the drum, I slowly emptied the remaining files into it. After about six or eight inches of paper, I opened a bag of the chemicals and spread its granular contents over the layer of paper. I repeated this process several times until all the files were in the drum, which now was just about full. Standing next to the drum, I removed the pin from the igniter, squeezed the lever, and dropped the igniter into the drum. With a loud whoosh, a sheet of fire shot up as high as the eight-foot ceiling. Luckily or prudently, I can't remember which, I had left the thick steel vault door open. I jumped backward through the doorway into the nar-

row hallway and tried to close the door. But I couldn't do it. The intense heat in the vault was sucking air in through the vents of the window air-conditioning unit that had been fitted into a space carved in the outer wall. The blast of hot air was so strong I couldn't push the door shut.

I was afraid that the fire would spread if I didn't get the door closed. In desperation, holding my arms against the door, I leaped up and kicked my feet out about a yard high against the opposite wall of the hallway. Using my leg muscles, I strained as hard as I could, got the door closed, and in the same motion pulled down on its handle.

The directions for the destruction procedures had neglected to warn that under no circumstances should the destruction kit be ignited indoors, especially in a small, enclosed space. In addition to burning the documents, I had come close to incinerating myself.

Breathing a sigh of momentary relief, I wondered what to do next. I could hear the fire burning fiercely. I decided I'd better have a look from outside the embassy. When I walked outside, Mafoudh was nowhere in sight. I went over to the vault side of the building. Oily black smoke was pouring out of the air conditioner. Two of Mafoudh's men, both dressed in fatigues and wearing red berets, came up to me. One asked in English, "What's that? What's going on?"

"I'm just burning some papers," I said, trying to be as casual as I could. He gave me a look of disbelief but said nothing as I turned and walked back inside the embassy. On the way up the stairs, I wondered how I would explain to the U.S. government that I had burned down the embassy.

Back in my office, I had another look around to be sure I had destroyed everything I needed to get rid of. I went back to the vault. It seemed to me that the sound of the fire had abated somewhat. I got the things I had put aside to take with me, went out the front door, locked it, and left the building. By now, only a wisp of smoke was coming out of the air conditioner.

A pleasant Ministry of External Affairs official named Rashad was waiting at my house when I got there. Armed guards were placed around the house. Rashad accepted my offer of a cold drink, and waited while I finished the packing I had begun the previous night. I chatted with him

Author being expelled from Zanzibar

for the next hour or so while we waited for the 5:30 P.M. arrival of the regularly scheduled East African Airways round-trip flight from Dar es Salaam.

At the airport, some uniformed security police hovered around me, making sure I did not mingle with anyone as I waited for the plane. Chinese news photographers were on hand to record the event on film. An English newspaperman later showed me a photograph in which one of Babu's men, a young bearded, uniformed Arab holding an automatic weapon, scowled as he guarded me. My clothes hung loosely on my skinny frame—I had lost more than twenty pounds. The other guards were good-humored, however, and we joked as they escorted me to the plane.

The flight on the Fokker Friendship twin-engine turboprop plane took about twenty minutes. Embassy officers met me at the airport and took me to the embassy. After talking to Leonhart and Carlucci, I began preparing an assessment for Washington of the Zanzibari leadership. I finished it the next day, after a good night's rest. Its main points were:

- Karume was president "in fact as well as in name." He had strong convictions, but was susceptible to the influence "of some of his more clever associates," particularly on complex international matters. A moderate, he wanted close ties with Tanganyika and favored a policy of nonalignment.

- John Okello appeared at cabinet meetings but did not actively participate. Karume considered him a madman and, when possible, would remove him from his place of power. Karume had to tread lightly, however, for fear that a too early attempt to depose Okello would divide the government and result in bloodshed.

- Some of the pro-Communists in the government had close ties with either the USSR or Communist China. Some were militant ideologues; others were not. Babu clearly was the leader of the pro-Communists. Although he expressed desire for friendship with the United States, his sympathies were with the Communist countries. If leftists in the ASP—Hanga, Moyo, and Twala—acted in concert with Babu, they would be a formidable threat to moderation in the government.

- It was unclear whether the prerevolution split in the ASP had been healed. Othman Sharif now played a minor role. Aboud Jumbe and other moderates in the cabinet were close to Karume. U.S. recognition and aid would help the moderates, but the pro-Communists "should not be underestimated." They had an opening and would exploit it to its limit.

With that done I caught a flight to Nairobi, arriving there that night. Despite the onset of flu symptoms, I had a happy reunion with Julie and the girls, but it was cut short. The following day, the twenty-second, Frank called to say that announcements of British and American recognition would be made simultaneously at three o'clock on the twenty-

third. I should fly to Dar the next morning so that he and I could take a charter flight to the island in the afternoon. I was not feeling very chipper; I had a slight fever and was beginning to feel a bit weak. But I was not about to miss the return to Zanzibar.

That same day, Leonhart had met with Nyerere to give him the news. Nyerere said he was delighted. He saw the decision as constructive and believed it would be of tremendous help to his efforts to promote genuine nonalignment on the part of the Zanzibar government. He said: "It is more important to me than to you that Zanzibar be nonaligned. The Chinese on Zanzibar threaten me more directly." Their threat, he explained, was "not only of subversion." In addition, skillfully employing their resources in such a small place, "they could make a success for Zanzibar. Then what happens to what I stand for in Tanganyika and what happens to this country? You Americans must help keep some sort of balance there."

Leonhart had never before heard Nyerere speak so openly about a threat from the Chinese. Nyerere's fear of the influence of Communist countries would continue to motivate him in the months to come. Eventually, however, he would regard the Chinese not as a threat but as a valuable help to his efforts to develop his country economically. When Western countries balked at providing him assistance to build a rail line to Zambia, he and the Zambians turned to the Chinese, who did the job for them.

Part 2
THE COLD WAR
COMES TO ZANZIBAR

10

Starting Over

In the course of further development of the international revolution, there will emerge two centers of world significance: a socialist center . . . and a capitalist center. . . . Battle between these two centers for command of the world economy will decide the fate of capitalism and of communism in the entire world.

—Joseph Stalin

The U.S.A. and the USSR had little in the way of common traditions, no common political vocabulary, precious few links. They looked upon themselves as rival models for the rest of mankind. They shared little except distrust.

—Daniel Yergin, *Shattered Peace*

The single-engine Cessna carrying Leonhart, Carlucci, and me passed over the sandbanks visible beneath their covering of pellucid water, made a direct approach to the runway, and landed at Zanzibar's airport at 1:30 P.M., February 23. We were not greeted by a parade of welcome, not that we had really expected one.

We met with Karume at State House. Several of his cabinet ministers (not including Babu, who was abroad) were with him. Leonhart for-

mally presented Carlucci as the new chargé d'affaires. Frank made a graceful statement about the importance of the occasion and the U.S. desire for friendly relations with Zanzibar. He read aloud the formal note of recognition and gave it to Karume.

Karume was genuinely pleased that the Americans, and British as well, had finally recognized the legitimacy of his government, and the meeting was all sweetness and light. He expressed his pleasure warmly, saying how delighted he was with the U.S. decision and with how quickly it had come since his previous meeting with us. "Today," he said, "is a very happy day for Zanzibar."

Karume's reaction to the recognition convinced us that although he was grateful that Communist countries had accorded speedy recognition to Zanzibar and welcomed their promises of aid, he wanted his country to be nonaligned. For one thing, nonalignment would give him a tool to reduce the power and influence of Babu and the leftists, whose ultimate aim he believed was to turn him into a figurehead and take control of the government.

After more pleasantries between Karume and Carlucci, we took our leave and went to the airport, where Frank and I saw Leonhart off. We then went to the embassy. Frank was pleased to see that the inside of the building was in good shape. Remembering where I had placed a number of small objects, I was reasonably certain that nobody had entered in my absence. A primary target of any search would have been the vault, and after we had seen it, we were doubly sure that I was right. When I had shut the vault door, I had not locked it. Frank carefully opened it. Every square inch of the vault's interior was covered in a layer of oily, dark-brown soot. There was no sign at all that the door had been previously opened. The now dark and slimy floor and inner surface of the door were completely unmarred.

The next morning, we set to with rags to clean the vault. After a short while, I suddenly felt weak and my head began to spin. I must have looked like death warmed over, for Frank, concern written on his face, asked me what was wrong. The fever, aching, and fatigue were more intense than before, and I felt so bad that I admitted as much to Frank. He told me to take the afternoon flight to Nairobi, where I could get

medical treatment. He would notify the embassy there to meet me and take me to where Julie and the children were staying.

That evening, I was back with Julie, Susan, and Julianne. The following morning, the doctor who came to see me diagnosed my ailment as a viral or bacterial infection and exhaustion. He prescribed an antibiotic and at least three days' bed rest. Four days later, I was well enough for us to visit the Nairobi Game Park, our first chance to see lions, giraffes, and other African animals in their natural habitat. The next day, we went downtown so I could buy some books and eat at one of Nairobi's good restaurants. Two days later, eager to get back to work, I left for Zanzibar.

While I was away, Frank had begun to work his magic on the Zanzibaris. A good example of this was when he called on Vice President Hanga. To many, myself included, Zanzibar's new vice president had been the personification of an evil-intentioned, militantly hostile pro-Communist. I had formed a judgment of him based mainly on the official reports I had read about him. I had met him only that time when he came with Karume to the embassy to talk to Fritz about the tracking station. What had really soured me on the man was his walking out of the session of the prerevolution parliament that had passed a resolution of sympathy for the family of President Kennedy.

Frank complimented Hanga on the way the government was getting itself organized and said he intended to maintain a sincere and friendly relationship with him. Smiling, Hanga said he was pleased that the United States had recognized Zanzibar. The delay had been a mistake, but all was now forgiven. They talked about the immediate goals of the revolution, and Frank drew Hanga out on his personal background. Hanga said he had had a scholarship to study at the University of Illinois in 1957 but had been refused a visa by the American embassy in London. As a result, he had studied in London and then later in Moscow. Frank reported to Washington that Hanga struck him "as intelligent, well-educated . . . and not lacking in personal charm. We parted with [an] African embrace and [a] promise to keep in close personal contact."

This, I would learn, was typical of Frank. He liked Africans and clearly showed them that he did. He put people at ease with his friendliness and openness and exhibited an honest interest in hearing what they had to

say. Good-humored, informal, and never one to mince words, Frank was totally lacking in false pretensions. And he was a tireless worker. Within days, he had befriended dozens of Zanzibari officials and before long had a wide range of contacts in the government, the Afro-Shirazi Party, and the Asian and British communities.

He had his work cut out for him. Despite Karume's pleasure that the United States and Great Britain had finally recognized his government, Zanzibar's new president continued to nurse some bitterness against the two countries for taking so long to acknowledge his legitimacy. Karume was increasingly self-assertive while at the same time aware of his relative ignorance of international affairs and his lack of managerial experience.

Most of the Revolutionary Council members were men of little ability, totally unschooled in the ways of government, and even less knowledgeable than Karume about the outside world. Among the better educated on the council, the pro-Communists were by and large the more skillful organizers and persuasive talkers. Without question, they were the most committed to using the power of government in the furtherance of ideological objectives. It was these men—Babu, Hanga, and trade unionists, Moyo and Twala among them—who at least initially exerted the most influence on Karume. Another important adviser to Karume was Salim Rashid, who had been a leading member of Babu's Umma Party and was now clerk of the Revolutionary Council.

In those days, if an African talked like a Communist, those of us in the Cold War trenches usually considered him or her a Communist. As time went by, even well before communism became a spent force on the world scene, the true depth of many Africans' professed commitment to communism, or for that matter to socialism, came into question. During the many years I spent in Africa, I came to see that wholly committed, deep-dyed Marxists were far outnumbered by people who believed they were Marxists but really did not know what Marxism was, had become disillusioned with Marxist socialism, or had merely jumped on the popular bandwagon of the time.

In the transition from the colonial era to independence in Africa, it was not surprising that many politically active Africans turned against the West—the source of colonial domination—and embraced what they

saw as the wave of the future: the new religion of Marxism. Primacy of the state over the individual and state control of the means of production were concepts that some new or aspiring political leaders found particularly appealing.

Of those who appeared to us to be pro-Communists in Zanzibar, I believe Babu was intellectually and emotionally committed to Marxism then and remained so throughout his life. We will never know how devoted to Marxism some of the others—Hanga and Twala, for example—were, for within a few years they were dead, executed for allegedly trying to supplant Karume as ruler of Zanzibar. Most, however, made peaceful transformations into the bourgeoisie. Moyo and another trade unionist, our erstwhile friend Adam Mwakanjuki, became fixtures in the Tanzanian political establishment and mirrored its increasing conservatism with the passing of time. Others were drafted into the Tanzanian diplomatic corps, and still others entered the world of commerce when free enterprise finally displaced socialism in Tanzania.

Regardless of what they became in the future, in 1964 the pro-Communists in the revolutionary government were fervent exponents of Marxism, and they urged their ideas on Karume. Impressed by at least some of their arguments, Karume was also subjected to pressures from the foreign Communists, whose diplomats and technicians were steadily increasing in numbers with each passing month. While the West had dithered, the Soviets, East Germans, and Chinese not only established diplomatic relations, but also made promises of aid, some of which was speedily delivered.[1]

Karume genuinely wanted Zanzibar to have a balanced relationship between East and West, but that did not mean sacrificing what he saw as valuable friendships with Communist countries just to mollify the United States and Great Britain. Nor did it deter him from accepting the advice he was getting to adopt a new, socialist course to transform Zanzibar into a people's paradise.

Julie and the children came home on March 7. Zanzibar's heat and humidity were in sharp contrast to the cool, dry air of Nairobi, but Julie

quickly adjusted to the weather, and the little girls seemed not to mind in the least. Julie was overjoyed, as she wrote in a letter home, that "our family is together again." There had not been much visible property damage in Zanzibar Town, and she said that someone coming to the island "for the first time would not believe we had a bloody revolution two months ago." She was sorry that many of our new friends had gone, but she was happy that all our household staff were alive and well. Shortly after she returned, they came back to work.

Mfaume, who had been working intermittently for me, took up where he left off, learning to become a cook. Before long, he would leave us to take a job with the government. Our guard, Jacobo, stayed for a while, then decided he did not like what Zanzibar was becoming and left for the mainland. Omari, who did the washing and other household tasks, stayed with us for the rest of our stay in Zanzibar.

The fears of the adults around her the day of and the day after the revolution had no doubt been communicated to Susie. The frightening noise of gunfire and the yelling of the people at the two roadblocks we had driven around had evidently had a further traumatic effect on the eighteen-month-old child. When we were at the English Club waiting for the *Manley* and while Susie was aboard the ship, she clung to her mother and screamed if Julie left her for even a few moments. She gradually became less fearful, but throughout the time they were in Tanganyika and Kenya, she continued to show signs of distress when Julie was not at her side.

Back home in Zanzibar, Susie was soon herself again and seemed happy when Agnes, our *ayah*, who had also come back to work, carried her or played with her. Six-month-old Julianne appeared not to have been affected by the excitement, presumably because she was only four months old during the trouble. Some months later, Agnes, unhappy with what was happening in Zanzibar, returned to the mainland; we quickly found another *ayah*, Mgeni, a kind and caring middle-aged woman.

With Julie back, I was eating well again and putting on some of the weight I had lost. A request that Julie made to my parents in a letter written on March 11 reveals that I was still pretty thin. It also is a reminder of what was a priority item of clothing for a transplanted

Californian in 1964. She wrote: "Don needs some Bermuda shorts, a couple of pair—one polished cotton (or light tan) and one conservative plaid, size 28."

I developed an immediate liking and respect for Frank. He had been in the service only four years longer than I, but his two African assignments and especially the extraordinary situations he had dealt with in the Congo put him light-years ahead of me in terms of experience as a political officer. And at that stage of my career, I was a long way from possessing his kind of self-confidence and decisiveness. As I got to know him, I considered myself lucky to have him as a friend and mentor.

Frank took me into his fullest confidence and provided me with daily examples of what it was to be an effective political officer and the officer-in-charge at an embassy. I had liked Fritz, too, and had admired his writing skills. Fritz, however, had not shared with Dale or me all that he learned from his contacts, and he had given us little scope for political work. Frank kept me fully informed. As a matter of course, he dealt with Karume and certain other officials, but he put no one off-limits to me and not only encouraged but also expected me to do political reporting.

In 1964, there were more than one hundred American embassies, a large increase over the fifty-eight diplomatic establishments (many of them legations, a level below a full-fledged embassy) that we had in 1940. When the United States emerged from World War II as the most powerful country in the world and was soon faced with a dangerous adversary that had swallowed up Eastern Europe and seemed to threaten the security of the United States and other Western countries, Washington believed it needed to have diplomatic representation in every country on the globe, even, it turned out, in as small a country as Zanzibar.

Had it not been for the revolution and its aftermath, in all likelihood Zanzibar would have been a backwater of little importance in the East-West struggle, and our embassy staff would probably have been no larger than the consulate's had been. Because of the arrival of the Cold War in Zanzibar, however, we would soon triple the size of the four-person American staff.

Now that we were on the front line of the conflict with the Communist world, a portion of our new team belonged to the CIA. It could not have been otherwise. With the coming of the Soviets, Chinese, and East Germans, soon to be followed by Cubans, Czechs, Poles, and Bulgarians, Zanzibar was awash with spies and agents of one kind or another trying to work their influence on Zanzibaris and to subvert Westerners. The American embassy was the primary target of opportunity for infiltration efforts.

We were not in a position to match the numbers and resources of our adversaries. However, thanks to what Frank and I were able to learn and report through our open contacts with Zanzibari officials, other Zanzibaris, our British diplomatic colleagues, and British and other expatriates, coupled with the CIA's covert intelligence gathering, the embassy was able to provide Washington with good-quality information.

There is an essential difference in the means employed by the Foreign Service and the CIA to collect intelligence from sources. The agency clandestinely gets information from paid agents. FSOs are strictly forbidden to do that and instead are to gather data openly from informed individuals, such as government officials, who are willing to pass it along. This is what Frank and I did in Zanzibar. I emphasize this because of the mistaken view that took root while Frank was in Zanzibar, and persisted after he left the island, that he worked for the CIA.

As I have noted, in his book on the revolution, British author Anthony Clayton included some erroneous information about the Americans. This certainly was the case in his assertion that Frank's "previous experience may have included Central Intelligence Agency work."[2]

In those days, it was commonly assumed that among FSOs were some who actually belonged to the CIA rather than the State Department. Enemy intelligence services believed this, and at least one of them produced a list of alleged CIA agents that included many FSOs, almost all of them political or economic officers. It was well known, of course, that CIA personnel were part of the diplomatic community and carried diplomatic titles. (In my experience, the cover for CIA agents attached to embassies was paper-thin. Our local employees usually had no difficulty figuring out who among the Americans were not bona fide State

Department employees.) However, none of the officers who, like Frank and me, had joined the Foreign Service and been commissioned as FSOs worked for the CIA.

All of us in the embassy were potential targets for recruitment by Soviet or other Communist-country intelligence officers. Throughout the world, the KGB made a special effort to turn communications specialists and secretaries. I don't recall that they tried to work their wiles on Lynn Derczo, the embassy's new American secretary, a willowy, attractive, and very able young woman. But they made a stab at ensnaring Chuck Cuenod, one of our communicators. Young and single, Chuck must have seemed to the Soviets vulnerable to sexual entrapment. What they did not know was that Chuck was fully aware that he might be a tempting target and was on his guard. So each time a pretty, young Zanzibari woman came knocking at his door—and this happened at least a couple of times—Chuck politely fended her off, and then promptly reported the approach to Frank.

If any of the Soviet officials I met ever tried to entice me into their fold, I never noticed it. They had probably concluded that I was too much of a straight arrow and not worth the effort. Nor would there be any use trying to lure me into the arms of some temptress, for they could see that I was happily married to a lovely and vivacious young woman.

They no doubt could also see that Frank was not someone whom they might have a chance of subverting. This did not mean that they stood clear of him, or of me for that matter. For example, the correspondent from TASS, the Soviet news agency, made a point of cultivating American embassy officials, Frank in particular. Unlike all but the highest-ranking of the Soviets in Zanzibar, he was not kept on a tight leash but roamed around as he wished. His wife, an attractive young woman was with him; this, too, was not the norm for the Soviet officials on the island at that time. He was urbane and spoke excellent English. With perhaps the exception of the ranking KGB officer in Zanzibar, Nicolai Tkachenko, the Soviets, including the ambassador, were deferential to him. All this indicated to us that he was more than just a TASS correspondent.

The Soviets were of two kinds: the professional diplomats and the KGB officials. The ambassador, Igor Chuvakin, a short, chunky, gray-haired man about sixty years old, was an old-line foreign ministry diplomat. Because he was high ranking, his presence in Zanzibar was evidence of the importance Moscow attached to what was developing on the island and the Soviets' intention to take full advantage of it. Chuvakin, like most of the people Frank encountered, took a liking to him. He tended to give Frank fatherly advice when they talked. High ranking though he was, Chuvakin was not the most important Soviet official in Zanzibar. Tkachenko, whose title was first secretary, was in fact the official in charge.

As eager as the Soviets were to get started in Zanzibar, the East Germans were even more intent on establishing a presence and forming close ties with the revolutionary government. Having diplomatic missions solely in the Communist world, the German Democratic Republic (GDR) saw Zanzibar as a golden opportunity to get a toehold in Africa and to begin to compete there with their West German rivals. Once the GDR was recognized by the government of Zanzibar, the East Germans could rest assured that they could do what they wanted on the island with no competition from West Germany (the Federal Republic of Germany [FRG]). This would be true because the West Germans adhered to the Hallstein Doctrine, which stipulated that the FRG would not have diplomatic relations with any country, except the Soviet Union, that recognized the GDR.

The Soviets, Chinese, and East Germans viewed Zanzibar as a unique possibility for showing the world, the Third World in particular, the advantages and blessings of the application of scientific socialism. They believed that because of its small size and its population of only a few hundred thousand, Zanzibar could be transformed with a relatively small outlay of resources. Zanzibar would be a model whose success would attract others into the socialist camp. To make this work as well as possible, it would be important to defeat any effort by the Americans and British to achieve good relations with the Karume government.

There no doubt was some coordination between the Soviets and the East Germans. Nevertheless, the East Germans seemed, in their desire

to gain legitimacy on the world scene, more avid than the Soviets to make a big splash in Zanzibar. Their aid projects, when announced, would appear to be the most ambitious and visible of the Communists' projects, clearly designed to win Zanzibaris' admiration and gratitude.

As time wore on, however, and it became apparent that the East Germans had bitten off more than they could chew, it was the Chinese who became favored in Karume's eyes. For one thing, it was important to him that Communist China was a Third World nation whose methods for achieving economic progress seemed pertinent to Zanzibar. He liked the Chinese proposal to develop state farms, especially for growing rice, the staple of Zanzibaris' diet. To him, the subsistence farming of tiny plots, the only land that had been available to Zanzibar's Africans, was unproductive and would perpetuate the backwardness of the majority of the island's people. He admired the Chinese work ethic and noted that Chinese aid technicians worked in the fields and had living accommodations no better than the rural Zanzibaris'.

For some reason, despite evidence of the growing split between the Soviet Union and Communist China, it was common for the U.S. government to refer to the "Sino-Soviet Bloc." That this was a fiction was clear to us in Zanzibar. The Soviets and the Chinese stayed clear of each other. They had rival bookstalls in Zanzibar Town, both of which we visited. I got a copy of Mao's treatise on guerrilla warfare and bought, at very low prices, some ideologically neutral children's picture books and fairy tales for the girls. But most of the material on display was pretty turgid stuff—treatises on Marxism-Leninism, for example—and appeared to be of little interest to most Zanzibaris.

If the Chinese stayed apart from the Soviets, then they shunned us like the plague. When Julie and I were walking in town, if any Chinese came strolling toward us, as soon as they saw the wicked imperialists, they crossed the street, averting their eyes. One day, we had left Susie and Julianne in the car while we stepped a few feet away into an alcove outside the post office where the mailboxes were located. As we started back to the car, we saw a group of young Chinese grouped about the VW, looking in the car and smiling at the two little girls. When they saw us approaching, the smiles vanished, and they bolted away.

This was a little extreme but not all that different from our own behavior. The U.S. government strictly enjoined American officials abroad from any contact with the Chinese, because the United States did not recognize Communist China. Perhaps an added reason for shunning the Chinese was that in the American lineup of Cold War villains, Communist China was seen as particularly nefarious. China's intervention in the Korean War in 1950 and its ill-treatment of American prisoners of war there were fairly recent and not forgotten. The U.S. involvement in Vietnam was escalating, and Americans tended to regard North Vietnam's Ho Chi Minh as a compliant tool of the Chinese. Mistaken though that view was, China was helping underwrite the war against the American-backed South Vietnamese government.

In Zanzibar, when American and Chinese diplomats attended a reception or other function given by the Zanzibar government, we would glance in each other's direction warily and be sure to keep as far apart as possible. More than once, the Zanzibaris seated me alongside a Chinese diplomat. The two of us would sit looking straight ahead or to the other side, never acknowledging the presence of our adversary. (This kind of Cold War role-playing made it seem all the more remarkable to me when, about fifteen years later when I was ambassador to Somalia, Julie and I found ourselves fast friends with the Chinese ambassador and his wife. The difference was even more pronounced when we were in Tanzania in the late 1980s. There the Chinese and the Americans became partners in an effort to rehabilitate the Chinese-built TanZam railroad, whose construction the U.S. government had strongly opposed in the 1960s.)

It quickly became apparent the word was out that Zanzibaris were to steer clear of the Americans. They had reason to be afraid to consort with us. Hundreds of people were still in detention. An intense anti-imperialist militancy was becoming more evident in revolutionary ranks. And within the Revolutionary Council, fears were looming that the American and British governments might support counterrevolutionary activities. No one, not even high-ranking government officials,

dared invite us to their homes, nor would anyone accept social invitations from us.

British high-commission personnel suffered the same ostracism. So it was that for many months, our social circle was limited to the Americans, the friends we had made with British diplomats and their families, a handful of Ghanaians and Nigerians, and the few British civilians who would manage to remain in Zanzibar, such as John and Lorna Cameron.

We did make some Zanzibari friends. However, during the long period of anti-imperialist, anticolonialist fervor, with its overtones of suspicion of American and British motives, those friendships were almost always made through the official and commercial contacts we had in the course of our work. They could rarely be nurtured in any social way.

Isolated from Zanzibaris, we necessarily looked to ourselves for a community existence and social life. Fortunately, we all got along well. As the weeks went by, the American men, women, and children in Zanzibar increased to about twenty. Frank's wife, Jean, arrived in early May with their two small children. Kent Crane, an economic officer, and his wife, Linda, had two little boys—more playmates for Susie. Along with Chuck Cuenod, we had a couple of other communications specialists. One was a very young-looking, tall, and thin redhead named Jerry Dewar. A romance between him and Lynn developed, and they got married a year later. Stu Lillico's replacement as the USIS public affairs officer was Harry Radday, who arrived in late June and was joined in July by his wife, Ellen, and their two small children. The Zanzibaris called Harry, a bright and amiable guy who stood six and a half feet tall, *Bwana Twiga*, Mr. Giraffe.

We all were in our mid- to late twenties or early thirties. The kind of social life we had for ourselves was typical of our generation and probably mirrored that of the average American suburbanite. We were joined by our British friends, especially Brian and Frances Banks of the British high commission—whose two little kids added to our stable of toddlers—and Harry and Caroline McBrinn, also of the high commission.

Outdoor barbecues, Sunday outings with the children to one of the beaches on the eastern side of the island, parties at someone's house—these would become the staples of our recreation. The parties were good

for letting off steam. We danced hard, and some of us drank fairly hard. One memorable night at a party at our house, I offered up a bottle of tequila that I had found packed away in our household effects. Having learned in Mexico the danger of the potent distilled cactus juice, I was careful to limit myself to just enough tequila sours for a good buzz. Kent Crane was not so cautious, and we didn't see him for two full days after the party.

If we played hard, then we worked even harder, regularly putting in long hours. No one was paid for overtime; it would be years before Foreign Service staff personnel and junior and some middle-grade officers would be accorded the right to receive overtime pay. But if any of us were bothered about the rigors of our work, I never heard complaints. Certainly for Frank and me, our jobs left little to be desired. Here we were, on an exotic tropical island, in the middle of a Cold War drama, with able and companionable coworkers in the embassy, and making new friends. For us, perhaps particularly Frank, who as chargé d'affaires was his own boss, Zanzibar was a great place to be.

Frank worked harder than any of us. I imagine he approached his work with the same determination that put him on the wrestling team at Princeton. He was a superb athlete. He taught me how to play squash (there was a court near the golf course that, after the British colonial officials left Zanzibar, hardly anyone used). Improve though I did, I could manage to win only a few points per game when we played. I had enough sense to not even try to play tennis with him.

Typical of this man who would one day be the national security adviser to the president of the United States and then secretary of defense was the way he learned to speak Swahili. I was continuing to study the language, taking lessons from an elderly Anglican nun. Frank began regular sessions with her, working with the Foreign Service Institute's Swahili manual and language tapes. I remember that just about every time I had reason to go to see him at night at his house, he would be sitting in the living room with the manual by his side and listening to tapes. Less than a year later, studying part-time, Frank had reached a high level of proficiency in the language. By any standard, Frank Carlucci was an exceptionally able and dedicated FSO.

11

Red Tide Rising

Anybody can win unless there happens to be a second entry.

—George Ade

I realized . . . that a serious fight for power was going on and someone wanted to emerge on top.

—John Okello

The outside world's picture of what was happening in Zanzibar continued to be opaque. For weeks after the expulsion of the Western journalists in January, only a few reporters from Western publications were permitted to come briefly to the island, and they were kept on a short leash. Joan Pasco, the *Tanganyika Standard* stringer, could get only anodyne stories past the censor. A window was opened when the Revolutionary Council restored normal diplomatic privileges to the American embassy in late February and later, when it reopened, to the British high commission. At last we could send and receive encrypted telegrams, enabling us to pass to Washington information of a sort that had been difficult or impossible for me to transmit over the open telephone line. To take advantage of this, we needed to obtain valid intelli-

gence. But because of the Zanzibar government's deepening suspicion of the U.S. government's intentions, it took us a while to develop new sources of reliable information.

On March 2, in one of his first encrypted messages, Frank cited the need to neutralize Okello, who continued to pose a danger of renewed violence. Babu's men, Frank believed, were politically the most dangerous element. Karume was "by far the most popular man on the island," but he was not exercising his political power. This was enhancing the possibilities for Babu, Hanga, Moyo, and Twala to expand their influence. The Soviets, East Germans, and Chinese were "pressing hard" and had met with some success. Sensibly, Frank cautioned that it "would be futile and wasteful for us to try to outbid the Communists," who were making lavish offers of aid. He said a better response would be to engage in nonpolitical fields that would contribute to long-range political and economic stability, such as education, agriculture, and fishing.

Worry about Zanzibar persisted in Washington and London. A memorandum written to Assistant Secretary of State Soapy Williams on March 5 said, "Pro-Communist elements . . . [are] steadily gaining ground at the expense of Karume and the nationalists." However, the memorandum noted, "The internal political situation is still murky." London was equally or even more unsure about the circumstances on the island. British high commissioner Crosthwait had delayed the high commission's reestablishment until March 5, citing a need for rest and leave and also a desire to avoid appearing overeager. This, Leonhart and Frank had written, just before Frank and I headed back to Zanzibar, was a curious attitude.

Through no fault of his own, Crosthwait was almost expelled for the second time. On the same day that he presented his credentials after returning to the island, the Zanzibar government ordered him to leave the country. His remarks during the credentials ceremony had included, at Duncan Sandys's insistence, criticism of a reference John Okello had made, during a Nairobi press conference, to Britons and Americans as devils. Although they had no love for Okello, Karume and others in the government viewed Crosthwait's words as interference in Zanzibar's

internal affairs. Fortunately for Crosthwait, Sandys, who was in Nairobi, had scheduled a visit to Zanzibar, and when he saw Karume and Babu on March 8, he convinced them to rescind the expulsion order. This affair, though, did further damage to Crosthwait's effectiveness.

John Okello and his unpredictability added to British and American uncertainty about Zanzibar. On February 20, the same day I was expelled from Zanzibar, Okello went to the mainland. He later wrote that he intended to meet with mainland government leaders, and he did, seeing Jomo Kenyatta and Milton Obote, as well as Nyerere.

In Nairobi in early March, Kenyan foreign minister Joseph Murumbi told visiting deputy assistant secretary of state Wayne Fredericks and American ambassador William Attwood that Okello had made a surprisingly favorable impression on Kenyan leaders. Murumbi said Okello was an angry and emotional young man but an African nationalist and not a pro-Communist. Murumbi believed that Okello could be convinced to provide support for Karume against Babu, whom Murumbi said was a dedicated Communist and a real menace.

Murumbi's idea about using Okello showed that he was ignorant of the political dynamics of postrevolution Zanzibar. Washington, however, evidently assuming that Murumbi knew what he was talking about, saw merit in what he had said and gave careful consideration to it.

Reacting to embassy reporting from Dar es Salaam, Nairobi, and Zanzibar, the State Department was by now alarmed that Karume was becoming more and more dependent on the advice of Babu and other pro-Communists. In a cable to the three embassies on March 6, the department, taking for granted that "for practical purposes" Babu was a "Communist and may lead Zanzibar into Commie camp," wondered how Karume could be convinced of this and how Babu's power could be "drastically reduced or eliminated."

The department accepted Frank's premise that the United States and Great Britain had negligible influence with the government of Zanzibar. It asked Fredericks, Attwood, Leonhart, and Carlucci—who were going to meet in Dar es Salaam on March 8—to consider an approach to Nyerere, Kenyatta, and Obote to enlist their intervention with Karume to get him to see the danger that Babu represented to him.

Picking up on Murumbi's assessment of Okello, the State Department suggested that, in the short run, it could be advantageous to have Okello return to Zanzibar. His dislike of Babu might slow down what Washington saw as Babu's drive for power. The department also asked Fredericks, Attwood, Leonhart, and Carlucci whether it would be useful to raise with Nyerere, "despite his previous objections, idea of Tanganyika-Zanzibar federation as possible way to strengthen Karume and reduce Babu's influence."

In a cable he sent to Washington after the meeting in Dar es Salaam on March 8 and talks the Americans had that same day with Tanganyikan and British officials (including Sandys), Leonhart reported that Fredericks, Attwood, Carlucci, and he had concluded that the situation in Zanzibar was "deteriorating in the Communists' favor with Babu emerging as effective power holder." There were other "inimical types" in the Zanzibar power structure, but Babu, they agreed, had "consolidated [his] leadership [of the] Communist faction." In their view, it was imperative that Babu be removed from his position of growing power.

Karume, they believed, did not sense the danger. And if he did come to see Babu as a threat, he himself would not have the means or capacity to deal with Babu and his supporters. Leonhart reported that he and the others believed that the way to get Karume to see the danger would be through the East African leaders. Kenyatta was the key; Obote was too far removed from Zanzibar, and Nyerere was "over-extended on interventions with Karume, probably also more indulgent of Babu, and disinclined to act unless Kenyatta willing to join in." The British had told the Americans that they had "milked Nyerere dry on Karume."

Leonhart, Fredericks, Attwood, and Carlucci examined the idea of bringing Zanzibar under the umbrella of a federation in order to smother the influence of Zanzibar's pro-Communists. Oscar Kambona had said that the Tanganyikans would be willing to consider a Kenya-Tanganyika-Zanzibar federation, but that unless Kenyatta was fully committed, Nyerere would not consider it. As it happened, Kenyatta was not interested.

In his cable, Leonhart reported that neither the Americans nor the British believed a smaller federation of just Tanganyika and Zanzibar was

a practical possibility. Leonhart said the others and he saw a short-term advantage of a return by Okello to Zanzibar, where he could help keep Babu in check. However helpful that might prove to be, though, "mainland influence [was] the critical factor and Kenyatta likely the determinant."

In the context of the information then available to the four American diplomats, their judgments made some sense. But in reality, they were woefully ill-informed about the willingness of East African leaders to intervene in Zanzibar. In the case of Attwood and Leonhart, the two ambassadors seemed to misread the intentions of, respectively, Kenyatta and Nyerere. It soon became apparent that as a group, the East African leaders would not exert any influence and Kenyatta would not get engaged at all. As for John Okello, his days in Zanzibar were swiftly drawing to a close.

For some time, Karume had been determined to rid Zanzibar of Okello. He didn't like Okello personally and, of course, saw him as a threat. In addition, the Ugandan's behavior had become a great embarrassment. By late February, Karume was ready. Okello played into his hands when he decided to go to the mainland for a time. Following visits to Uganda and Kenya, where he had favorably impressed Murumbi, he flew to Dar es Salaam. It is not clear how long he initially planned to stay there. Frank and I heard later from a source close to Okello that among other things that he wanted to do there, he was going to pick up the scores of copies of a photographic portrait of himself that he had ordered.

By this time, the discord between Okello and Karume had become clearly evident. When Okello was ready to return to Zanzibar, Nyerere, who was in accord with Karume that Okello had to go, and Kambona persuaded him to remain in Dar until Karume came there and their differences could be resolved. Karume had conspired with Nyerere to keep Okello off the island as long as possible.

On March 5, Frank reported that during the previous week, Karume and the police in Zanzibar had "succeeded in disarming and disbanding about 750 of Okello's group of approximately one thousand. Remaining

250 now undergoing intensive [paramilitary] training." Okello did not know it yet, but he was finished.

On the afternoon of the eighth, Sandys met with Karume and Babu in Zanzibar. They let him know that they did not want Okello to return. This, and talks Sandys had with members of the British community, convinced Sandys that it would not, after all, be useful for Okello to go back to Zanzibar. In Dar es Salaam that night, he expressed this to Leonhart and Attwood.

By this time, the issue was moot. The next day, March 9, Okello and two of his lieutenants flew from Dar to Zanzibar on a scheduled East African Airways flight. Karume, together with a few members of the Revolutionary Council and some armed men, met the plane. Karume told Okello that the two of them would fly back to Dar in a Tanganyikan government aircraft. Okello's two associates were not allowed to disembark from the East African Airways plane, which left for Mombasa. The government aircraft soon arrived and took Karume and Okello to Dar. Karume parted from him there and shortly afterward returned to Zanzibar.

Okello's nonperson status was made clear to him during the few days he was in Dar. From there, Kambona took him to Nairobi. Whatever good impression Kenyatta and Murumbi seemed to have had of Okello was no longer evident. The fearful reputation he had acquired for himself by his actions and pronouncements in Zanzibar was still alive, and it made him unwelcome wherever he went in East Africa. Not allowed to remain in Kenya, he traveled back to his home country of Uganda. At a press conference in Kampala on March 16, Okello said he had been expelled from Zanzibar because he was a Christian and a Ugandan. He announced that he intended to visit Ghana, Ethiopia, and Egypt for consultations with African leaders about plans to liberate places such as Angola, Mozambique, Southern Rhodesia, and South Africa.

The American embassy reported that the Ugandan government was "extremely uneasy regarding Okello's presence" and that ways to contain him were being discussed. "It is likely," the embassy stated, "that he will be encouraged to continue on his African tour." Later, while trying to

transit Tanganyika to go to the Congo, where he intended to get involved in revolutionary activities, he was arrested and deported back to Uganda.

In subsequent years, Okello was imprisoned in both Kenya, for illegal entry, and Uganda. In 1971, he was seen with Idi Amin, shortly after the infamous dictator came to power. Then John Okello disappeared from sight, never to be seen again. It is logical to assume that Amin saw Okello as a possible danger and had him eliminated along with the countless others whom Amin murdered during his bloody reign.

In London, Duncan Sandys told Ambassador Bruce that the UK and the three East African governments should do everything they could to strengthen Karume's position. Bruce reported to Washington that Sandys believed the East African leaders were interested in supporting Karume, "particularly since they do not want Zanzibar to become a nest for subversion against their own countries." Sandys accurately described Karume as the most popular political figure in Zanzibar but mistakenly believed that he was not a dynamic leader. In Sandys's opinion, Kenyatta, who had shown a cooperative attitude on the issue, would "serve as a stabilizing influence against Babu and pro-Communist elements."

Sandys was wrong. A planned early-March meeting in Dar es Salaam of Kenyatta, Nyerere, and Obote with Karume never took place. Kenyatta, like Obote, did not comply with a request from Karume that the Kenyan and Ugandan governments each supply Zanzibar with seventy-five police officers.

Throughout March and into April, the impression in Foggy Bottom and the White House and in Whitehall and Number 10 Downing Street steadily grew that Karume was being outmaneuvered and more and more influenced by the cleverer Babu and other pro-Communists. The Americans and British became increasingly worried that, unless this was checked, Zanzibar would definitely become a launching pad for Communist subversive activities in the African continent. Unfolding events, reported by the American embassies and British high commissions in Zanzibar and Dar es Salaam, intensified Western anxieties.

On March 8, I went to the playing fields on the outskirts of town near the site where, only three months earlier, the independence ceremony had been held. Some 10,000 people stood sweltering in the midafternoon sun while President Karume spoke. Karume was presented by Babu, who himself had been introduced to the crowd by Ali Mafoudh, dressed as usual in his Cuban combat fatigues. That it was these two, and not any of the African nationalists, who shared the dais with Karume was not a good sign.

Working my way to the front of the crowd so I could hear clearly, I took notes as Karume, speaking forcibly in good Swahili, declared that thenceforth, "the People's Republic of Zanzibar" was a one-party state. The Afro-Shirazi Party would be the only political party in the country. Next, he announced that all land was nationalized and that all property, including plantations, that former governments had given or sold to capitalists now belonged to the government. All racially based private clubs—"Hindu, Bohora, Arab, Comorian, etc., etc."—were nationalized.

Karume got his loudest applause when he told the crowd the new government promised that by June 1, 1964, less than three months away, every inhabitant of Zanzibar would have a better way of life. He spoke extemporaneously. Two days later, the government released a statement with further details of the new policy. It explained that the better way of life by June 1 included a promise of full employment for all the people of Zanzibar and Pemba. Furthermore, the government would immediately set up good homes for the care of the elderly, and promised that "every modern equipment will be installed in these homes." These promises would turn out to be the first of many that Karume's government would be unable to fulfill.

The statement referred to previous governments as "reactionary" and "puppets" and labeled capitalists as "exploiters." The Communist jargon, nationalization of all land, and seizure of private property were seen in the West as clear signs that Babu and company were calling the shots and that Karume was under their spell. The worry in Washington and London about where Zanzibar was headed went up a notch.

Of more direct concern to us in Zanzibar was one immediate effect of Karume's announcement. That night, only a few hours after he spoke, armed men—irregulars, not uniformed policemen—took over all private clubs. Included among them was the English and American communities' favorite watering hole, the Sailing Club.

I had dropped by there for a beer and some conversation before going home. I wasn't a member of the Sailing Club, but as an official of the American embassy, I had bar privileges. Less than an hour earlier, after his meeting with Karume and Babu and prior to leaving for the airport to fly back to Dar, Duncan Sandys had been at the nearby English Club for a meeting with British civilians and officials who were still working in government ministries. I was talking with someone about this when Ali Mafoudh and several men armed with carbines barged in. Mafoudh said the Sailing Club now belonged to the government and that we would have to leave. We did, but not until we finished our drinks.

The weekly sailboat races, which had ended with the revolution, were never resumed; those people who owned boats—all of which were small, one-masted sailing craft—got them to the mainland or otherwise disposed of them. The bar's stock went to the revolutionaries, who, after the stock was depleted, stopped frequenting the former club.

The golf course and its adjacent tennis court, which were run by the English Club, were also nationalized. Until further notice, no one was allowed to use them. In a private letter to the editor of the *Tanganyika Standard*, Joan Pasco wrote: "The nationalization of the clubs has of course been a great blow to the minorities of Zanzibar, particularly the European who since the Revolution has depended upon the sailing and English Clubs for all recreation. Now there is just nowhere to go and nothing to do."

It wasn't quite that bad, but I wrote home that "we cannot play golf or tennis, nor is it possible to have any social functions. However, we'll get along—we still have the beaches and the movies have started showing again." I neglected to say that the only beaches we could use were those close to town; travel across the island to the better beaches on the East Coast was prohibited.

In her letter, Joan said racism had nothing to do with the closure of the clubs, "since almost all clubs had for some time been open to all races." People were convinced, she added, that "the true object was to prevent people getting together." To an extent, she was correct. Gatherings of more than a few people outside their homes were not permitted. But the Africans viewed the private clubs in a very negative light, seeing them as perpetuating a discriminatory system that found them at the bottom of the ladder.

It was true that the clubs had become, in theory, open to all races. But in practice, they had remained racially exclusive or close to it. This was especially true of the Asian clubs. The English Club and Sailing Club had opened their doors to a small number of Zanzibaris, but Africans were not among them. Once the Africans came to power, it was inevitable that the clubs would be abolished.

Ironically, the Communist successors to the colonial officials and European civilians would be as much or more clannish, the members of each nationality sticking very much to themselves. With notably few exceptions, Communist-country diplomats and technicians were not permitted by their governments to mingle with Zanzibaris except in the line of work and certainly not with the Americans or British. As for the new elite, the Zanzibari leaders began to practice what could be termed reverse discrimination against the Arabs and Asians. And their attitude toward the West became increasingly xenophobic.

On March 14, following a visit to Zanzibar by Oscar Kambona, approximately one hundred additional Tanganyikan police were flown to the island. The now three hundred Tanganyikans answered to Karume through Police Commissioner Eddington Kisassi. They were only lightly armed, however, possessing no automatic weapons. In a showdown, they would have been no match for Babu's followers, a good number of whom had automatic weapons and had received military training in Cuba. Babu's men referred to themselves as the mobile police; the local populace called them "the comrades."

With Okello gone and most of his men disarmed and the remainder undergoing training, tension in Zanzibar Town lessened a great deal. Nevertheless, armed patrols were much in evidence, and roadblocks continued to be manned on roads leading out of town. We heard of the occasional shooting incident. We Americans had no run-ins with armed men, but some of the British suffered from harassment now and then. They, like us, were not permitted to travel outside the environs of Zanzibar Town without express permission from the government.

In a cable to Washington on March 11, Frank warned, "Communists and pro-Communists have Karume completely surrounded." Illustrating his concern, he said: "Junior minister Twala, as nasty a character as I have met here, has office in Karume's house; Salim Rashid, young, bright and bitterly anti-U.S., spends most of his time there; Cuban-trained Ali Mafoudh is never far from Karume's side; and Moyo acts as general agitator and utility infielder."

Six days later, he cabled that East African governments were showing little inclination to become further involved in Zanzibar. It was "highly improbable," he said, "that a reasonable excuse could be found for UK intervention." That being the case, he suggested that the United States "think in terms of longer-term operation in Zanzibar." Salim Rashid, Frank noted, had told him "that the tactics of the pro-Communist element will be to harass us until we withdraw completely."

During the night of March 15, a freighter arrived in the harbor. Because the anchorage at dockside in Zanzibar harbor was too shallow to take deep-water vessels, lighters were used to unload them. That night, Bill Hall, who worked for Smith, Mackenzie, a British export-import trading company that staffed the wharfage company at the port, and others at the port were ordered to lay on lighters to discharge cargo from the ship that had arrived. Once that was done, they were told that their services were no longer required for the unloading. The port was cordoned off, and the cargo was taken from the ship and stored in secrecy. Before long, however, we obtained information about the ship—it was from the Soviet Union—and its cargo: arms, military equipment,

and ammunition. This came as no surprise but nonetheless added to Western apprehensions about Zanzibar.

In late March, Frank flew to Pemba on the *Bamboo Bomber*. What he found there added to his belief that Zanzibar and Pemba were undergoing a rapid transformation into a Marxist state. Pemba was governed by a regional commissioner who had three area commissioners subordinate to him. All four were pro-Communists with close ties to Babu. During his two-day stay, Frank stayed at the house of Area Commissioner Ali Sultan Issa. Issa told him he had been schooled in London by the British Communist Party, spent some time in Cuba, and received extensive training in Peking. An engaging man in his early thirties, Issa was an enthusiastic booster of communism; he went so far as to try to convert Frank. His house was decorated with pictures of Mao Tse-tung, Stalin, and Lenin. His daughter was named Fidela. In 1964, there was no more zealous Marxist in the whole of Zanzibar.

Proud of his handiwork, Issa treated Frank to what Frank termed "a demonstration of how Communists can use popular revolution to indoctrinate people." With Issa, Frank "attended youth cadre meetings, peoples mobilization meetings, party rallies and even danced in mud with work battalion." Issa expounded Communist dogma in simplified language suitable for his unsophisticated audiences. He exhorted one gathering to shout to Frank, "Tell the American people we are building a people's paradise in Zanzibar and Pemba."

Issa was not a cruel man, and his parishioners must have been happier with his rule compared to the barbarism they had suffered under Okello and his band. Others in Pemba were not so lucky. Area Commissioner Ahmed Diria Hassan, for example, was not averse to having people flogged. Many Pembans were still in detention, and a general air of militancy and oppression blanketed the island.

In a cabinet reshuffle announced on March 25, moderates Hasnu Makame and Othman Sharif were dropped. Makame was named to head Zanzibar's mission to the United Nations in New York, and Sharif was slated to become high commissioner in London.

In the early days after the revolution, British colonial holdover officials had played a key role in restoring normal functioning of govern-

ment departments. Karume recognized their valuable efforts, but as vestiges of the colonial era, these officials were expendable. The Zanzibar government announced on March 26 that almost all the remaining British civil servants would have to leave Zanzibar by April 30. Twelve officials—engineers, doctors, ship officers, and the island's only dentist—were exempted. The government made clear that it intended to replace the British with experts from Communist countries. Already, an East German had been appointed permanent secretary in the Ministry of Finance, replacing Henry Hawker, and other East German, Soviet, and Chinese technicians were arriving.

Looking at the sum of what had happened during the five weeks he had been in Zanzibar, Frank told Washington on the twenty-sixth that we had reached a point where it no longer was practical to think of Zanzibar as a "non-aligned member of the African family." Communists and pro-Communists occupied key positions in the government and controlled the most effective military forces.

The Communist diplomats, advisers, and technicians, who were "flowing in at an ever increasing pace," were promising massive aid programs in an effort to make Zanzibar a Communist showcase of Africa. More military equipment was on the way. Frank accurately forecast that it was just a question of time before Communist-country military advisers would arrive and begin their work in the training camps that were already being set up. He said there were signs that his movements were under surveillance, and he expected that "our future activities will be severely proscribed."

He noted that although East African governments were now becoming alarmed, they had no program for concerted action. By this time, High Commissioner Crosthwait doubted that even a strong approach by Kenyatta would be effective. He believed, he told Frank, that Karume had thrown in his lot with the Communists and would tell Kenyatta he was satisfied that the aid he was getting from Communist countries was a sincere offer of friendship.

Appearances supported Crosthwait's pessimism. Frank acknowledged to Washington that Karume, in addition to falling more under the pro-Communists' influence, distrusted the British and Americans. He

said Karume's attitude was conditioned by a conviction that the "West in general and U.S. in particular tried and still trying undermine revolution." Karume apparently believed that the United States had supported the previous regime and that the four American journalists who had arrived illegally during the revolution were "CIA counterrevolutionaries." Karume repeatedly and vehemently denounced the delay by the Americans and British in according recognition to his government. He rebuffed tentative offers of assistance from the United States and United Kingdom.

Carlucci, however, was not ready to concede that Karume was a lost cause. Frank had met a number of times with Afro-Shirazi Party general secretary Thabit Kombo. A tall, slightly stooped, courtly man whose narrow face was framed by a trim white beard, Kombo, who was in his seventies, was moderate in his political outlook and wanted Zanzibar to have good ties with the West. He told Frank that Karume was aware of the danger that Babu and the other pro-Communists posed to him.

The British saw the downgrading and expatriation of Makame and Sharif as an unmistakable sign that Karume was being increasingly isolated from moderates in Zanzibar. Because the cabinet changes could not have taken place without Karume's approval, the British concluded that he was being manipulated by the pro-Communists. That may have been true, but it is also likely that Karume needed little encouragement to get rid of Sharif, who had openly broken with him and had resigned from the ASP on January 2, and Makame, who had allied himself with Sharif.

Messages back and forth between the British and American governments at the end of March reflect that London and Washington were thoroughly alarmed by this and the other recent developments in Zanzibar. The British embassy in Washington asked the State Department whether the U.S. government would consider a joint approach to the East African governments. The department said it favored individual approaches, suggesting that the UK lead the way and the United States follow.

A note of desperation appeared in some of the U.S.-British exchanges. President Johnson wrote Prime Minister Douglas-Home on

March 29 that their two governments needed urgently to consider what action, if any, they could take. Responding the following day, Douglas-Home said the situation in Zanzibar "is going from bad to worse, and I agree with you that we must consider very urgently what action, if any, we can take." But the British had no new ideas, and Douglas-Home told Johnson, "Our best course would seem to be to try to induce Karume to seek military help either from Britain or from the East African mainland governments, or both."

Earlier that day, Duncan Sandys had sent instructions to High Commissioner De Freitas in Nairobi to see Kenyatta at once and spell out again the "increasing danger that Zanzibar may become a fortified Communist stronghold from which subversive activities of all kinds in East Africa will be organised." If Kenyatta shared the British concern, De Freitas was to warn him that if Karume were deposed, any possibility of intervention would disappear. It was "a case of now or never."

If Kenyatta was still interested at this point in De Freitas's presentation, then the British diplomat was to tell him that there seemed to be only two ways to get Karume to ask for intervention. One would be for Kenyatta or a "trusted emissary" to visit Zanzibar, see Karume with Babu not present, and get Karume's signature on a written request for intervention. The other would be to get Karume to come, without Babu, to the mainland for a meeting with the three East African presidents.

If Kenyatta did not share the British anxieties or was clearly opposed to any outside intervention, De Freitas was not to press him.

The records I have seen do not include telegrams reporting the results of the British and American representations to the East African governments. But it is clear that Kenyatta did not act on the British proposal. Despite his concern about the turn of events in Zanzibar, he did not meet with Nyerere and Obote on the issue, he and they did not jointly approach Karume to give him a warning or seek his agreement for outside intervention, nor did Kenyatta pursue the matter by himself.

Inexplicably, Sandys persisted in his mistaken belief that Kenyatta could still be influenced to get Karume to ask for British intervention. It should have been apparent to him by the time that he sent his instructions to De Freitas that Kenyatta was more than reluctant to become

involved. Kenyatta had not even responded to Karume's request for seventy-five policemen, and he had not arranged for a meeting in early March between himself, Nyerere, and Obote with Karume. As for Nyerere, he had made it clear to the British that he was not interested in making a case to Karume on their behalf.

There was more than a tinge of arrogance in Sandys's unsolicited advice to Kenyatta and the other two presidents as to how they should handle the Zanzibar situation. That Sandys would continue to believe it possible to get Karume to ask for British military intervention indicates that he was badly misreading the Zanzibari leader. Karume may have been concerned about Babu and his followers, but he distrusted the British and would have had to be in extremis, which he was not, even to consider asking them to intervene.

It was taken as gospel in those days and for years afterward that the British knew Africa much better than the Americans. The British, after all, had their long experience of colonial rule to draw on. Through the lens of that experience, they could make sounder judgments than we could on how to deal with African issues. In the many years I worked in Africa, I came increasingly to question this conventional wisdom. Certainly now, in looking back on decisions that were being made in London and Washington in 1964 regarding the Zanzibar crisis, it is clear that the British were flailing around just as badly as the Americans in trying to find a way to counter Zanzibar's growing ties with Communist countries.

Washington, feeling a need to do more than just support Sandys's plan of action, sought to enlist a number of African leaders, other than Kenyatta, Nyerere, and Obote, to help counter the Communists' inroads into Zanzibar. On March 30, the State Department sent a cable to the American embassies in Ethiopia, the Congo Republic, Liberia, and Tunisia. It informed the ambassadors to those countries that the situation in Zanzibar had deteriorated to the extent that "chances of a Communist takeover have materially increased." They were instructed to urge their respective host governments to establish a diplomatic presence in Zanzibar as soon as possible.

The ambassadors were to stress that the government of Zanzibar was aligning itself with the "Eastern bloc in the Cold War," a development that was contrary to the "desires and policy [of] African states" that favored nonalignment. In addition to providing the four governments with details of the Communists' activities in Zanzibar, the ambassadors were to point out that the United States and Britain were the only two Western countries with diplomatic representation there and Ghana the only African country. (Ghana, which had no mission in Zanzibar before the revolution, had sent a chargé d'affaires to the island in March.)

Just as nothing would come of the effort to energize the East African leaders to get Karume to ask for British intervention, the U.S. attempt to get staunch African friends to agree to establish diplomatic relations with Zanzibar failed. Whether they viewed the Zanzibar question as less foreboding than the Americans saw it or were simply unwilling to assume the financial costs of setting up new embassies, none complied with the American request.

In London, David Bruce, ever an activist when it came to Cold War matters, had been advocating some kind of joint Anglo-American covert action to change the course of events in Zanzibar. He rightly believed that British military intervention was not feasible. He told Washington on March 31 that he could see no reason "to think that the three East African leaders would give their public approval to such an undertaking nor, indeed, that Karume could be induced to ask for intervention." Bruce advised that with overt political action impractical, "covert activity appears to be the best opening for us." He thought the Zanzibar situation offered "an intriguing challenge to test the mettle of clandestine operators." But his suggestion fell on deaf ears; nothing came of it.

In less than a month, Nyerere and Karume, acting on their own, would confront the threat that Babu represented to Karume's control of power in Zanzibar. And they would do this without consulting with Kenyatta or seeking the advice or support of either Britain or the United States.

12

Union

The first step on the way to victory is to recognize the enemy.

—**Corrie Ten Boom (1892–1983), Dutch evangelist**

Our first concern was the growing Communist presence and, second, the danger of the Cold War coming in. . . . The problem was how to isolate Zanzibar from the Eastern countries, yet not be used by the West for its own purposes.

—**Oscar Kambona**

U.S. leaders pressed for the union in order to stem the revolutionary tide before it swept throughout East Africa and beyond.

—**Abdulrahman Mohamed Babu**

The hot northeast monsoon *(kaskazi)* was ending, and the long rains *(masika),* which lasted from about March until June, were beginning. By the latter part of March, the rains had not yet begun in earnest, but they were sufficient to add to the misery of the some 2,200 Arab detainees. For more than two months, they had been kept in detention camps at several locations near Zanzibar Town that lacked sufficient shelter. Red Cross workers from Tanganyika, Kenya, and Britain were look-

ing after them, distributing blankets and clothing, as well as food. Hundreds of women and children whose male relatives were in detention had no way of providing for themselves. They were camped in various places and were also being cared for by the Red Cross. Julie spent her mornings working as a volunteer at a feeding center for the refugees.

Many among the detainees were Manga Arabs, previously so feared and detested by the Africans. The Revolutionary Council decided to expel as many of them as possible by dhows. It mattered not to the council members that most of these Arabs had been born in Zanzibar. Dhow captains, some of whose boats were of questionable seaworthiness, were paid to take the human cargo.

In mid-April, Frank wrote in an airgram that the Zanzibar government had by that time deported from 1,500 to 2,400 Arabs, "most of them in badly overcrowded dhows. Maximum capacity of the dhows is 50 passengers; those leaving at the present time often carry 200." He said that, according to a Red Cross official, "women below decks were so crowded they were unable to sit up straight." The dhow captains had been compelled to sign an undertaking, Joan Pasco learned, "not to enter port until they reach the Persian Gulf area."

The first four dhows, packed to the gunwales—150 people per dhow—departed in the last week of March. Of this and later sailings, Frank reported that word came back to Zanzibar that at least one vessel had sunk. He wrote that "even if the rest complete the journey it can be assumed that a large number of prisoners will die en route." By mid-April, 1,500 Arabs had been inhumanely deported from Zanzibar in dhows. Ultimately, several thousand would leave the island in this way.

With the exodus of the Arabs and the marginal role that those who remained played in the economy, to all intents and purposes the centuries-old dhow trade between Zanzibar and the area to the northeast extending past the Gulf of Aden, into the Arabian Sea and the Persian Gulf, and reaching as far as the Malabar Coast, ceased. Years later, it revived, but only to a limited extent.

As time went on, many other Arabs left Zanzibar and Pemba of their own volition. Drawing on various sources of information, more than a

year later, I estimated that by the end of the summer of 1965, Zanzibar's prerevolution Arab population of 50,000 had been halved.

Many weeks passed before we saw Arabs at the market or elsewhere in town. Two photographs that I took of Arabs, one in December 1963, the other in April 1965, stick in my mind as graphic illustrations of the change in status of Arabs in Zanzibar. The first shows a group of men at the airport waiting for Ali Muhsin, who was returning from a trip to Cairo. Turbaned, bearded, and dressed in white *jellabiya* robes, each wore a curved dagger in an ornate sheath tucked into a sash at the waist. They had an independent, almost fierce air about them. The picture taken almost a year and a half later is of three men at the market. Instead of turbans, they wore caps. Over their *jellabiya*s, they wore black suit coats. They carried umbrellas. They were huddled together, one of them seeming to be glancing nervously to one side. Any sense of arrogance or fierceness is absent in this photograph, which instead captures an impression of timidity.

Zanzibar's Asians did not fare as badly as the Arabs did during the revolution in the sense that only a relatively small number were killed. Although some were imprisoned in Pemba, none were put into the detention camps near Zanzibar Town. However, the life of the Asians was far from easy. Africanization of the civil service hit the Asians particularly hard, costing many of them their jobs. Fearful of the consequences of a decree that gave Zanzibar's president power to confiscate all immovable property without compensation, the Asian mercantile community stopped importing goods. Some months later, the formation of a state trading corporation spelled the end of Asian firms dealing in imports and exports.

The nationalization of their clubs, an important part of the Asians' social fabric, had caused dismay. An even more telling blow to some families occurred when the government revised the list of children who had passed the secondary schools' entrance examination. Eighty percent of the children who had passed, most of them Asians, were dropped from the list so that places could be made for African children.

To the vast majority of Asians, the future looked bleak. In an airgram I wrote on April 7, we reported to the State Department that "large

numbers of Asians have already left the country; others have sent out their families and are waiting for the most propitious time to depart with a minimum of financial loss." The Indian high commissioner to Kenya visited Zanzibar and Pemba and reported that there had been innumerable cases of looting of Asians' homes and seizure of their property.

In a cable dated April 15, Frank reported that all members of the Asian Muslim community had suffered from harassment, looting, or flogging. The Ismaeli sect, followers of the Aga Khan, were hardest hit. "During the revolution their businessmen bore [the] brunt of looting, houses were stripped of furniture, and approximately eleven were killed and many more wounded."

Money and valuables were being smuggled out of Zanzibar by whatever means possible. Departing Asians were frequently forced to strip and surrender jewelry and funds in excess of four hundred shillings (about fifty-six dollars). As conditions for them worsened, more Asians opted to leave, many of them to join relatives on the mainland. By the latter part of 1965, an estimated 10,000 of Zanzibar's 20,000 Asians had departed. Most of the remainder would leave in future years.

Living though we were in a situation of political turmoil and violence, Julie and I were entering into as happy a time as we would have in our married life. We took much joy in our two little girls, we had a growing number of good friends, and I had a great job. As March gave way to April, Julie, Susie, and Julianne had been back for almost a month. I spent as much time as I could with them. Julie and I often took the girls to the seashore. Susie and Julianne loved paddling in the ocean, which along the gradually sloping shoreline near Zanzibar Town gently lapped the sandy beaches.

With the cooler weather, we turned off the air-conditioning unit upstairs and began using the large overhead fans in the bedrooms and in the living room downstairs. The sibilant sound of the fans gently turning was much preferable to the loud whirring of the air conditioners. At night, we opened the sliding door that led from our bedroom onto a veranda directly over the one off the living room downstairs. Except for

the occasional cry of a bird or a monkey or the shriek of a bush baby, the nights were still.

Then one night, we had an intruder. We were just falling asleep when we heard and felt a thump on the mosquito net that enclosed the bed. Startled, we sat up. Another thump thoroughly alarmed us. I cautiously reached out of the net and turned on my bedside lamp. A bat! A large bat had flown into the room and, disoriented, was flying frantically around, heading in every direction except the right one that would take it outside. After some minutes, with the bat continuing to collide with the net, I decided I had to act.

I must have forgotten that Zanzibar's bats, at least those in our area, were harmless fruit bats. I had the average American's fear of bats that stemmed from Halloween stories and horror movies. The image in my mind must have been of a frightful rabies-infested, fanged creature. I jumped out of bed, ran out into the hall, took a broom from the closet, reentered the bedroom, and began flailing away at the bat. Finally, I whacked it a glancing blow, knocking it to the floor. While it lay there stunned, I grabbed a wicker wastebasket, put it over the bat and slid it out to the veranda, took away the basket, jumped back into the bedroom, and quickly closed the door. The next morning, the bat was gone. Long before then, my momentary flush of success at getting rid of the bat had given way to sheepishness as I remembered the harmlessness of the bats and their usefulness in eating insects.

The animal life near our house was augmented by a couple of monkeys. Red colobus monkeys and blue monkeys inhabited various parts of Zanzibar, but before the revolution there were none in our area. A British couple that had recently left Zanzibar had kept the two that appeared at our house. When the couple departed, they freed their two charges.

We thought it was nice to have monkeys swinging from the branches of the tall trees in our yard and those nearby. But then one day, we forgot to close up the house when we went to town. When we returned, we found that the kitchen had been trashed. The monkeys had come in and torn the place up, leaving behind remnants of food, broken dishes, ripped-up cartons, and monkey shit.

We stopped looking on the monkeys with benevolence after that, especially not long afterward when one jumped from a tree, landed a few feet from Susie, who was playing on the veranda, and shrieked, scaring the daylights out of the little girl and her mother, who was sitting nearby reading a book. Julie chased the monkey away. Later, the monkeys disappeared, going where we neither knew nor cared.

Although we had to take some care to keep possible animal intruders from getting into our house, we had no worries about break-ins by humans. The revolution was a stark reminder that Zanzibaris, like people everywhere, were capable of violence and cruelty toward their fellow human beings. And the revolution's aftermath brought many instances of maltreatment of people by some members of the Revolutionary Council and their followers. But this was not the norm for Zanzibar, which still in many ways was a safe place to be. In fact, for us it was, apart from the days of the revolution, the safest of the nine African posts to which I would be assigned during my Foreign Service career.

Zanzibar Town was the only African city in which we lived where we did not have night watchmen, except for the short time that Jacobo had worked for us. After the worst of the violence of the revolution had ended, we could leave the house for the day without locking it. We would drive downtown, park the car, leave it unlocked, windows open, even with our belongings inside, and never fear that anything would be taken. Dar es Salaam, we knew, was almost as safe.

All this would change. Although Zanzibar would not become as crime-ridden as Dar became, in the years ahead it would no longer be the safe place it was during our time there. A guidebook published in 1998 warned: "A few pickpockets operate in the main market, and some tourists have had bags and cameras snatched while walking around the narrow streets of Old Town [Stone Town]. There have also been attacks and robberies on some of the beaches around Zanzibar Town and the East Coast beaches popular with travelers. It is best not to go to the beach alone, especially at night."[1] But none of that was either present or foreseen when we were in Zanzibar.

Frank and I had full days at work. April would turn out to be even more eventful for us than March had been. Frank met with Karume as often as he could and with a wide range of Zanzibaris, including Babu and some of his followers. He and Babu had an amicable personal relationship. In a letter to an official in the State Department, Frank said, "Babu is intelligent, quick to get a nuance, witty and [has] a boisterous sense of humor." The two men, however, were far apart on their views of international issues and on where Zanzibar ought to be heading. Frank had no illusions about Babu's anti-Western bias and his ability to further the Communists' aims in Zanzibar.

The State Department proposed that it would be in the interest of the United States to develop a public relations campaign that would portray Babu as a threat to Zanzibar's nonalignment. Frank responded in a cable on April 1 that this was not a good idea. Though acknowledging that Babu was both "a threat and Communist-oriented," Frank told the department that more than the other pro-Communists in the government, "[Babu] understands need to maintain normal relations with West." Frank wrote, "If USG [U.S. government] should become associated with personal attacks on him, our activities here would be severely restricted. Even possible embassy would be closed."

He suggested that instead of going after Babu or any other of the Zanzibari pro-Communists, Washington could emphasize the influx of Communist arms, advisers, and diplomats. He said, "The question could surely be asked why small remote island like Zanzibar should find it necessary develop [Communist-] equipped army, in addition to existing adequate police force, unless aggression intended."

In an earlier message, Frank had taken what I considered as a reasoned approach to what we were facing in Zanzibar at that time. He said that for the time being, we would have to live with Babu and like-minded individuals in the government. He continued:

> In this situation, it important that we demonstrate our continuing interest in island, both to protect position of moderates and to maintain a posture which will enable us to take advantage of Communist errors or factional disputes. As first priority we must be ready indicate willingness to

follow through on commitments made to previous GOZ. . . . At same time believe we must look for other areas in which our assistance would be welcome.

We could not begin to compete with the Communist countries, which, it appeared, intended "to try to make Zanzibar a showcase," but we could nonetheless be an "active player" in the effort to influence the Zanzibar government.

One day, Frank and I drove to Mkokotoni, a village near the northern tip of Zanzibar Island. We were able to travel there, despite the government's restrictions on travel, because a celebration was being held in honor of Karume. Scheduled sporting events were rained out, but we sat next to Karume in a large tent and enjoyed the food that was passed around. Although it meant nothing in the greater scheme of Zanzibar's foreign relations, we took some satisfaction in being the only diplomats present, as inexplicably the Communist embassies were not represented. The Soviets, East Germans, and Chinese must have heard about this and been mortified; corrective measures were taken, and never again were Communist diplomats not in attendance at official functions.

On the drive up and back, with the U.S. flag flying from the flagstaff of the car, we received warm greetings from the hundreds of people who lined the road to hail Karume as he passed; men and children cheered, and women ululated. The goodwill shown to us that day was repeated again and again throughout the time I was in Zanzibar. Even when anti-American propaganda was at its most intense level and most vitriolic in content and when the government organized anti-American demonstrations, ordinary Zanzibaris were consistently friendly to us.

President Karume believed that Zanzibaris would need to work harder than they customarily did if they were to raise their standard of living. He had concluded that the Communist model of communal farms made good sense for Zanzibar. On a Sunday morning in early April, at Kinumoshi, a village northeast of Zanzibar Town, a ceremony took place to demonstrate the kind of self-help that Karume expected of his people. Present at a large weed-covered field just outside the vil-

Frank Carlucci at hoeing ceremony

lage were Karume, several thousand Zanzibaris, government and ASP functionaries, and most of the diplomatic corps, including Frank and me.

The president gave the diplomats a pep talk, praising the value of hard work. He said photographs would be taken to record for history a scene of diplomats of various countries working together. He led the Soviet, Chinese, East German, and American chiefs of diplomatic missions, along with various Zanzibari officials, to the center of the field. The diplomats, gripping their hoes tightly and casting sidelong glances at each other, were placed in the front row.

On command, the hoes were raised. "Take pictures!" Karume commanded. Then down crashed the hoes in unison. Frank, who as a construction worker years earlier had plenty of experience with a hoe, showed good form. The Soviet ambassador made up for his lack of skill by hacking away enthusiastically. The East German ambassador seemed totally unacquainted with a hoe and chopped hesitantly and ineffectively at the weeds in front of him. The Chinese chargé d'affaires worked the hardest, possibly to impress his ambassador, who had not yet presented his credentials and was watching from the sidelines. Up and down, the Chinese's hoe flashed at a furious pace. For some reason, he concentrated on one spot and consequently dug a deep hole.

After several minutes, Karume halted the work and took the diplomats to a nearby building where they were given *madafu* (coconut water) to drink. Then we all went home, except for the dogged East German, who rushed back to the field, joined the hundreds of Zanzibaris who were working the field, and resumed his hoeing.

I was spending a fair amount of my time those days gathering information for a report on the economy. With pro-Communists taking over the jobs of some of the departing British civil servants and the Asians who had been fired, I had some difficulty getting all the data I wanted from government offices. But there were sufficient sources available from the Clove Growers' Association, banks, and other commercial firms to give me the facts and figures I needed.

In my economic report, I informed the State Department about the Asian mercantile community's lack of confidence and the consequent drastic drop in imports. Customs duties on imported goods accounted for 30 to 35 percent of the government's revenues. The marked decline in imports would mean, then, a larger than expected budget deficit. The British government had planned to finance half the deficit, but that would no longer be the case. I wrote that "the most likely solution to this difficulty will be for someone else to pick up the tab." There already were indications that the Chinese would be that someone else.

The Revolutionary Council did not care what happened to the Asian businessmen and seemed unworried about the demise of private commercial transactions. In the report, I said that if the current trend continued, all foreign commerce and much of internal commerce would "become functions of the state." In fact, it was not long before this came to pass.

I ended the report by asserting that if the government showed it was "willing to prop itself up financially with aid from Communist countries, it [could] probably avoid any immediate financial collapse." I pointed out, however, that the government would find it difficult not to continue to be dependent on this outside assistance.

We continued to see additional signs that Zanzibar was going, from the U.S. standpoint, in the wrong direction. A one-party state, a feature of Communist countries, was rapidly becoming a reality. Membership in

the ASP was made compulsory for all adult Zanzibari citizens. No one was allowed to leave Zanzibar without producing his or her party membership card. At a meeting at the old Arab fort on April 2, the regional commissioner for Zanzibar Town told a meeting of Stone Town residents, mostly Asians, that anyone who failed to join the ASP would be "severely punished." A picture of President Karume had to be displayed in every house. We learned that the government, taking a lesson from its new totalitarian friends, had set up a system of paid informants within each government department. Each informant was paid five hundred shillings per month.

In a conversation with an embassy officer in Dar es Salaam, Tanganyikan minister of home affairs Job Lusinde confirmed the veracity of reports we had received that fifty Soviet military advisers were now training the Zanzibar army. (A Chinese military training team had also arrived.) Ali Mafoudh, he said, was prominent in the army. In fact, Mafoudh would soon emerge as the army's de facto commanding officer.

Although downplaying the removal of Othman Sharif and Hasnu Makame from the government, Lusinde agreed that "Communist-dominated Zanzibar was a threat to the mainland." He said the Communist countries represented in Zanzibar were making an effort to attract exiled African political organizations to Zanzibar in order to undermine the Organization of African Unity's Liberation Committee.

Alluding to the growing problem of urban poverty in Dar es Salaam, Lusinde pointed out that during the army mutiny in January, the only place where mob violence had taken place was in the capital. He declared that the stability of the Tanganyikan government depended on immediate visible economic development in Dar. Lusinde worried that if the Communists, through their aid programs, made Zanzibar a showplace, the contrast in Dar would exacerbate the Tanganyikan government's problems.

After Karume and the Revolutionary Council had given permission in February for us to keep the air conditioners running at the Project Mercury tracking station, I had gone out to Tunguu a couple of times.

The government and security forces had not interfered with Ernest Clark's periodic visits to ensure that all was well. These concessions by the revolutionary government did not, however, assure us that operations at the tracking stations could be resumed. Frank and I were mindful that Babu's Umma Party had denounced the station, calling it a rocket base, and that Karume had never repudiated the ASP's prerevolution condemnations of the presence of the tracking station in Zanzibar. Less than a month after the revolution, the Revolutionary Students' Union, an offshoot of the Umma Party, demanded the removal of the station.

In his talks with Frank, Karume was noncommittal about the future of the station. He did, however, grant a U.S. request that George Burch of the Bendix Corporation and Tom Spencer of NASA be permitted to return to Zanzibar to look after the station facilities at Tunguu and Chwaka. We mistakenly took this as a hopeful sign that Karume was not wedded to the idea that Project Mercury had to go.

The belief that Zanzibar was moving closer to becoming a Communist satellite was deepened when, on April 7, Karume ordered the removal of the tracking station from Zanzibar. Before making a public announcement, Karume called Frank in to tell him of the decision. Recounting what Karume said, in a letter to my parents Julie wrote, "He said that he was sorry to ask us this because our countries are friends, but that every day the people of Zanzibar go to see him and ask him to remove Project Mercury." Karume told Frank that his decision had been precipitated by unfavorable remarks about Zanzibar that the American ambassador to Kenya had made in a speech he gave in New York. The essence of Ambassador Attwood's remarks was that the Communists were preparing to use Zanzibar as a base for subversive activities in Africa.

Burch and Spencer, in consultation by radio with Bendix and NASA, had been making preliminary plans for dismantling the station if its closure were ordered. They estimated that it would take two months or more to do the job right. When Frank mentioned that to Karume, he said we could have sixty days. He would soon renege on this, however.

Two days after Karume's announcement on the seventh, the government organized a demonstration that began at the People's Palace.

Karume addressed the crowd. The more-in-sorrow-than-in-anger Karume who had talked with Frank was not evident. He said concern about "the establishment of an imperialist rocket base on our small island" had been expressed as early as 1959. Then he took aim at Ambassador Attwood: "Recently, the U.S. ambassador to Kenya left Nairobi for New York. He told the people there that Zanzibar is a Communist country, and he also uttered dirty words about Zanzibar. He insulted the government of Zanzibar. . . . This was aimed at sowing the seeds of discord among the East African governments and making us quarrel and despise one another." This had catalyzed the decision to rid the island of the tracking station. Karume said:

> We told the Americans to remove their base immediately. In reply, they said that they would require about three months to remove the base. We assure you today that this base will have been removed in not more than seventeen days. We assure you that your government has no master. [The former] masters are no longer here today. It will therefore be contrary to our wish to make the United States our second master.

His next remarks would be in tune with the content of an impending intensified barrage of anti-American invective in the newspapers, *Kweupe* and *Zanews*, and on Radio Zanzibar. He said: "Today we are removing the U.S. base and we will remove forthwith everything owned by the United States that is likely to cause dissension in our country or discord between us and our neighbors. . . . If the United States or any other country attempts to bring about dissension between African governments, it is just wasting its time."

Why did Karume, who seemed to want to improve Zanzibar's relations with the United States, decide to demand removal of the tracking station? For one thing, the ASP's opposition to Project Mercury's presence in Zanzibar had been a matter of record for years. The party's position had jelled even more after the ZNP-ZPPP government let it be known that it favored allowing the tracking station to remain after independence. It is possible, moreover, that Karume had come to believe at least part of the Communist propaganda that painted Project Mercury in a sinister light. No doubt Babu, Hanga, Twala, Moyo, and other pro-

Communists in his government influenced Karume. And either through them or directly, Communist diplomats must have been urging Karume to close down the station.

But why did he go back on his assurance that we could have sixty days to dismantle it and then permit, if not encourage, anti-American demonstrations and vitriol? The likeliest answer to these questions is that Karume's power was circumscribed. He apparently did not yet have the political strength to ignore the demands or urgings of not just Babu and the other overtly pro-Communists in the Revolutionary Council, but also probably a majority of the other members. Many of these men were barely educated, some were illiterate, and most were open to the arguments and blandishments of their more worldly colleagues and the hardworking diplomats and agents of the Soviet, Chinese, and East German governments. Once the bulk of the council had adopted a harsh stand against the United States, Karume felt compelled to go along with it.

The crowd at the People's Palace marched down past the Beit el-Ajaib and the old Portuguese fort and through a narrow street onto Kelele Square. While we watched from the embassy's second-story balcony, several hundred men, women, and children marched past, some carrying signs with anti-American slogans—for example, "Amerika ni adui ya Afrika" (America is the enemy of Africa). They were orderly and seemed to be having a good time doing something different from their usual daily pursuits. To give an impression of a large number of demonstrators, the organizers had them march out of the square, around the block, back into the square, and past the embassy two or three more times.

Two days later, on April 11, another demonstration took place, this one organized by the Federation of Revolutionary Trade Unions (FRTU). Carrying the same signs and chanting "Yankees go home," the demonstrators were even fewer in number than before; it was evident that the whole population of the area had not turned out as instructed.

Once more, Frank, two other Americans, and I stood on the balcony and waved at the people as they passed. *Zanews* reported that the cowardly Americans hid behind pillars during the demonstration. The pillars

were four inches wide. In an airgram, I pointed this out and enclosed copies of photographs that had appeared in the *Tanganyika Standard* showing demonstrators in the foreground and, beyond them, a clear shot of three of us standing at the front of the balcony, enjoying the parade. I commented in the airgram that the pictorial evidence upheld American honor.

On April 8, Radio Zanzibar quoted the Revolutionary Students' Union as stating, "U.S. imperialism [is] the greatest enemy of all progressive forces in the world . . . but [it] will fail in Zanzibar as it has done in Cuba and elsewhere." The next day, the radio station commented that removal of the tracking station "was a step towards safeguarding the people of Zanzibar from the ulterior motives of American imperialism and neocolonialism."

Most of the April 9 edition of *Kweupe* was devoted to anti-American articles. One charged that the American government wanted to keep the previous Zanzibar regime in power to "perpetuate imperialism" and to keep the "dangerous rocket base" in Zanzibar. The headline article of the April 11 edition of the newspaper declared, "The American rocket base will be rooted out right away." The paper referred to Americans not as *"Marekani"* but as *"Kimarekani,"* a term of contempt (literally, "little Americans"). The anti-American campaign would continue undiminished for another ten days or so.

The State Department recognized that the removal of the tracking station was not necessarily just a Communist-inspired act. It concluded, however, that the pro-Communists had forced Karume's hand, compelling him to act when he did and in the manner he did, going back on his word after giving us sixty days to complete the dismantlement and engaging in harsh anti-American rhetoric.

The adverse trend of events continued. On the twelfth, the government's Information Office ordered us to close the USIS library. The library had been a popular place for many educated young Zanzibaris, who had very little access to books and up-to-date Western newspapers, magazines, and other publications. But it was anathema to Zanzibari pro-Communists and particularly to the Communist embassies now established on the island.

The only good that came from the closure was that I was able to fire an employee of the library who had, we knew, been an informant of the government. We had kept him on the payroll to keep pressure off our other Zanzibari employees, but with the closure of the library, that was no longer necessary.

That same day, Frank sent a cable describing a meeting he had had the previous night with Wolf Dourado and the visiting Indian high commissioner to Kenya. The three men agreed that "Zanzibar was for all intents and purposes completely Communist-dominated," that the "situation had deteriorated even more rapidly" in the three weeks since the high commissioner's previous visit, and that "normal diplomatic action" was unlikely to have any effect on the course of events.

In Dar es Salaam, Job Lusinde was becoming increasingly pessimistic. He remarked to an embassy officer that the mainland coast was uncontrolled, and agents sent from Zanzibar would have no difficulty entering Tanganyika or Kenya. He said that Kenya, beset by tribalism and unemployment, was even more explosive than Tanganyika, itself vulnerable to "subversive agitation" because of its unstable political conditions. Lusinde had supported the Zanzibar revolution, expecting the postrevolution government to be dominated by ASP moderates. He said that he and others in the Tanganyikan government had not foreseen the preeminent role that Babu and other pro-Communist Umma Party adherents would assume.

Washington's and London's views of Zanzibar were getting gloomier by the day. The State Department's guidance to the American delegation attending an April 15 NATO meeting on Zanzibar said that instead of pursuing African nationalist, nonaligned policies, the Zanzibar government had "chosen Communist China, East Germany and USSR as principal benefactors and political allies." Already, there were "signs that Zanzibar agents are penetrating Tanganyika." Babu, the guidance said, had emerged as the "dominant political figure with [his] own security force and own lieutenants in key GOZ positions." Reversing a decision by Karume to establish ties with West Germany, Babu had engineered the recognition of East Germany, making Zanzibar the only non-Communist

country in the world to have done that. The Soviets were establishing a military training mission and supplying Zanzibar with military hardware.

In recommending what NATO members might do to deal with the Zanzibar problem, the department persisted in its vain quest to get additional Western and friendly Third World countries to establish embassies on the island. (In the coming year, only France would do this. Its one-man embassy would be too small and French aid too insignificant to make any difference in the international political equation in Zanzibar.) Virtually giving up on changing the situation in Zanzibar, Washington stressed that it was "very important for the West to enhance efforts [to] bolster East African regimes politically."

In London, Ambassador Bruce talked with Duncan Sandys on April 20. Sandys was still beating the drum for getting Kenyatta and Nyerere to urge Karume to ask the British to intervene. He told Bruce he believed that the British representatives in Kenya had considerable influence on Kenyatta. His dogged pursuit of the chimerical notion that Kenyatta would finally become more activist and that Karume would

consider seeking help from Britain could have stemmed only from blindness to the realities of the Zanzibar situation.

Frank went to see Karume at State House on the morning of April 20. He found the Zanzibari president "bubbling over with self-confidence, enthusiasm and friendship." In no way did Karume present a picture of a man who had any worries about his place in the Zanzibar power structure. And his friendly attitude was far divorced from what might have been expected of the man who had just days earlier lashed out at the United States for its wicked ways and demanded the removal of the tracking station.

Karume brought his fourteen-year-old son into his office, presented him to Frank, and said he planned to send him to the United States for his studies. Then he asked Frank about the U.S. aid project for Zanzibar that had been agreed to with the previous government but put on hold by the revolution and by Karume's own coldness toward U.S. assistance

Presidents Karume and Nyerere

of any form. The project included the construction and furnishing of a teacher training college. Karume said he wanted it built and asked that construction begin as soon as possible. That same morning, I met with Minister of Education Idris Wakyl, who also asked about the project and requested U.S. scholarships and teachers.

Frank told Washington that he hoped this startling change was linked to Karume's visit to Dar es Salaam two days earlier. But he did not know what might have happened there to account for Karume's ebullience and affability. Within a few hours, we knew the answer.

That afternoon in Dar, the Tanganyikan government announced that Tanganyika and Zanzibar had agreed to form a political union. The announcement said the articles of union had been signed that day by Presidents Nyerere and Karume. Four days later, on April 26, following ratification by the Tanganyikan National Assembly and Zanzibari Revolutionary Council, the union came into effect. Soon afterward, it was titled the United Republic of Tanganyika and Zanzibar.

Karume and Nyerere had played their cards very close to their chests. Nyerere took Oscar Kambona and Attorney General Roland Brown into his confidence and also probably Vice President Rashidi Kawawa, but few

if any others. Lusinde, for example, was kept in the dark. It seems that Kambona informed Leonhart of the merger plan a few days before it was announced and that Leonhart passed this on to the State Department. Leonhart and Washington, however, played no role in the decision to form the union, doing nothing more than indicating support for the plan. They did not inveigle Nyerere into creating the federation, as Babu would allege years later.

Like Nyerere, Karume was circumspect on the merger question. He entrusted Hanga and Twala to work with the Tanganyikans. The two flew to Dar on the twenty-first to confer with Nyerere and Kambona. The two Zanzibaris were pro-Communists, to be sure, but they were loyal to Karume and the ASP and were as wary as their leader about Babu's growing strength. Not coincidentally, the last stages of the plan to create the union and the announcement of its consummation took place when Babu was on a trip abroad.

Karume was much more alive to the danger that Babu posed to him than the British, the Americans, or anyone else gave him credit for. He knew how close Babu was to the Chinese Communists, and he certainly was fully aware of how well armed Babu's followers were. Karume was not at all uncomfortable with the Marxist policies that his new foreign friends were advocating. However, he may well have worried that Zanzibar would be too dominated by the Communist countries and that it could become embroiled in the East-West struggle.

A merger with Tanganyika would provide Karume the protection of the stronger mainland government and its military and police forces if they were needed. But most important, it would give him greater freedom of action in relation to the dynamics of Zanzibar politics. Union would clip Babu's wings, and it would also provide Karume a means of isolating others whom he did not trust. From then on, Karume would steadily increase his personal power in Zanzibar.

Nyerere had become increasingly alarmed at what was happening in Zanzibar. Lusinde's comments to American embassy officers had reflected Nyerere's fears about the ascendance of Babu and other pro-Communists in Zanzibar and the influence that they and the foreign Communists could exert on the mainland. A nonaligned union of Tanganyika and Zanzibar

would give the Tanganyikan president, working with Karume, a mechanism for controlling the situation.

It is quite likely, as Leonhart reported from Dar, that the turning point in the Karume-Nyerere move to unite their two countries came in Nairobi on April 10 and 11 during talks that Nyerere, Kenyatta, and Obote had regarding creation of an East African federation. The federation proposal, already beset with difficulties, foundered over the issue of inclusion of Zanzibar. Kenya was strongly opposed. A Tanganyikan proposal for a subsequent meeting of Tanganyika, Kenya, and Uganda to consider what to do about Zanzibar was rejected. From then on, Nyerere focused on a union between Tanganyika and Zanzibar, and he found a willing partner in Karume.

The announcement came as a total surprise to Kenyatta. At first, he was vexed because Nyerere had not informed him. But after a three-hour meeting with Kambona on the night of the twenty-third, he said he understood the reasons for the action and pledged his support. The next day, he sent one of his cabinet ministers with Kambona to help get the support of Obote, who, like Kenyatta, was miffed at being kept in the dark.

Washington was pleased and relieved by the turn of events. So was London. Bruce saw Sandys on the morning of the twenty-fifth. Sandys intimated that British pressure on Kenyatta and Nyerere had played a part in what had occurred. This was, to say the least, highly dubious. Any effect the British might have had was marginal at best. The facts are that Kenyatta had eschewed a direct role in trying to solve the Zanzibar problem and that Nyerere needed no advice from the British as to the danger that Zanzibar posed to Tanganyika. Sandys admitted to Bruce that the union came as a complete surprise to the British government.

In Zanzibar, the announcement of the union left Babu's followers dismayed and dejected. Many were angry. Salim Rashid's reaction was typical. Looking glum, he told an acquaintance that he had sent a cable to Babu advising him to cut short his trip abroad and return to Zanzibar. Rashid complained that the terms of the union involved a complete surrender of Zanzibar's sovereignty and gave nothing in return. "We will fight," he said. He alleged that Karume believed only a loose federation

was intended. Taking leave of his acquaintance, Rashid vowed that the union would never go through.

Babu was in Pakistan when word of the union reached him. He had arrived in Karachi on the twenty-third and been met by Foreign Minister Zulfikar Ali Bhutto, who accompanied him to Rawalpindi. They returned to Karachi on the night of the twenty-fourth, and Babu left for home the next morning. There is no doubt that Babu was floored by what had happened, but he tried to put the best face on it. According to the Pakistani press, just before his departure, Babu looked "tired and agitated and was extremely reticent about developments in Zanzibar during his absence." Pressed by reporters for some comment, he said that he favored the concept of African unity and that he had foreknowledge of the union.

The Tanganyikans, not to mention the Americans and British, were concerned that Babu's forces would resort to arms to prevent the union from becoming a reality. Furthermore, as Leonhart noted in a cable, there was uncertainty about how the Soviets might react. In the days leading up to the union, the Tanganyikan police had been given semiautomatic rifles. Following the announcement of the union, the British government offered to send troops if Nyerere wanted them, but the Tanganyikans fervently hoped there would be no need for them.

It is doubtful that the Soviets, East Germans, or Chinese intended even to consider the use of force to undo what Karume and Nyerere had done. Had they supported any such effort by the Zanzibari pro-Communists opposed to the union and it had failed, their position on the island would have been untenable. And if in the unlikely event an effort succeeded, they would have suffered disastrous political consequences on the mainland.

In a letter to my parents, Julie wrote from Dar es Salaam on the twenty-fourth that Frank and I had decided that morning that it would be prudent for her and the children "to leave the island just in case of some trouble." Only a few days earlier, she and I had represented the embassy at a celebration held in President Karume's honor at Makunduchi, on the southeastern tip of the island. That trip had been possible because of the improved security situation. But the uncertainties that had arisen from the union announcement caused us to take precautions.

Susie cried at the airport when she saw that I was not going with them. She soon got over it, though, and seemed to be somewhat reassured when they arrived at a place familiar to her, the same house by the beach in which they had stayed when they were in Dar es Salaam in January. Julie wrote that she planned to return to Zanzibar on Monday, and it turned out that she was able to do so. In a letter I wrote that same day, I said we at the embassy hoped Babu and his followers would realize "it will be hopeless to resort to arms."

On the twenty-sixth, Frank notified Washington that "outwardly situation normal and strategy of local pro-Communist elements will be determined by Babu, who only just arrived." Frank said he thought there was a good chance that Babu would be impressed with the odds against him, would decide to accept the union in principle, and then would work "to poison Karume and others against [the Tanganyikan government]."

Once home, Babu saw that Karume and Nyerere had outmaneuvered him and that there was nothing he could do about it in the short term. He, Salim Rashid, and others may have planted some doubts in the minds of Karume and other ASP leaders, but Karume was wedded to the fact of the union. Babu had lost face and was fully aware of it. Some of his followers had gone so far as to desert him and give their allegiance to Karume. Babu had no choice but to accept his appointment as one of the twenty-two cabinet ministers of the United Republic of Tanganyika and Zanzibar, and, after a time, he had to move his residence to Dar es Salaam.

Babu would hold various ministerial positions in the union cabinet for eight years, never again holding political power in Zanzibar. His stature in the union government was much lower than it had been in Zanzibar, and he grew to despise Nyerere, with whom he had deep philosophical and political differences. Babu's loss of influence and authority left him bitter for the rest of his life. He would claim that the Americans engineered the union, and he falsely portrayed Nyerere as little more than a British-American puppet.

13

Ups and Downs

Zanzibar Still Drifts into Communist Camp

　　　　　　　　　　　　—*Los Angeles Times,* July 26, 1964

Red Influence Is Spreading in Zanzibar. Union with Tanganyika Fails to Halt Red Advances in Indian Ocean Islands.

　　　　　　　　　　　　—*Washington Post,* November 9, 1964

The highlight of postrevolution Zanzibar's first May Day celebration was a parade on the airport road for a stretch that paralleled the golf course. It began at ten o'clock in the morning and ended at noon. The morning sunlight, filtered by the trees along the road, laid a dappled pattern of light and shadow on the people in the procession. Groups of workers of various kinds and members of the ASP and its women's and youth organizations marched by, carrying banners and signs proclaiming solidarity with the revolutionary government and bearing anti-imperialist, anti-Western slogans.

Of greatest interest to all, though, and certainly to Frank and me, was the military portion of the parade. The new Zanzibar army was on display for the first time. A company of men dressed in olive-drab tropical

May Day-celebration effigies

battle dress and carrying Soviet AK-47 automatic rifles stiffly at their chests led the procession. They were followed by several Soviet-made army trucks bearing troops sitting in the open beds of the vehicles. The soldiers were also carrying small arms. The trucks pulled either how- itzers or antiaircraft guns. We later learned that the Soviet arms and equipment consisted mainly of obsolete castoffs. But in comparison to what we had been used to seeing in Zanzibar, the men and the weapons in the parade that day looked pretty formidable.

After the parade, Julie and I drove around town with the girls. We stopped to have a close look at displays of effigies that some townspeo- ple had made and placed by their houses. They depicted scenes of the revolution, most of them showing Arabs being attacked by Africans. They were grim reminders of the recent violence and the still-strong anti- Arab sentiments. A panel of judges rated the displays, and winners received cash prizes.

May Day saw Julie and me plunged into a socialist social whirl, as we attended various celebrations of Zanzibar's entry into the fraternity of countries in which May Day was a major holiday. That night, we went to a dinner that the government held at the People's Club, which in its pre- vious life had been the Karimjee Jivanjee Club. The food was good, and,

somewhat at variance with socialist Spartanism, the liquor flowed freely. By the time we left, two of Okello's former fighters who were now on the Revolutionary Council had passed out.

The next day, we drove across the island to the town of Chwaka to take part in a luncheon given by local officials. It was the first time since the revolution that either of us had been able to drive to the East Coast, except for the day in February when I had gone to Chwaka to check on the status of the Project Mercury building there. We now were free to travel again. The only restriction placed on the movement of Westerners was to certain areas where military training was taking place.

Although Zanzibaris could not come to American social functions, they were free to accept invitations to attend affairs put on by Communist-country diplomats. That evening, we went to a reception at the Soviet embassy; many Zanzibaris were in attendance. From there, after dinner with a few friends at home, we drove to the People's Club for the first State Ball given by the Karume government.

The ball was, I wrote home, "a real rouser." It must have been a far cry from state occasions under British colonial rule. Because I was a mere vice consul, and perhaps because we were newcomers, Julie and I had not been invited to receptions and dinners given by the British resident or other top British officials. But from what our British friends told us and the impressions I had gained from the events I did attend during the pre-independence day celebrations, we knew that occasions of state were somewhat starchy affairs marked by decorum and protocol. All that ended with the passing of the colonial era and the overthrow of the previous government.

Everyone, ourselves included, had a good time. The club was crowded with government officials, Revolutionary Council members, diplomats, visiting Communists, and ordinary Zanzibaris. Once again, alcoholic beverages were plentiful and gratis. Julie and I were greeted enthusiastically by the head of the Cuban delegation. We had met him at the May Day parade, and he, who spoke neither English nor Swahili, was so happy to find someone who spoke Spanish that he did not care that I was an American diplomat.

Karume seemed to be enjoying himself immensely. Much of the music the band played was a Zanzibar version of West African high life.

During one of the numbers, Karume got people into a conga line and led us around the floor. The party was still going strong when Julie and I left at one in the morning.

Establishment of the United Republic of Tanganyika and Zanzibar did not mean clear sailing for us, although we did benefit in some ways. The anti-American propaganda campaign eased off. I made a trip to Pemba. Frank and I began getting a friendlier reception in government offices. In June, Karume gave us permission to reopen the USIS library. Overall, however, we were fighting an uphill battle to get Karume and his government to become truly nonaligned, and initially our successes were few and were outshone by the progress that our Communist adversaries were making.

Under the terms of the agreement between Nyerere and Karume as ratified by the Tanganyikan National Assembly and the Zanzibar Revolutionary Council, Julius Nyerere became president of the United Republic, with Abeid Karume and Rashidi Kawawa first and second vice presidents, respectively. Zanzibar maintained control of the essentials of its domestic affairs: agriculture, banking, commerce, education, health, justice, and police. National defense, foreign affairs, and control of foreign-exchange reserves were to be responsibilities of the union government.

It soon became clear, however, that Karume and Nyerere had different notions about what union meant. Nyerere envisioned an eventual complete merger of the two countries into one sovereign state. Karume saw it as a partnership in which Zanzibar would retain a great deal of autonomy. In Zanzibar, he continued to be called "president of Zanzibar."

Nyerere soon found that he had little actual influence over Zanzibar. All of Zanzibar's ministries remained virtually autonomous, and the Zanzibar government kept control over Zanzibar's immigration and emigration, its foreign-exchange reserves, and its armed forces. Zanzibar dealt with foreign governments in the manner of a sovereign country. For years, the ASP did not merge with the Tanganyikan African National Union, Nyerere's political party, as Nyerere and Kambona had

hoped. Faced with increasing domestic problems, for a time Nyerere turned his attention away from his difficulties with Zanzibar. However, particularly because of the two-Germanys issue, he could not ignore it for long.

Tanganyika had enjoyed a warm relationship with West Germany. Nyerere wanted to maintain that relationship, which, through West German aid, had very much benefited Tanganyika and would now benefit the United Republic. The West Germans had helped establish an air wing of the Tanganyikan military and a naval police force and provided technical advice and equipment for both. Other technical assistance experts and more than fifty volunteers were present in the country, working on health and education projects. West German capital assistance in various fields, especially agriculture and housing, was substantial.

Karume was equally happy with his relationship with East Germany, the first country to recognize his government. He had no intention of giving up the considerable amount of aid promised by the East Germans. But Nyerere could not agree to recognize East Germany, knowing that if he did, West Germany would have to break relations with the United Republic of Tanganyika and Zanzibar, because of the Hallstein Doctrine. Months would pass before the issue was resolved.

The questions raised about the future of the union made our diplomatic status unclear. With the East Germans leading the way, the Communist countries represented in Zanzibar insisted that they continue to maintain embassies rather than revert to consulates. A change to consular status was the correct thing to do, since embassies are located only in the capitals of countries and Dar es Salaam was the capital of the United Republic. However, with the Communists so insistent and because of his desire to keep his ties with them firm, Karume went along with their wish on this issue. This move notwithstanding, for some weeks, it seemed possible that Nyerere and Karume would resolve their differences on the German question in such a way that would result in closure of all the foreign missions in Zanzibar.

With the ending of the *masika* rains, we were entering into the nicest time of the year to be in Zanzibar, roughly from May or June to October.

The winds of the southwest monsoon *(kusi)* brought relatively cool days and balmy nights.

Dismantlement of the tracking station had gone smoothly. Once Karume and the Revolutionary Council had ordered the removal of the station by the end of April, NASA and the Bendix Corporation had geared up to meet that deadline. Joining George Burch and Tom Spencer, American technicians came over to Zanzibar from the mainland. Among them were some of the men who had been evacuated on the *Manley*. A couple of them were bitter about the property they had lost because their houses had been looted. They blamed the embassy and the State Department for ordering the evacuation. They seemed to have forgotten that when we were gathered at the English Club on January 12 and 13, they were scared and only too happy to be taken off the island by the *Manley*. None of the Project Mercury people had voiced any desire to remain in Zanzibar.

NASA and Bendix made the end-of-April deadline. Karume was pleased not only by the speed with which the station was dismantled, but also by the competence and lack of fuss shown by the Americans as they went about their business. He also seemed suitably impressed and grateful that we left the station's power generator in place and turned it over to his government. If properly used and maintained, the generator was capable of providing electricity for a large part of the rural area in the vicinity of Tunguu.

The American technicians left the island just before the end of the month, and Julie and I said good-bye to George Burch. He and Teresa had become good friends of ours. Soon afterward, we also said farewell to departing British friends. In early June, the Irish doctor who had cared for Julie during her pregnancy left Zanzibar. He was one of the dozen British colonials who at first had been exempted from the expulsion order but then were also told to go. An East German replaced him at the hospital. Many of the new medical personnel were Chinese, including an acupuncturist. The name of the hospital also underwent a change. Originally named after the Indian philanthropist who had helped

finance its construction, the Karimjee Jivanjee Hospital became the V. I. Lenin Hospital.

The British community, about five hundred strong at the time of independence, had shrunk to a handful. The total number of Westerners in Zanzibar, including men, women, and children, now amounted to only about sixty souls: Britons, Americans, and a few people of other nationalities.

The golfers among us were happy when the golf course was reopened. Now named the People's Golf Club, it was under the management of former caddies, some of whom were excellent golfers. The grass on the fairways had grown quite high, which was a formidable challenge. The caddies finally managed to get the loan of the island's only mowing machine, which belonged to the Zanzibar Town municipality. After one or two uses of the machine, however, the municipality refused to let the caddies have it again. The national government was unsympathetic to the caddies' request for help—golf was viewed as a capitalist sport.

The final blow to the People's Golf Course came when members of the Chinese embassy who were learning to drive used the course as a place to practice. It was an ironic sight: young Chinese Communists zooming around the fairways in Mercedes sedans. Disgusted, getting no help from the authorities to keep the course open for business, and with only a few golfers left on the island—not enough to meet the costs of running the course—the caddies gave up. The golf course was closed, never to reopen.

Although we lost the golf course, we still had the cinemas. Closed for a while after the revolution, Zanzibar Town's three cinemas were open for business again in April. A decision by the government to nationalize them drew an immediate and furious protest from ordinary Zanzibaris, who loved going to the movies, and the decision was revoked.

Gone forever were the days when British colonials dressed formally when they went to see a movie. Invited to accompany some of our new friends to the cinema, Julie and I had done this a couple of times before the revolution—she in a long dress and me wearing the de rigueur "Red Sea rig," which consisted of tuxedo trousers, a long-sleeve formal white

shirt, a bow tie, and a cummerbund; in deference to the heat, white dinner jackets were not worn. We felt silly but obliged to observe the local custom.

Now, in the postcolonial era, we dressed casually. The seating was still segregated, with the masses downstairs and the elite—Communists and capitalists alike—occupying the balcony. The Zanzibaris enjoyed in particular spaghetti westerns, hollering with great gusto at action scenes. One week, we were looking forward to watching an early James Bond film, *From Russia with Love*. Unfortunately, the Soviet embassy got wind of it and protested to the government. The film was not shown, and from then on, the government censors were careful to ban any motion picture that might portray a Communist country in a bad light.

The summer months rolled by, but we were only vaguely and occasionally aware that it was summer elsewhere. Our lives were governed by the monsoons and the periods of rain between them. In those days, long before satellite television came into being and when telephone calls to the United States were virtually unplaceable, I found that if I had reason to think about something in the United States, then I would have to make a mental calculation about what month it was at the time and then transpose that into a picture of what the weather would be like at wherever it was that I was thinking about.

While we waited to see what decision would be made about diplomatic representation in Zanzibar, Frank, our still growing staff, and I kept hard at work. Frank focused on strengthening his relationship with Karume and other important people in the government and the ASP, getting Washington's concurrence for moving ahead on our school construction project, adding to his sources of information, reporting on political developments, and learning Swahili. I supported him in every way I could, did my own reporting, handled my administrative and consular duties, and also worked on improving my fluency in Swahili.

Karume had told Frank he preferred that the school the United States had planned to build for Zanzibar be changed from a teacher training college to a vocational high school. After talking this over with John

Cameron, who was the architect for the project, and conferring with USAID officers from Dar, Frank proposed to Washington that we go along with Karume's preference. The State Department and USAID agreed. Within the USAID bureaucracy, however, there were some who opposed going ahead with the project. They believed that Zanzibar was a Communist satellite and that any aid to it would be benefiting communism. Frank and I did not know this at first, but as time went on and we kept running into bureaucratic hurdles, we learned what lay behind them. Throughout 1964, Frank struggled to overcome this resistance within USAID.

Frank and I attended a gathering that Karume addressed outside the ASP headquarters building in early June. We reported in a cable that the crowd in attendance that afternoon applauded vigorously when he announced: "Today we are happy because we have received a gift from the Americans: a gift of a secondary school they will build. It will be a technical secondary school." The crowd applauded even more energetically, we reported, when Karume said, "We have another reason for happiness: China has extended us a five million pound loan with no interest."

Our Communist adversaries continued to outdo us on the aid front, but that was all right. As Frank had told Washington earlier, it would make no sense for us to try to compete with the Communist countries, which were lavishing aid on Zanzibar. Our aid project was well designed, would meet one of the country's pressing educational needs, and would keep us in the game.

It was a measure of Karume's political strength that he could leave Zanzibar whenever he wished with no fear that his power and position would be usurped during his absence. On the morning of June 12, shortly before flying to Dar es Salaam to meet Ethiopia's Haile Selassie, he received Frank at State House. He was delighted when Frank gave him a gift of a Zenith shortwave radio. Karume was enthusiastic about the proposed curriculum for the secondary school, and he asked that construction begin immediately.

After telling Karume that the United States continued to support the union, Frank brought up Pemba. He told Karume that on his most

recent visit there, he had found the situation very bad. He had learned of many instances of looting of Asians' homes, seizure of their property, and forcible stripping from people of possessions they had on their persons, including even wedding rings. The Asians were not the only victims. Under the rule of Pemba's regional commissioner, Rashid Abdullah, people were tried and punished by kangaroo courts. Corporal punishment was common.

Since becoming president, Karume had yet to visit Pemba. He said he had heard there were difficulties there, but he was unacquainted with details of the Pemba situation. A few days later, Karume admitted to Associated Press correspondent Dennis Neald that things were bad in Pemba. He said numerous people had talked to him about it. He told Neald that he planned to dismiss the present commissioners and "replace them with good men."

Reporting to Washington, Frank said he was impressed by Karume's goodwill but "distressed by his inadequate understanding of what is taking place in Zanzibar." He went on to say:

> While he still our best hope on local scene, Karume is uninformed, lacking in skills needed to control a government organization and easily influenced. I believe his sense of insecurity stems as much from his feeling of personal inadequacy (despite his forceful mannerisms) as it does from rumors of unrest in Zanzibar. This in part may explain Karume's unpredictability.

However, he added, "While he presently under Communist influence Karume, in my opinion, is still attracted by the siren call of African nationalism."

Karume's relationship with the Revolutionary Council was complex and was shaped by sometimes conflicting political and ideological influences. It was not the council as a whole that wielded political power, but Karume himself and certain of the council's members, notably those in the cabinet. A mixture of moderates and radicals, they favored, in varying degrees of intensity, a Marxist approach to the economy and strong friendships with Communist countries.

Of the original thirty-one members of the council, Okello and Babu were gone. About a third of the remainder were former "freedom fighters" who had given their allegiance to Okello. Politically naive and in some cases not very intelligent, these men did not figure prominently, if at all, in the government's decisionmaking. Even though they had been politically marginalized, however, Karume wanted to retain as many allies as possible and went out of his way not to alienate them. They were given places of honor at public functions and received other forms of deference. To a large extent, they were allowed to do as they pleased, as long as their activities did not seriously interfere with the government's objectives.

The loose rein on some of the wilder of former revolutionaries led to some problems. Said Idi Bavuai and A. S. Natepe were allowed to seize Arab property as they wished for their personal use. With this precedent, others took whatever they wanted from Arabs or Asians whenever they chose. And some seemed to enjoy harassment for harassment's sake.

Said Wa Shoto was an especially ill tempered man who liked to throw his weight around. One day in April, when some British officials were still around, he decided to search the offices of the Clove Growers' Association. Discovering a picture of a former sultan, he arrested the nearest European, engineer Bill Belcher. When Wa Shoto arrived at a police station with his prisoner and ordered that he be locked up, he was ignored. A government minister was called, came to the station, apologized to Belcher, and left with Wa Shoto, apparently explaining to him that his action was not helpful.

Later in the year, Wa Shoto confronted a taxi driver and berated him for saying Wa Shoto did not have the right to act as he did. The driver denied saying this. When Wa Shoto threatened to put him in prison until he confessed, the driver admitted his guilt. Wa Shoto gave him twenty lashes with a whip. One day, Wa Shoto and Idi Bavuai, both packing side arms, leaped into their car when they saw Frank driving by and followed him out to the American school project. Evidently satisfied that Frank was not engaged in some kind of skullduggery, they drove off after a short while.

The worst offense committed by one of the Revolutionary Council's wild men occurred in September. Mohamed Abdulla entered an Ithnasheri mosque and shot dead four worshipers and wounded five others. He said the men in the mosque were plotting against the government, a patent lie. After being held for a brief time, Abdulla was freed. Two other Ithnasheris were arrested and charged with being a part of the nonexistent plot. Karume got nowhere in trying to convince the Revolutionary Council to prosecute Abdulla.

Karume went to Dar to discuss the matter with Nyerere. The next day, an editorial, probably written by Nyerere, appeared in the government-oriented newspaper, the *Nationalist*. It condemned the killings. Back in Zanzibar, a few days later Karume publicly lamented the killings and promised that the crime would be punished. Curiously, he denied that the shooting took place in a mosque. Abdulla, who was in the audience, seemed unconcerned. Asians refused to believe Abdulla would be punished. He never was and, unrepentant, continued to go about his business. Julius Nyerere was infuriated, but there was nothing he could do about it.

In July, the anti-American campaign in the media heated up again. Articles in *Kweupe* and *Zanews* frequently contained violent criticisms of U.S. foreign and domestic policies. The worse that the United States could be portrayed, the better. Almost all the material that was used came from either the Soviet or the Chinese news agencies.

Because of fears of government retribution, Zanzibaris continued to treat Westerners socially as if we were pariahs. This would persist as long as I was in Zanzibar. No matter how many times we tried, invitations from Frank or me to Zanzibaris to attend a dinner or party at our houses went unanswered and produced no results.

The danger of getting too close to Zanzibaris was driven home in June, when a member of the British high commission staff was declared persona non grata because he was regarded as being too friendly with government officials. He, too, had been inviting some of them to his house. We learned that the Revolutionary Council believed he was trying to instigate plots against the government.

Frank had been unsuccessful in trying to establish a social relationship with one of his next-door neighbors, Aboud Jumbe, who was now a min-

ister of state in the government. After getting a diploma in education from Makerere College in 1945, Jumbe had taught school for fourteen years. In 1960, he stopped teaching to work full-time for the ASP. Despite his alcoholism, Jumbe played a significant role in the party and remained a cabinet minister throughout Karume's presidency. One night in June, Jumbe phoned Frank and asked him to come to his house. Arriving there, Frank found that "as usual, Jumbe had been drinking to excess." Perhaps that accounted for his temporary courage in daring to meet with Frank. Reporting on their talk, Frank said Jumbe "apologized for not having become socially acquainted earlier but said that 'If I had visited your house, I would have been shot.'"

The Communist diplomatic missions to Zanzibar increased with the arrival of Polish, Czech, Cuban, and Bulgarian diplomats and technicians. By late summer, there were about sixty Soviets, fifty East Germans, and forty Chinese on the island, along with a smattering of Cuban and assorted Eastern Europeans. More would continue to arrive.

All the Communist missions offered scholarships and overseas training opportunities for young Zanzibaris. The Soviets had a military training unit and continued to provide arms and equipment. They bought a large amount of cloves. The Chinese interest-free loan was appreciated, as was their military training and agricultural technical assistance. The East Germans were slow to get off the mark on their housing project, but the promise of it kept the Zanzibari leaders happy for the time being. The East Germans were also developing a plan to build a radio transmitter.

Julie and Jean Carlucci flew over to Dar in early June. It was the first time that Julie had traveled off the island for a reason other than her safety. She and Jean went to buy food items that we could not get on the island. Fruits, vegetables, and fish were generally in good supply, but dry goods in shops were getting scarce, and good meat was hard to find. Shortages would persist throughout the remainder of our stay in Zanzibar.

Shipments of consumer goods began arriving from Communist China, but many of the items were of poor quality or of no use to any-

one. The first ship from China brought, for example, thousands of cans of talcum powder, an item that few Zanzibaris were interested in buying. The talcum powder was consigned to Bizanje, the newly created State Corporation for External Trade. Before long, the stuff, sitting on shelves fully exposed to Zanzibar's heat and humidity, congealed.

Free to travel, Julie and I did some more exploring. Among the places we visited on the West Coast with the girls was the beach at Mangapwani. We drove north from town, stopping about halfway to our previous house at Mtoni to have a look at the Marahubi Palace. Built of coral stone and wood in 1882 for Sultan Barghash, the palace was said to have housed his wife and ninety-nine concubines. Destroyed by a fire in 1899, all that remained of the palace were a bathhouse and huge stone pillars that supported the upper story. It was still an impressive sight, the row of reddish brown pillars in a setting of deep-green foliage, thick growth of lilies, and bright-red flowers of flamboyant trees.

We passed our former house and, several miles up the road, the palace at Kibweni that was popularly called the sultan's summer palace. It was now used as an official residence by the government. Mangapwani was several miles farther north. Arabs had lived in the area through which we drove, and we saw empty houses, some badly burned, their doors hanging open, mute reminders that the inhabitants were probably dead.

The clean sands of Mangapwani curved around a cove. At one end was the Slave Cave. It was a square cell cut out of the coral and had been used to store slaves. After being unloaded from boats, some of the slaves that were brought from the mainland were kept there before being transshipped to Zanzibar Town or elsewhere.

The southwest monsoon wind blowing off the Zanzibar Channel could sometimes be blustery, and the best beach weather was on the East Coast. That summer and fall, until about the end of November and the onset of the northeast monsoon, we and some of our American and British friends and their children began what would continue to be regular Sunday trips to one of the East Coast beaches when the weather permitted.

We would often dig a large hole in the beach and cut a channel to it from the sea to allow the water to flow into the hole, giving the chil-

dren, all of whom were very young, a pool to splash around in. When
we were not swimming, talking, eating, or drinking, we sometimes
used a cricket bat and a tennis ball to play a game vaguely resembling
cricket. Our pleasures were simple, and our days together at the beach
were something we all valued a great deal.

In late June, we were still an embassy. Nyerere and Karume had not been
able to reach an agreement about the status of the East Germans. For
more than two months, the GDR, the Soviet Union, and probably China
had urged Karume to stick to his guns on the issue of recognition of the
GDR. Karume needed little encouragement. He was receiving aid from
the East Germans and big promises of more to come. Zanzibar was getting nothing from West Germany. No contest.

The Communist diplomats continued to hope that the union would
fail, and for a while it seemed that it might. But by June, it had become
increasingly apparent that Tanganyika and Zanzibar were going to remain
politically merged, despite the union's imperfections and Karume's and
Nyerere's different views about the meaning of political and economic
integration. Finally, in July, all the embassies in Zanzibar were notified
that they had to become consulates. The Communists were chagrined,
but had to comply. Ambassador Chuvakin complained to Frank that he
was too high ranking to be a consul, and some months later he left
Zanzibar.

As high commissioner, Timothy Crosthwait was the equivalent of an
ambassador. Therefore, Tanganyikan foreign minister Kambona had
asked in May that he be transferred in order to set a precedent for transferring from Zanzibar the Soviet, Chinese, and East German ambassadors. Crosthwait was probably not sorry to hear of the request. By his
own admission, he suffered from his inexperience in Africa.

Crosthwait did not have a smooth relationship with Karume—far
from it. He was handicapped by his obligation to give top priority to the
needs of the departing British. He also had to emphasize such matters as
settlement in Britain of the sultan and pensions for policemen who had
opposed the revolution. His talks with Karume usually dealt with UK-

Zanzibar differences and seldom with the nature of the problems in Zanzibar and Karume's needs. As Crosthwait put it in a message to Duncan Sandys summarizing the Zanzibar situation in late July, his defense of British interests and protection of individual British subjects brought him "into frequent and sometimes stormy conflict with Karume and his authorities."[1] It did not help that he could be, as one of his staff told me, arrogant at times.

Crosthwait's feelings about Karume probably added to his lack of rapport with the Zanzibari president. He was disdainful of what he regarded as Karume's inadequate background for the leadership position he had assumed. Crosthwait said Karume "is a simple and rather stupid man easily misled by the Communists who surround him and sensitive moreover to pressures from the ignorant, bigoted members of the Revolutionary Council." Frank Carlucci felt that Crosthwait overlooked Karume's sense of independence, innate political shrewdness, and ability to maintain popular support.

Crosthwait left Zanzibar in late July. He was replaced by James Bourn, a Swahili-speaking former–colonial service district officer and a man who, unlike Crosthwait, had great empathy for Africans. As deputy high commissioner and later as British ambassador to Somalia, Jim proved to be a superb diplomat. The good-humored and outgoing Jim Bourn and his gracious wife, Isobel, were welcome additions to the small Western community.

The change in diplomatic status had no significant effect on us. Frank relinquished his chargé d'affaires title and became the American consul. We took down our embassy sign and replaced it with the old consulate sign.

The question of recognition of the GDR continued to bedevil relations between Karume and Nyerere. The East Germans kept pushing for diplomatic status within the union, not just in Zanzibar. Nyerere and Kambona resisted them. In August, the Tanganyikan Foreign Ministry issued a statement that rejected the Zanzibari claim that the GDR had an embassy on the island. Still, Nyerere knew full well how important the East German relationship was to Karume, and he tried to find a satisfactory compromise.

While the stalemate on this issue continued, the East Germans persisted in jockeying for a better position. By September, they got the Zanzibaris to agree that the GDR consulate would be elevated to consulate general. Although this had no practical effect, it gave the East Germans mission more prestige and put them at the top of the diplomatic pecking order on the island. In response, the Soviets and Chinese became consulates general. So, perforce, did we—which meant that we had to get the Department of State to send us a consulate-general sign.

In early 1965, Nyerere and Karume reached agreement that the East Germans would be allowed to open an "unofficial" consulate general in Dar es Salaam. Nyerere believed this would be acceptable to the FRG, but it was not. The government of Chancellor Ludwig Erhard indicated that if this plan was adopted, the flow of West German aid would be adversely affected. This did not sit well with Nyerere.

On February 19, the Tanzanian government announced that the GDR would open a consulate general in Dar es Salaam but that this would not constitute official recognition. West Germany immediately canceled its military aid and recalled its air and naval training teams. In ham-handed fashion, the FRG cabinet announced that it would consider further pressures on Tanzania.

Nyerere's response was equally swift. Infuriated, he asked the West Germans to cancel all remaining aid, including a promised multimillion-dollar new aid program. All the FRG aid personnel, including the volunteers, were to be sent home. This was avoided only after assiduous negotiations by concerned individuals in both governments.

Later, the Tanzanian government ordered all the consulates general in Zanzibar to revert to consulate status. For what would be the last time, we changed our sign again.

Harry Radday reopened the library and hired an African to run it. Harry's ability to counter the anti-American campaign was limited, however, since USIS was not permitted to distribute informational materials or news releases. Even if we had permission do this, Information Officer Ahmed Qullatein, a close associate of Babu, would

have made sure that none of the media would have used whatever we gave them. Harry worked hard on getting around town, meeting as many Zanzibaris as possible and giving people information about the United States and its foreign policy, especially as it applied to Zanzibar.

Antagonism against the United States soon got worse. In July 1964, the president of the Democratic Republic of the Congo, Joseph Kasavubu, faced with widespread disorder in his country, asked Moise Tshombe to form a new government. Tshombe, who had earlier attempted to separate the mineral-rich Katanga Province from the rest of the country, was regarded by many Africans as a tool of Western governments and financial interests—Belgium's Union Minière in particular—and despised for it. Nyerere, among other African leaders, saw Tshombe's assumption of power as a betrayal of Africa by the West.

Most African countries turned down Tshombe's and Kasavubu's appeals for military aid to enable the central government to defeat rebellions organized by anti-Tshombe elements. The United States, however, responded to the appeal by sending arms and military equipment in August. This produced a negative reaction, which was fueled by the Communists throughout much of the Third World.

On August 23, we again watched demonstrators marching by our building. About 2,000 people participated in the demonstration. This time, they were led by several cabinet ministers. The ASP, the Youth League, the Revolutionary Students' Union, and the Federation of Revolutionary Trade Unions were represented. Chanting "Yankee go home" and other slogans, the crowd marched past the consulate three times. Representatives of the four organizations presented a letter to Frank condemning the United States for interfering in the Congo's internal affairs and demanding an end to U.S. aid to the Congolese government. The letter ended with a threat to ask Nyerere and Karume to sever diplomatic relations with the United States if U.S. policy did not change.

Press attacks took on a new intensity. After describing the demonstration, the August 25 edition of *Zanews* carried some statements attributed to prominent Zanzibaris at a predemonstration rally. Mtoro Rehani, vice president and a respected moderate elder of the ASP, was quoted as declaring that U.S. imperialism was "the butcher of the

Congolese patriots" and asking the crowd, "Shall we drive out those who have come to suck our blood?" *Zanews* said he was referring to the American consul.

Frank and I went to see Rehani to discuss the Congo. Frank showed the *Zanews* article to him. Rehani was outraged. He said that although he had addressed the crowd, he had made no such statement. He sent word asking ASP general secretary Thabit Kombo to come to his office. After reading the article, Kombo called Karume and made an appointment for Rehani and us to see him immediately. At first, Karume was angry, thinking that Rehani had made the statement. When he understood that this was not the case, Karume nonetheless chided him for having participated in the affair.

Karume called in Information Officer Qullatein and rebuked him for fifteen minutes. He said information obtained from foreign sources, whether Russian, American, Chinese, or British, should no longer be used by the Zanzibar news media. Zanzibar was nonaligned and wished to be friends with all nations. He said the continual attacks on the United States made it appear as if the people of Zanzibar, himself included, hated Americans. Zanzibaris must wonder how the government could accept U.S. assistance—the secondary school—from such a bad country. The portrayal of the United States was false, he said, and he repeated to Qullatein that there would be no further use of foreign news materials.

The anti-American propaganda did not end, but it became much less frequent and its content less inflammatory. Karume had to continue to guard against its resurgence. In early September, Frank and I attended a ceremony at which Karume opened a new ASP branch office at Kizimkazi, a village at the southwestern end of the island. Government ministers, Revolutionary Council members, and diplomats were among those in attendance. During the ceremony, schoolchildren sang a song that included a denunciation of Project Mercury as a weapon the Americans had directed against Zanzibar.

In a speech later in the program, Karume ordered the Information Service to cut the anti-American references out of the broadcast tape. He told the crowd that the government had misunderstood the objectives of Project Mercury and now knew that the project was for peace-

ful purposes only. He said it was necessary for him to apologize to the Americans. He then explained emphatically that Americans were friends of Zanzibar who were assisting Zanzibar by building a secondary school. Propaganda against them should cease. At an indoor reception following his speech, Karume ceremoniously crossed the room to hand Frank a refreshment. A small victory perhaps, but it did show that we were making progress in reducing the suspicion of U.S. motives and the government's hostile actions against the consulate. Karume seemed to be succeeding in his effort to make Zanzibar truly nonaligned.

Near the end of September, in another meeting, Frank told Karume that we planned to move the USIS library closer to Ng'ambo, where most of Zanzibar Town's Africans continued to live. It would be much more accessible to our target audience of young Africans there than at its present location in the consulate. Karume did not object.

Not long afterward, on a flight to Dar es Salaam, Frank had a chance encounter with Thabit Kombo. Kombo, who probably was Karume's closest associate, described how Karume's attitude toward Americans had changed from the early days of the revolution, when he had believed we were working against him. According to Kombo, Frank's presentation of the radio to Karume had, strangely enough, been a major factor in changing Karume's disposition toward us. But the key element was his satisfaction with the progress being made on building the school. Kombo told Frank that Karume was using the example of the school to try to persuade his colleagues that the United States was a friend of Zanzibar, not an enemy.

Joel Kalonzi, the commissioner of prisons, was one of the few moderates in the government who did not hesitate to have contact with us. He openly expressed dissatisfaction with what he saw as a rush to embrace Communist ideas. He told Frank that Karume was no longer uncritically accepting the advice of the pro-Communists around him. Kalonzi believed that the impression our school was making was "bringing the pendulum back toward the center."

The political environment may have been better for us, but life for most Zanzibaris continued to fall far short of their revolutionary expectations. The economy remained depressed, there were few new jobs,

unemployment grew, and political repression increased. Although the camps of Arab detainees had long since been emptied, many Arabs remained in prison. Arabs and Asians who could emigrate continued to leave the island.

Some Revolutionary Council members kept Zanzibaris, especially Asians and Arabs, in a jittery state as they continued to nationalize houses and cars and to commit acts of brutality. Said Wa Shoto, among others, made a sport of on-the-spot floggings. The council expanded its network of informants. Selected members of the council stationed themselves at various locations throughout Zanzibar Town and passed out a few shillings to people who brought them information. At night, a council "duty officer" circulated around town to make sure no subversive meetings were taking place.

Zanzibar had great potential for tourism. It had barely begun to be scratched before the revolution, but the number of tourists who came was sufficient to provide the island with a significant amount of foreign exchange and a livelihood for a good number of Zanzibaris. Now tourism was dead. In one of his meetings with Karume, Frank told the president that increasingly stringent requirements for entry permits— fourteen days' prior notice, for example—delays in processing applications, and many refusals made it next to impossible for tourists to come to Zanzibar. Karume said he wanted tourists, and he promised to look into the matter.

Nothing much changed, however. Security concerns stemming from fears of counterrevolution and the pro-Communists' aversion to tourism as a bourgeois institution were creating a xenophobia that would intensify. Reports reaching the outside world about events in Zanzibar must have discouraged all but the most adventurous of tourists. In November, for example, many people, perhaps hundreds, were rounded up on the basis of unsubstantiated reports of a plot to overthrow the government. From several sources, we heard that some of those detained had been tortured. The government announced that five men had been executed and nine others sentenced to prison terms. From a variety of sources, we had reports indicating that the number of people put to death far exceeded five.

On October 29, the United Republic of Tanganyika and Zanzibar was officially renamed the United Republic of Tanzania. *Tanzania* had been chosen following a nationwide contest to pick a new name for the country.

The first major problem that the United States had with Tanzania was not with the troublesome Zanzibar but with the mainland. In November, Foreign Minister Oscar Kambona released a series of documents that he said were proof that the United States, in league with Portugal, was plotting to overthrow the Tanzanian government. Nyerere had received the documents from his ambassador to the Congo and passed them on to Kambona, asking him to make them public. Kambona's announcement was followed by publication of the documents in TANU's newspaper, the *Nationalist*. Kambona made a series of statements denouncing the alleged plot as an example of American imperialism. All this unleashed a surge of anti-Americanism throughout much of Tanzania. Nyerere's and Kambona's rush to judgment was a mistake, for it soon became clear that the documents were phonies. A document authentication expert from Washington showed the Tanzanians that the documents in question contained more than fifty errors—obvious and in part crude forgeries.

The readiness to believe the worst of the United States had made the Tanzanians look foolish and should have been deeply embarrassing to Nyerere. He expressed regrets to Ambassador Leonhart but, possibly to avoid laying any public blame on Kambona, stopped short of formally apologizing. Nyerere's refusal publicly to exonerate the United States tarnished his reputation within the U.S. government, although it would still be years before his mystique would be permanently and deeply eroded.

It was not this issue, however, that caused grief for us in Zanzibar that November. In the Congo, rebels who had seized Stanleyville (later renamed Kisangani) were holding hostage between 1,500 and 2,000 whites, many of them missionaries and teachers. Most of the captives were Belgians, but they included a significant number of Americans and other nationalities. In a rescue operation, Belgian paratroopers were flown to the city by American air force aircraft. Some sixty of the hostages, including Dr. Paul Carlson, a well-known American mission-

ary, were killed, but all the rest were freed, and Stanleyville was captured.

Nyerere, typically, reacted emotionally. Noting that the Organization of African Unity had been negotiating for a cease-fire in Stanleyville, he went too far in equating the rescue mission with the Japanese attack on Pearl Harbor. But in comparing the West's lack of concern about the killing of many Africans by Tshombe's white mercenaries with its action to save a relatively small number of whites, Nyerere made a valid criticism. He and other African leaders were chagrined at the ease with which Western powers could intervene in Africa.

Considering Nyerere's condemnation and the criticism throughout Africa and other parts of the Third World of the U.S. government's Congo policy, another government-organized anti-American demonstration in Zanzibar Town came as no surprise. This time, Frank and I, in a less than astute move, decided on the spur of the moment to go outside the consulate to view the procession. We may have believed we could talk to leaders of the demonstration. The officer in charge of the policemen who were keeping the demonstrators at a distance from our building was not happy to see us.

We had been outside for only a few moments when, catching sight of us, the marchers suddenly took on the attitude of a mob and began to surge toward us . The officer yelled at us to get back inside. A couple of rocks flew by. We needed no further advice and reentered the building. Our coworkers, who had thought we were crazy to go out, had "we told you so" looks on their faces but were relieved to see us back unharmed.

The United States was fair game for pro-Communist propagandists once more. This latest campaign continued into December. The Afro-Shirazi Youth League issued a denunciation of American policy in the Congo. It had the earmarks of having been written by the Chinese. Referring to a recent statement by Mao Tse-tung vilifying American participation in the Stanleyville rescue mission, the Youth League said:

> Chairman Mao Tse-tung, the great beloved leader of the Chinese people, has taken very seriously the armed aggression by U.S. imperialism against

Carlucci and Petterson (hidden by demonstrators)

the Congolese people. . . . He stated the voice of the 650 million Chinese people against U.S. villainies in the Congo Leopoldville. . . . Thus U.S. imperialism has been shaken to the core. . . . The peoples of Africa, Asia, Latin America and the whole world will unite and totally defeat the most evil force of oppression and exploitation of man by man—imperialism headed by the United States.

At a Youth League seminar a few days later, Twala, now Zanzibar's finance minister, said Zanzibaris should know that their enemies were Great Britain, the United States, and West Germany. Seif Bakari declared that the United States was "the worst enemy of mankind." The pro-Communists, who did not agree at all with Karume's policy of non-alignment, were taking full advantage of the Congo affair to get their licks in against us. Karume may have been unaware of the extent and nature of some of the vituperation, or he may have believed that he should let the pro-Communist Youth Leaguers have their say on the Congo issue. In any event, the anti-American outburst soon largely subsided.

Which is not to say that the overall atmosphere was getting a lot better for us. Frank alluded to this in a letter to the State Department's desk officer for Zanzibar, John Meagher: "Life in Zanzibar in many respects is close to what I understand it is in an iron curtain country. Although I am not followed, our telephones are tapped, my movements are reported on and our consulate is watched at night. Virtually all Zanzibaris are afraid to have contact with us."

14

⚛

Déjà Vu

The curse of man, and the cause of nearly all his woe, is his stupendous capacity for believing the incredible

—H. L. Mencken

We made too many wrong mistakes.

—Yogi Berra

"But I am not guilty," said K.; "it's a misunderstanding."

—Franz Kafka, The Trial

Julie and I enjoyed our second Christmas in Zanzibar. The hot *kaskazi* northeast wind of the monsoon was blowing, but we were used to the island's heat and humidity and not bothered by the change in the weather. Nineteenth-century European residents of Zanzibar had described Zanzibar's weather as enervating; they would spend the middle of the day indoors and inactive, more or less prostrated by the heat. The climate then was no different from the 1960s. But dressed as they were in heavy woolen garments totally unsuitable for the sultry weather, and lacking either overhead fans powered by electricity or air-conditioning, it is no wonder that the Europeans were so affected by it.

Julie, Susan, and Julianne

We continued to take great delight in our two daughters: Susie was old enough to show pleasure over the doll she got for Christmas; Julianne was now walking and expanding her vocabulary. We visited with our friends and capped the holiday season with a New Year's party at Brian and Frances Banks's. Frank and I had reason to believe we had made some progress in furthering U.S. interests in Zanzibar. Everyone seemed to be in good spirits, looking forward to 1965.

Frank and I were fighting a battle. The enemies were middle-level bureaucrats in USAID and the Department of State's Bureau of Educational and Cultural Affairs (or CU, as it was labeled in the State Department). Working with USAID officers from the embassy in Dar es Salaam who came over from time to time to consult on the school project, Frank had made progress in overcoming the objections to it from within USAID in Washington.

The problem with CU arose when the consulate nominated Aboud Jumbe to be invited to visit the United States. CU administered U.S.

government–funded scholarships awarded to foreign students to study at American universities and a visitor program that brought people from various walks of life to the United States, primarily to expose them to what America was all about—both its good and its not-so-good features. It was a highly successful program that gave visitors a chance to make their own judgments about the United States after having seen it instead of relying on hostile views put forth by governments and individuals antagonistic toward American values and institutions.

Frank was disappointed when CU turned down our recommendation on Jumbe. We had recently sent a report to Washington about the many Zanzibaris who were going to Communist countries on scholarships and visitor programs. In a letter to John Meagher, Frank said he hoped the report would help Meagher "in doing battle with CU." He added: "Quite honestly, to arouse the interest of any Zanzibar official in visiting the United States is such a major breakthrough that I find it incredible that CU should balk at the Jumbe visit." We could figure only that in CU, as in USAID, there were officials who regarded Zanzibar as virtually a Communist country and did not want anything to do with it.

Together with Bob Gordon, the deputy chief of mission at the embassy in Dar es Salaam, Frank was involved in another battle of sorts concerning a matter of protocol. It all started when Frank sent a cable to Ambassador Leonhart in December suggesting that President Johnson send a congratulatory message to President Karume on January 12, the first anniversary of the revolution. He believed Karume would see this as another sign that Washington was not hostile toward him.

Leonhart responded negatively. He believed any greeting from President Johnson should be limited to a message to President Nyerere commemorating Tanganyika's independence day, December 9. Carlucci suggested as an alternative for Zanzibar a message from Vice President Humphrey to Karume. Leonhart did not like this idea either.

In a telex message to Gordon on January 6, Carlucci informed him that Zanzibar's January 12 revolution-day celebration had been postponed until February 12 because January 12 fell within the Muslim month of fasting, Ramadan. Frank reasoned that official congratulations would be appropriate for the later date.

Frank went to Dar es Salaam on January 9 and while there discussed the matter further with Gordon. From their talk, he got the impression that the U.S. government would send a message to Karume on February 12. Accordingly, in his personal message to the Zanzibari president, which he sent to Karume on January 11, Frank said U.S. official congratulations would be sent in February. It turned out, however, that he had jumped the gun.

Later that same day, after talking with an official of the British high commission in Dar es Salaam, Gordon sent a cable to Frank telling him that the British would probably *not* send a second message on February 12. They would reconsider, Gordon said, only if heads of state of many British Commonwealth countries sent messages to Karume.

That night, still faced with the task of convincing Leonhart and the State Department to send an official message to Karume on February 12, Frank called Bob Gordon. Aware that the telephone lines at either end could be tapped, the two men spoke in a manner—improvising code words, for example—to disguise the meaning of their conversation. Frank conveyed to Gordon that he believed the British decision not to send a message to Karume for the February 12 celebration would not be right for the United States under the circumstances. He referred to his commitment to Karume.

Replying, Gordon indicated that he did not know what he should recommend to Ambassador Leonhart or what the State Department would agree to for the "second twelfth" because a lot would depend on what the Commonwealth countries would decide to do. Continuing to use code words, he conveyed to Carlucci that the ambassador had been thinking about a message from Assistant Secretary of State Soapy Williams if one were to be sent to Karume. Gordon judged that this would be an appropriate level, but Carlucci favored getting someone at a higher level in the government to sign off on the message.

The essence of what Gordon said next was that if on the next day, January 12, many high-level messages were delivered to Karume, then Gordon and Carlucci might have the ammunition necessary to persuade the ambassador and the State Department that a high-level message from the U.S. government should be delivered on the "second twelfth." Just

how Gordon conveyed this speaking elliptically is not precisely known, but he did use the words *ammunition* and *delivery*. He or Frank, or both of them, may have referred to Williams or a higher-level official as "the big gun."

When Frank heard the word *ammunition,* he told me years later, "a bell went off in my head." He realized that what he and Gordon were saying could be misconstrued if, as was likely, someone was listening. The use of code words, he said to me, "was the dumbest thing I ever did."

He told Gordon that they should meet again in Dar es Salaam. On the fifteenth, he caught the East African Airways flight to the Tanzanian capital.

Ambassador Leonhart was called to State House that same afternoon. Nyerere received him in his office. With Nyerere were Second Vice President Rashidi Kawawa and Secretary to the Cabinet J. A. Namata.

Nyerere was somber. He said that the Tanzanian government had clear and certain evidence that Consul General Carlucci and Deputy Chief of Mission Gordon were plotting the armed overthrow of the government of Zanzibar. Nyerere said the plot involved contact with dissident Zanzibaris, a clandestine arms shipment, and an uprising on January 12, the anniversary of the Zanzibar revolution.

An incredulous Leonhart listened as Nyerere gave further details of the charges against Carlucci and Gordon. The operation, called the "Second Twelfth," misfired, Nyerere said, when Gordon was unable to arrange for the shipment of arms. Both men had been under surveillance for some weeks. Kawawa had brought final proof of the plot to Nyerere on the fourteenth, when the president returned to Dar es Salaam from a meeting with Kenyatta and Obote in Nairobi. The evidence indicated that Gordon and Carlucci were operating on their own, without the knowledge or approval of Washington or the embassy in Dar es Salaam. Nyerere said his information showed that they intended to bypass Leonhart and to seek approval at the last moment from Assistant Secretary Williams. The Tanzanians seemed to believe that the use of the phrase *the second twelfth* was particularly damning.

Leonhart was astonished. How could Nyerere, who had been burned only two months earlier, when he had at first believed the authenticity of the forged documents alleging a U.S. plot, be taken in again by such an unbelievable accusation? Leonhart told Nyerere, Kawawa, and Namata that the charges were fantastic and mistaken. He asked to see any evidence bearing on them. Nyerere answered that Leonhart had only to question Gordon and Carlucci using the information he had just provided. They would know that the Tanzanian government had the full facts and would acknowledge their guilt.

Continuing to remonstrate, the ambassador told the three Tanzanians he was confident that the charges rested on serious misunderstandings and that Gordon and Carlucci would certainly deny the false allegations. He offered to bring both to Nyerere or Kawawa for a face-to-face meeting. Nyerere refused to see either of them. When Leonhart continued to press for further details or the nature of the evidence, Nyerere said he could not provide anything further without compromising Tanzanian intelligence sources. He said he was confident that the CIA would advise President Johnson that the charges were true.

Leonhart appealed to Nyerere to reconsider. He said that apart from an injustice to two fine officers who had his full faith and confidence, the way the Tanzanians were handling the affair could have a grave effect on U.S.-Tanzanian relations.

He would have been angered and appalled had he known how much worse the Tanzanians were about to make the situation. At the same time that he was talking with Nyerere—and before he could have a chance to look into the facts and present the U.S. government's side of the story— the Tanzanian government was announcing publicly that Nyerere had called Leonhart in and demanded that Gordon and Carlucci leave the country. The story was carried on the radio then, and it appeared in the press the next day.

In response to Leonhart's restated appeal that he reconsider, Nyerere said emotionally that because of the false allegations that had been made against the United States in November and the resulting strain in U.S.-Tanzanian relations, and his appreciation of the restraint that Washington had shown, neither he nor his government would have made the decision

on this matter without overwhelming proof. He and his closest advisers had met throughout the day and had no alternative but to request that the two Americans leave Tanzania within twenty-four hours.

Leonhart continued to argue, emphasizing the seriousness of the step Nyerere was taking and asking for an extension of the twenty-four hours. This would allow the U.S. government to comment and give Nyerere the chance to reconsider in light of what he would hear then. Nyerere said it was impossible for him to reconsider. The two would have to leave. It would not be safe for Carlucci to remain in Zanzibar longer, inasmuch as information about him and Gordon was now widely known, Nyerere claimed.

Returning to the embassy, Leonhart met with Gordon, who, Leonhart reported to Washington, "completely and categorically denies any foundation whatever for charges." The reference to the "second twelfth" made it clear that the accusation stemmed from a wiretap of the January 11 telephone conversation between Gordon and Carlucci. In his cable, Leonhart said that the two men had been framed and that it was obvious Nyerere had been duped again.

In the meantime, Frank was with embassy political officer Jack Mower at Mower's house that afternoon. They were listening to the radio when the startling news of the demand for Frank's and Bob's expulsions was announced. Frank called the embassy, talked to Leonhart, and rushed over to see him.

When he got there, he joined Leonhart and Gordon. The three of them went over all the exchanges between Carlucci and Gordon and between the embassy, consulate, and State Department on the question of the congratulatory message. This further cemented Leonhart's conviction that the Tanzanians had blundered, drawing an incorrect conclusion from the content of the January 11 telephone conversation.

In a cable to Washington, Leonhart said he knew that, in view of the repeated news broadcasts about the expulsions, the possibility that Nyerere would change his mind was "negligible." Nevertheless, he determined to try one last time to give the Tanzanian leader an opportunity to remedy the injustice to the two officers and limit further damage to U.S.-Tanzanian relations. He called State House and asked to see Nyerere again. An appointment was set for that night.

He was back in Nyerere's office at eight-thirty. Cabinet Secretary Namata was with the president. The ambassador related to them what he had learned, showed them copies of the cables and the telex messages, and gave them, as he told Washington, "categorical assurances" that there was "nothing whatever to 'second twelfth' except concern for appropriate protocol."

Leonhart told Washington that Nyerere, "now nervous, agitated, stammered, finally said this was plausible story which Washington might accept, but he could not." Nyerere insisted that there was too much other evidence against Gordon and Carlucci. He sat silently after Leonhart pressed him to give him the substance of this other information.

Namata broke the silence. He said the Tanzanians had evidence that Gordon and Carlucci had discussed clandestine ship movements and the unloading of munitions before January 12. When Leonhart asked whether this alleged exchange between the two had been written or verbal, Namata declined to answer. Nyerere then spoke up to state that the explanation that Leonhart had offered was incompatible with what his government knew about plans that were under way on Zanzibar for an armed revolt. He said the Tanzanians had sufficient evidence regarding individuals and sites involved to link Gordon and Carlucci with the plot.

After more discussion, Nyerere said he had confidence in the U.S. government and the embassy; he was convinced that the two officers were acting on their own. Because he had to protect national security, he could offer no further details. He understood and regretted the seriousness of the matter but could not change the decision that had been made.

Because it was clear even before this meeting that there was virtually no hope that the expulsion order would be dropped, arrangements for Frank and Bob to leave for Washington had been made. Frank would have to wait in Dar es Salaam until the following morning to catch the regular flight to Zanzibar so he could help Jean pack and also see Karume before leaving for the United States.

That night, Julie and I were having a small dinner party at home for a few friends. None of us had happened to listen to the radio that afternoon or evening. We were at the table when, at about eight, the phone

rang. It was Frank calling from Dar es Salaam. He told me what had happened and said he would be returning the next day to pack and leave. He had called Jean just before calling me.

I was stunned. I understood what Frank was saying but found it hard to accept. He did not give me much detail, but later when he did, I wondered how the Tanzanians could be so foolish as to believe that two American officials would, on their own, concoct some crazy counter-revolutionary plan, be able—again, on their own—to get the military resources to carry it out, and discuss the plan on an open telephone line.

It was probable that one of the Communist intelligence services, perhaps one that had provided expertise for tapping the phone line, had taped the Carlucci-Gordon phone call. There is no reason to doubt that someone edited portions of the tape to take out material that would tend to reveal the true nature of the discussion and whose deletion would make the remaining words as damning as possible.

A story about Tanzania in the January 1, 1965, issue of *Time* magazine could have contributed to Frank's expulsion. The *Time* article, written in a smarmy style and replete with inaccuracies, featured a visit by Nyerere to the island. Both Nyerere and Karume were made to appear somewhat ridiculous. If they read the piece, they no doubt would have been annoyed. In a letter to Meagher just after the article appeared, Frank had commented: "I thought I had explained to [correspondent Peter] Forbath of Time Magazine the need for responsible reporting on Zanzibar, but the article appearing in the January first issue which was probably rewritten by the desk back in the United States was a disaster. It probably set our efforts back by many months."

The article noted that when Nyerere and Karume spoke in Swahili, Frank answered in kind while GDR ambassador Guenther Fritsch ("wincing behind his sunglasses") needed an interpreter. It also made an unflattering comparison between the GDR housing project and the American technical-school project. In doing so, it portrayed Frank very favorably and made the East Germans look like idiots. There was belief at the time that the piece in *Time* infuriated the East Germans and Zanzibari pro-Communists as well, possibly adding to their determination somehow to vanquish Frank Carlucci.

At ten-thirty the next morning, the sixteenth, shortly after he arrived back in Zanzibar, Frank met with Karume at State House. We had had no difficulty getting the appointment on short notice. Frank told Karume he was leaving that afternoon but before going wanted to tell him that the accusations against him and Gordon were "lies and utter nonsense." Karume nodded sympathetically. He said the allegations and the evidence behind them had come from Tanganyika; he had nothing to do with it and was consulted about it only a few hours before the action was taken.

Frank outlined the details of his telephone conversation with Bob Gordon. He reminded Karume of the letter of personal congratulations that he had sent to him on January 12 and said he was sure Karume could understand his desire that another letter be sent on February 12. Surely, he said, Karume would not think that if he opposed the government of Zanzibar he would be so foolish as to discuss it over a telephone line he knew was tapped. Karume agreed.

By releasing the news to the media at the same time he was talking to Ambassador Leonhart, Frank told Karume, Nyerere had eliminated an opportunity for the Americans to defend themselves. That and Nyerere's refusal to show the evidence were, Frank said, grossly unfair.

Karume seemed surprised and asked for details of the timing of the news release. After they talked some more, he repeated that this affair was not his doing. He said he would be willing to travel to Dar es Salaam to intercede with Nyerere if the United States could convince Nyerere to accept a statement by the American secretary of state that no plot existed. In the cable he sent reporting the conversation, Frank said he and Karume "parted on very cordial terms."

All the staff of the consulate, our families, and other friends of the Carluccis went to the airport late that afternoon to see Frank, Jean, and the children off. Their flight departed at 5:15. I went to the consulate and sent a telegram to Washington and Dar es Salaam informing them of the departure. I reported that there had been no hostile acts against Americans, and no indications of possible violence to the consulate or to

American homes. I said that in view of the "calm situation here and Karume's conversation with Carlucci, I doubt we will have trouble."

The story continued to play out in Dar es Salaam. That afternoon, Leonhart went to see Nyerere again. He delivered a letter from Secretary of State Dean Rusk to President Nyerere. In his letter, Rusk asked for the information on which the allegations of subversive activity was based. He proposed a joint U.S.-Tanzanian examination of the relevant information, which he said would demonstrate the falsity of the charges. Rusk expressed astonishment at the ultimatum on the expulsion and distress at the simultaneous press release. He asked that the ultimatum be suspended, pointed out the harm that insistence on immediate departure of the two officers would inevitably have on U.S.-Tanzanian relations, and said, "such action could only be viewed by the United States as unfriendly."

Nyerere was shaken by what he read. He said he could only ask Leonhart to inform Secretary Rusk that he appreciated the seriousness of the affair but could not alter his decision, for he was "in an impossible dilemma."

Leonhart told Nyerere of Karume's statement to Carlucci that he would be willing to come to Dar es Salaam to reopen the matter. By this time, Nyerere was weeping. He said, almost inaudibly, that Karume could not help; neither of them could change the decision.

The ambassador implored Nyerere to take a straightforward action to resolve the problem. He asked him to consider carefully the consequences for U.S.-Tanzanian relations. He recalled how Nyerere had expressed thanks for the restrained manner in which the U.S. government had reacted to the false accusations the Tanzanians had made against the United States in November.

Nyerere responded, "This is one more damn period we've just got to get through." Leonhart closed the conversation by saying that with all the goodwill in the world, the Americans could not try to help Nyerere unless he tried to help himself.

The publicity that the Tanzanian authorities had given to the accusation that U.S. officials had plotted to overthrow the Zanzibar government worried Washington. There was concern that it could lead to vio-

lence against Americans on the island and on the mainland. The Defense Department agreed to a State Department request to alert a United States Navy destroyer at Madagascar, other U.S. vessels in the eastern Indian Ocean, and all nearby U.S. government aircraft to stand by for a possible evacuation of U.S. nationals in Zanzibar or Tanganyika. When nothing happened after a couple of days, the alert was withdrawn.

On February 1, Ambassador Leonhart and his wife departed Dar for Washington. The Johnson administration had, in reaction to the expulsion of Carlucci and Gordon, recalled him to Washington for consultations. In addition, it expelled a diplomat from the Tanzanian embassy in Washington. In a show of support for Leonhart and the U.S. government, more than 150 Americans and the heads of Western embassies were at the airport to see the Leonharts off. After six weeks and an exchange of letters between Presidents Johnson and Nyerere, the ambassador returned to Dar es Salaam.

Nyerere would head the Tanzanian government for another two decades. Relations between him and the U.S. government would never again be as warm as they had been before his ill-considered decision to expel Frank Carlucci and Bob Gordon. This was not, to be sure, the only reason for the change, but it was a major element and perhaps the turning point in the relationship.

As for the putative plan by dissident Zanzibaris for an armed revolt following arrival of a clandestine arms shipment, this was as untrue as the allegations against Frank and Bob. Neither the shipment nor the plan was ever brought to light. There was no public revelation of the plan, and no arrests of suspected dissidents.

For the second time, I found myself, still a junior officer, in charge of the post. January 16 was, within a day, exactly one year since Fritz Picard had been expelled from Zanzibar. And now, under different circum-

stances, Frank was compelled to leave. It was a blow to us at the consulate, for we knew how much his abilities and his leadership had meant to us. Of all of us, I had worked most closely with him and would be the most affected professionally by his departure. But my unhappiness stem-

med more from the injustice that had been done to someone whose friendship I valued highly.

Taking over as head of the post was quite a different matter this time than it had been a year earlier. Then I was the only American. I had no means of communicating, except by telephone. I had no management issues to contend with, no responsibilities outside of trying to find out what was going on, report as best I could, and do as much as possible to look after American properties. Now I was in charge of a consulate staff of about ten Americans and twice that many Zanzibari employees. The issues we had to deal with were more multifaceted and required managerial as well as political decisions. Although I was still wet behind the ears as an executive, I had one thing going for me: I had learned a lot from Frank.

The next morning, I went to State House to deliver a farewell letter Frank had written to Karume. I told him I was very distressed by the events of the previous two days. He replied in kind. The charges against Frank, I said, were absolutely false. Responding, Karume repeated the substance of what Frank had told him about the evidence and made it clear he agreed that nobody in their right mind would have discussed a plot over the telephone.

Karume said he was sure of America's friendship. He said he believed that after the U.S. and Tanzanian governments exchanged intelligence-information reports and a report by Carlucci and Gordon, the problem could be resolved favorably. Tempers were high now, and it was best to wait until reason prevailed before making decisions that could affect bilateral relations. Continuing in a reasonable vein, Karume asked rhetorically, "Does the United States want to reimpose Arab slavery on Africans?" then answered his own question: "Of course not; there could be no possible reason for this, no benefit for the U.S. government." He spoke of his belief in U.S. goodwill for himself and Zanzibar.

I brought up the safety of Americans and American property, pointing out that those in Zanzibar who disliked the U.S. government might seize the opportunity to cause trouble. He assured me that nobody would do anything against any American. As I took my leave, he warmly said his friendship with Frank extended to me, and he invited me to come see him whenever I wished.

Karume's reaction to the expulsion and his words to both Frank and me led me to think that things for us Americans on the island would fall into place without much disruption, that we could begin to breathe more or less easily again.

Two days later, I had a call from State House. President Karume wanted to see me. Because I would be going to State House, I attached the metal flagstaff with its small American flag to the car, which I still considered Frank's car. The drive there took only about a minute. Karume received me in his office. Although he greeted me in friendly-enough fashion, he looked solemn. What, I wondered, now?

He said he was sorry to have to tell me that one of the consulate's officers had been guilty of inappropriate behavior. Without mentioning Harry Radday's name, Karume said the USIS officer had been seeing the wrong kind of people, people who were not friendly toward the revolution, and he had been saying some hostile things about the Zanzibar government. He would have to leave Zanzibar.

I said I was deeply sorry to hear what he had told me. I could not believe that Harry Radday was guilty of any of the charges against him. He was a highly competent officer who had no animus against the government and who was carrying out his responsibilities in a wholly professional way. We had just been through the business with Frank Carlucci that had involved untrue, fabricated allegations. Were we going to have this happen again? I asked Karume to reconsider his decision.

He replied that the decision was made by the Revolutionary Council and could not be changed. He went on to say that the matter would be kept quiet; there would be no publicity whatsoever. He added that he would not press the issue; he would not insist that Radday leave right away. I repeated that Radday had done no wrong. I told Karume I would inform Washington and get back to him.

At a USIS public affairs officers' conference in Zambia, Harry had been astounded to hear the news of the Carlucci-Gordon expulsion. He had just returned from there, and when I went to see him, he asked, "What happened to Frank?"

"Harry," I said, "I'm afraid I've got some bad news for you."

He was dumbfounded by Karume's accusation. He said the charges were totally untrue and made no sense at all. We could conclude only that Karume, like Nyerere, had been duped by manufactured false-intelligence reports. I was convinced that the order to expel Harry came about because he was highly, and visibly, effective in meeting a wide range of Zanzibaris and providing them with a source of information other than the steady diet of propaganda they received from their own government.

After Harry, Kent Crane, and I had talked things over, I sent a cable to Washington and Dar es Salaam recommending that Harry's withdrawal be delayed until February 15 at the earliest. I explained that some Zanzibaris could construe an earlier departure as being linked to the expulsion of Carlucci and Gordon. I said that this could add to perceptions that the United States was working against the government of Zanzibar.

Noting that Karume was not demanding urgent action by us, I suggested that I tell him that, although the U.S. government did not believe Radday was guilty of any indiscretion, in deference to Karume's wish, we would withdraw him. I would then request that Harry's departure be delayed until about February 15 to avoid a hardship for him and his family and allow sufficient time for a replacement to be found.

After the State Department agreed to this suggestion, I went to see Karume again, on January 26. He was in general agreement with the proposal but said he wanted the withdrawal to take place sooner. After more discussion on the timing, he said he would allow Radday to remain for one week after the Zanzibar government received an official response from Washington.

A week earlier, the Zanzibaris had put a ban on the entry of American officials. I brought this up with Karume and protested. He indicated that the ban had been imposed for security reasons but said he would have it lifted. I asked whether his permission for us to move the library still held. He said it did. He turned down my request for particulars of the charges against Radday, telling me that to give them would compromise security measures taken by his government.

The State Department's take on the Radday expulsion reached us on January 28 while I was visiting the embassy in Dar es Salaam. I was told to express to Karume appreciation for the quiet manner in which the affair had been handled. I was to reiterate, however, that the U.S. government did not believe the accusation was true. Washington was aware of some of the problems Karume faced, but if the good relations that had been built over the past several months were to continue, they had to be "fostered in an atmosphere of mutual trust and confidence." We considered him a friend, but "normal practice among friends is to provide some evidence to support allegations as serious as those he had made in the Radday case."

I had flown to Dar that day to discuss the Radday situation with Ambassador Leonhart. I told him that a delay of more than several more days might make Karume suspicious and cause him to handle the matter in a less circumspect way. Leonhart sent a cable to Washington suggesting that I see Karume again about February 3 and give him Washington's concurrence for Radday's departure about February 10.

Carl Rowan, the director of the United States Information Agency (USIA), the parent organization of USIS missions abroad, was not pleased with the way the Radday affair was being handled. He questioned whether it was in the interest of the United States to withdraw Radday quietly. A meek withdrawal, Rowan believed, would be inconsistent with the sharp attitude we had taken concerning Gordon and Carlucci. He also said that a compliant acquiescence would offer only a thin hope of keeping Karume friendly toward us. Rowan did not believe there was any realistic hope of keeping the matter quiet. A cable from Washington on the first of February said USIA was convinced that the Radday withdrawal could have adverse psychological repercussions in Tanzania and elsewhere in Africa. Furthermore, it would increase the suspicions of the United States that existed following the Gordon-Carlucci expulsion and the earlier forged-document affair.

It seemed to me that USIA was piqued that the administration was not making a fight for a USIS officer as it had done for State officers. I saw no reason that Radday's withdrawal could not be kept quiet. And in my

view, USIA's case that the withdrawal would have widespread repercussions was much overdrawn.

The cable continued that USIA believed I should be asked to attempt to persuade Karume to hold off for a few weeks until he could talk to Rowan, who would be visiting the area at that time. Because of Karume's strong feelings about Radday, I doubted that an attempt to get a delay would succeed. However, I tried out the suggestion on Karume, and, to my surprise, he agreed to it.

We went ahead with the quiet withdrawal in mid-March, when Harry, Ellen, and their two children left on a ship that took them to Greece en route to the United States. Harry's departure attracted no undue attention, received no mention in the media, and had no repercussions in Zanzibar or elsewhere.

The February 12 celebration of the revolution was reminiscent of the previous year's May Day celebration, with a parade of the People's Liberation Army and squads of marchers representing workers and various organizations. I sat behind Karume and his most notable guest, the famous Cuban revolutionary, Che Guevara, at the football stadium during a bullfight. Part of Zanzibar's and Pemba's Portuguese heritage was retention in Pemba of a form of bullfighting. Its main difference from traditional bullfighting was that a long, thick rope was tied around the bull, and when he got too close to the bullfighter, men on the other end of the rope prevented him from doing any damage. It may have been tame by bullfighting standards, but nobody got hurt, including the bull, which was not dispatched at the end of the "fight."

Guevara was at the State Ball that night. At one point, he said hello to Julie and was delighted when she responded in Spanish. He asked her where she was from, and when she told him, he said, "That's nice, a girl from Mexico. What are you doing here?"

"My husband is the American consul," she answered. Guevara's mouth dropped open; he stared for a moment, then without further word turned around and walked away.

In April, Harry's successor arrived. Barney Coleman, a gregarious man of about forty, tried to pick up where Harry had left off. He had been an effective and popular USIS officer at his previous post, Lagos. The USIS program continued to be a successful means of countering the Communist propaganda campaign against the West in general and the United States in particular. But within several months, Barney was gone.

Once again, the Zanzibar government accused our USIS officer of inappropriate behavior. In early August, we received word from a reliable source that pro-Communists in the Afro-Shirazi Youth League were peddling vicious rumors that Coleman was a spy whose USIS work was aimed at luring people into his office for questioning on intelligence matters. Worse, the smear alleged that Barney was a sexual deviate who had ulterior motives in attracting the large number of children who flocked to the library.

In what had become a familiar routine, I went to Karume, and Leonhart took the matter up with Nyerere. Nyerere made sympathetic noises but said it was a Zanzibar matter that Karume would have to settle. Karume, for his part, listened attentively but made no commitment to act in Barney's favor. Soon afterward, Karume told me that under the circumstances, it would be best if Coleman were withdrawn.

Like Radday's, Coleman's departure was done without fanfare. It seems likely that in both cases, one of the Communist missions, with the willing help of pro-Communist Zanzibaris, concocted bogus information and had it presented to Karume. That Karume and others who were not antagonistic toward the United States were taken in by the fraud indicates that the Communists had created clever pieces of misinformation.

I believe that Radday and Coleman were targeted because the Communists despised USIS. The USIS library, with its film shows and stock of books and periodicals, attracted young Zanzibaris; scholarships to American schools were highly sought after; and visitor programs were also popular. USIS provided people with a window to the outside, Western, world that gave them a view that was far different from that which was portrayed by Communist propaganda. The Communists in Zanzibar did not like the competition.

15

⤬

Kwaheri

Revolution: in politics, an abrupt change in the form of misgovernment.

—Ambrose Bierce

Revolutions have never lightened the burden of tyranny: they have only shifted it to another shoulder.

—George Bernard Shaw

I thought my two-year assignment would be finished in July. However, although a replacement for Frank had been picked, mine would not be available until about the end of the year. Because of that and since my next assignment was uncertain, in March the State Department extended my tour of duty to November. I was also informed that I would be elevated in title to consul from acting consul and remain in charge even after Frank's successor arrived. Maybe the department felt they owed me that much, or perhaps the African Bureau and Personnel had decided that, in view of the expulsion of my previous two bosses, it would be tempting fate to provide me with another one.

In April, Thomas Pickering, his wife, Alice, and their two children came to Zanzibar. Tom would work with me until my assignment ended and then would take charge of the consulate. I had been told that Tom, who was working with the Arms Control and Disarmament Agency in Washington, was considered to be an FSO of great potential—an assessment that turned out to be wholly correct. I wondered how a high flyer like Tom, who had been in the Foreign Service longer than I and who outranked me, would take to working for several months as my second-in-command.

I soon knew that there would be no problem. Tall, good-humored, and extremely intelligent, Tom was generous to a fault and totally without any hang-up about outranking me but not being in charge. Within a short time, he assumed much of the reporting workload and picked up the bulk of the consular and administrative duties. Julie and I were happy to have Tom and Alice as our newest friends on the island.

Tom Pickering, like Frank Carlucci, would go on to have an extraordinary career with the U.S. government, serving as an ambassador to six countries and the United Nations in New York, and becoming, in 1997, under secretary of state for political affairs. Between 1964 and 1979, when it closed, the American consulate in Zanzibar produced no less than seven future ambassadors.[1] For a post that small, that was a remarkable record. I would not go so far as to say that an assignment to Zanzibar was a launching pad for successful careers in American diplomacy, but it certainly did not hurt.

I maintained a close relationship with Karume. We always spoke in Swahili when I met with him, and he patiently corrected my occasional errors or helped me find a word I was searching for. He had given me his direct phone number, and I used it now and then to bypass the bureaucratic phalanx that would normally have made it difficult or impossible for me to see him on short notice.

Much of what Tom and I reported in 1965 dealt with Karume's consolidation of his political power. More of those people whom he, or he and Nyerere, saw as potential dangers to Karume's hold on political power found themselves in jobs on the mainland. The ASP became entrenched, unfortunately, for like sole political parties in one-party

states everywhere, it would become both an expression of and a vehicle for political intolerance and, eventually, corruption.

Karume's growing strength, the moderation of ASP elders, the union with Tanganyika, and the limitations in education—and in some cases intelligence—of Revolutionary Council members combined to prevent the council from completely controlling the government. Nyerere and Karume probably agreed to keep the council in check but to move slowly so as to avoid the danger of a direct clash.

Although some of the council's wild men may have been shorn of political power, far abler and strongly pro-Communist council members remained in positions of high authority. And Karume continued to rely a great deal on their advice, while they in turn maintained close ties with foreign Communist diplomats and advisers. There was no lessening of the strong Communist influence over Zanzibar in 1965.

One result of that influence was a persistent belief by many in the government that the United States was backing a counterrevolution. In late June, Karume told me, "Some people think Americans are helping Arab counterrevolutionaries, but I do not believe this." In spite of repeated assurances of this kind, there were indications that Karume did indeed harbor suspicion of us. Some Revolutionary Council members appeared convinced that we were up to no good, and more than once, we learned, they called for the removal of the consulate from Zanzibar.

With even the moderates in Zanzibar now leaning more toward the East than the West, it was not surprising that pro-Communist and anti-American propaganda would continue to be seen in the press and heard on the radio. Karume interceded from time to time to inject some balance into the media output and the public pronouncements by pro-Communists. Speaking to members of youth organizations—the Young Pioneers and the Women's Army—one day, he warned them not to listen to those who said that certain foreign nations were bad. He pointed to the diplomatic representatives present and said the Americans, British, French, East Germans, and Chinese were all in Zanzibar to help the people of the islands. He declared they should be called *sheikhs*, a term he said was reserved for respected and important men.

In a speech he delivered in June, when Chou En-lai had visited Zanzibar, Karume emphasized the independence and nonalignment of Tanzania. Speaking several days later at British deputy high commissioner Jim Bourn's reception honoring the queen's birthday, the Zanzibari leader stressed Tanzanian nonalignment again.

A few months later, when anti-Americanism had become epidemic once more, I talked to Karume. Afro-Shirazi Youth League and Federation of Revolutionary Trade Unions officials had been condemning "American imperialism." I reminded him that inasmuch as the ASYL and FRTU were now integral units of the ASP, people might think that their public declarations had government approval. Karume replied that the statements were ridiculous and had been written "by fools." He said that because ASYL and FRTU leaders were getting money from the Chinese, they were prone to denounce the United States whenever an opportunity arose. He said there would be no repetition of what had happened. I knew, however, that he did not exercise close control over the pro-Communists, and I reported that unfavorable portrayals of the United States were not going to end.

Whatever Karume may have believed about the Americans, he seemed to have no doubt that a counterrevolutionary threat was real. He and others in his government believed that some of Zanzibar's Arabs who had left the island had gone somewhere in the Arab world, been trained, and returned to East Africa, principally Mombasa, where they were waiting until the time was right to come back in force to Zanzibar. The regime's fear of being overthrown was a cause of recurrent tension and persistent political instability. I reported that this fear had been "manifested by continued political arrests and searches of houses and cars by police looking for hidden weapons." A Zanzibari who had been released from prison told us that there were some two hundred political prisoners in Ziwani prison.

Karume's distrust of Othman Sharif did not abate. Some of Sharif's Shirazi followers came under suspicion, and some were imprisoned. Even though he was Tanzania's ambassador to the United States, Sharif was seized and imprisoned while he was home on a return visit to Zanzibar. No charges were lodged against him. Nyerere, once again dismayed by an

action taken by Karume, had to intervene several times before succeeding in getting Sharif released and returned to the mainland.

In the short run, Karume's concerns about security made him more reliant on the pro-Communists in the ASP. In the years to come, however, their political and ideological differences with him led him to suspect them of disloyalty. This would have fatal consequences for some of them, including Hanga and Twala.

The government's management of the economy did not go well, compounding Zanzibar's internal problems. Confiscation of property and strict controls on imports and exports added to the woes of the merchants, most of them Asians, who had already curtailed or entirely stopped bringing in goods because of the fear they would be confiscated. As more traders went out of business, the people they employed joined the growing ranks of the unemployed. Few if any of those who lost their jobs found new employment with the state trading corporation, Bizanje, which had only a small workforce.

With tourism all but nonexistent, those Zanzibaris who had previously been engaged in it remained out of work. The government had taken charge of the tourist trade, and the new bureaucracy was a study in ineptitude. Government controls and tourism just did not mix. Despite the tourism office's claim that increasing numbers of tourists were visiting Zanzibar, it was obvious to everyone that only a handful were coming to the island.

Clove harvesting was another source of employment adversely affected by Marxism in action. The government took over plantations but did a poor job of organizing for the harvest of the clove crop. And with a large surplus of cloves stored in a warehouse, the government was not interested in buying all the cloves that did get harvested.

The growth in unemployment and the government's unfulfilled promises about economic progress worried Zanzibari leaders, instilling fears that the government would lose popular support. This made them all the more prone to believe what they heard about dissident activities, adding to the political tension.

Given its political fears and economic woes, the government depended all the more on Communist aid. As the second anniversary of

the revolution approached, Zanzibaris were discovering that there was a big difference between the promise and the reality of Communist aid programs.

The Soviets supplied military hardware and advisers but no economic development projects. And although Zanzibar's share of the Soviet aid to Tanzania as a whole was spelled out in an aid agreement signed in 1964, none beyond the military assistance had materialized.

The Zanzibari leaders had been led to believe, or led themselves to believe, that the East Germans would provide housing for all of Zanzibar Town's 40,000 Africans. By late 1965, all that had been definitely promised were 150 two- or three-bedroom apartments. Construction was going very slowly, there were disagreements with the local labor force, and construction materials available in Zanzibar were brought from the GDR.

The Chinese shipped in large quantities of nonessential consumer goods. They bought copra from the Zanzibar government at a low price and sold it elsewhere for a profit. They imported high-priced, poor-quality rice. Like the East Germans, the Chinese tarnished their image with Karume and ASP moderates by their sometimes clumsy effort to proselytize Zanzibaris.

Whatever pleasure we might have taken at the discomfort the Communists might have been experiencing as a result of their mistakes was tempered by our knowledge that they had done a lot to repair their record. The Chinese gave a cash grant of 1 million pounds, which the Zanzibar government sorely needed and much appreciated. However meager the Chinese rice production was turning out to be, Zanzibar's leaders seemed favorably impressed by it. Additional Chinese medical personnel were expected to join those who were working at the hospital.

Soviet, as well as Chinese, military advisers continued to train Zanzibari soldiers. Both countries brought in more arms, equipment, and ammunition.

The East Germans tried harder on their housing construction. They brought in additional medical and other technicians and teachers and delivered an armed patrol boat and several small fishing boats.

All told, even though the Zanzibaris had expected more than they were getting, the Communist aid program was having a considerable impact. We had to accept that the Communists were going to continue to be present in relatively large numbers and exert a significant influence on the government of Zanzibar. This remained a matter of concern to Washington. However, the hysterical edge to American and British anxiety about what was happening in Zanzibar had pretty much dissipated when Zanzibar merged with Tanganyika.

Tom, Ambassador Leonhart, and I were in agreement that the United States should continue the low-key approach we had been following. Frank's advice that there was no point in trying to compete with the Communists' aid to Zanzibar was still sound. By going ahead with construction of the technical secondary school, we were demonstrating at a low cost our goodwill for Zanzibar and our support for Karume and the moderates in his government and the ASP.

The gap between form and substance of the union of the mainland and the island was apparent. The pro-Communists on the Revolutionary Council continued to oppose the union and did what they could to influence Karume and others to weaken if not scuttle it. Karume himself was reluctant to give up some of the powers of an independent state. But although some important union matters remained in fact outside the union government's control, significant cementing steps had been taken. A signal accomplishment was the integration of the police forces of Tanganyika and Zanzibar. Near the end of 1965, the first moves were made toward eventual amalgamation of the armies. Possibly the most cohesive element of the union was the union government's budgetary support for the government of Zanzibar.

Not long before I left Zanzibar, I wrote in a message to Washington that "if the pace of effecting a true union has been slow it has at the same time been steady." I said all indications were that the union would remain intact and commented, "In the long run, Zanzibar's future seems inextricably linked with mainland Tanzania."

In July, the birth of our third child was imminent. Despite the presence of the Chinese medical personnel at the V. I. Lenin Hospital, the quality of care, especially nursing, had deteriorated. Julie was advised to have the baby in Dar es Salaam. So, accompanied by her close friend Frances Banks, she flew there in early July. Mgeni, the children's *ayah,* took care of Susie and Julianne during the day, and I spent as much time as I could with them. John, our first son, was born on July 13. Julie was overjoyed to have a boy. I was used to the idea of having girls and thought I wanted another, but once I saw and held the new baby, I was very happy to have a son. (Our last child, Brian, was born fourteen years later, when we were in Somalia.)

In September, Julie and I took our first and only vacation during the more than two years we were in Zanzibar. We flew to Moshi in the northern highlands of Tanganyika. From there, we drove to Lake Manyara. Two days later, we drove to Ngorongoro Crater. In later years, we would visit the same area and also travel to other locations of African wildlife, but the four days we spent at Manyara and Ngorongoro are etched in our memories. After two years of the warm-to-hot and humid air of Zanzibar, we luxuriated in the dry highland weather—the days warm, the nights chilly enough to warrant a fire in the lodges' fireplaces.

Both places were teeming with game and very short on tourists; we and our guide, Daudi, saw only one other vehicle during each of the two days we were on the floor of the immense crater that encloses the Ngorongoro game park. Twenty-two years later, we found to our sadness that Manyara, in particular, had suffered from the effects of poor park management and drought. But our four days in 1965 were perfect, and we left with rolls of film capturing images of elephants, rhinos, lions, cheetahs, hippos, wildebeests, water buffalo, zebra, antelope of various kinds, and a profusion of bird life.

In October, Julie and the three little children departed for Mexico. To enable them to spend more time with her family in Mexico City, we decided that she and the kids would leave a month earlier than I. The large number of people who came to the airport to see her off and the emotional farewells showed how much our friends cared for her.

In mid-November, on the day that I departed, I went to State House to see Karume for the last time. Tom came with me. As usual, Karume

was friendly, and he told me I could leave Zanzibar knowing that I had helped improve relations between our two countries. I thanked him for the help he had given me, told him the United States respected his wish to pursue a policy of nonalignment, and reiterated that Washington wanted to maintain friendly relations with Zanzibar. I said that within his government, there were those who were working against that. I hoped he could do something to change the existing situation in which Zanzibaris were afraid to be seen with Americans.

Karume restated his friendship for the United States. He said he was not much concerned about those in the government who acted as if they disliked Americans. He explained that this was not their true belief but merely a show for their Communist friends. He said Africans reacted to deeds, not words, and if East Germans built houses for them, then East Germans were friends. Neither communism nor capitalism had meaning for Africans, who were just interested in achieving a better life for themselves. He wished me good luck.

It wouldn't have been Zanzibar if I didn't have a last bit of trouble before saying *kwaheri* (good-bye) to the island. An hour of so after meeting with Karume, I drove around town to take a few snapshots. Parking in front of State House, I took a picture of the old cannon on the lawn by the building. Immediately, three plainclothes security policemen rushed out of the entrance and demanded that I turn over my camera and film. A minute later, I was still arguing with them when a State House official came out and convinced them to drop the matter. It was not the dignified leave-taking I had anticipated.

Reunited in Mexico, Julie, the children, and I then went to California, where we spent most of December and a few days in January 1966. From there, we flew to Washington so I could make final arrangements for our onward travel. We were going to Nigeria. When I had stopped in Washington en route to Mexico, I had asked to go to the Congo, which I was sure would be an interesting assignment. But Charlie Whitehouse, the FSO who was responsible for my assignment, told me I had had enough excitement in Zanzibar. Referring to Frank, he said that if you put yourself into tight spots too often, then you probably pay a price. He also took note of my experience of being in charge of a post at such an

early stage in my career and concluded that I should get back into a more usual career pattern. He believed I should have the experience of being a political officer in a larger embassy and in a country that was stable. He chose for me the number-two political-officer slot in the three-person political section at the embassy in Lagos.

The airplane carrying us to our new post approached the airport at Lagos on the morning of January 15. As the plane entered the flight pattern, the pilot made an announcement. He said there had been a coup d'état, and the government seemed to be in the hands of the military. The airport had been seized by armed troops, and we might have a problem getting into town.

Epilogue

Revolutionary upheavals may change how the world looks but seldom change the way the world works.

—Richard Nixon

The concentrating [of powers] in the same hands is precisely the definition of despotic government.

—Thomas Jefferson

Abeid Amani Karume was assassinated while playing cards at the Afro-Shirazi headquarters building in April 1972. By the end of his reign, popular support for Karume had given way to fear; Zanzibar had become a police state. Employing his GDR-trained secret police—known as *panya* (rats)—Karume tolerated no opposition, no dissent. He dismissed Revolutionary Council members who did not see eye-to-eye with him, replacing them with more compliant men. He gained international attention briefly in 1970 when he forced Asian teenagers to marry Revolutionary Council members. I still find it hard to reconcile the man who had shown me many kindnesses and courtesies

while I was in Zanzibar with the sometimes-cruel despot who emerged during his eight-year reign.

Karume's oppressive ways generated plots to overthrow him. Among those accused of subversion were **Abdulla Kassim Hanga** and **Othman Sharif**. Hanga had been a minister in the union government. Stripped of his position in 1967, he was arrested in Dar and accused of trying to subvert military personnel. Released in 1969, he was rearrested, along with Sharif, who by then was a businessman in Dar. Nyerere, foolishly believing assurances that they would receive a fair trial, allowed them to be flown to Zanzibar, where they and two others were executed soon afterward. At some point, **Abdul Aziz Twala** was also executed.

Abdulrahman Mohamed Babu remained in the union government until 1972, when he was dropped from the cabinet. Following Karume's assassination, Babu was arrested and charged with planning to overthrow the government in Zanzibar. He was kept in prison for six years. Nyerere, knowing that Babu would be executed if he were returned to the island, refused to accede to requests by the Zanzibaris to have him sent there. After being freed, Babu went to the United States, lecturing and teaching at Amherst College. London became his home in 1984, and he lived there, teaching and doing freelance writing, until his death in 1996.

Aboud Jumbe conquered his drinking problem, succeeded Karume, and was president of Zanzibar and first vice president of Tanzania until 1984, when he resigned. During Jumbe's presidency, political repression was eased, and economic reforms were instituted. Initially much closer to Nyerere than Karume had been, Jumbe was agreeable to Nyerere's merger in 1977 of the ASP with Nyerere's TANU into a single party for all of Tanzania, the Chama Cha Mapinduzi (CCM) (Party of the Revolution). He was succeeded by an even more moderate politician, Ali Hassan Mwinyi, who was a strong believer in the union.

After a successful career with the mainland government, in 2001 **Adam Mwakanjuki** became minister of state in the office of the president of Zanzibar.

Julius Nyerere was reelected president of Tanzania several times. Perhaps because most Tanzanians continued to admire him, he would have been kept in office even if he had been opposed. But in Tanzania's one-party state, no other candidates were permitted, and Nyerere's reelection was a foregone conclusion.

His belief in the viability of a one-party democracy came under increasing criticism as his government degenerated into misrule and corruption.

Untainted by corruption himself—he lived simply and had no interest in the spoils of government—Nyerere was, however, responsible for stubbornly sticking to a failed statist economic policy and not rooting out the corruption it spawned. His legacy in the 1980s was an economy that could be labeled only a gigantic failure. Much of the economy's decline could be blamed on the deterioration of Tanzania's terms of trade. But the heart of the failure was an unworkable mixture of egalitarian social policies lacking popular support, cockeyed economic ideas (for example, an aversion to outside investment in Tanzania), a proliferation of parastatal organizations, and growth of a bloated, inefficient, and finally corrupt government bureaucracy.

Much to his credit, Nyerere voluntarily gave up the presidency in 1985. He kept the chairmanship of the Chama Cha Mapinduzi, however, for five more years and influenced the selection of his successor, Tanzania's first, and as yet only, Zanzibari president, Ali Hassan Mwinyi.

After relinquishing the CCM chairmanship in 1990, as a generally esteemed elder statesman, Nyerere continued to play a role in both Tanzanian and African affairs. He was instrumental in the selection of Mwinyi's successor, Tanzania's current president, Benjamin Mkapa. At the age of seventy-seven, Julius Nyerere died in late 1999.

By 1967, Nyerere had come to distrust **Oscar Kambona**. Although there was never any evidence that he was disloyal, Kambona had become increasingly dissatisfied with what he saw as his progressive marginalization in Tanzanian politics. After Kambona surreptitiously left the country and exiled himself and his family in the Netherlands, he and Nyerere became bitter enemies, exchanging vitriolic public denunciations.

One Zanzibari who can testify with authority that Nyerere had feet of clay is **Wolf Dourado**. The feisty lawyer of unquestioned integrity remained loyal to Zanzibar, serving its various governments until the 1990s, when he retired from public office. Because of his honesty and his outspokenness, Dourado was in and out of hot water at various times and was well acquainted with the inside of prison. At one point, his opposition to some of Nyerere's policies landed him in jail, and at others, it was his differences with the Zanzibar government that got him into trouble.

Judgments made about **Fritz Picard**'s actions during his time in Zanzibar severely damaged his Foreign Service career. He might have resurrected it, but he did not hit it off well with his superiors at the American embassy in Nigeria. Fritz had been assigned there in 1967; ironically, he replaced me as the number-two officer in the three-person political section. Unfortunately, he had not conquered his drinking problem. He left the service, worked for a charitable organization, then took a job with a large multinational company that sent him to Tehran. He died there in the mid-1970s.

Frank Carlucci was assigned to Brazil after he left Zanzibar. After his tour of duty there, Frank departed from the usual career path of an FSO, rising to become director of the Office of Economic Opportunity; deputy director of the Office of Management and Budget; under secretary of health, education, and welfare; ambassador to Portugal; deputy director of the CIA; deputy secretary of defense; assistant to the president for national security affairs; and secretary of defense. A highly successful businessman, he is a partner of Carlyle Associates.

Tom Pickering's career was also prestigious. Before he left the Foreign Service in 1997, Tom had been ambassador to Jordan, Nigeria, El Salvador, Israel, India, the United Nations, and Russia. Between his stints in Jordan and Nigeria, he was assistant secretary of state for oceans and international environmental and scientific affairs. Shortly after his retirement, he was asked to return to public life to take the post of under secretary of state for political affairs. In 2001, he became the Boeing Aircraft Company's senior vice president for international relations.

From the sea, the skyline had not changed. When we went ashore, Zanzibar Town appeared, at first glance, much the same as when Julie and I had last seen it. She, our seven-year-old son, Brian, and I had come over from Dar on the Norwegian hydroplane ferry. It was early 1987. I was the American ambassador to Tanzania, and Zanzibar was part of my parish. Julie and I had been looking forward to coming to the island since our arrival in Dar a couple of months earlier. The consulate had been closed in 1979 as a result of a State Department cost-cutting exercise, but the embassy retained the consul's house.

When we looked more closely, Julie and I saw that the passing years had not been kind to the town. Not required to pay rent or to maintain the properties, squatters who had replaced the Arab and Asian residents of Stone Town had let many buildings go to ruin. Over the years, the rains had literally melted down many of the coral and lime structures. On Kenyatta Road, the former Main Street, the few shops that were open for business had but a fraction of the kinds of wares they had featured in prerevolution days. There was a forlorn air about Stone Town stemming from decline, neglect, and apathy.

In Ng'ambo, we viewed the German Democratic Republic's monument to socialism, a broad avenue lined with Stalin-era architectural monstrosities. The East Germans had not provided housing for all the residents of the old African quarter of Zanzibar Town, but they had erected multistoried apartment buildings that at one time housed as many as a few thousand people. The apartments

were destined to become instant slums. Apartment living was a totally foreign concept to the Africans who came to live in them; they never really liked living in high-rise apartments, and neither many of them nor the government managers cared enough to keep the apartments well maintained.

The countryside was much the same as before. Conspicuously absent were the communal farms proposed by the foreign Communists and started up by the revolutionary government. The good roads we had known were in terrible shape, showing the effects of virtually no maintenance over a twenty-year period. I was to learn that poverty in Zanzibar in the late 1980s was worse than it was before the revolution.

The Cold War, now in its waning days, had long since left Zanzibar. The Communist countries' apparent victories in 1964 and 1965 had, it turned out, amounted to nothing of significance. The Cold War's legacy was a government that had become too dependent on foreign aid handouts, was presided over by a feckless bureaucracy that routinely mismanaged the economy, and was for years obsessed with security. Tensions had arisen out of a political struggle between those who were comfortable with the union and those who wanted greater autonomy for Zanzibar.

But if, like mainland Tanzania's, Zanzibar's economy had deteriorated to an appalling state, then change was in the air. Socialism had failed and was discredited. Zanzibaris were looking for something better. There was an entrepreneurial spirit alive that apparently lacked only know-how to get it off to a good start. Epitomizing the new look of things, at a reception given in my honor, Ali Sultan Issa, the most ardent of Zanzibar's self-proclaimed Communists we had known, showed up wearing a three-piece suit and presented me with his business card. Ali now owned a restaurant in town and was promoting the construction of a hotel in the Mtoni area.

By the end of my assignment to Tanzania three years later, Zanzibaris, still handicapped by political tensions, were groping to find a way out of poverty. Since then, there has been some progress, but not much. At the beginning of the twenty-first century, grinding poverty is still the lot of most of the people of Zanzibar and Pemba.

Foreign aid, from whatever source, had made no lasting impression.

With the price of cloves having plummeted, aid from Communist countries having virtually dried up, and Western aid having been curtailed because of human rights violations, Zanzibari officials turned to tourism for salvation. Many hotels, some of them luxury class, have been erected, the number of tourists has vastly increased, and the islands' roads and communications infrastructure have been improved.

Tourism in Zanzibar, like tourism everywhere, is not an unmixed blessing. In Zanzibar, most of the employment that has come with the growth of tourism

has been of the low-wage variety. The relative boom in tourism has not yet transformed the economy. Nor is it likely, on its own, to do so. Then, too, the presence of large numbers of tourists has been accompanied by environmental stresses and, many islanders charge, an erosion of their blend of Islamic and Swahili cultures.

Discontent in Zanzibar erupted in January 2001, carrying with it an echo of 1964: an unpopular political party—the party in power—had won an election that many believed it should have lost, and violence had followed. In October 2000, on both the mainland and Zanzibar, the Chama Cha Mapinduzi had been returned to power in general elections. The elections in Zanzibar had been marred by numerous irregularities, including tampering with ballot boxes. Three months later, more than thirty people died in Zanzibar when Tanzanian police used force to put down demonstrations against the elections' outcome. The authorities arrested many people afterward, and allegations of police brutality arose. Some 2,000 Zanzibaris fled to Kenya.

It was situation in a way reminiscent of 1964, yet fundamentally different. Western governments and human rights organizations expressed concern, but, unlike in 1964, most of the world neither heard nor cared about what had happened in Zanzibar. Bad though the violence was, it did not approach the scale of the violence of the revolution. This time, there was no deep ethnic divide underlying the troubles. And the government, however unpopular it may have been, was a far cry from the oppressive, often brutal Revolutionary Council.

Different though Zanzibar's political unrest in 2001 was, it had roots in the revolutionary era. The governing political party was the Chama Cha Mapinduzi, the lineal descendant of the ASP and TANU, still in power thirty-four years following its inception. Had it not been for the revolution, there would have been no union, no Chama Cha Mapinduzi. The new president of Zanzibar was Aman Abeid Karume, former president Karume's son. He had been a Tanzanian diplomat and a cabinet minister in the previous Zanzibar government. Karume, a moderate who believes in consensual politics, was more popular than his party.

The political unrest at the end of the twentieth century had an obvious link to the past, in that it arose from the Chama Cha Mapinduzi's unwillingness to tolerate genuine political opposition. But the past also appeared to carry a message that political exclusivity and repression have unacceptable consequences. In any event, in the waning months of 2001, the moderation of President Aman Abeid Karume was evident and was having positive results. In October, the

Zanzibar government dropped all charges against people who had been involved in the January riots. Later that same month, the CCM and the opposition party signed a reconciliation agreement aimed at ending hostility between them. By early November, almost all the 2,000 who had fled to Kenya had returned to Zanzibar and Pemba.

Because of Africa's great diversity, neither Zanzibar nor any other one country should be regarded as a metaphor for Africa and its present afflictions. There are, however, common threads to the Zanzibar story and the experiences of many countries. The hopeful expectations that came with independence have vanished for the most part, replaced by popular despair or discontent. In too much of Africa, the political norm has been self-perpetuating authoritarian, repressive, corrupt governments. Although Zanzibar's recent governments have not been that bad, they have a miserable record of achievement and have not exactly been paragons of democracy and enlightenment. True economic progress in most of Africa, Zanzibar included, has been relatively rare, and basic infrastructure and public services have drastically deteriorated. Malaria, tuberculosis, gastrointestinal diseases, and, of course, AIDS take a terrible toll.

The West had centuries to evolve from feudalism to industrialization. Africa did not. In the middle of the twentieth century, Africans set out on a hopeless journey to try to achieve virtually instant modernization. Given Africa's centuries of isolation from the rest of the world, its generally bad colonial experience, its harsh physical environment and widespread debilitating diseases, its unfavorable terms of international trade, its lack of a sufficiently large middle class of people trained to cope with the exigencies of modernization, and the tensions arising from deep-seated ethnic allegiances, is it any wonder that failures far overshadow successes?

There are instances of real progress in Africa today, and the future is not uniformly dismal. However, for most of Africa, the outlook for decades ahead, at least, is bleak. Only when the talents and energies of African peoples are given scope and their hunger for education and a decent shot at advancement is fulfilled will a better picture emerge.

Zanzibar is one place that can prosper, but only if those who lead it or would lead it can shuck off the legacy of the past. As that story unfolds, the polyethnic, polycultural atmosphere will remain, sustaining Zanzibar's exotic flavor. And though explorers, slavers, sultans, colonialists, revolutionaries, and Cold Warriors have come and gone, the physical beauty of Zanzibar—its azure sea, verdant landscape, and beaches of white sand—will endure.

Westview Press is grateful to the following agencies and publishers that have generously granted permission to use the photographs and figures in this book:

Page 2   Map of Zanzibar Island. By permission of Oxford University Press from *History of Zanzibar: From the Middle Ages to 1856* by Sir John Gray, (London: Oxford University Press, 1962).

Page 5   Map of the East African Coast. From *Zanzibar: Tradition and Revolution* by Edward Bradley Martin (London: Hamish Hamilton, 1978).

Pages 10, 21, 48, and 124   Photo of Arab Notables, maps of Zanzibar Town, and photo of Main Street, Stone Town. From *A Guide to Zanzibar* (Nairobi: East African Printers, 1961). Permission granted by Crown Agents' Archivist Philip Knights.

Pages 40 and 212   Photos of Prerevolution Government of Zanzibar and May Day effigies. From *Revolution in Zanzibar* by Field Marshal John Okello (Nairobi: East African Publishing House, 1967).

Page 70   Photo of Field Marshal John Okello. From *Revolution in Zanzibar* by Field Marshal John Okello (Nairobi: East African Publishing House, 1967). Permission for photo granted by Africapix.

Page 77   Photo of Adam Mwakanjuki and Rebel Companion. Permission granted by AP/Wide World Photos.

Notes

Preface

1. Anthony Clayton, *The Zanzibar Revolution and Its Aftermath* (London: C. Hurst, 1981). Two other works are excellent sources regarding the circumstances leading up to the revolution: Michael Lofchie, *Zanzibar: Background to Revolution* (Princeton: Princeton University Press, 1965), and Richard M. Preece, "Constitutional Development and Political Change in the Zanzibar Protectorate, 1890–1962" (Ph.D. diss., Johns Hopkins University, 1975).

Prologue

1. David Reed, "Zanzibar: Laziest Place on Earth," Reader's Digest 81, no. 487 (November 1962): 302. The political entity Zanzibar (known in Swahili as Unguja) consists of the islands of Zanzibar and Pemba and the islets within their territorial waters. In this book, the context makes it clear whether I am referring to Zanzibar as a whole or just Zanzibar Island.

Chapter 1

1. Richard F. Burton, *Zanzibar: City, Island, and Coast*, vol. 1 (1872; reprint, New York: Johnson Reprint Corporation, 1967), 27-28; David Livingstone, *The Last Journals of David Livingstone in Central Africa from 1865 to His Death* (London, 1874), 6–7.
2. Michael Lofchie, "Party Conflict in Zanzibar," *Journal of Modern African Studies* 1, no. 2 (1963): 1.
3. Rodger Yeager, *Tanzania: An African Experiment* (Boulder: Westview Press, 1982), 21.
4. Michael Lofchie, *Zanzibar: Background to Revolution* (Princeton: Princeton University Press, 1965), 18, 20.
5. Lofchie, "Party Conflict in Africa," 10.

Chapter 2

1. The usual five-year waiting period for American citizenship could be waived by a federal judge for the spouses of Foreign Service personnel.

2. *A Guide to Zanzibar* (Nairobi: East African Printers, 1961), 30.

3. Sir John Gray, *History of Zanzibar: From Middle Ages to 1856* (London: Oxford University Press, 1962), 105–6.

4. Alan Moorhead, *The White Nile* (New York: Harper, 1960), 13.

5. Gray, *History of Zanzibar*, 224.

6. Any account of the revolution and of John Okello's role in it must draw from his autobiography, bearing in mind that he had a lot of help in writing it and that by omission and commission he paints a favorable portrait of himself (*Revolution in Zanzibar* [Nairobi: East African Publishing House, 1967]). Hyperbole aside, the essentials of his story ring true. Anthony Clayton draws heavily on the Okello book in *The Zanzibar Revolution and Its Aftermath* (London: C. Hurst, 1981). Clayton, like many others, myself included, does not doubt the primary role Okello played in the genesis and execution of the military action that overthrew the Zanzibar government, and in the early days that followed. I have meshed some parts of Okello's and Clayton's accounts with what I learned from people who were in Zanzibar and from my own observations and my encounters with Okello.

7. Okello, *Revolution in Zanzibar*, 58.

8. Ibid., 76.

9. Ibid., 73.

10. Clayton, *Zanzibar Revolution*, 68.

11. Keith Kyle, "How It Happened," *The Spectator* 212, no. 7077 (February 14, 1964): 202; Clayton, *Zanzibar Revolution*, 68 n. 35.

12. *Washington Star*, May 4, 1964.

Chapter 3

1. Anthony Clayton, *The Zanzibar Revolution and Its Aftermath* (London: C. Hurst, 1981), 15.

2. Because of scheduling problems, the U.S. diplomatic courier service to Zanzibar had been suspended for a couple of months that summer.

Chapter 4

1. British ambassadors to Commonwealth countries are titled "high commissioner" instead of "ambassador."

2. Michael Lofchie's research provided the basis for his book, *Zanzibar: Background to Revolution* (Princeton: Princeton University Press, 1965). Lofchie departed Zanzibar in late 1963.

Chapter 5

1. Associated Press, January 17, 1964.

2. The U.S. Foreign Broadcast Information Service, which monitored foreign radio broadcasts worldwide, recorded and translated Okello's words.

3. John Okello, *Revolution in Zanzibar* (Nairobi: East African Publishing House, 1967), 151.

4. I have seen nothing in available material that would explain why the embassy in Nairobi, which did have voice communication with the *Manley* and was receiving all the cables from Dar, did not, or was unable to, keep the ship better informed. It also is unclear why Washington was not doing a better job of communicating pertinent facts to the *Manley*.

5. Newsletter 2001 (Droitwich, England: Zanzibar Association, 2001).

6. For example, see Anthony Clayton, *The Zanzibar Revolution and Its Aftermath* (London: C. Hurst, 1981), 107. Apparently (he cited no sources), Clayton was reflecting the opinion of former British colonial officials.

Chapter 6

1. The numbers substituted for the letters of the two words *Zanzibar Embassy* in the above sample encryption were derived from the following table:

```
a 7 4 3 9 0 2 4
b 2 6 1 0 8 3 9
e 0 9 8 0 3 1 5
i 4 5 1 7 4 9 9
m 1 4 7 2 0 1 8
n 8 2 6 6 3 4 1
r 7 8 2 0 5 9 6
s 6 0 7 5 3 7 2
y 2 0 4 8 3 9 6
z 3 9 7 5 4 1 8
```

Using this table, the number for the first *z* in the word *Zanzibar* is 3, the number for the second *z* is 9. If the word *Zanzibar* appeared again in the message, the number for the first *z* would be 7, and the next would be 5, and so on. Because of its random nature, this system was foolproof (in those days, anyway) unless the enemy had access to either the sender's or the receiver's pad.

Chapter 7

1. Richard M. Preece, "Constitutional Development and Political Change in the Zanzibar Protectorate, 1890–1962" (Ph.D. diss., Johns Hopkins University, 1975), 394; *Observer* (London), March 8, 1964, cited in ibid., 395.
2. Known as a *despatch* until about 1960, when the term *airgram* was adopted, this form of written communication was sent in the diplomatic pouch.

Chapter 8

1. U.S. Department of State, "Guidelines for Policy and Operations, Africa," March 1962, p. 1. Quoted in Paul Schraeder, *United States Foreign Policy Toward Africa* (London: Cambridge University Press, 1994), 15.

Chapter 9

1. House of Representatives, Frances P. Bolton, *Congressional Record* (February 25, 1964), daily ed., p. 3478.
2. This and other exploits of Frank Carlucci when he was in the Congo are recounted in Perter Lisagor and Marguerite Higgins, *Overtime in Heaven: Adventures in the Foreign Service* (Garden City, N.Y.: Doubleday, 1964).

Chapter 10

1. East Germany was the first country to recognize Zanzibar. In addition to the Soviet Union and Communist China, other Communist countries that quickly recognized Zanzibar were Cuba, Czechoslovakia, Yugoslavia, Bulgaria, Albania, North Vietnam, and North Korea.

2. Anthony Clayton, *The Zanzibar Revolution and Its Aftermath* (London: C. Hurst, 1981), 107 n. 128.

Chapter 12

1. David Else, *Guide to Zanzibar* (Bucks, England: Bradt Publications, 1998), 61.

Chapter 13

1. Declassified confidential despatch dated July 22, 1964, from the British high commission to the secretary of state for Commonwealth relations, Commonwealth Relations Office, London.

Chapter 15

1. In addition to Carlucci and Pickering, the other ambassadors were Jack Matlock, David Halstead, Ellen Shippy, Charles Cecil, and the author.

Index

Abdulla, Mohamed. *See* Mosque murders

Abdullah, Rashid, 220

Abdullah, Seyyid Sultan, 42

Africa, since independence, 271

Africans in Zanzibar, 8
 antipathy toward Arabs, xviii, 12, 19, 25, 40, 41, 212
 place of in pre–revolution society, 9–11
 socio-political groupings of, 10–11

Afro-Shirazi Party (ASP), 40
 and 1963 elections, 12
 founding of, 11, 35
 internal frictions of, 12, 28, 29, 30, 36
 and merger with TANU, 214, 266
 opposition of to tracking station, 39
 as sole political party, 178, 199

Aley, Juma, 41, 69, 80, 81, 95, 106

American consulate/embassy, Zanzibar, 93, 119
 changes in diplomatic status of, 215, 225, 227
 and Communist Chinese diplomats, 167–168
 description and location of, 20, 22
 diplomatic privileges restored, 171
 Foreign Service inspection of, 38,
 history of, 4, 21–22
 increase in staff of, 163
 social life and recreation, 169–170, 224–225

Anglican cathedral, 23

Anglo-German agreement of 1896, 8, 9

Anti-American demonstrations, 200, 202–203, 228, 233

Anti-American media campaign, 201, 203, 222, 228–229, 233–234, 257–258

Arabs in Zanzibar
 arrive in East Africa and Zanzibar, 6–7
 contemptuous of Africans, 28, 39, 41
 decrease in population of, 191
 in detention camps, 106–107, 189
 emigration, escape, or expulsions of, 107, 190, 231
 Manga, 40–41, 64, 190
 nationalism of, 11
 Omanis, 6, 23
 place of in pre-revolution society, 9–10
 rebel atrocities against, 3–4, 64, 76, 94, 121–122, 190
 See also Said, Sultan Seyyid

Asians in Zanzibar, 19
 decrease in population of, 192
 effects of revolution on, 191–192, 231
 mistreatment of, 121–122, 192
 place of in pre-revolution society, 9–10, 11

ASP. *See* Afro-Shirazi Party

Attwood-Carlucci-Fredericks-Leonhart assessment, 173–175

Attwood, William, 173–175, 200, 201

Babu, Abdulrahman Mohamed, 30, 50, 99, 100–101
 on aims of revolutionary government, 109–110
 background and description of, 30, 108–109
 and Carlucci, 195
 and Chinese Communists, 31, 109
 and evacuation of Americans, 83–84
 and expulsion of Picard, 100
 flees to Dar es Salaam, 31,

returns, 74
followers of, 55, 98, 126, 180, 208
and Karume, 160, 207
later years and death of, 210, 266
and Marxist beliefs of, 108, 161
and Nyerere, 83–84
and Okello, 74, 106
during onset of in revolution, 55, 63,
    65
and Petterson, 102, 109–110, 131–132,
    134
post-revolution influence of, 55, 126,
    172, 204
and tracking station, 38, 110
and union of Tanganyika and Zanzibar,
    207, 209, 210
on U.S. recognition, 135
Bakari, Seif, 26, 27–28, 49, 64–65, 234
Ball, George, 96
Bamboo Bomber, 61
Banks, Brian, 169, 238
Banks, Frances, 169, 238, 262
Bavuai, Said Idi, 221–222
Belcher, Bill, 53, 221
Bendix Corporation, 50, 54, 216
Bourn, James, 226
British colonial officials
    attitude of toward Zanzibar ethnic groups,
        9, 11,
British colonial rule, 9–12
    and class system, 36,
    and indications of trouble, 31, 45, 60
    and Okello, 25
    post-independence exodus of, 45
    post-revolution departures of, 183, 216
    quality of, 36–37
British community, post-revolution, 107,
    181, 216
British government, 186
    asks Nyerere to intervene, 139
    on Babu, 63
    and Communist influence in Zanzibar, xi,
        96, 128, 172, 177, 178, 184–185, 204
    and evacuation of British nationals, 63, 78
    gives asylum to Jamshid, 106
    on military intervention, 62, 63, 115
    on recognition of Zanzibar, 95, 114, 115,
        123, 135, 146

and Tanganyika army mutiny, 116
and union of Tanganyika and Zanzibar,
    208
British High Commission, Zanzibar 69, 169,
    222, 225
Bruce, David, 128, 208
    recommends covert action, 187
Burch, George, 50, 53–54, 132, 141
    and dismantling of tracking station, 200,
        216
    during evacuation of Americans, 67–68
Burch, Teresa, 50, 54, 216
    and Cuban involvement in Zanzibar, 73
    during evacuation of Americans, 67–68
Burton, Sir Richard, 7–8
Butler, R.A., 136

Cable and Wireless, 22, 51, 62, 80
Cameron, John and Lorna, 53–54, 66, 169
Carlucci, Frank C., III, 196–197
    advocates visitor program, 239
    and anti-American demonstrations, 228,
        233
    arrives in Zanzibar with Leonhart, 148
    assesses Zanzibar internal affairs, 172,
        204, 183–184
    and Babu, 195, 210
    background of, 147
    begins assignment in Zanzibar, 157–158
    on British intervention, 181
    and CIA, 164–165
    and congratulatory message to Karume,
        239, 241
    diplomatic title of, 226
    expelled from Tanzania, 241–244, 246
    and Hanga, 159
    and Jumbe, 223
    and Karume, 195, 196, 219–220, 231,
        246
    on Karume, 183–184, 220, 226
    and Kombo, 184
    meets with Attwood, Fredericks, and
        Leonhart, 173–175
    modus operandi of, 147–148, 159–160,
        170, 218
    and Petterson, 158, 163
    policy recommendations of, 186,
        195–196, 219

reports of to Washington, 172, 181, 183,
204, 210
subsequent career of, 268
on surveillance and phone taps, 183, 235
and Swahili language, 170, 218
on *Time* article, 245
and USAID project, 219
visits Pemba, 182
Carlucci, Jean, 169, 223, 244, 245
Centaur, HMS, 116
Chama Cha Mapinduzi (CCM), 266, 267,
270, 271
Chuvakin, Igor, 166, 197, 225
CIA, 55–56, 164–165
Clark, Ernest, 113–114, 132, 200
Clayton, Anthony, xi, 29, 36, 164
Cloves, 8, 9, 18–19, 259
Cold War, 127–128, 269
Coleman, Barney, 254
Committee of Fourteen. *See* Bakari, Seif
Communist China, 128, 161
aid to Zanzibar of, 199, 223, 260
aims of regarding Zanzibar, 166
Babu and, 31
favored by Karume, 167
Nyerere and, 154
rivalry of with Soviets, 167
and union of Tanganyika and Zanzibar, 209
Communist Chinese embassy/consulate,
attitude of toward Americans, 167–168
changes in diplomatic status of, 215, 225,
227
number of personnel of, 223
Communist diplomatic missions in Zanzibar,
164, 180, 183, 223, 261, 275(n1, Ch.
7)
See also specific missions
Congo crisis, 228, 232–233
Conley, Robert, 98, 99
See also foreign journalists
Counterrevolution, fears of, 140, 231–232,
257, 258
Crane, Kent, 169, 251
Crosthwaite, Timothy, 108, 111, 119
background of, 123
difficulties of during assignment,
172–173, 225–226
and evacuation of British subjects, 63,

88–89
expulsion from Zanzibar, 144, 148
on Karume, 183, 226
and Petterson, 119, 122–123
and Picard, 51, 58, 97
during revolution, 63, 66, 83, 88–89, 123
transferred from Zanzibar, 225–226
Cuban involvement in Zanzibar revolution
evidence refuting, 73, 86
Leonhart on, 87–88
reports regarding, 86, 97
Cuenod, Chuck, 165

De Freitas, Geoffrey, 114, 185
Dhow trade, 7
Douglas, Brigadier Patrick Sholto, 116
Douglas-Home, Sir Alec,
meets with President Johnson, 130, 136
sees Communist threat in Zanzibar, xi,
184–185
Dourado, Wolf, 108
background and description of, 110–111
on Communist inroads, 204
as external affairs ministry official,
108–112, 119, 120, 133, 141
later years of, 111, 267
and Petterson, 111–112, 133, 143

East African federation, 208
East Germany (German Democratic
Republic), 161
aid to Zanzibar of, 223, 260, 268–269
aims regarding Zanzibar of, 166
recognition of, 166, 204, 215, 225,
226–227
and union of Tanganyika and Zanzibar, 209
East German embassy/consulate in Zanzibar,
245
changes in diplomatic status of, 215, 225,
227
number of personnel, 222
Elections of 1961 and 1963. *See* Zanzibar,
elections
Encryption, 100
English Club, 66–68, 81, 180
Evacuation of Americans and others, 73–74
completed in Dar es Salaam, 86
decision on, 72, 77

implementation of, 84–85
negotiations for, 83–84
opinions on need for, 88
preparations for, 66–67
Evacuation of British subjects, 63, 78, 88–89,
102, 108

Fathiya, 68–68, 85
Federation of Revolutionary Trade Unions,
202, 228, 258
Feinsilber, Mischa, 74, 75
warns Picard, 30
Foreign journalists
arrive, detained, expelled, 97–102
praise Picard, 118
Foum, Mohammed Ali, 149–150
Franck, Thomas, 138
Fredericks, Wayne, 173, 174
French embassy/consulate, 205
Fritsch, Guenther, 197, 245
FRG. *See* West Germany (Federal Republic of
Germany)

German colonial rule of Zanzibar, 9
Ghanaian consulate, 187
Goan community, 110–111
Gordon, Bob
and congratulatory message to Karume,
239–241
expelled from Tanzania, 241–244
Guevara, Che, 253

Hall, Bill and Monica, 103, 107, 181
Hallstein Doctrine, 166
See also, West Germany
Hampton, B.P., 92, 119
Hanga, Abdul Kassim, 44–45, 69, 94, 99, 119
background of, 39, 159
and Carlucci, 159
execution of, 161, 266
flees to Dar es Salaam, returns, 54, 74
influence of, 160, 172
and tracking station, 39
and union of Tanganyika and Zanzibar,
207
Harriman, Averill, 128, 136
Hassan, Ahmed Diria, 182
Hawker, Henry, 60, 81, 183
Hebe, HMS, 63, 108

Helgoland. *See* Anglo-German Agreement of
1886
Hennemeyer, Bob, 87, 88, 117, 126
Independence ceremony and celebration,
xviii–xix, 43
International Red Cross, 93, 107, 113,
189–190
Issa, Ali Sultan, 182, 269

Jamshid, Seyyid Sultan, 42–43,
escape of, 56–57
exiled, seeks U.S. help, 105–106
Johnson, Lyndon B., 110, 239
meets with Douglas–Home, 130, 136
message to Karume, 146–147
sees Communist threat in Zanzibar, xi,
128, 130, 184–185
Jumbe, Aboud, 98, 222–223
as president of Zanzibar, 266
during revolution, 81–82, 84, 85

Kalonzi, Joel, 230
Kambona, Oscar, 174, 175, 176, 180
and alleged U.S. plot, 232
later years of, 267
during Tanganyikan army mutiny, 116
and union of Tanganyika and Zanzibar,
206–207, 208
Karume, Abeid Amani, 41, 51, 66, 214, 239,
240
anger of toward U.S. and Britain, 133,
135, 160, 184
arrests Picard and Petterson, 99–101
assassination of, 265
and Babu, 160, 207
background and description of, 34–35
and Britain, 186
and Carlucci, 196, 219–220, 230, 246
and Communist China, 167, 197
Communist pressures on, 138, 161, 178,
181, 202
consolidates political power, 207, 219, 256
constraints on power of, 202
and counterrevolution, 140, 257, 258
declares one-party state, 132, 178
despotic behavior of, 258–259, 265–266
and East Germany, 215, 225, 226–227
and evacuation of Americans, 83–84
and expulsion of Carlucci, 246

and expulsion of Crosthwait and
    Petterson, 144, 147, 148
and expulsion of USIS officers, 250–251,
    253, 254
and foreknowledge of revolution, 28
and mosque murders, 222
nationalizes land and properties, 178
on non-alignment, 158, 161, 229, 258
and Nyerere, 214, 222, 226–227
and Okello, 27, 74, 126, 137–138, 174,
    176
opposes anti-American propaganda,
    229–230, 257
and Pemba violence, 220
and Petterson, 34, 113, 118, 134, 144,
    249–250, 254, 256
and Picard, 39
president of Zanzibar, 214
and recognition of Zanzibar, 118, 133,
    135, 160, 184
during revolution, 54, 66, 74, 83–84
and Revolutionary Council, 220–221
seeks mainland assistance, 177
speeches of, 133, 141, 144
and tourism, 231
on tracking station, 39, 200–202, 216
and union of Tanganyika and Zanzibar,
    206–208, 210
and United States, 230, 249, 257
and U.S. aid 205–206, 219, 230
Karume, Aman Abeid, 270
Kawawa, Rashidi, 206, 241–243
Kennedy, John F., 44, 128
Kenyatta, Jomo, 63, 95, 117, 174
    and East African federation, 208
    declines to intervene in Zanzibar, 177, 185
    supports union of Tanganyika and
        Zanzibar, 208
KGB, 165
Khalifa bin Harub, Seyyid Sultan, 42
Kisassi, Eddington, 112–113, 180
Kiswahili. *See* Swahili language
Kombo, Thabit, 184, 230
Kweupe, 132, 201, 203, 222
Kyle, Keith, 29

Leonhart, William, 51, 93, 117, 252
    and arrests of Picard and Petterson, 101,
        102

and congratulatory message to Karume, 239
and Cuban involvement in Zanzibar revo-
    lution, 87–88
and expulsion of Carlucci and Gordon,
    241–244, 247
and expulsion of Petterson, 145
flies to Zanzibar with Carlucci, 148,
    157–158
meetings of with Nyerere, 63–64, 95,
    114, 129, 130, 135–136, 140
praises Picard, 118
recalled to Washington, 248
and union of Tanganyika and Zanzibar,
    207, 208
on U.S. policy toward Zanzibar, 127, 261
Lillico, Stuart, 29, 34, 53, 65
    during evacuation, 71, 73, 80–81
Livingstone, David, 7–8
Lofchie, Michael, 55, 274(n1, Ch. 4)
Lusinde, Job, 199, 204, 207

MacDonald, Sir Malcolm, 114
MacKnight, Jesse, 72, 93
    recommends U.S. recognition, 115
Mafoudh, Ali, 149, 179, 199
Makame, Hasnu, 182, 184, 199
Malindi police station, 53, 64, 65, 69
Manga. *See* Arabs in Zanzibar
Manley, USS, 62, 83, 92, 94
    landing party of, 79, 80, 84–85
    ordered to carry out evacuation, 72, 77
    sails from Mombasa to Zanzibar, 78–79
    takes evacuees to Dar es Salaam, 86
Marahubi Palace, 224
May Day 1964 celebration, 211–214
Meagher, John, 235, 239, 245
MI5, 74, 75
Miles, Stephen, 63–64, 95, 144
Monsoons, 6, 7, 43, 189, 216, 237
Mooring, Sir George, 36
Mosque murders, 222
Moyo, Hassan Nasser, 44–45, 161
    influence on Karume, 160, 172, 181
Mshangama, Maulidi, 68
Muhsin, Ali, 29, 30, 43
    background and description of, 28
    disdainful of Africans, 28, 39
    imprisoned, 106
    as minister of external affairs, 41

during revolution, 51, 69, 81, 82, 84
    threatens Babu and Umma Party, 31
Murumbi, Joseph, 173
Mutinies in Kenya and Uganda, 117
Mutiny in Dar es Salaam. *See* Tanganyikan
    Army mutiny
Mwakanjuki, Adam, 34, 77, 161, 266

Namata, J.A., 241–243, 244
NASA. *See* National Aeronautics and Space
    Administration
Natepe, A.S., 221
National Aeronautics and Space
    Administration (NASA), 21, 54, 115
Nationalization, effects of, 179, 191, 259
Neald, Dennis, 100, 220
New England, trade with Zanzibar, 4
N'gambo, 48, 268
    See also Zanzibar Town
Nugent, John, 98, 101–102
    See also foreign journalists
Nyerere, Julius, 75, 105, 174
    and alleged U.S. plot against Tanzania, 232
    and Babu, 83–84, 130
    background of, 129–130
    British ask to intervene, 139
    on British policy, 130
    on Communist China, 154
    condemns Stanleyville operation, 233
    on evacuation of Americans from
        Zanzibar, 83–84
    and expulsion of Carlucci and Gordon,
        241–244, 247
    and expulsion of Petterson, 145
    failed economic policies of, 267
    and FRG and GDR, 215, 225–226, 227
    and Karume, 138, 214, 222, 226–227
    later years and death of, 266–267
    and Leonhart, 63–64, 95, 114, 129, 130,
        135–136, 140
    and Okello, 94, 113
    on recognition of Zanzibar, 95, 114, 136,
        140
    and relations with the United States, 248
    and Sandys, 139, 145
    sends police to Zanzibar, 113
    on Shamte request for intervention,
        63–64
    and Tanganyikan army mutiny, 116
    and union of Tanganyika and Zanzibar,
        206–208, 210, 214

Obote, Milton, 95, 117, 174, 177, 208
Okello, John, 42, 51, 66, 72, 78, 112, 113,
    117, 126
    appoints leaders of new government, 69
    arrival in Pemba and Zanzibar, 26
    and attack on Manga Arabs, 190
    and Babu, 74, 1266
    background and description of, 25–26, 82
    banishes Sultan Jamshid, 105
    declares himself field marshal, 52
    dreams of, 25, 26
    and evacuation of Americans, 82–84
    erroneous reports about, 74–75
    and Karume, 54, 69, 126, 137–138, 175
    leads attack on Ziwani, 49–50
    life and death of after Zanzibar, 176–177
    meets with mainland leaders, 173
    ousted from Zanzibar, 176
    and Petterson, 141–143
    prepares for revolution, 26–27, 42
    press conference of, 75
    radio broadcasts of, 52, 57, 65, 69,
        75–76, 95, 108
    and reign of terror, 94, 113, 121–122, 131
    on relations with United States, 108
    seeks U.S. and UK recognition, 70
    seizes Ziwani prison, 57
    sends greetings to Khrushchev, 75
    and Swahili language, 26, 52
    on Sultan Jamshid, 43
    taste for power, 94–95
    travels to Dar es Salaam, 114, 175
Oman. *See* Arabs in Zanzibar.
One-party state, 178, 199
Ostracism of Westerners, 168–169, 222
Owen, HMS, 63, 101, 102, 108

Pasco, Joan, 122, 171, 178, 190
Pemba Island, 5, 7, 29, 220
    atrocities and misrule in, 121–122, 123,
        182
People's Golf Club, 212, 217
People's Liberation Army. *See* Zanzibar's
    post-revolution security forces

Petterson, Brian, 262

Petterson, Don

  and anti-American demonstration, 233

  arrested by Karume, 100–101

  assessment of Zanzibar leaders, 153

  and Babu, 102, 131–132, 134, 135

  and Carlucci, 158, 163

  chooses to remain in Zanzibar, 102

  communications of censored, 107, 110,
    119, 122, 126, 131,133, 134

  and Communist Chinese diplomats,
    167–168

  and Crosthwait, 119, 122–123

  departure from Zanzibar, onward assign-
    ment of, 262, 263

  destroys classified materials, 143, 145,
    150–151

  detained with journalists, 97–98

  on economy of Zanzibar, 198

  education and training of, 13–14, 15–16

  during evacuation, 71–74, 76–77,
    80–86

  expelled from Zanzibar, 144–146, 148,
    149–153

  and expulsion of Carlucci and Gordon,
    245

  and expulsions of USIS officers, 250–253,
    254

  family and social life of, 44, 126,
    192–194, 218, 238

  and Karume, 34, 118, 134, 249–250,
    254, 256, 263

  in Mexico, 15

  mistakes of, 120, 133

  and Okello, 141–143

  and Picard 20, 68–69, 92–93, 163

  and protection of American property,
    110, 111–113, 119, 126, 132,
    133–134

  reports of to Washington, 108, 110, 113,
    114, 119, 123, 125–126, 132, 134,
    256, 261

  returns to Zanzibar in 1987, 268–269

  during revolution's first day, 50–53,
    58–59, 60–62, 66–69

  and sources of information, 123–125

  and Swahili language, 15–16, 93, 218, 256

  travels of in Zanzibar, 19, 224

  travel to and early days of in Zanzibar,
    16–19, 37–38, 43

  on union of Tanganyika and Zanzibar, 261

  on U.S. policy, 131, 132, 261

Petterson, Julianne, 37, 58–59, 84–85, 115,
    162, 238

Petterson, Julie, 161–162, 190, 223

  birth of children in Zanzibar, 37, 262

  and Che Guevara, 253

  courtship and marriage of, 15

  and Cuban involvement in Zanzibar,
    73

  and departure from Zanzibar, 262

  evacuation of from Zanzibar, 84–85

  family and social life of, 44, 192–194,
    218, 238

  in Kenya, 117

  and mutiny in Dar es Salaam, 115–116,
    117

  returns to Zanzibar in 1987, 268

  during revolution, 50–53, 58–59, 66–67,
    72

  sent to Dar es Salaam second time,
    209–210

  travels in Zanzibar of, 19, 224

  travel to and early days in Zanzibar,
    16–19, 37, 43

  in Washington, DC, 15–16

Petterson, Susan, 15, 34, 58–59, 84–85, 115,
    162, 210, 238

Picard, Frederick P. ("Fritz"), 23, 29, 38,
    44

  during revolution's early stage, 50–53, 58,
    60–62, 66, 68–69

  arrest and expulsion of, 100–102

  on Babu, 30

  background of, 20

  career of damaged, 118

  checks airport for evacuation, 61

  courage of, 83, 84

  and Crosthwait, 51, 58, 92

  in Dar es Salaam, 117

  and evacuation of Americans, 51–52, 58,
    62, 66, 72–74, 76–77, 80, 82–86

  and Karume, 38, 94, 99–100

  later years and death of, 267

  offers U.S. assistance to Zanzibar, 94

  praised by journalists and others, 118

post-revolution actions of, 91–94, 97–102
pre-independence reports by, 20, 29, 30, 31
questionable behavior of, 34, 68–69, 76, and Rex Preece, 55–56
warned by Feinsilber, 30
Picard, Shoana, 20, 33, 59, 60, 117
Pickering, Thomas, 262
    background and abilities of, 256
    subsequent career of, 268
    on U.S. policy toward Zanzibar, 261
Pitcher, Dennis, 56
Police Mobile Force, 41, 49
Portuguese era, 6
Povenmire, Dale, 22–23, 33, 37, 38, 56, 163
Povenmire, Marilyn, 33, 37, 38
Preece, Richard ("Rex"), 59, 67
    and CIA, 55–56
    illness and near-death of, 56, 80, 85
    and Picard, 55–56
Project Mercury tracking station, 33, 39, 97, 113, 115, 125, 132, 134, 199–200, 229
    Anglo-American agreement to establish, 22
    mandated closure of, 200, 216
    political attacks on, 38
    ZNP/ZPPP government support for, 38

Qullatein, Ahmed, 56, 227, 229

Radday, Harry, 169
    expelled from Zanzibar, 250–253
    USIS work of, 227, 228
Raha Leo, 48, 49, 82–84, 98–99
Rashid, Salim, 149, 160, 180, 208–209, 210
Reader's Digest article on Zanzibar, xviii
Rehani, Mtoro, 228–229
Revolution. See Zanzibar revolution
Rhyl, HMS, 63, 78
Rowan, Carl, 252, 253
Ruchti, Jim
    aboard the Manley, 77–79
    comments on talk with Petterson, 126–127
    expresses concern about Picard, 117
    during evacuation, 80, 82–85
Rumbold, Jack, 60

Rusk, Dean, 110, 136
    sends letter to Nyerere, 247
Said, Sultan Seyyid, 6, 7, 8, 23
    Salah, Ibuni 106
Sandys, Duncan, 172
    on British intervention, 128–129
    and expulsion of British diplomats, 145
    low regard of for Karume, 138–139, 177
    meets with Karume and Babu, 173, 176
    and Nyerere, 139, 145
    and recognition of Zanzibar, 96, 139
    seeks Kenyatta intervention, 177, 185–186, 208
    and union of Tanganyika and Zanzibar, 208
Scots Guards, xviii, xix, 12
"Second Twelfth", 240, 241
    See also Carlucci, expulsion of
Shamte, Mohammed, 29, 38, 39, 58
    refuses to flee, 60
    requests British military intervention, 62, 63
    resigns, 81
Sharif, Othman, 69, 99–100, 184, 199
    breaks with and denounces Karume, 36, 39
    execution of, 266
    imprisoned and released, 258–259
    loses cabinet position, 182
    in protective custody, 55
    resigns from ASP, 36, 39
Shirazis, 11
Slavery in Zanzibar, 4, 6–7, 8, 23–25
Smithyman, M.V., 59–60
Soviet embassy/consulate, 166
    changes in diplomatic status of, 215, 225, 227
    efforts of to subvert Americans, 165
    and "From Russia With Love", 218
    number of personnel of, 222
Soviet Union, 127–128, 161
    aims of regarding Zanzibar, 166
    aid to Zanzibar, 181–182, 199, 212, 223, 260
    and rivalry with Communist China, 167
    and union of Tanganyika and Zanzibar, 209
    and Zanzibar recognition of East Germany, 225
Speight, Ray, 79

Spencer, Tom, 132, 141, 200, 216
Stanleyville rescue operation, 232–233
State Corporation for External Trade
(Bizanje), 224, 259
Stone Town, 21, 51, 56, 123–124, 268
See also Zanzibar Town
Sullivan, J.M., 53, 56
Swahili language, 16

Tanganyikan African National Union (TANU),
129, 214
and merger with Afro-Shirazi Party, 215,
266
Tanganyikan army mutiny, 115–117, 199
Tanganyikan police, 113, 131, 180, 209
TanZam railroad, 154, 168
Tanzania. *See* United Republic of Tanzania
Time magazine articles on Zanzibar, 117,
245–246
Tkachenko, Nicolai, 165, 166
Tracking station. *See* Project Mercury
tracking station
Trimble, William, 114
Tshombe, Moises. *See* Congo crisis
Twala, Abdul Azziz,
condemns Western countries, 234
execution of, 161, 266
influence on Karume of, 160, 172, 180
and Petterson, 142, 149
and union of Tanganyika and Zanzibar, 207

Umma Party, 38
banned, 31, 40
condemns tracking station, 38
founded by Babu, 30
opposes Zanzibar government, 31
Union of Tanganyika and Zanzibar, 174, 175
aspects of, 214
establishment of, 206
opposition to, 208–209, 261
United Republic of Tanganyika and Zanzibar,
206
United Republic of Tanzania, 232
United States Agency for International
Development (USAID)
project in Zanzibar, 45, 205 206, 219, 238
United States government
approves evacuation, 72
on British intervention, 128

on Carlucci/Gordon expulsion, 248
and Communist influence in Zanzibar, xi,
30, 172, 177, 178, 184–185, 186, 204
policy on contacts with Communist
Chinese, 168
and recognition of Zanzibar, 95, 96, 114,
139, 146
sends arms to Congolese government,
228
and union of Tanganyika and Zanzibar, 208
United States Information Service (USIS),
252–253
library, 22, 203, 214
USAID. *See* United States Agency for
International Development
U.S. Department of State, 62, 80, 96, 118
on Babu, 204
Bureau of Educational and Cultural Affairs
(CU), 238
cables to Petterson, 102, 110, 112, 120,
132
and Carlucci/Gordon expulsion, 248
on Communist influence in Zanzibar, 128,
173–174, 186–187, 205
instructions to Bruce, 128
instructions to Leonhart, 129
on Okello, 174
and Radday expulsion, 251–252
and recognition of Zanzibar, 139–140
USIS. *See* United States Information Service

Voice of Zanzibar (radio station), 48, 49, 52,
203

Wa Shoto, Said, 221–222
West Germany (Federal Republic of
Germany), 225, 227
aid of to Tanganyika of, 215
and recognition of East Germany, 136,
204, 215, 227
Whitehouse, Charlie, 263–264
Williams, G. Mennan, 43–44, 240
and recognition of Zanzibar, 115
on U.S. policy toward Zanzibar, 96
Zanews, 132, 201, 222
Zanzibar
colonial era, 8–12
dependence on foreign aid, 259, 269
descriptions of, 4–5, 19

economic problems of, 9, 20, 231, 259, 269
elections, xviii, 12, 30
independence of, xviii, xix
inhabitants of, 5–6, 10
in 1980s and afterward, 268–270
political unrest in 2001, 270
tourism in, 231, 259, 269–270
Zanzibar and Pemba Peoples Party (ZPPP), 12, 29, 76
Zanzibar National Party (ZNP), 11, 28, 29, 76, 109
Zanzibar revolution
    airport seized, 62
    atrocities during, 3–4, 64, 68, 76, 121–122
    attacks on police stations, 49, 53, 64
    commences, 49
    death toll of, 107
    first anniversary celebration of, 253
    foreknowledge of limited, 20, 27–28, 29, 31, 45, 56, 60
    looting during, 65, 71, 76, 92
    communications facilities seized during, 51, 52
    See also Okello, John
Zanzibar Revolutionary Council, 133, 250
    assessment of, 160
    established by Okello, 81–82
    and evacuation of Americans, 83–84
    expels Arabs, 190

and Karume, 125, 220–221
members of, 125–126, 221, 257
misdeeds of some members, 221–222
power of circumscribed, 257
suspicious of U.S. motives, 168, 172
and tracking station, 202
and union of Tanganyika and Zanzibar, 261
Zanzibar's post-revolution security forces, 211–212, 253
Zanzibar Town
    in aftermath of revolution, 131, 181, 194
    descriptions of, 7–8
    during revolution, 51, 65, 68, 71, 72, 76, 84
    layout of, 20–21(map), 47–48(map)
    in 1980s, 268–269
    See also N'gambo, Raha Leo, Stone Town
Ziwani police headquarters, 49, 50
Ziwani prison, 49, 57
ZNP. See Zanzibar National Party
ZNP/ZPPP coalition government, xviii
    attitude of toward Africans, 12
    establishment of, xviii, 12
    fate of ministers of, 59, 60, 69, 80, 81, 106
    ineptitude of, 27, 41–42
    policies of, 12, 40, 41–42
    support of for tracking station, 38
Zolo, Irv, 66–67, 79
ZPPP. See Zanzibar and Pemba Peoples Party